INDIANA
Math

www.hmhschool.com

HOUGHTON MIFFLIN HARCOURT
School Publishers

THE WORLD ALMANAC FOR KIDS

Printed in the U.S.A.

ISBN 13: 978-0-15-385675-4
ISBN 10: 0-15-385675-0

1 2 3 4 5 6 7 8 9 10 1678 18 17 16 15 14 13 12 11 10 09

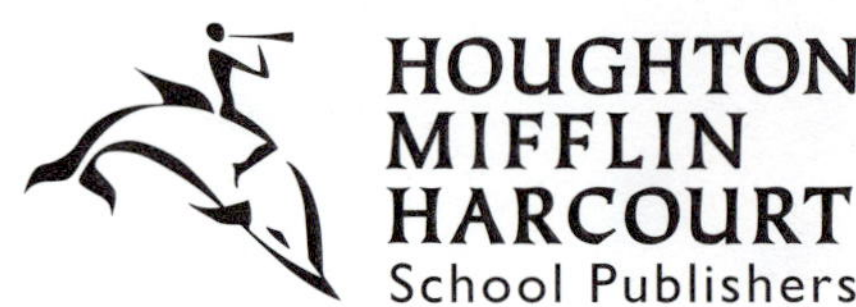

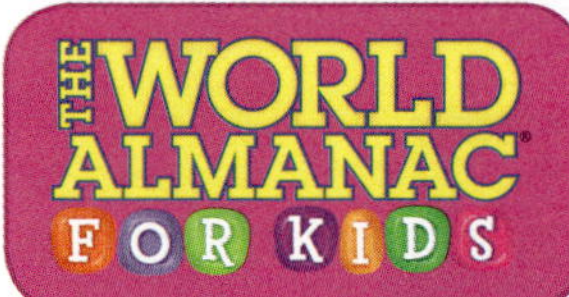

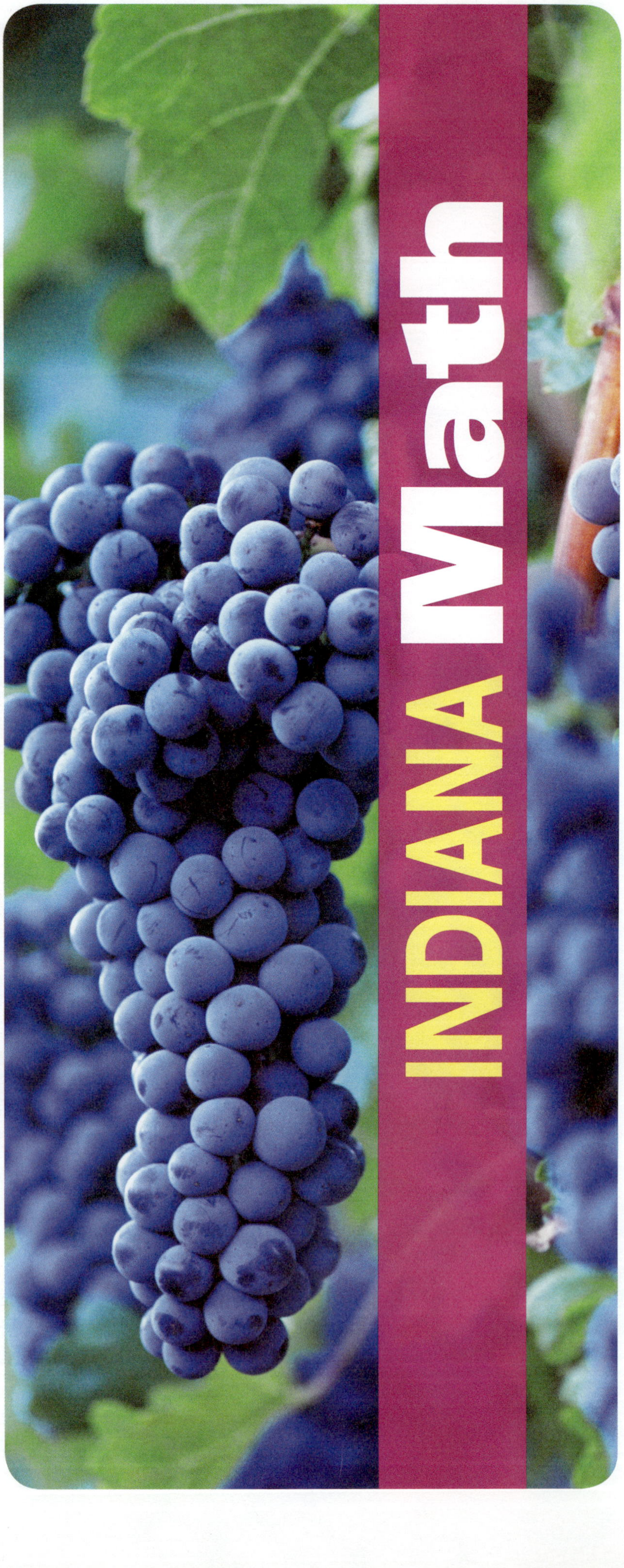

INDIANA
Math

Program Authors

Juli K. Dixon
Associate Professor of
Mathematics Education
University of Central Florida
Orlando, Florida

Matt Larson
Author-in-Residence
K-12 Curriculum Specialist
for Mathematics
Lincoln Public School District
Adjunct Professor, University
of Nebraska–Lincoln
Lincoln, Nebraska
Visiting Adjunct Professor,
Columbia University
New York, New York

Dr. Miriam A. Leiva
Distinguished Professor of
Mathematics Emerita
University of North Carolina
Charlotte, North Carolina

Joyce McLeod
Visiting Professor, Retired
Rollins College
Winter Park, Florida

www.hmhschool.com

CHAPTER 3

Meaning of Subtraction   55

Theme: On the Playground

Unit 1

THE WORLD ALMANAC FOR KIDS

Indiana Standards

A

What I Know About Math

1. I can count to _______.

2. I can draw these shapes.

3. I can measure length.

_______ inches

4. I can tell time.

_______ :00   _______ :00

Take a Survey

1. Ask 8 friends which activity they like the best.
Draw a circle for each response.

2. **Math Talk** What is the favorite activity on your picture graph?

Numbers and Number Words

1. Write the number.

 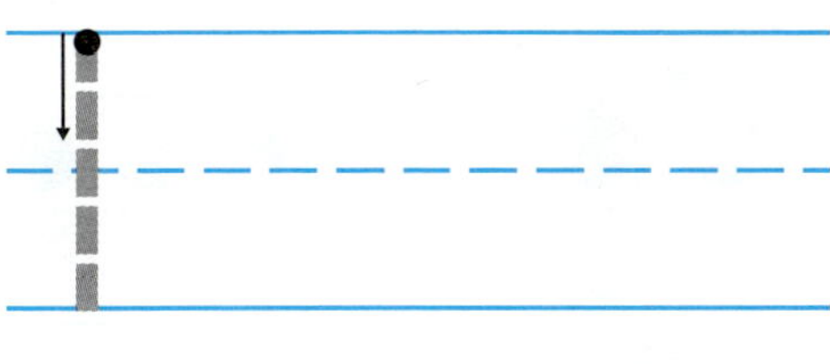

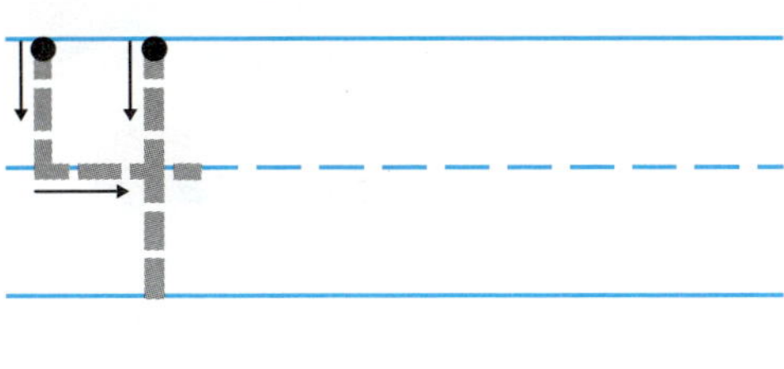 

 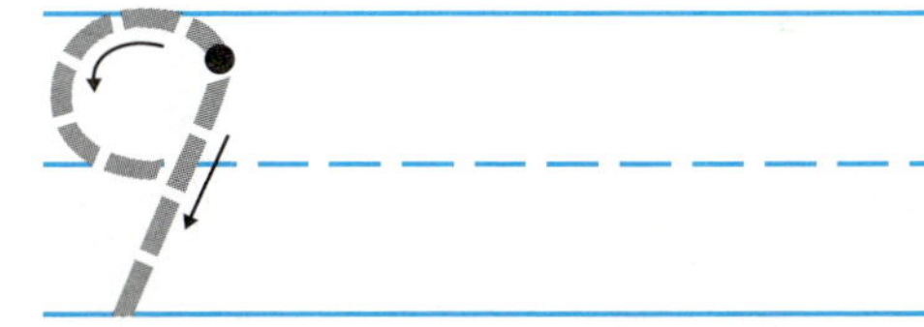

2. Match the number word and the number.

six	10
ten	14
fourteen	6

3. **Math Talk** When you count, what number comes before 3?

D

Different Ways to Show Numbers

1. Circle the ways that show 5.

 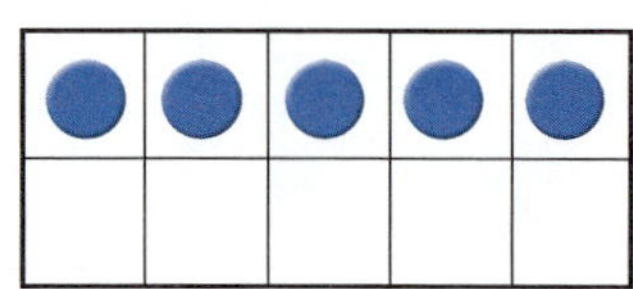 $4 + 2$ 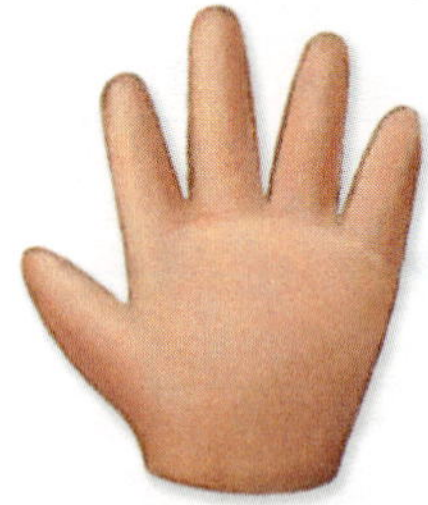

 $2 + 3$ 

2. Draw an X on the ways that show fewer than 8.
   Circle the ways that show more than 8.

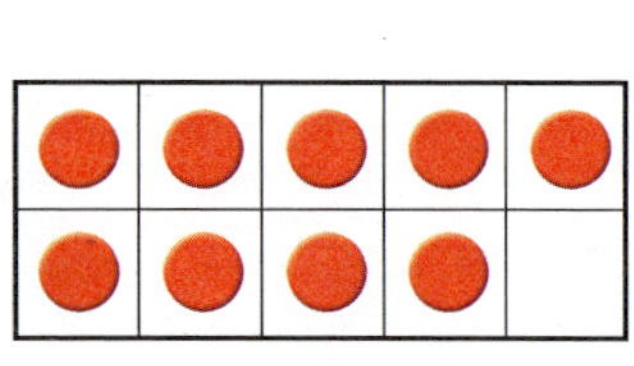 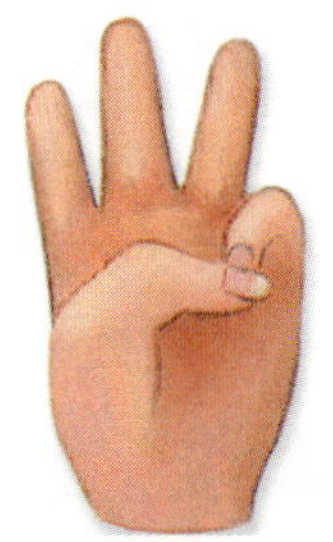 5 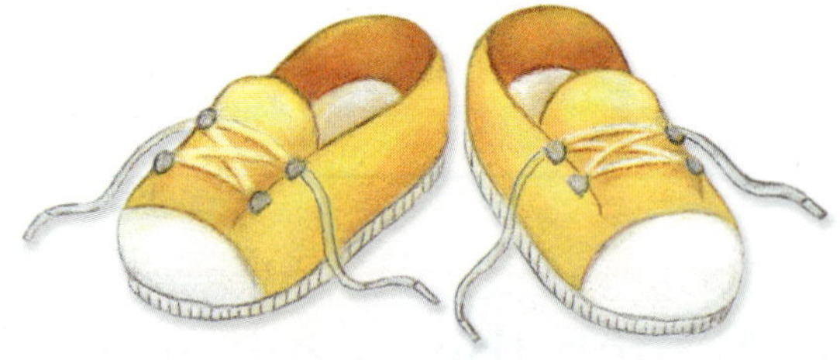

3. **Math Talk** What is the greatest number shown
   on this page? How do you know?

E

Ordinal Numbers

1. Circle the first child red.

2. Circle the ninth child orange.

3. Circle the sixth child blue.

4. **Math Talk** What is the pattern with boys and girls?
Would a boy or girl come next in line?

5. What other patterns do you see?

F

Use Position Words and Classify

I. Listen to your teacher.

2. **Math Talk** How are the objects on each shelf alike? How are they different?

Comparing Sets

1. Draw a set with the same number.

2. Count the coins. Write the numbers. Circle the set that has more.

3. Draw a set with fewer than 5.

4. **Math Talk** How do you know when a set has more than another set?

Name ____

Calendar Time

Use the calendar.
Circle the answer.

1. Look at the blue row.
What does it show?

month   week

2. Today is Tuesday.
What day is tomorrow?

Wednesday   Monday

3. The calendar shows July.
Circle the season.

winter   summer

4. Look at the green day.
What date is it?

July 16   March 16

5. **Math Talk** How can you tell if there are more Mondays
or Thursdays in the month shown above?

I

Estimating

Look at the 10 beads in the pan.

About how many beads are shown? Circle the answer.

1.

more than 10   fewer than 10   about 10

2.

more than 10   fewer than 10   about 10

3.

more than 10   fewer than 10   about 10

4. **Math Talk** What helps you make an estimate?

Name ________________________________

Geometry

1. Write how many.

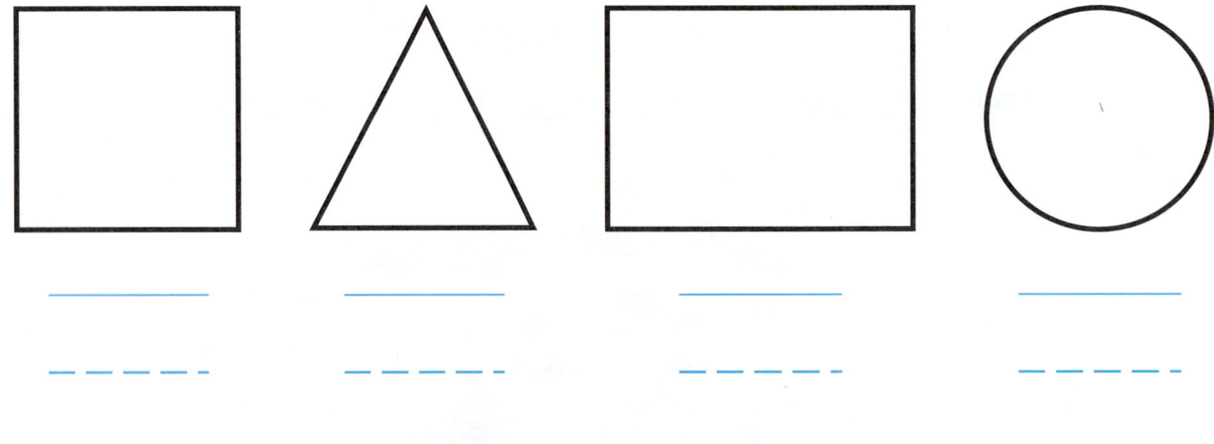

2. **Math Talk** What shapes can you see in your classroom?

K

Name ___________________________

Patterns

Circle the one that is likely to come next.

1.

2.

3.

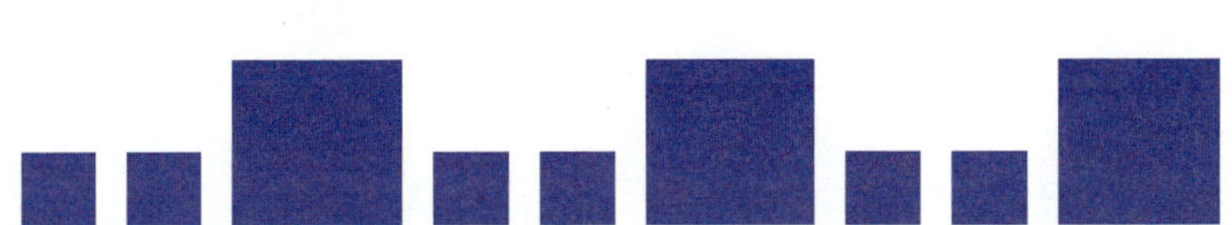 

4.

5. **Math Talk** How could you make a pattern with claps and stomps?

L

Position Words

Use the picture.
Circle the correct word to fill in the blank.

1. The ball is ___________ the sandbox.　　near

far from

2. The bird is ___________ the tree.　　above

below

3. The child is going ___________ the slide.　　down

up

4. The dog is ___________ the tree.　　behind

next to

5. **Math Talk** What words would you use to describe where you sit in your classroom?

M

Name _______________________

Time

1. Circle the one that comes first.

2. Circle the activity that is shorter than an hour.

3. Write the hour the clock shows.

 ___ :00
 ___ :00

4. Write the half hour the clock shows.

 ___ :30
 ___ :30

5. **Math Talk** What do you do before you go to school? What do you do after school?

Name _______________________

Measurement

1. Circle the one that is longer.

2. Circle the one that is shorter.

3. Circle the one that is heavier.

4. Circle the one that is lighter.

5. Circle the one that can hold more.

6. **Math Talk** Which can hold more water: a bathtub or a swimming pool? How do you know?

30

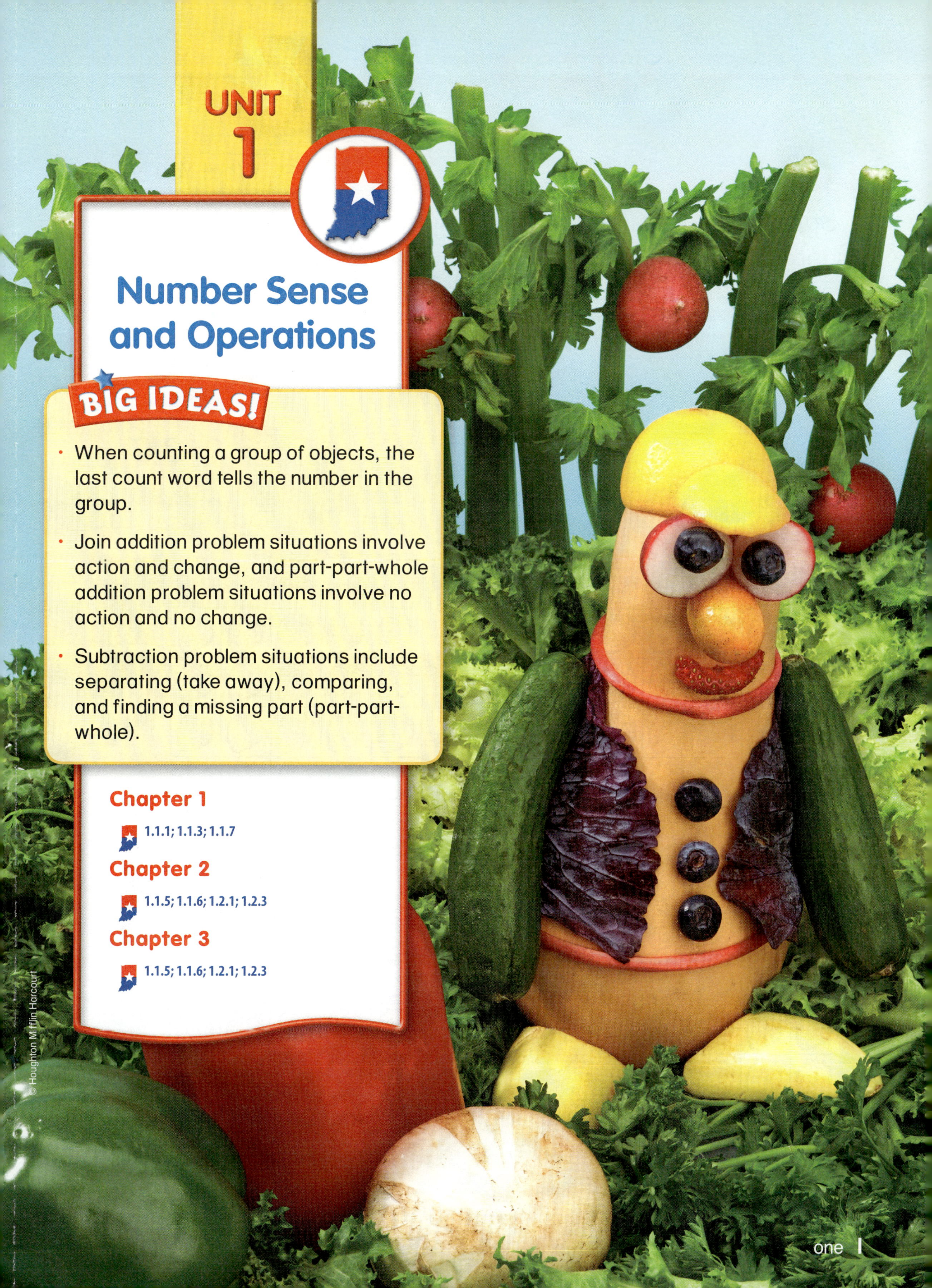
UNIT
1

Number Sense
and Operations

BIG IDEAS!

· When counting a group of objects, the
last count word tells the number in the
group.

· Join addition problem situations involve
action and change, and part-part-whole
addition problem situations involve no
action and no change.

· Subtraction problem situations include
separating (take away), comparing,
and finding a missing part (part-part-
whole).

Chapter 1
1.1.1; 1.1.3; 1.1.7
Chapter 2
1.1.5; 1.1.6; 1.2.1; 1.2.3
Chapter 3
1.1.5; 1.1.6; 1.2.1; 1.2.3

Berry Basket

1. Spin the spinner and color that many berries on your card.

2. Take turns. The winner is the first player to color all 50 squares.

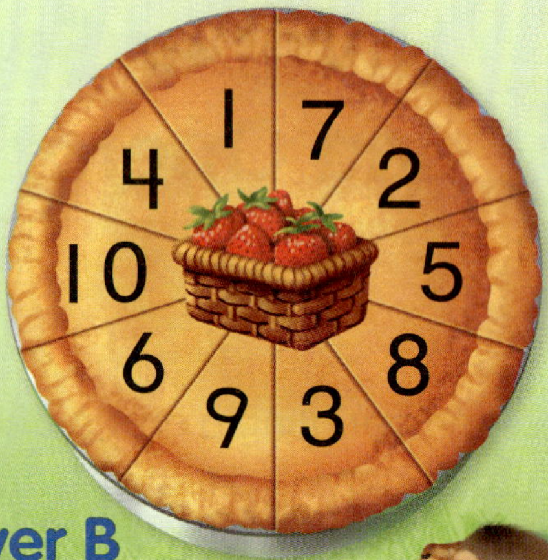

Player A

Player B

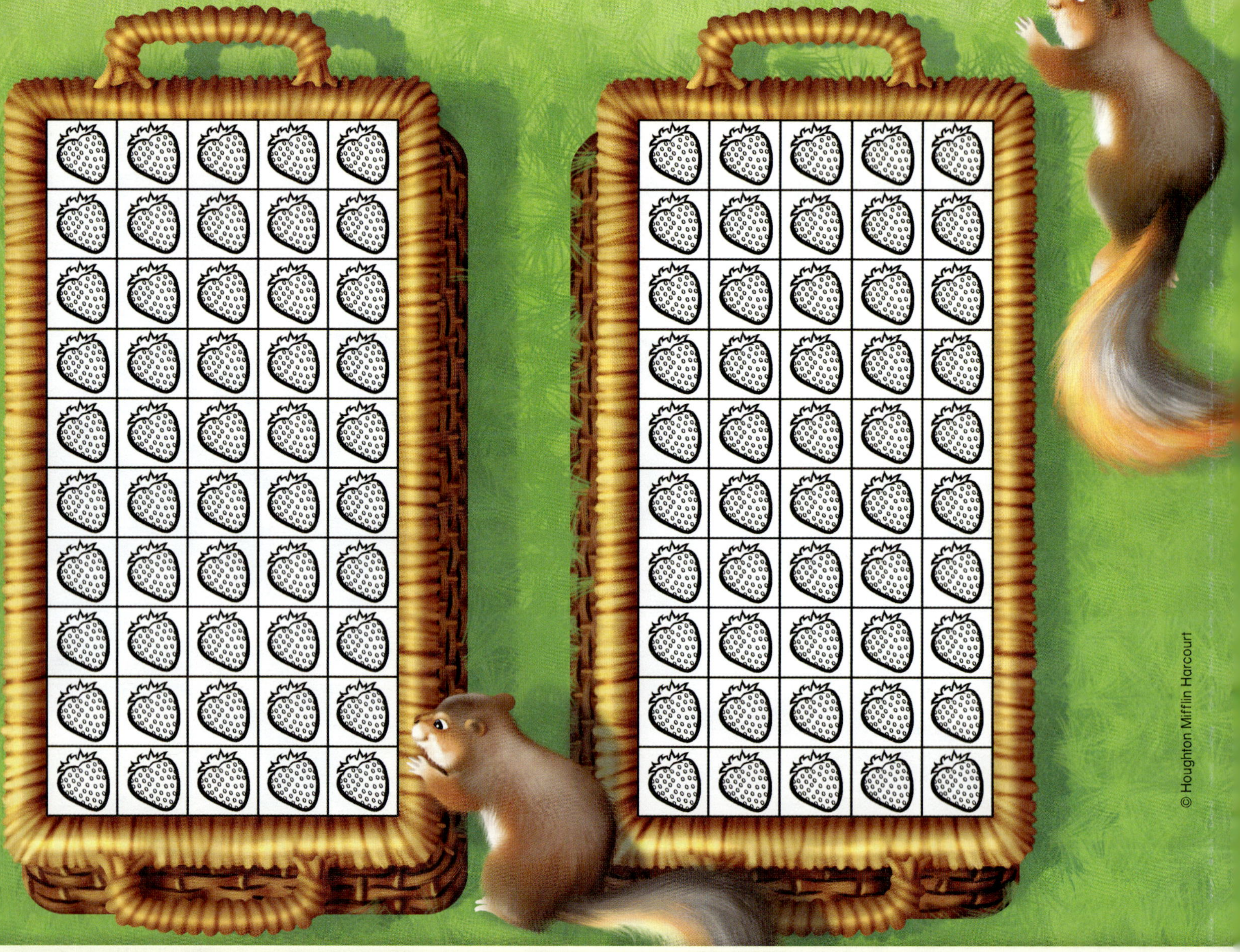

2

Math at Home

Dear Family,

My class started Unit 1 today. In the next few chapters, I will work with numbers to 20 and learn to add and subtract to 10. Here are vocabulary words and activities for us to share.

From,

____

Vocabulary

$2 + 1 = 3$ is an **addition sentence**.

$$2 + 1 = 3$$

The **sum** tells how many in all.

$5 - 4 = 1$ is a **subtraction sentence**.

$$5 - 4 = 1$$

The **difference** tells how many **are left**.

Family Math Activity

Put 5 marbles in a clean egg carton. Close the lid and shake the carton. Then open the lid. Have your child count the marbles in each of the two rows of egg cups and make an addition sentence.

$$3 + 2 = 5$$

Let your child use up to 10 marbles to make other egg-carton addition sentences.

Literature

These books link to the math in this unit. Look for them at the library.

- **Adding**
  by Rozanne Lanczak Williams
  Illustrated by Michael Jarrett
  (Gareth Stevens Publishing, 2004)

- **Adding It Up at the Zoo**
  by Judy Nayer

- **Springtime Addition**
  by Jill Fuller

Math at Home

Chapter 1

Have your child print the names of each family member on different cards. Ask your child to order the cards from least to greatest by the number of letters in each name; for example, Lu, John, Christy.

Chapter 2

As you are reading a story or discussing a picture, ask questions such as these: How many (objects) do you see? If 2 more were shown here, how many would there be altogether?

Chapter 3

Provide 6 balls and a box. Have your child try to roll each of the balls into the box. After all the balls are rolled, record a subtraction sentence to show how many total balls were rolled, how many balls were rolled into the box, and how many balls are outside the box.

At Home These activities are designed for you to work with your child at home.

You Can Count on Fun!

written by Jo Sumara and Kris Derrico

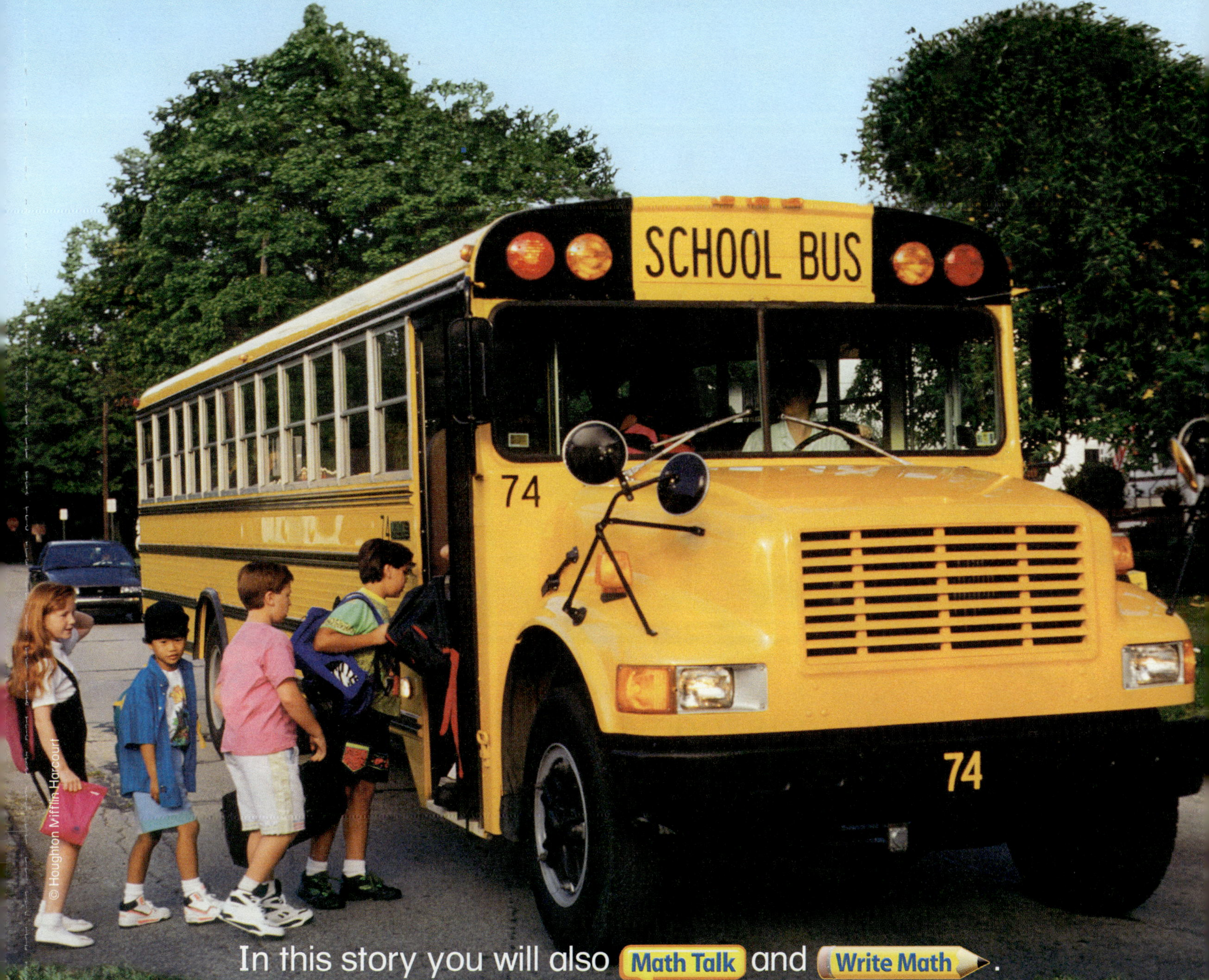

In this story you will also Math Talk and Write Math .

At Home This story will help your child review counting.

A

27 28 29 30 31 32 33 34 35 36 37 38 39 40 41 42 43 44 45 46 47 48 49 50 51 52 53 54 55 56 57 58 59 60 61 62 6
Aa Bb Cc Dd Ee Ff Gg Hh Ii Jj Kk Ll Mm Nn C
1. Raise Your Hand.
2. Share with others.
3. Take Turns.
© Houghton Mifflin Harcourt
School starts today. That is good news.
Count the rules that we will use. ______
B
Why do we have rules?

The teacher asks, "Who will help me?"

How many raised hands does she see? _______

Why do we raise our hands?

c

Why do we share with others?

At school we all take turns to read.

How many books does our group need? _____

Why do we take turns?

I like first grade. It is so much fun!

Just count the smiles on everyone! ______

F

Why do we work together?

Name _______________________

Look at the picture.
Draw three more smiling faces.

How many smiles are there now? _______

Write Math ▶ How did you find your answer?

G

How Many Ears?

1. How many blue crayons are there? ______

2. How many yellow crayons are there? ______

3. How many blue crayons and yellow crayons are there in all? ______

4. Draw green crayons to show a different number.

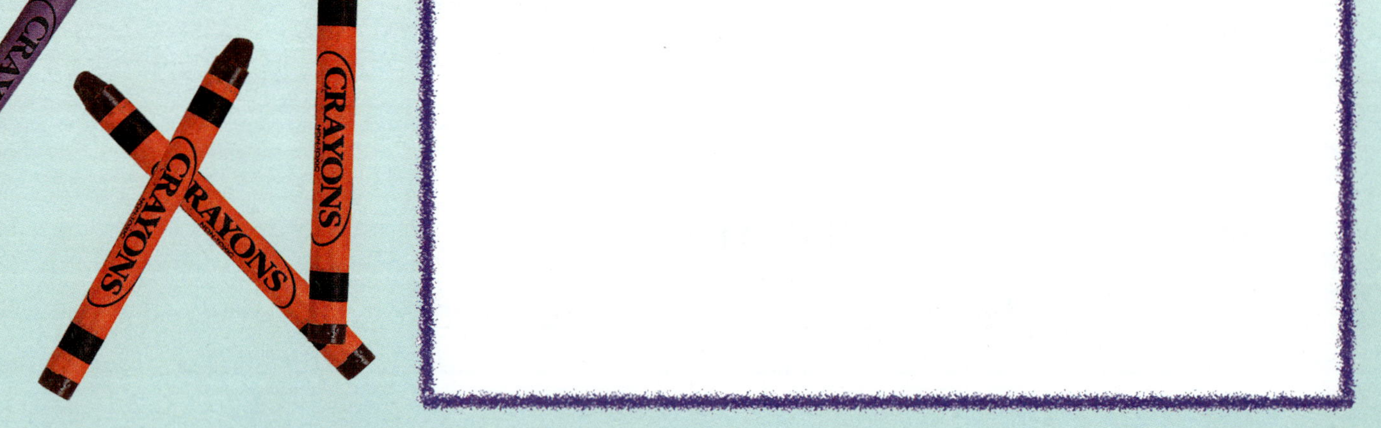

5. How many green crayons are there? ______

6. How many purple crayons and red crayons are there in all? ______

Write Math ➤ Write a question about the green crayons and another group of crayons on the page. Write the answer.

H

Number Sense

Theme: Getting to Know You

Fun Fact

You are special. There is no one in the world just like you.

Investigate

Look at the picture. Tell how you could count all of the eyes.

GO ONLINE
Technology
Student pages are available in the Student eBook.

Show What You Know 

Circle the row that has more.

1. 

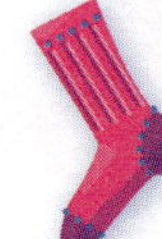

2. 

Circle the row that has fewer.

3. 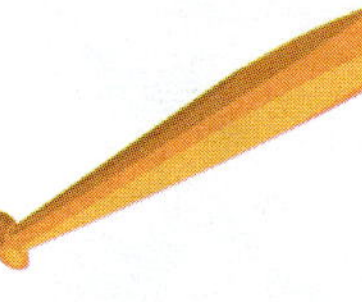

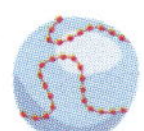

4. 

Circle the 2 groups that are equal.

5. 

At Home This page checks your child's understanding of important skills needed for success in Chapter 1.

Chapter 1 Lesson 1

Numbers to 10

▶ **We Learn**

There are different ways to show numbers.

Here are some ways to show
the number 5.

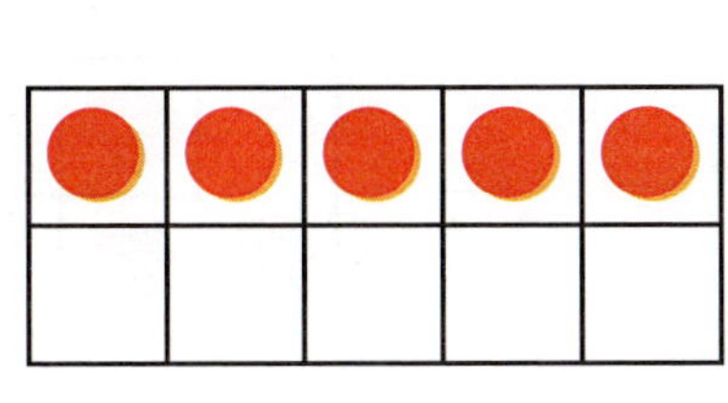

5   five
number   **word**   **counters**   **pictures**

Essential Question
What are some different ways to show numbers?

THINK!
1	one
2	two
3	three
4	four
5	five
6	six
7	seven
8	eight
9	nine
10	ten

▶ **Share and Show**   

Circle the ways that show the same number.
Write the number.

1. (three)   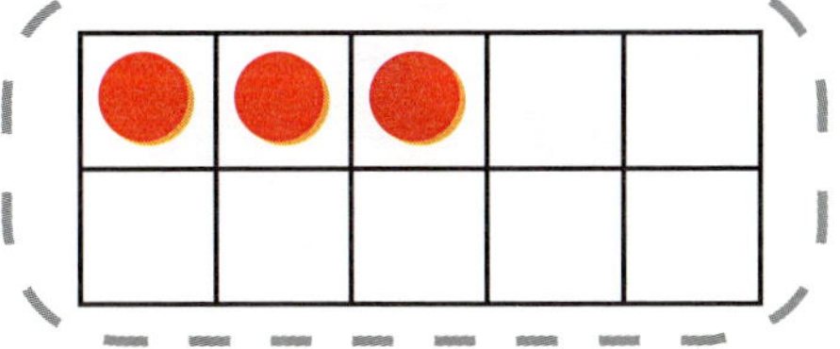      3

2.    five      _______

3.    one      _______

4.         seven   _______

5. **Math Talk** Tell how to make each way in Exercise 2
   show the number 4.

Circle the ways that show the same number.
Write the number.

1.  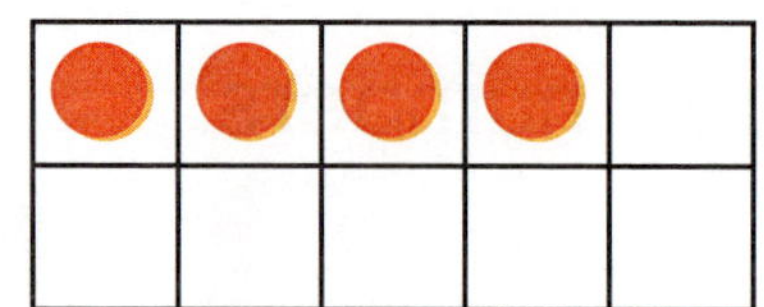 (two) 

2. six  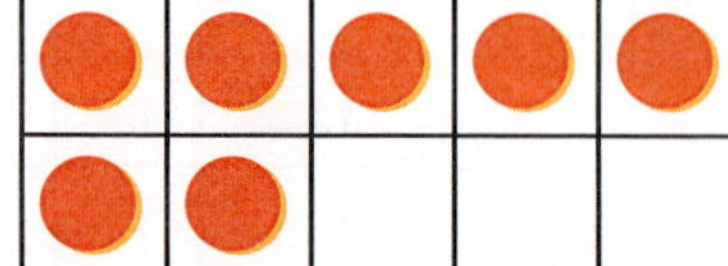 _______

3. 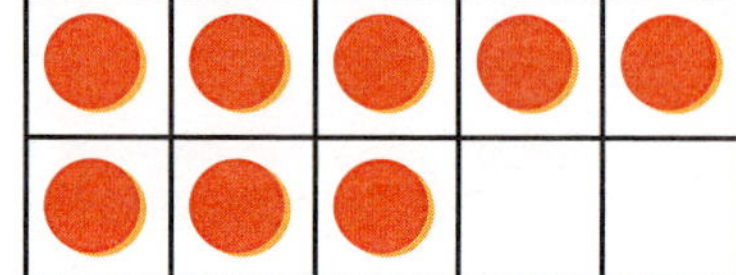 eight 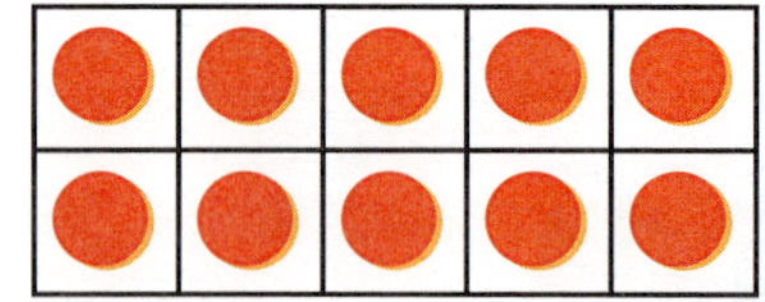 _______

4.   ten _______

5. 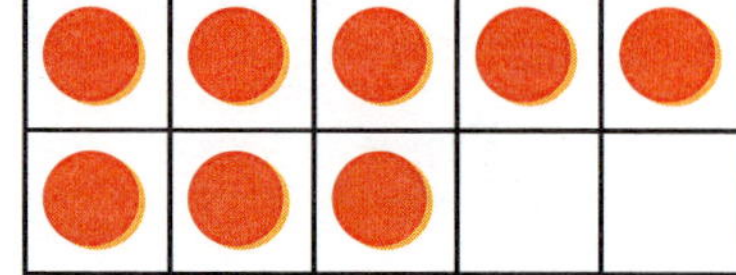 nine _______

Math Board

Problem Solving: Application

6. Count the pennies. Circle the amount.

8¢   9¢   10¢

Write the numbers from 1 to 10.
Write each number word.

Chapter 1 Lesson 2

Numbers to 20

These are some ways to show 12.

12
twelve

Circle the number word that tells how many.
Write the number.

1. 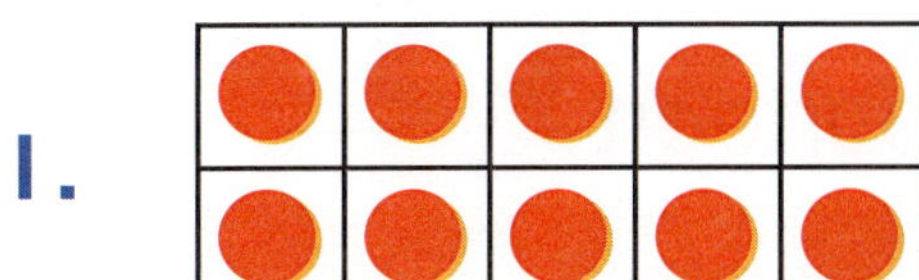
   eleven
   eighteen
   ___11___

2. 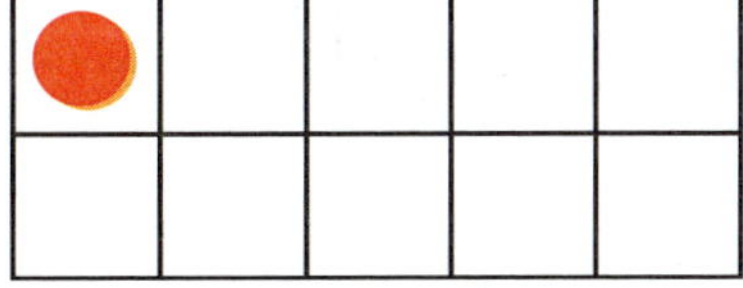
   fifteen
   fourteen
   ____

3. 
   fifteen
   nineteen
   ____

4. 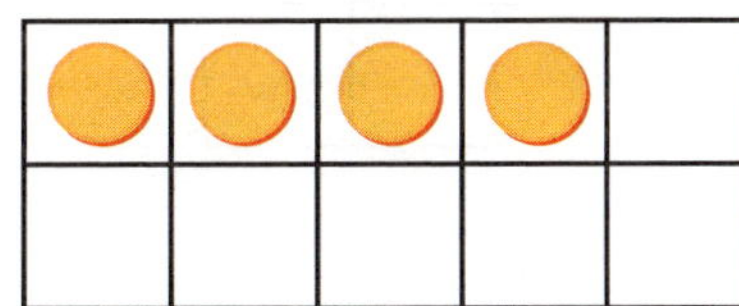
   twenty
   thirteen
   ____

5. **Math Talk** Describe what is the same about the models in Exercises 1–4.

1.1.1 Count, read, write, order, rename and compare whole numbers to at least 100.

Circle the number word that tells how many.
Write the number.

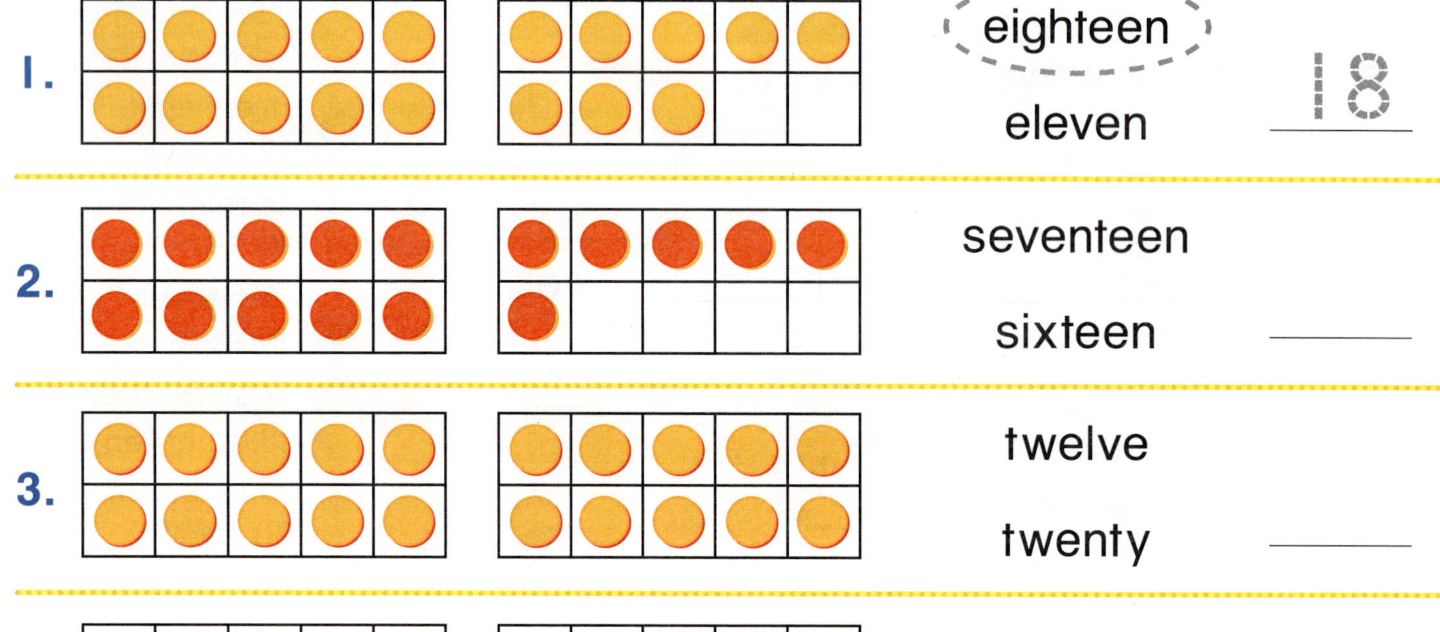

1. eighteen
eleven
18

2. seventeen
sixteen
______

3. twelve
twenty
______

4. nineteen
fourteen
______

5. fifteen
seventeen
______

Problem Solving: Visual Thinking

6. Complete each sentence.

16 is 4 less than ______.

16 is 6 more than ______.

How many more counters do you need to
make 20? Explain.

10

At Home Tell your child a number between 11 and 20. Have
him or her count out that number of pennies and write the
number. Repeat with other numbers.

Chapter 1 Lesson 3

Compare Numbers to 20

▶ Explore

You can compare numbers.

6

9

11

Hands On

Essential Question
How do you compare numbers?

Vocabulary
is greater than
is less than

▶ Connect

Use ▢ to show each number.
Circle **is greater than** or **is less than**.

1. 2 is greater than 4.
(is less than)

2. 3 is greater than 1.
is less than

3. 4 is greater than 5.
is less than

4. 6 is greater than 13.
is less than

5. 10 is greater than 8.
is less than

6. 11 is greater than 14.
is less than

7. 12 is greater than 7.
is less than

8. 11 is greater than 19.
is less than

9. **Math Talk** What number is greater than 12 and less than 14?
Use ▢ to show how you know.

1.1.1 Count, read, write, order, rename and compare whole numbers to at least 100. *also* **1.1.2**

Use 🎴 if you need to.

Circle **is greater than** or **is less than**.

1.

5 (is greater than) 2.
   is less than

2.

4 is greater than 8.
   is less than

3.

6 is greater than 10.
   is less than

4.

12 is greater than 16.
    is less than

5.

19 is greater than 9.
    is less than

6.

17 is greater than 14.
    is less than

7.

15 is greater than 16.
    is less than

8.

18 is greater than 20.
    is less than

 **Problem Solving: Reasoning**

9. Circle the numbers that are less than 15.

Explain how you know which numbers to circle.

Chapter 1 Lesson 4

Order Numbers to 20

You can put numbers in order.

7

8

10

7   8   10

least   greatest

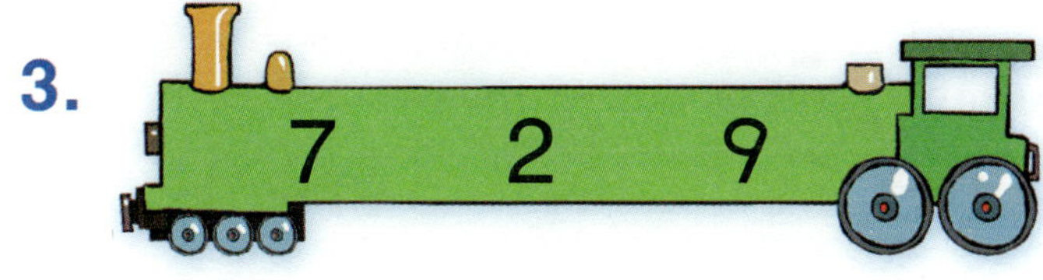

Hands On

Essential Question
How do you order numbers?

Vocabulary
least
greatest
is less than
is greater than

Connect

Use ⬛ to show each number.
Write the numbers in order from least to greatest.

1.

4   5   6

least   greatest

2.

_____ _____ _____

3.

_____ _____ _____

✓**4.**

_____ _____ _____

✓**5.**

_____ _____ _____

6. **Math Talk** Which number is least? Explain.

20   10   11

1.1.1 Count, read, write, order, rename and compare whole
numbers to at least 100. *also* **1.1.2**

Share and Show

Write the numbers in order from least to greatest.
Use 🔴 if you need to.

1. 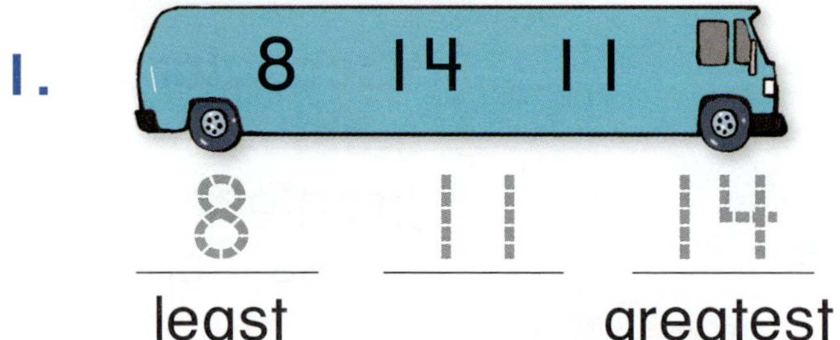

8 ___ 11 ___ 14 ___
least   greatest

2. 

___ ___ ___

3. 

___ ___ ___

4. 

___ ___ ___

5.

___ ___ ___

6. 

___ ___ ___

7.

___ ___ ___

8. 

___ ___ ___

Problem Solving: Application

9. Write the numbers in order from least to greatest.

___ ___ ___ ___

Will this order change if 

is added? Explain.

Chapter 1 Lesson 5
Ordinal Numbers

▶ **We Learn**

You can use special number words to tell position.

first   second   third   fourth   fifth   sixth   seventh   eighth   ninth   tenth

▶ **Share and Show** 

Circle to show position.

1. first

second   seventh   ninth

2. first

third   fourth   eighth

3. first

first   fifth   tenth

4. first

second   sixth   seventh

5. **Math Talk** You are the tenth person in line.
How many people are in front of you? Explain.

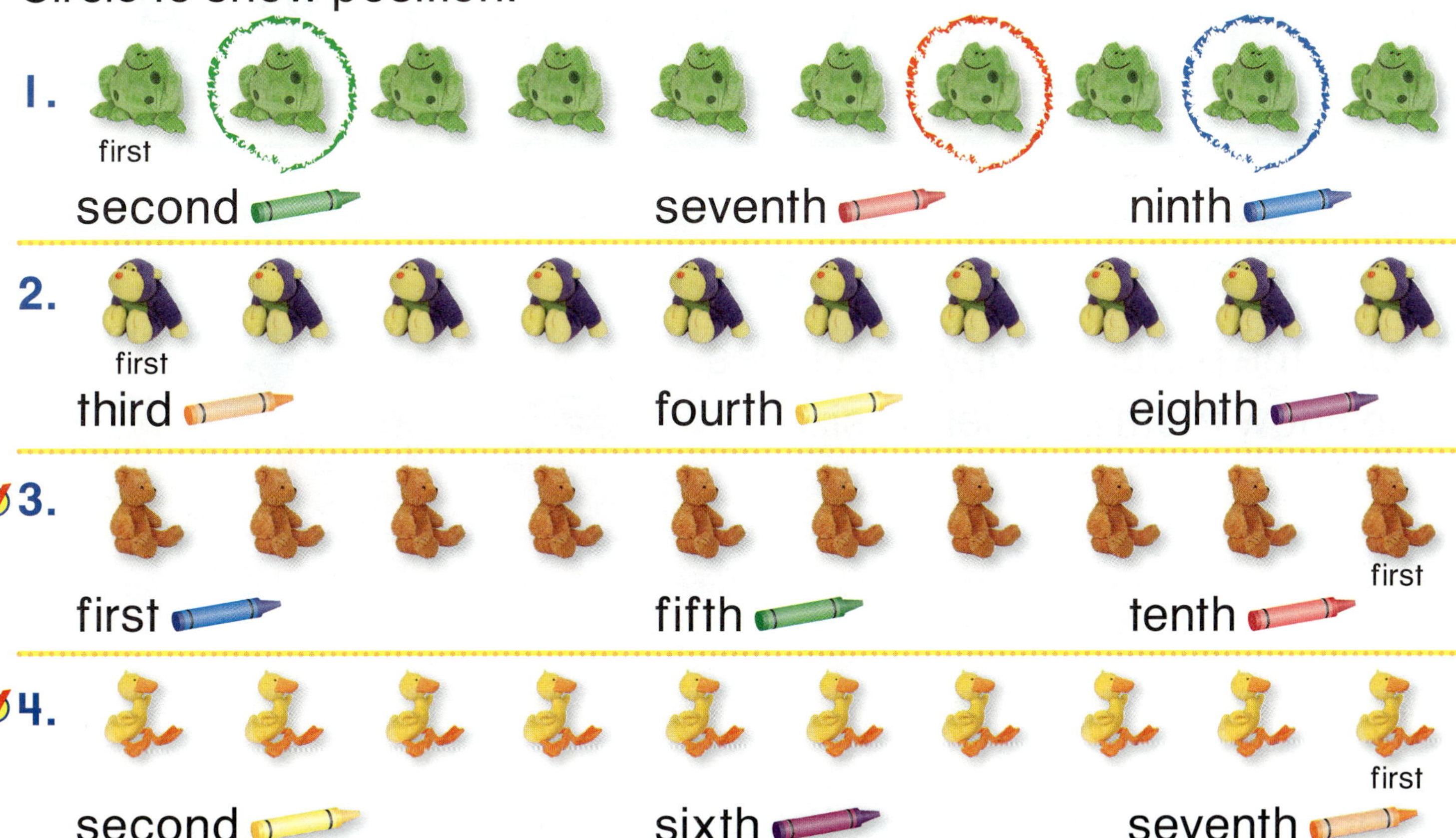

1.1.3 Match the ordinal numbers first, second, third, etc. with an ordered set to at least 10 items.

1. Color to show order.

first   second   third   sixth   eighth   tenth

Problem Solving: Application

2. Use the picture. Copy the circles to show them in order by size.

first   second   third   fourth   fifth

Tell how you decided which circle was first.

© Houghton Mifflin Harcourt

Problem Solving Workshop

Skill: Use Data from a Graph

Problem Solving

Essential Question

How do you read a graph?

Use the picture graph.

Write how many.

1. ___6___ 

2. ______

3. ______

Circle the lunch that has the least number.

4.

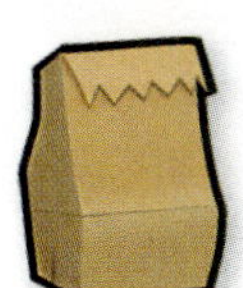

Circle the lunch that has the greatest number.

5.

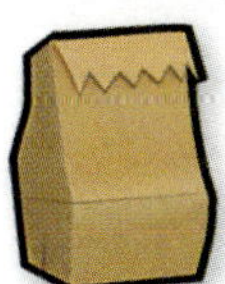

6. **Math Talk** Tell how you use the data from this graph.

1.1.7 Pose a question and collect and represent data using pictures or picture graphs to answer the question posed. *also* **1.1.1; 1.1.4**

Problem Solving Skill Practice

Use the picture graph.

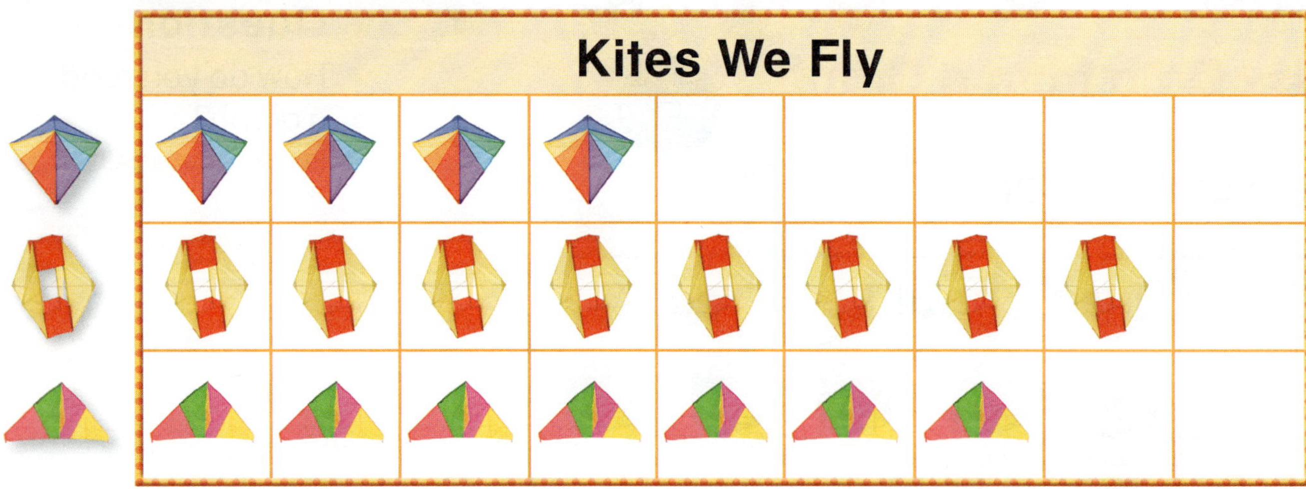

Kites We Fly

Write how many.

1. _4_ 

2. _____ 

3. _____ 

Circle the kite that has the least number.

4. 

Circle the kite that has the greatest number.

5. 

Name ___________________________

Extra Practice

1. Circle the ways that show the same number.
Write the number.

six 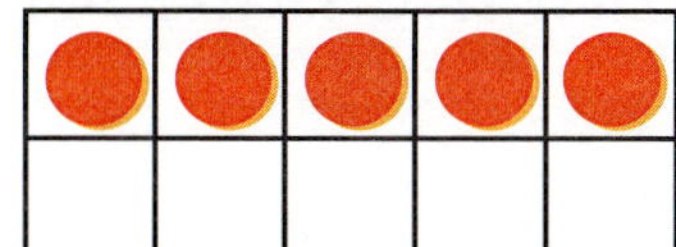    
    ______

2. Circle the number word that tells how many.
Write the number.

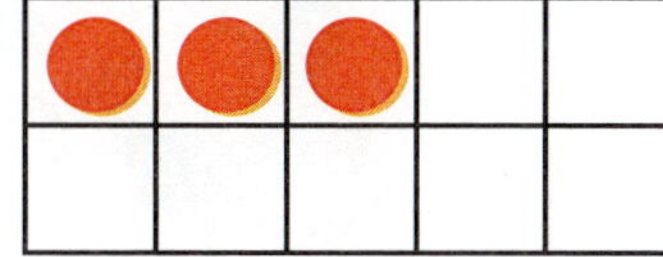

thirteen
fourteen   ______

Use ▦.
Circle **is greater than** or **is less than**.

3. 17   is greater than / is less than   7.

4. 15   is greater than / is less than   18.

Write the numbers in order from least to
greatest. Use ▦ if you need to.

5. 14   18   9
______ ______ ______

6. 16   14   15
______ ______ ______

Problem Solving

Use the picture graph.

7. Write how many.

______ 🍎

______ 🍌

______ 🍊

Fruit We Like

Multistep Problems 
Chapter 1

1. You can show numbers in different ways. Choose a number that is greater than 2 but less than 6. 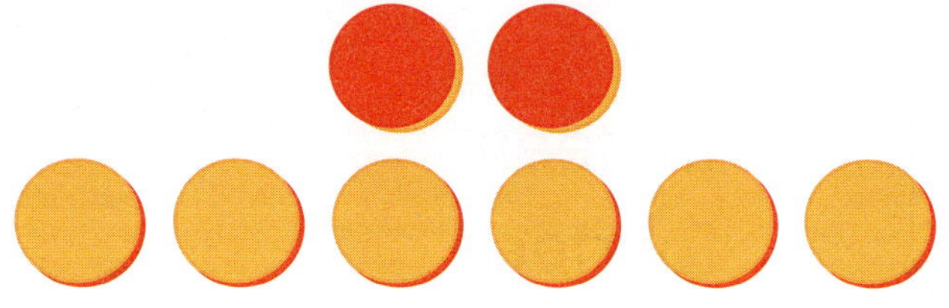 1.1.1

- What is your number?

- Write your number in words.

- Use counters. Show your number.

2. Count the number of  . 1.1.1

- How many ducks are there?

- What number comes after 11?

- What number comes before 11?

- Write a number that is less than 16.

 # Standards Quick Check

1. Circle the ways that show 6.

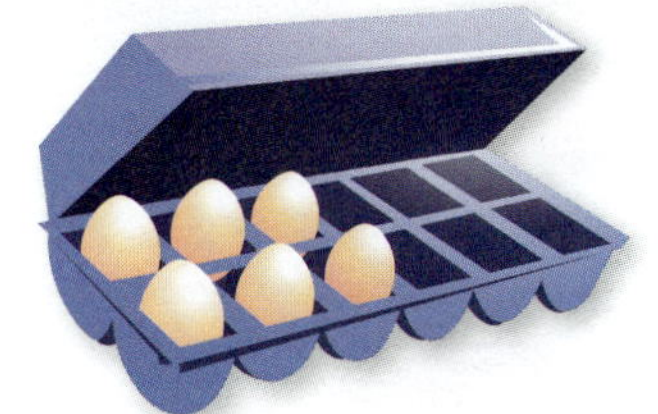

Count. Write the number.

2.   **3.** 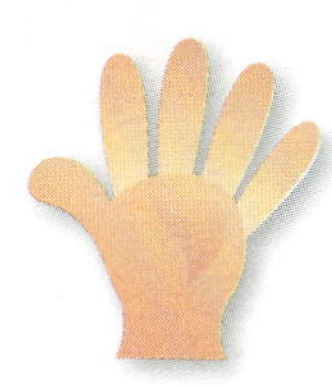   **4.**    **5.** 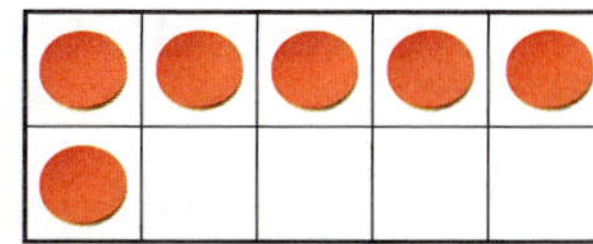

_______   _______   _______   _______

Challenge H.O.T.

Sara used tally marks to show how many 
and ✏️🖍 she has. Count your ✏️
and 🖍. Complete the chart.

Pencils and Crayons		
Sara's ✏️	||||	4
Sara's 🖍	卌 卌 卌 |	16
1. My ✏️		
2. My 🖍		

Juice is a liquid. You can pour liquids. You can freeze liquids to make solids. Frozen juice makes good ice pops!

Count. Write the number. Write the number word.

1. Lian makes ice pops.

______

____

2. Melvin pours juice.

______

____

3.

|| 12 13 14 15 16 17 18 19 20

Anne works at after-school daycare.
She gives out 18 juice pops.
Which number is just before 18?

______

____

 # Looking Ahead to the ISTEP+
Chapter 1

Mark the best answer for questions 1–5.

1. Which is more than

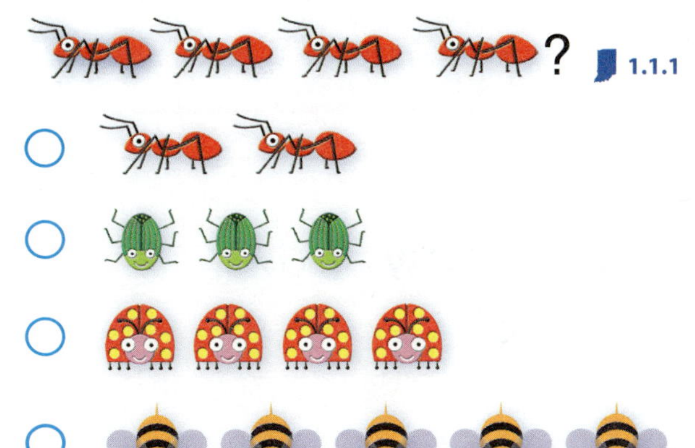

? ▌1.1.1

○
○
○
○

2. Which shows the same number as 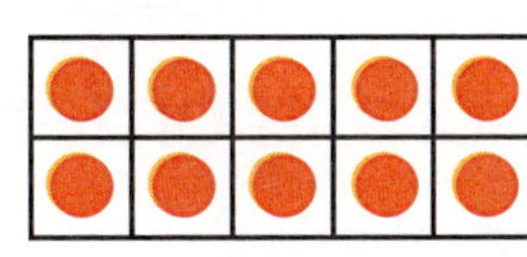 ? ▌1.1.1

○ 6
○ 8
○ 10
○ 16

3. Which has the same number as 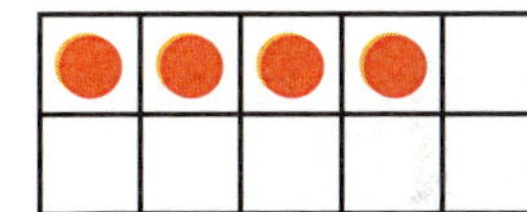 ? ▌1.1.1

○
○
○
○

4. Which number tells how many? ▌1.1.1

○ 4
○ 10
○ 14
○ 15

5. Which is another way to show eleven? ▌1.1.1

○ 1
○ 10
○ 11
○ 12

Mark the best answer for questions 6–8.

6. Which is greater than 12?

1.1.1

- ○ 2
- ○ 10
- ○ 12
- ○ 14

7. Which is less than 16? 1.1.1

- ○ 15
- ○ 16
- ○ 17
- ○ 19

8. Which numbers are in order from least to greatest?

1.1.1

- ○ 10, 6, 13
- ○ 6, 10, 13
- ○ 6, 13, 10
- ○ 13, 10, 6

Open Ended

Use the picture graph.

Write how many. 1.1.7

9. _______ 

10. _______ 

11. _______ 

12. Circle the juice that has the least number. 1.1.7

13. Circle the juice that has the greatest number. 1.1.7

Chapter 2
Meaning of Addition
Theme: In the Classroom
Fun Fact
Most people like the blue crayon best.
Investigate
Ask 5 of your classmates if they like blue, red, or yellow the best. How many like red or yellow the best?
GO ONLINE
Technology
Student pages are available in the Student eBook.
© Houghton Mifflin Harcourt

Show What You Know

Write the number that tells how many.

1.
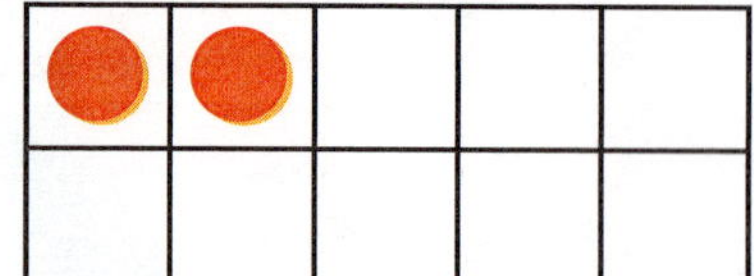
____

2.
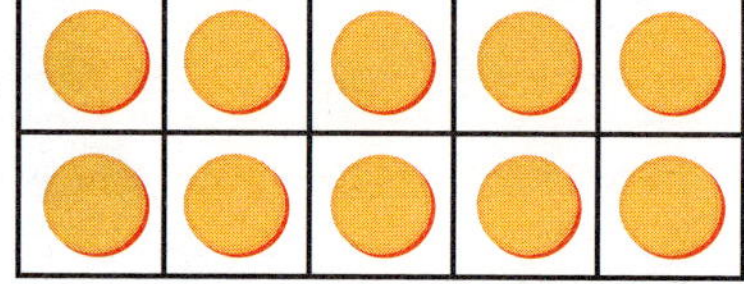
____

3.

____

4.
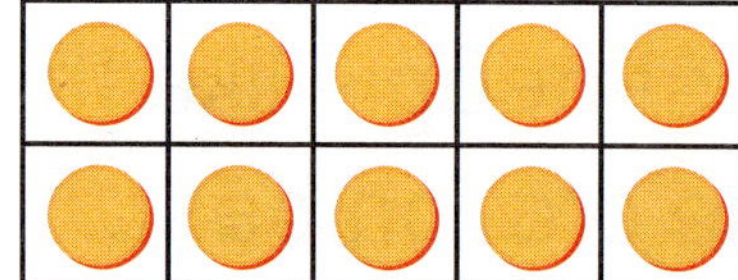
____

Write how many fish in each bowl.

5.

____

6.

____

7.

____

8.

____

At Home This page checks your child's understanding of important concepts and skills needed for success in Chapter 2.

Name ______________________________

Chapter 2 Lesson 1

Model Addition

Hands On

Essential Question

How do you model an addition problem?

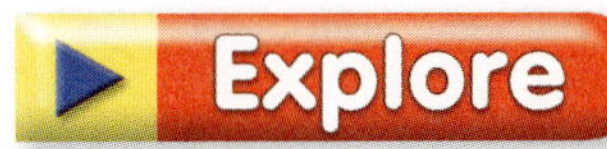

Explore

Use ● to show the addition story.

Draw the ●.

Write how many in all.

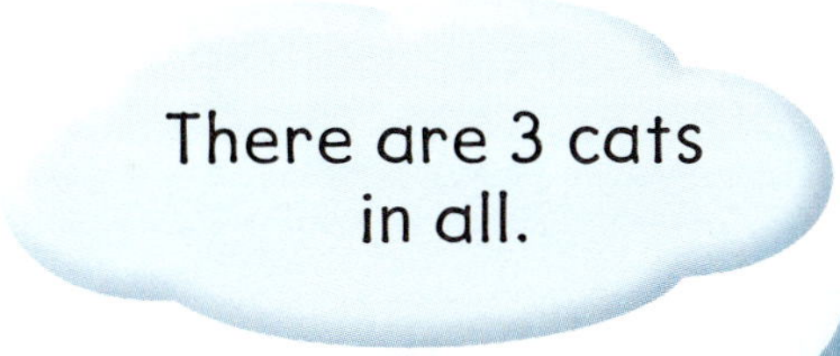

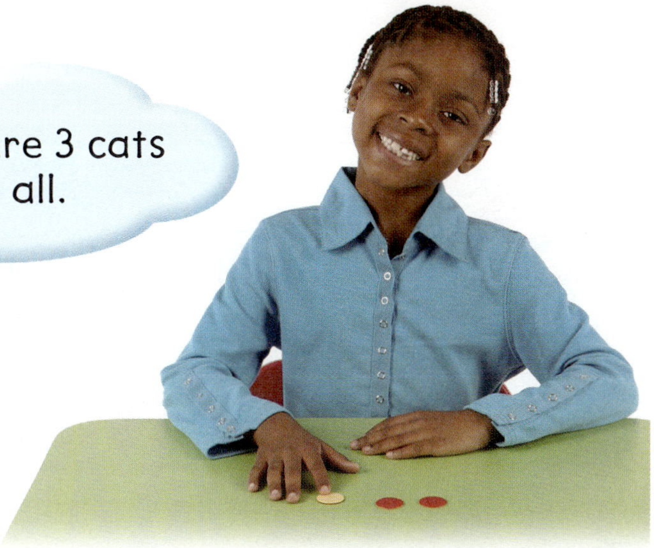

2 cats   1 more cat   __3__ cats in all

Connect

1.

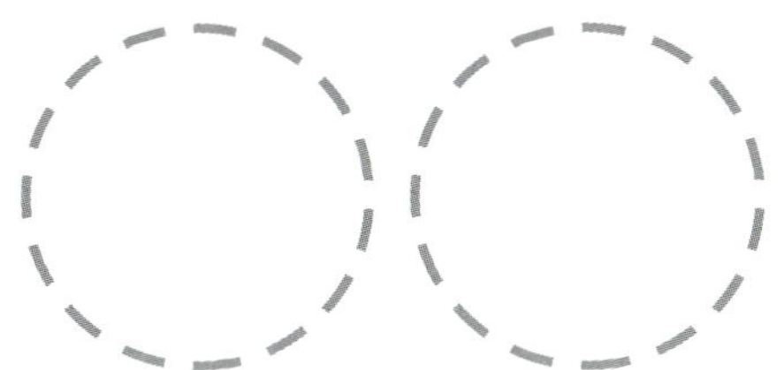

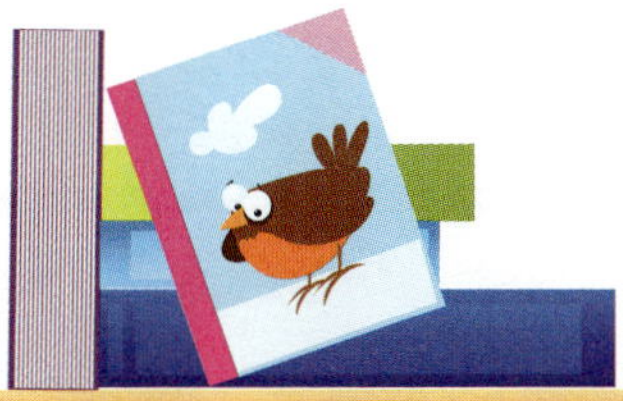

1 bird   1 more bird   _____ birds in all

2.

2 fish   3 more fish   _____ fish in all

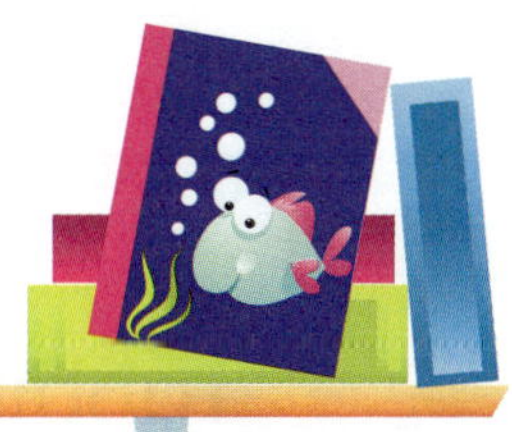

3. **Math Talk** How do you find how many there are in all? Explain.

1.1.5 Solve problems involving addition and subtraction by modeling addition of numbers to at least 100 and by modeling the inverse operation of subtraction using objects. *also* **1.1.6**

Use ● to show the addition story.
Draw the ●. Write how many in all.

1.

○ ○ ○ ○

2 puppies   2 more puppies   ____4____ puppies in all

2.

3 ants   1 more ant   ______ ants in all

 Math Board

Problem Solving: Application

3. Try your own story. Choose two numbers.
Draw the ●. Write how many in all.

______ rabbits   ______ more rabbits   ______ rabbits in all

Look at Exercise 3. Choose two different
numbers. Draw a picture to show your story.

 Have your child use stuffed animals or other toys to show 3 animals.
Then have 2 more animals join the group. Ask how many animals there are in
all. Repeat for other combinations of animals with totals of up to 6.

Use Symbols to Add

See

Write

Say

2 plus 1 is equal to 3.
The sum is 3.

Share and Show

Use the picture. Write the addition sentence.

1.

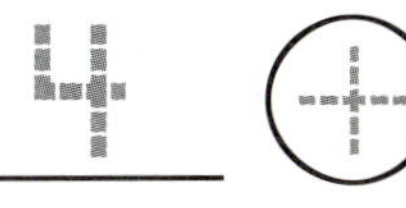  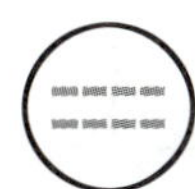 

2.

3.

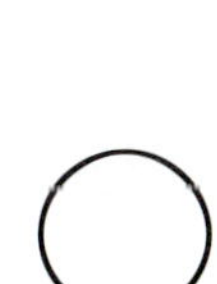 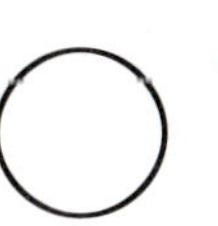

4.

5. **Math Talk** How can you use pictures to help you
write addition sentences? Explain.

Essential Question
What symbol tells you to add?

Vocabulary
plus (+)
is equal to (=)
sum
addition
sentence

$2 + 1 = 3$ is an addition sentence.

1.1.6 Demonstrate fluency with addition facts and the corresponding subtraction facts for totals to at least 20. *also* **1.1.5; 1.2.1**

Use the picture. Write the addition sentence.

1.

______ ◯ ______ ◯ ______

2.

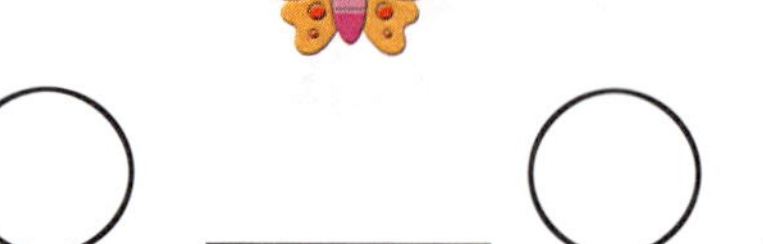

______ ◯ ______ ◯ ______

3.

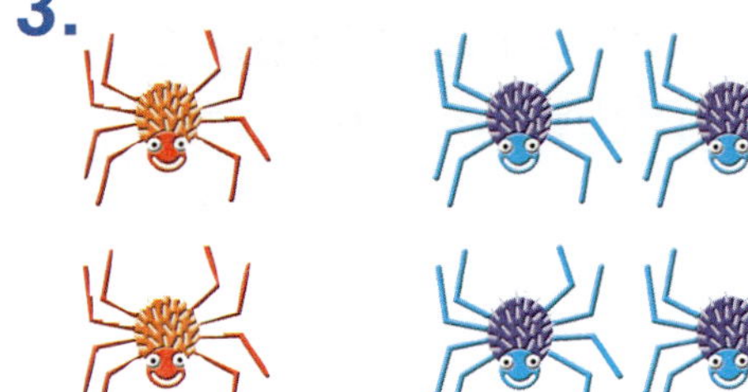 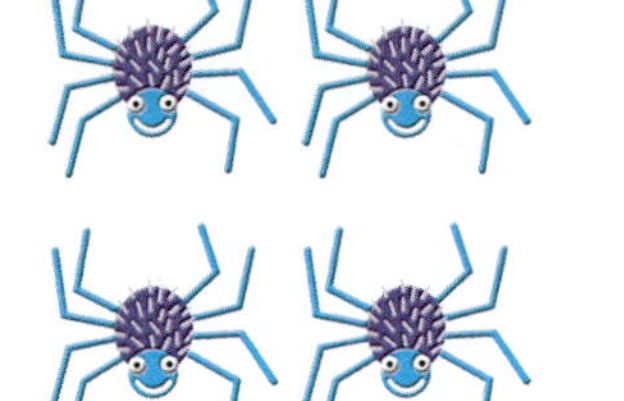

______ ◯ ______ ◯ ______

4.

______ ◯ ______ ◯ ______

5.

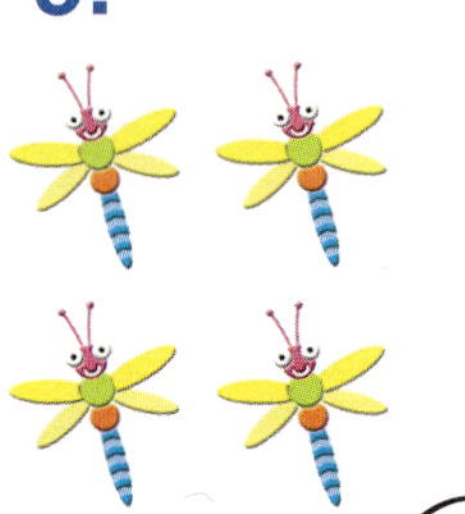 

______ ◯ ______ ◯ ______

6.

______ ◯ ______ ◯ ______

Problem Solving: Visual Thinking

7. Circle the picture that shows $3 + 1 = 4$.

Draw a picture to show $5 + 1 = 6$.

Model Part-Part-Whole

 **Explore**

3    I 

How many crayons are there in all?

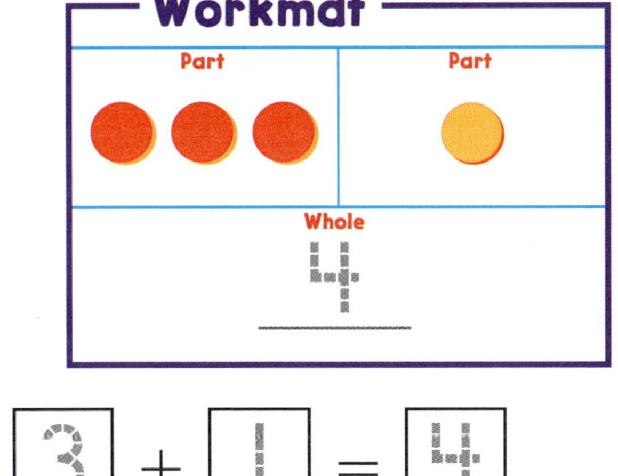

 **Hands On**

Essential Question
How do you model a part-part-whole problem?

Vocabulary
add
part
whole

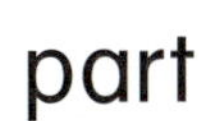 $3 + 1 = 4$

part   part   whole  4 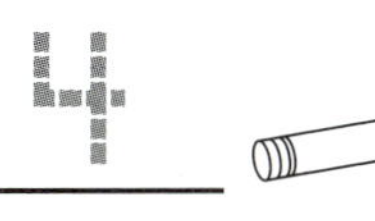 in all

Connect

Make up an addition story. Use Workmat 9 and .
Write the addition sentence. Write how many in all.

I.   2    I 

☐ + ☐ = ☐

part   part   whole   ______  in all

2.   4 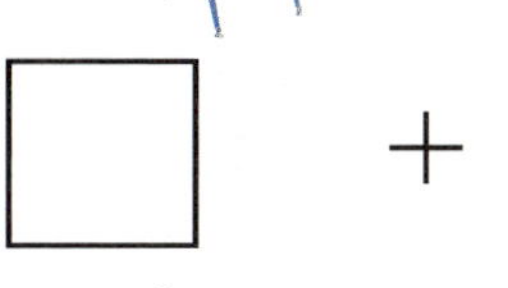   2 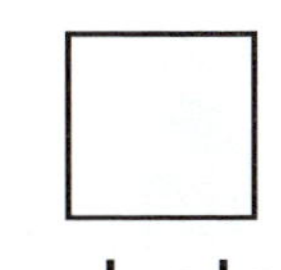

☐ + ☐ = ☐

part   part   whole   ______  in all

3. **Math Talk** How do you find how many there are in all? Explain.

1.1.6 Demonstrate fluency with addition facts and the corresponding subtraction facts for totals to at least 20. *also* **1.1.5; 1.2.1**

Make up an addition story. Use Workmat 9 and ⬤.
Write the addition sentence. Write how many in all.

1. 2 🔵 4 🟡

$$\boxed{2} + \boxed{4} = \boxed{6}$$

part   part   whole   ______ 🥤 in all

2. 3 📎 2 📎

$$\boxed{} + \boxed{} = \boxed{}$$

part   part   whole   ______ 📎 altogether

3. 2 ✏️ 2 ✏️

$$\boxed{} + \boxed{} = \boxed{}$$

part   part   whole   ______ ✏️ in all

4. 1 📘 5 📙

$$\boxed{} + \boxed{} = \boxed{}$$

part   part   whole   ______ 📖 altogether

 **Math Board**

Problem Solving: Application

5. Use the bears to tell a story. Write how many in all.

  ______  in all

Look at the bears. Explain what happens to the
whole when you add the two parts.

At Home Have your child collect a group of up to 6 small
objects and use them to make up part-part-whole addition
stories.

Chapter 2 Lesson 4

Algebra: Add 0

When you add **zero** to a number, the sum is that number.

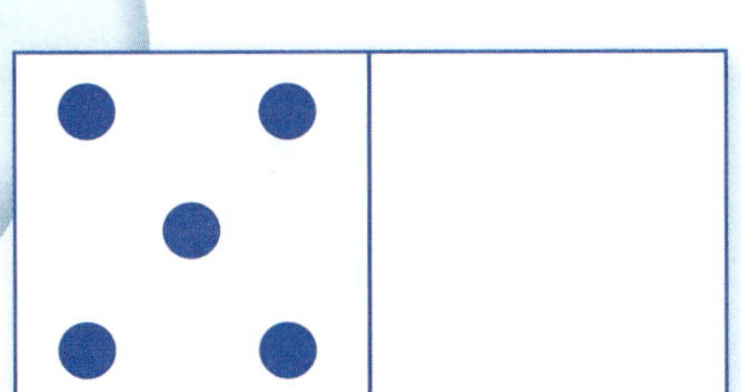

When you add a number to zero, the sum is that number.

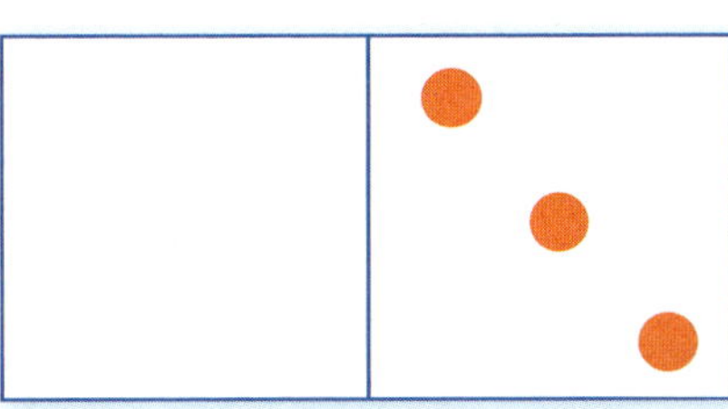

$5 + 0 = \underline{\quad 5 \quad}$
sum

$0 + 3 = \underline{\quad 3 \quad}$
sum

Write the sum.

1.

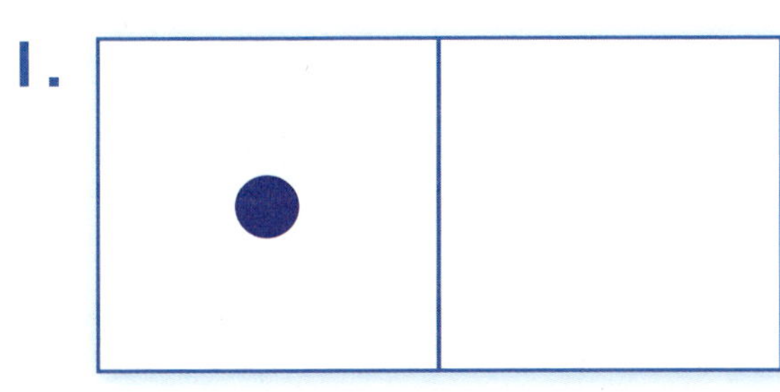

$1 + 0 = \underline{\quad\quad}$

2.

$0 + 2 = \underline{\quad\quad}$

3.

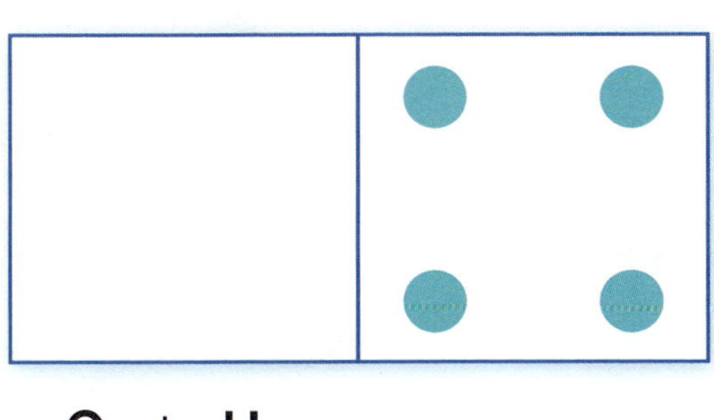

$0 + 4 = \underline{\quad\quad}$

4.

$6 + 0 = \underline{\quad\quad}$

5. **Math Talk** What happens when you add 0 to a number? Use  to prove your answer.

1.2.3 Solve problems using the identity principle for addition and subtraction. **1.1.6** Demonstrate fluency with addition facts and the corresponding subtraction facts for totals to at least 20. *also* **1.1.5; 1.2.1**

Draw circles to show each number.
Write the sum.

1.

$2 + 0 = \underline{\quad 2 \quad}$

2.

$0 + 1 = \underline{\quad 1 \quad}$

3.

$1 + 2 = \underline{\quad 3 \quad}$

4.

$0 + 5 = \underline{\qquad}$

5.

$3 + 1 = \underline{\qquad}$

6.

$0 + 6 = \underline{\qquad}$

7.

$3 + 0 = \underline{\qquad}$

8.

$1 + 4 = \underline{\qquad}$

9.

$4 + 0 = \underline{\qquad}$

10.

$5 + 1 = \underline{\qquad}$

11.

$1 + 3 = \underline{\qquad}$

12.

$5 + 0 = \underline{\qquad}$

Math Board

Problem Solving: Real World

13. Solve.

Mike has 3 books.
Kim does not have any books.
How many books do they have
altogether?

_______ books
What happens when you add 0 to the
number 0? Explain.

Chapter 2 Lesson 5

Algebra: Add in Any Order

You can change the order of addends.
The sum is the same.

$$\underline{1} + \underline{3} = \underline{4}$$

└ addends ┘ sum

$$\underline{3} + \underline{1} = \underline{4}$$

└ addends ┘ sum

Use 🔴 and 🔵 to add.
Color to match. Write each sum.

1.

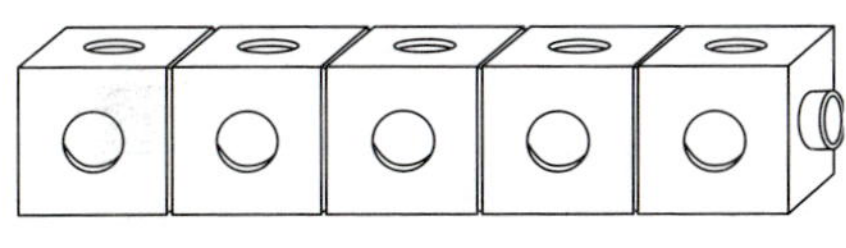

$2 + 3 = \underline{\hphantom{00}}$

2.

$3 + 2 = \underline{\hphantom{00}}$

3.

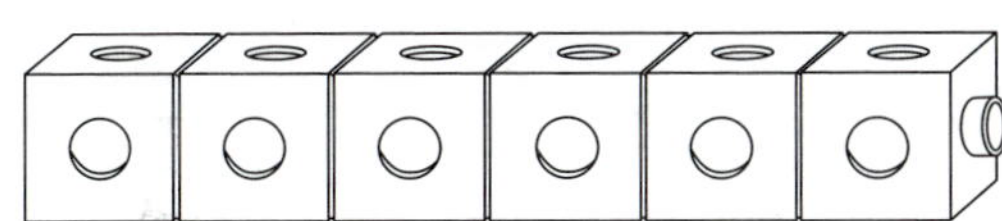

$2 + 4 = \underline{\hphantom{00}}$

4.

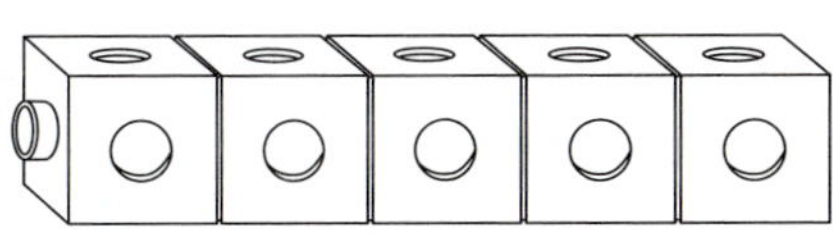

$4 + 2 = \underline{\hphantom{00}}$

5.

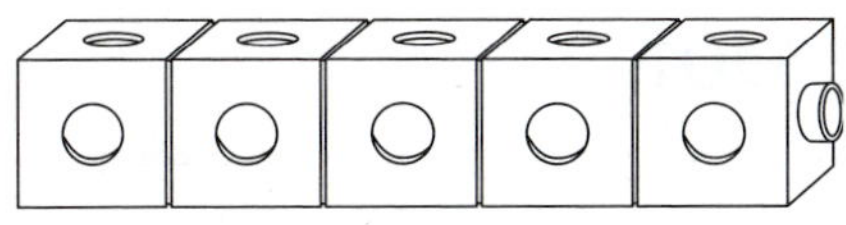

$4 + 1 = \underline{\hphantom{00}}$

6.

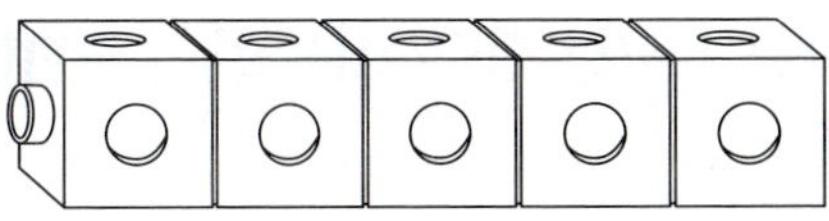

$1 + 4 = \underline{\hphantom{00}}$

7. **Math Talk** How is $4 + 0 = 4$ the same as $0 + 4 = 4$?
How is it different? Use 🔴 🔵 to prove your
answer.

Essential Question
Why can you add numbers in any order?

Vocabulary
order
addend

⭐ **1.1.5** Solve problems involving addition and subtraction by modeling
addition of numbers to at least 100 and by modeling the inverse operation
of subtraction using objects. *also* **1.1.6; 1.2.1**

Use 🟥 and 🟦 to add.
Write the sum. Circle the addition sentences
in each row that use the same addends.

  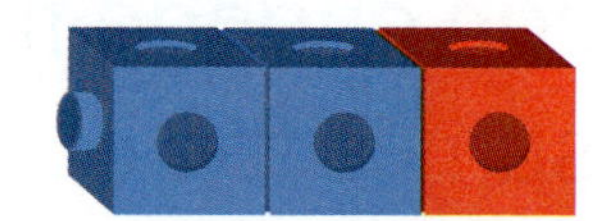

1. $1 + 2 = \underline{3}$ 2. $1 + 3 = \underline{4}$ 3. $2 + 1 = \underline{3}$

4. $1 + 5 = \underline{\hphantom{0}}$ 5. $4 + 2 = \underline{\hphantom{0}}$ 6. $2 + 4 = \underline{\hphantom{0}}$

7. $3 + 2 = \underline{\hphantom{0}}$ 8. $2 + 3 = \underline{\hphantom{0}}$ 9. $3 + 3 = \underline{\hphantom{0}}$

10. $3 + 1 = \underline{\hphantom{0}}$ 11. $4 + 1 = \underline{\hphantom{0}}$ 12. $1 + 4 = \underline{\hphantom{0}}$

13. $0 + 6 = \underline{\hphantom{0}}$ 14. $6 + 0 = \underline{\hphantom{0}}$ 15. $5 + 1 = \underline{\hphantom{0}}$

Math Board

Problem Solving: Visual Thinking

16. Write two addition sentences that tell about
the picture.

$$\underline{\hphantom{00}} + \underline{\hphantom{00}} = \underline{\hphantom{00}}$$

$$\underline{\hphantom{00}} + \underline{\hphantom{00}} = \underline{\hphantom{00}}$$

Explain how you know what addition
sentences to write.

Chapter 2 Lesson 6

Algebra: Ways to Make Numbers to 8

Ways to Make 7

▶ **Connect**

Hands On

Essential Question
How many ways can you show the parts of 8?

Vocabulary
pattern

$7 = \underline{7} + \underline{0}$

$7 = \underline{6} + \underline{1}$

$7 = \underline{5} + \underline{2}$

Use 🟥 and 🟦 to make 7. Color to show a pattern. Complete the addition sentence.

1. $7 = \underline{4} + \underline{3}$

2. $7 = \underline{3} + \underline{}$

3. $7 = \underline{} + \underline{}$

4. $7 = \underline{} + \underline{}$

5. $7 = \underline{} + \underline{}$

6. **Math Talk** Look at the colored cube trains. What pattern do you see? Explain.

1.1.6 Demonstrate fluency with addition facts and the corresponding subtraction facts for totals to at least 20. **1.2.1** Write and solve equations involving addition. *also* **1.1.5**

Use 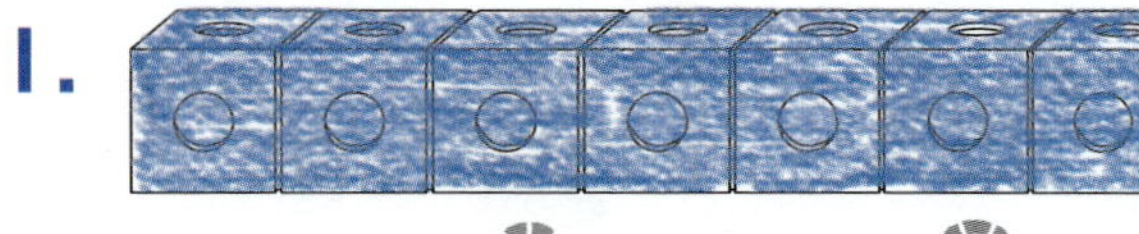 and ▮ to show all the ways
to make 8. Follow the pattern. Color.
Complete the addition sentence.

1.
$$8 = \underline{} + \underline{8}$$

2. 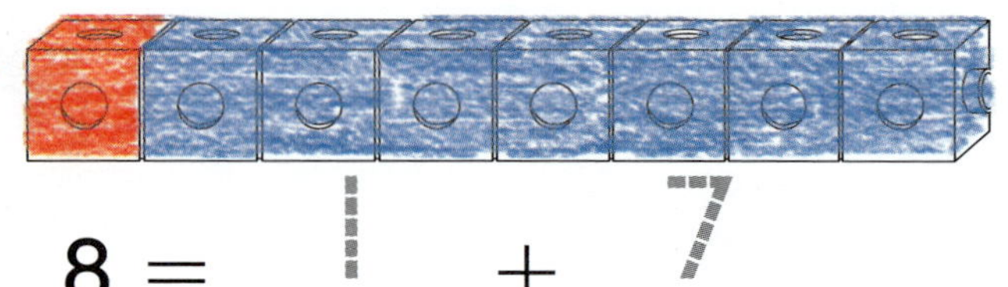
$$8 = \underline{1} + \underline{7}$$

3. 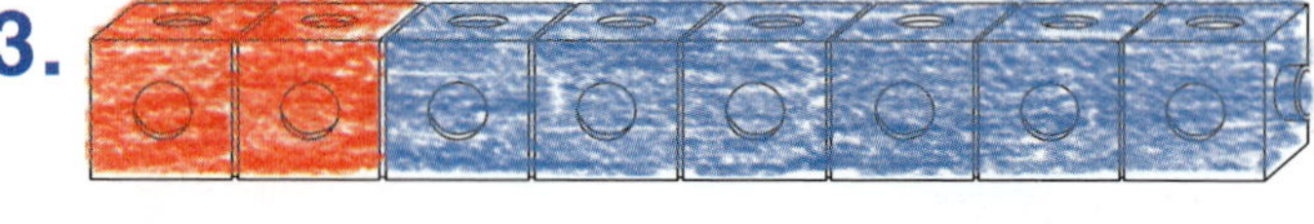
$$8 = \underline{} + \underline{}$$

4.
$$8 = \underline{3} + \underline{}$$

5.
$$8 = \underline{} + \underline{}$$

6. 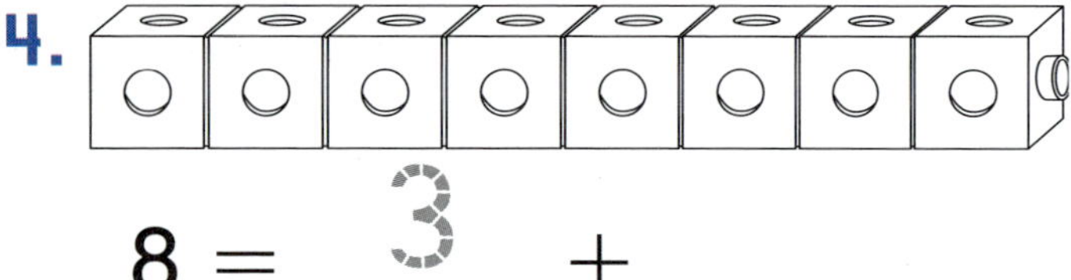
$$8 = \underline{} + \underline{}$$

7. 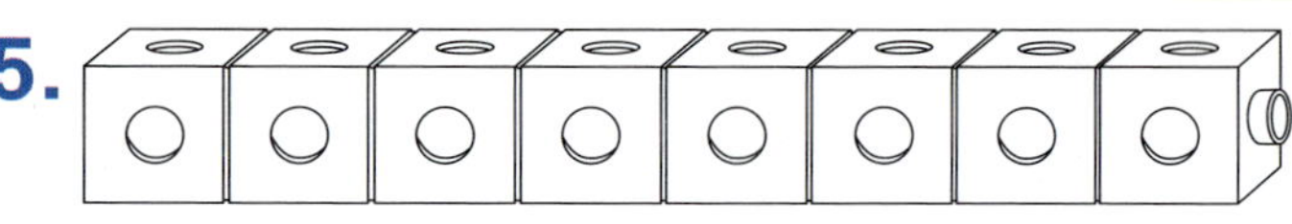
$$8 = \underline{} + \underline{}$$

8. 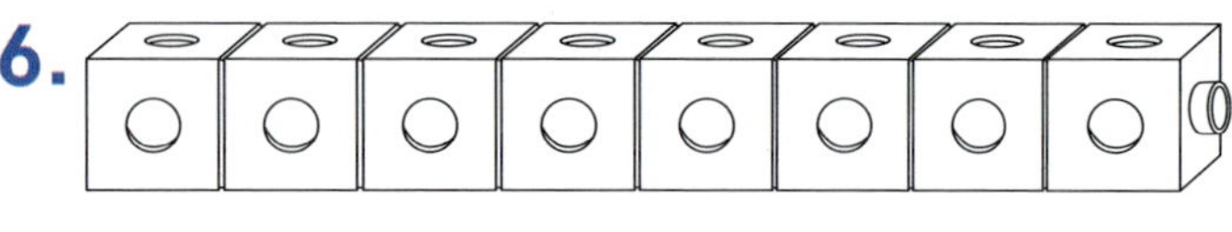
$$8 = \underline{} + \underline{}$$

9. 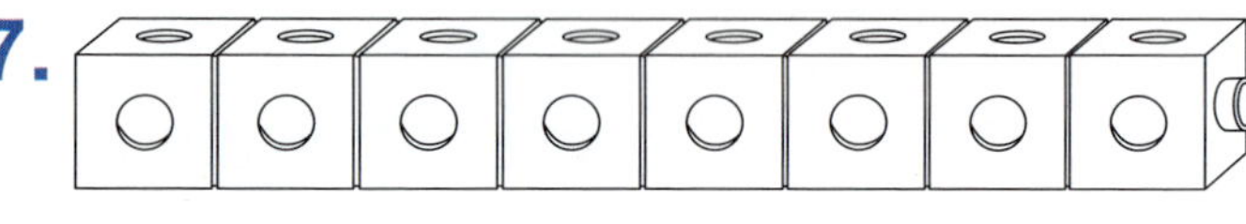
$$8 = \underline{} + \underline{}$$

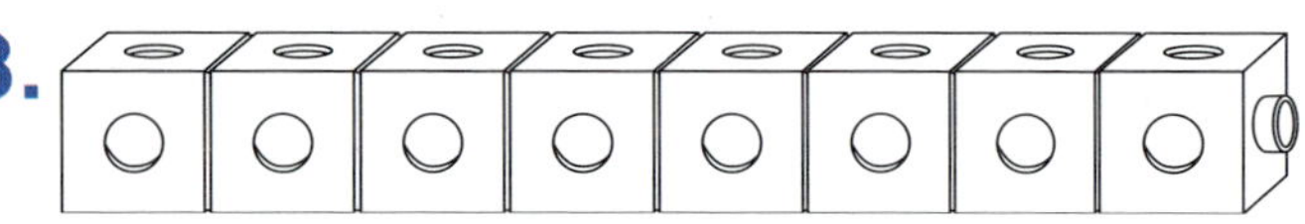
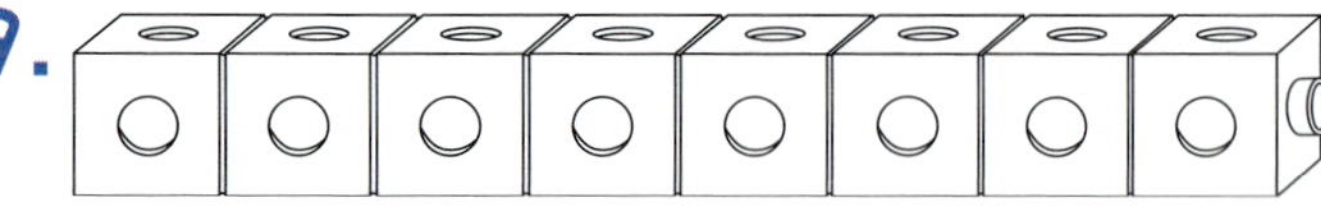

Problem Solving: Visual Thinking

10. Use the picture.

Write an addition sentence.

$$\underline{} + \underline{} = \underline{}$$

How does knowing how to make numbers
help you solve this problem? Explain.

At Home Write 10 = 9 + 1. Model the problem with small objects. Ask your
child to make 10 another way. Take turns until you and your child model all the
ways to make 10. See if your child follows a pattern. Now show ways to make 9.

Vertical Addition Sentences

Add across.

Add down.

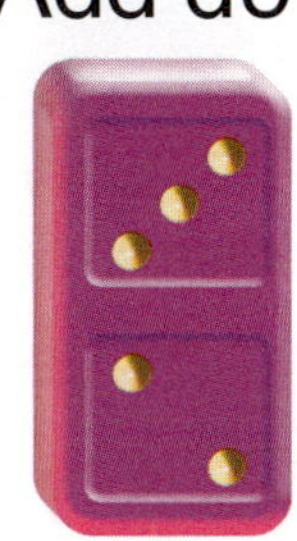

3 + 2 = 5

3
+ 2
5

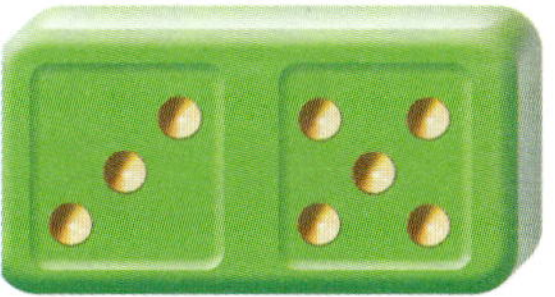

Write the numbers to match the dots.
Write the sum.

1.

_____ + _____ = _____

+

2.

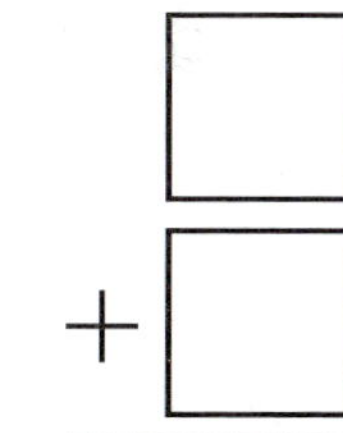

_____ + _____ = _____

+

3.

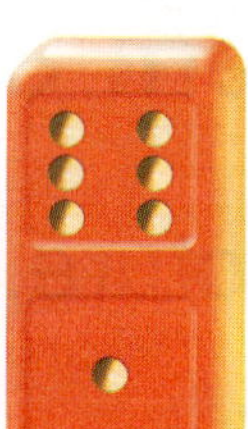
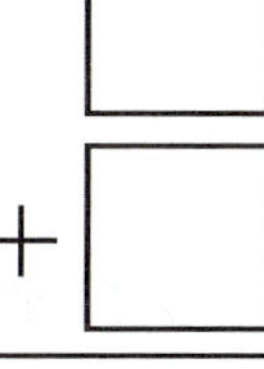

_____ + _____ = _____

+

4. **Math Talk** Why is the sum the same whether you add across or add down?

Write the numbers to match the dots.
Write the sum.

1.

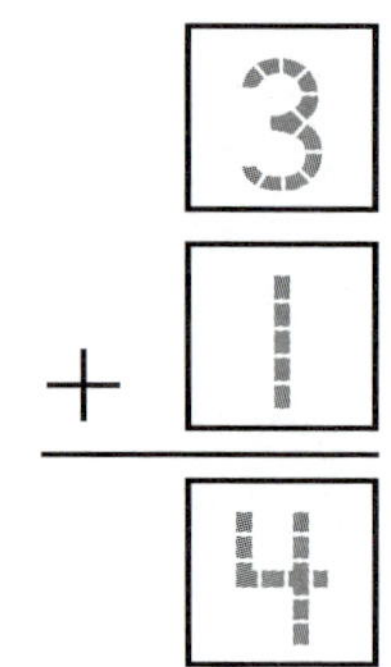

$$3$$
$$+\ 1$$
$$4$$

$$\underline{3} + \underline{1} = \underline{4}$$

Write the sum.

2. $\begin{array}{r} 1 \\ +2 \\ \hline \end{array}$ **3.** $\begin{array}{r} 2 \\ +2 \\ \hline \end{array}$ **4.** $\begin{array}{r} 0 \\ +3 \\ \hline \end{array}$ **5.** $\begin{array}{r} 1 \\ +1 \\ \hline \end{array}$ **6.** $\begin{array}{r} 6 \\ +2 \\ \hline \end{array}$

7. $\begin{array}{r} 0 \\ +4 \\ \hline \end{array}$ **8.** $\begin{array}{r} 2 \\ +5 \\ \hline \end{array}$ **9.** $\begin{array}{r} 8 \\ +0 \\ \hline \end{array}$ **10.** $\begin{array}{r} 2 \\ +3 \\ \hline \end{array}$ **11.** $\begin{array}{r} 0 \\ +5 \\ \hline \end{array}$

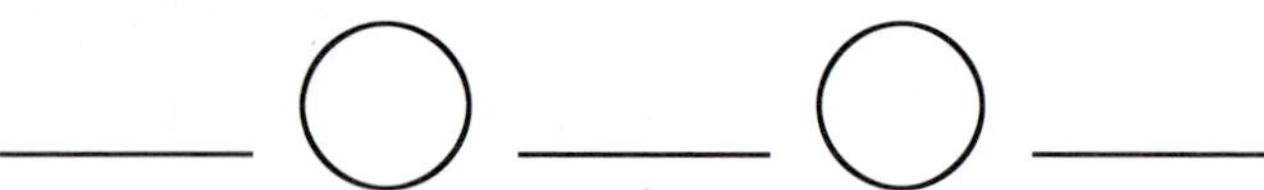

Problem Solving: Visual Thinking

12. Use the picture. Write an addition sentence
both ways.

____ ◯ ____ ◯ ____

$$+ \ \square \atop \square$$

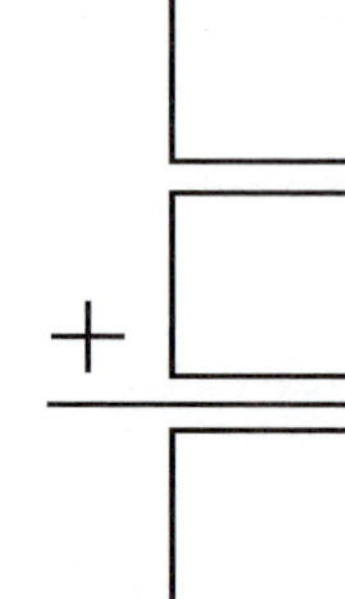

How does the picture help
you write an addition sentence?

Chapter 2 Lesson 8

Algebra: Ways to Make Numbers to 10

You can make the number **8** in different ways.

$$3 + 5$$

$$9 - 1$$

Connect

Use 🟥 and 🟦. Circle the ways that make the number.

1. **6** $(2 + 4)$ $(5 + 1)$ $6 - 1$ $(8 - 2)$

2. **4** $5 - 2$ $2 + 2$ $4 + 1$ $8 - 4$

3. **5** $0 + 5$ $7 - 2$ $6 - 3$ $1 + 4$

4. **7** $10 - 3$ $9 - 1$ $10 - 2$ $3 + 4$

5. **9** $8 + 2$ $3 + 6$ $10 - 1$ $7 + 2$

6. **8** $4 + 4$ $10 - 1$ $9 - 2$ $0 + 8$

7. **10** $6 + 4$ $8 - 2$ $2 + 8$ $10 - 0$

8. **Math Talk** What are all the ways to make a sum of 8?

Circle the ways that make the number.

1. **3**   7 − 3   1 + 2   3 − 1   0 + 3

2. **5**   6 − 1   2 + 3   9 − 4   7 − 1

3. **7**   5 + 2   9 − 6   10 − 3   5 + 4

4. **9**   3 + 5   10 − 1   2 + 5   6 + 3

5. **8**   10 − 2   5 + 3   4 + 4   0 + 8

6. **4**   3 + 1   10 − 6   4 + 0   9 − 3

7. **6**   10 − 2   6 − 0   3 + 3   5 + 4

8. **10**   7 + 2   7 − 3   9 + 1   8 + 2

Math Board

Problem Solving: Number Sense

9. Color the flowers that make the same number.

What is the number? _____

Write two more ways that make the same number.

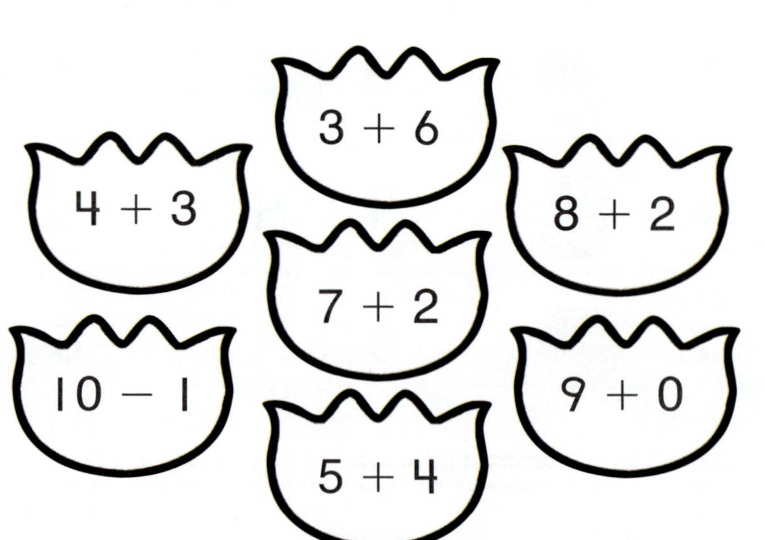

Chapter 2 Lesson 9

Explore Equality

▶ **We Learn**

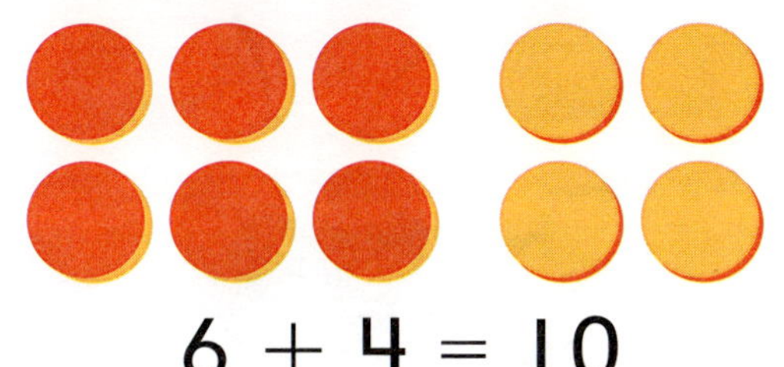

$$6 + 4 = 10$$

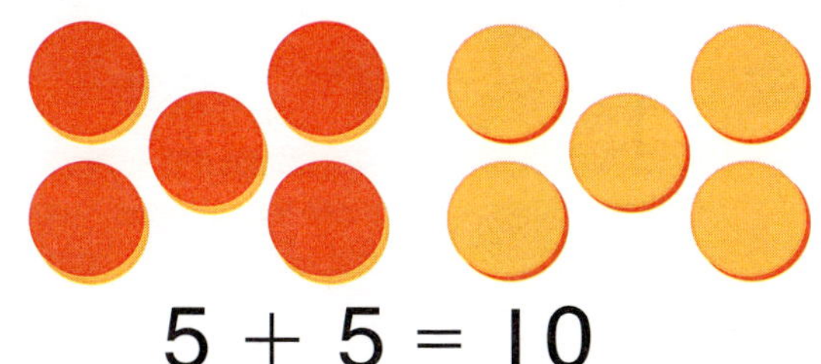

$$5 + 5 = 10$$

6 + 4 is equal to 5 + 5

$$6 + 4 = 5 + 5$$

↑

equal sign

▶ **Share and Show**   Math Board

Add each side.
Write = inside the ◯ if both sides are equal.

1. 7 + 1 ◯ 3 + 4

2. 7 + 3 ◯ 5 + 5

3. 8 + 1 ◯ 1 + 4

4. 2 + 2 ◯ 4 + 6

5. 6 + 2 ◯ 4 + 4

6. 8 + 1 ◯ 3 + 6

7. 5 + 2 ◯ 3 + 4

8. 5 + 2 ◯ 1 + 9

9. **Math Talk** Is the number sentence 5 + 1 = 3 + 3 true?
Explain.

1.2.1 Write and solve equations involving addition.

Draw lines to match the facts that are equal.

1. $2 + 3$ $4 + 5$

2. $8 + 1$ $4 + 4$

3. $3 + 4$ $5 + 5$

4. $5 + 3$ $5 + 2$

5. $6 + 4$ $1 + 4$

Problem Solving: Real World

6. Sue plants 3  and 2  .

   Rob plants 4 🌷 and 1 🌷 .

   Write facts to show if Sue and Rob plant an equal number of flowers.

   _____ + _____ ◯ _____ + _____

   How do you know if these two amounts are equal?

Problem Solving Workshop
Strategy: Make a Model

Essential Question

How does making a model help you solve a problem?

You can make a model to help solve a math problem.
Use ● for people and things.
This model shows $3 + 2 = 5$.

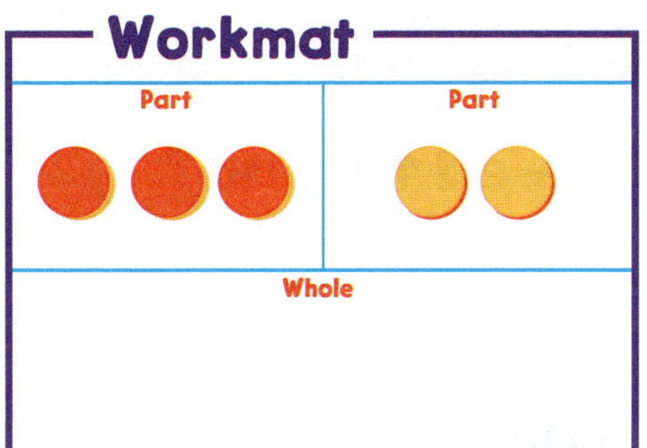

Make Your Math Model

Use ● to make a model.
Find the sum.

There are 2 red flowers in a pot.
There are the same number of
yellow flowers as red flowers.

Math Talk How many flowers are there in all? Explain.

Use the Strategy • Make a Model

Hana sees 3 flowers on one plant.
She sees 5 flowers on another plant.
How many flowers does Hana see in all?

 Unlock the Problem

What do I need to find?

how many flowers
Hana sees in all

What information do I need to use?

3 flowers on one plant
5 flowers on another plant

Show how to solve the problem.

Write a number sentence: _____ + _____ = _____

Hana sees _____ flowers in all.

Math Talk How did your model help you find how many flowers Hana saw in all? Explain.

Problem Solving Strategy Practice

Use ● to make a model.
Write the number sentence.

1. Mark has 4 blue pencils and 2 red pencils. How many pencils does he have in all?

pencil

$$4 + 2 = 6$$

_____ 6 pencils

2. There are 3 children at the gym. The same number of children join them. How many children are there?

child

_____ + _____ = _____

_____ children

3. One poster shows 4 leaves. Another poster shows 3 leaves. How many leaves are there in all?

leaf

_____ + _____ = _____

_____ leaves

Try Your Own Problem

4. Tia read _____ books at school. She read the same number of books at home. How many books did she read in all?

book

_____ + _____ = _____

_____ books

At Home Change the numbers in one of the problems above. Have your child use small objects to make a model to show how to solve the problem.

Mixed Strategy Practice

Choose a way to solve each problem.
Write or draw to explain.

Choose a Strategy
- Act It Out
- Draw a Picture
- Make a Model

1. There are 2 bees.
3 more join them.
How many bees in all?

bee

______ bees

2. 6 red crayons.
4 blue crayons.
How many crayons
altogether?

crayon

______ crayons

3. Roger sees 5 bunnies.
Then he sees 3 more
bunnies. How many
bunnies does he
see in all?

bunny

______ bunnies

4. Kate has 3 and 1 .
Todd has 2 and 2 .
How many
do they have in all?

______ cubes

5. You have 5 and 2 .
How can you use to
show 7 another way?

______ cubes

______ cubes

48

Name _______________________

Extra Practice

Use and to add. Write the sum. Circle the addition sentences that have the same addends.

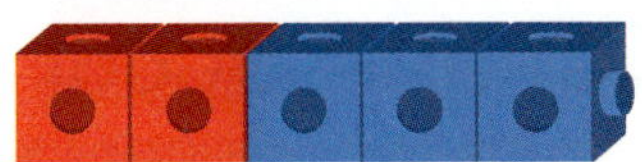

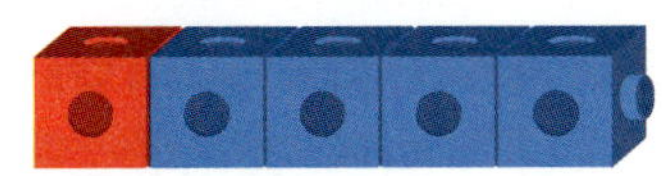

1. $2 + 3 =$ _____   **2.** $1 + 4 =$ _____   **3.** $3 + 2 =$ _____

Color to show two ways to make 7.
Complete the addition sentences.

4. $7 =$ _____ $+$ _____

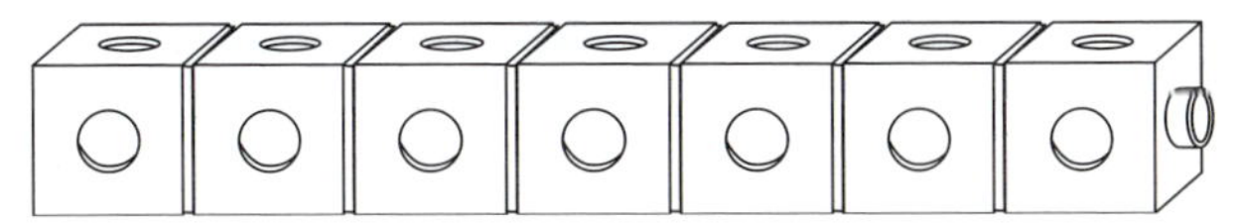

5. $7 =$ _____ $+$ _____

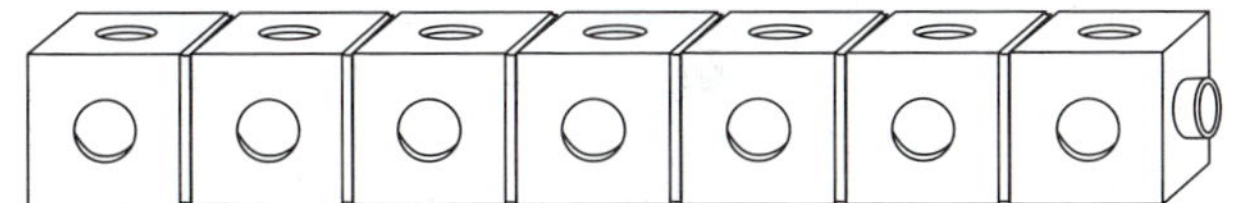

Write the numbers to match the dots.
Write the sum.

6.

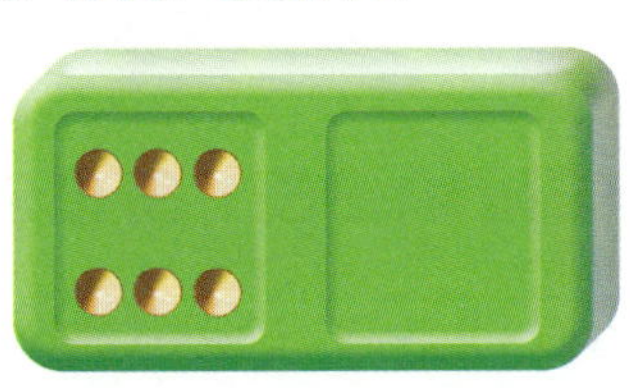

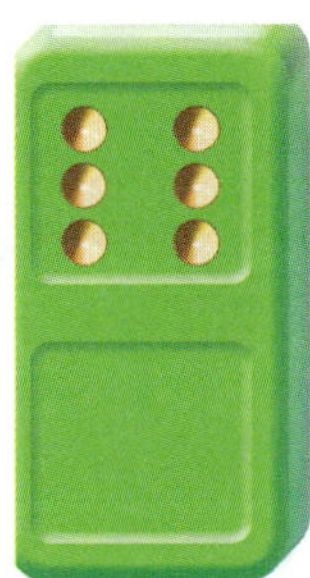

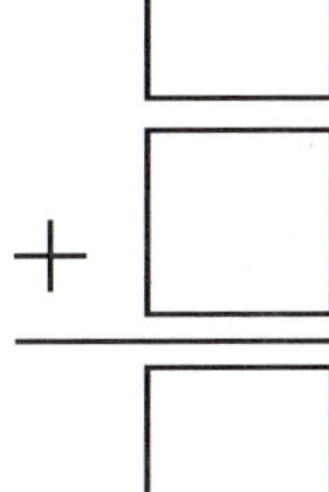

_____ $+$ _____ $=$ _____

Problem Solving

Use ● to make a model. Write
the number sentence.

7. Sam has 4 red cars and
3 yellow cars. How many
cars does he have in all?

_____ $+$ _____ $=$ _____

_____ cars

Multistep Problems
Chapter 2

1. Use the picture to answer the questions.

1.1.5, 1.1.6, 1.2.1

- How many purple flowers are there?

- How many red flowers are there?

- How many flowers are there in all? Write an addition sentence.

2. Nia has 2 soccer balls. Her brother brings 3 more soccer balls 1.1.5, 1.1.6, 1.2.1

- How many soccer balls are there in all?

- Write an addition sentence to show how many soccer balls there are in all.

- What is another way to write the addition sentence?

Name _______________________

 # Standards Quick Check

Read the story. Write an addition sentence to solve.

1. There were 3 green peppers.
   There were 5 red peppers.
   How many peppers were there altogether?

   _____ + _____ = _____

   _____ peppers

Add.

2. $4 + 6 =$ _____

3. $3 + 1 =$ _____

4. $4 + 3 =$ _____

5. $7 + 2 =$ _____

6. $4 + 4 =$ _____

7. $8 + 2 =$ _____

1. Write your own addition story.

   ____

   ____

   ____

2. Write an addition sentence to solve your story.

   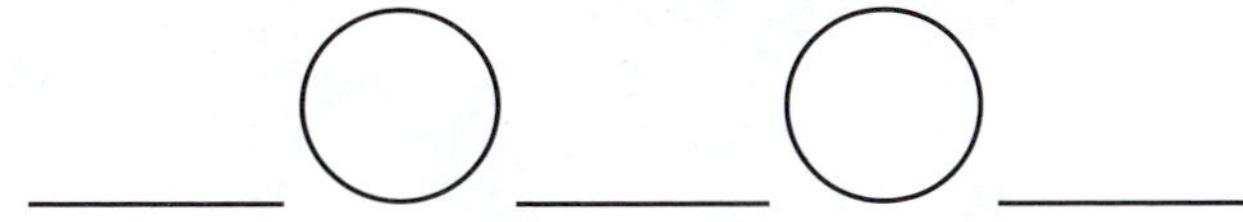

Organic farmers plant seeds. They water the ground. They pull weeds. They pick food when it is ripe. They pack it in boxes. They sell it at a farmer's market.

Draw to add.
Write the addition sentence.

1. 2 tomatoes are in the box.
Benito puts in 4 more.
How many tomatoes in all?

_____ ◯ _____ ◯ _____

_____ tomatoes

2. Julie digs up 4 onions.
Then she digs up 4 more.
How many onions in all?

_____ ◯ _____ ◯ _____

_____ onions

Looking Ahead to the ISTEP+
Chapter 2

Mark the best answer for questions 1–5.

1. How many are there in all?

1.1.5

- ○ 2
- ○ 3
- ○ 4
- ○ 5

2. Which addition sentence tells about the picture? 1.1.6

- ○ $1 + 4 = 5$
- ○ $1 + 5 = 6$
- ○ $2 + 4 = 6$
- ○ $3 + 3 = 6$

3. What is the sum for $6 + 0$?

1.2.3, 1.1.6

- ○ 0
- ○ 4
- ○ 6
- ○ 7

4. Which shows the same addends in a different order?

1.1.5

$$2 + 3 = 5$$

- ○ $2 + 5 = 7$
- ○ $3 + 2 = 5$
- ○ $3 + 5 = 8$
- ○ $4 + 2 = 6$

5. Which shows a way to make 7? 1.1.6, 1.2.1

- ○ 
- ○ 
- ○ 
- ○ 

Mark the best answer for questions 6–7.

6. What is the sum? 1.2.1

$$4 + 4 =$$

- ○ 5
- ○ 6
- ○ 7
- ○ 8

7. Which number sentence matches the story? 1.1.6

Kim has 2 blue pencils and 4 yellow pencils. How many pencils does she have in all?

- ○ $2 + 3 = 5$
- ○ $2 + 4 = 6$
- ○ $4 + 3 = 7$
- ○ $4 + 1 = 5$

Open Ended

Draw ● to make a model. Write a number sentence. Solve. 1.1.6

8. Adam has 3 brown caps and 2 blue caps. How many caps does he have in all?

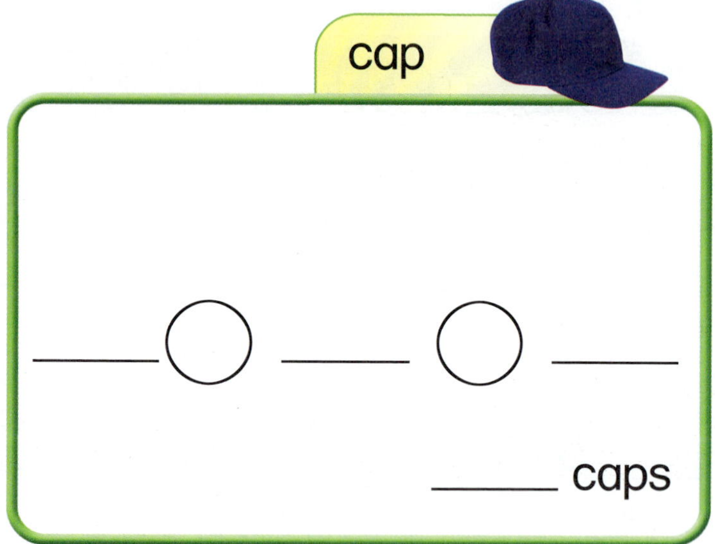

Use ● to make a model. Write the number sentence. 1.1.6

9. There are 5 children in the library. 2 children join them. How many children are there in all?

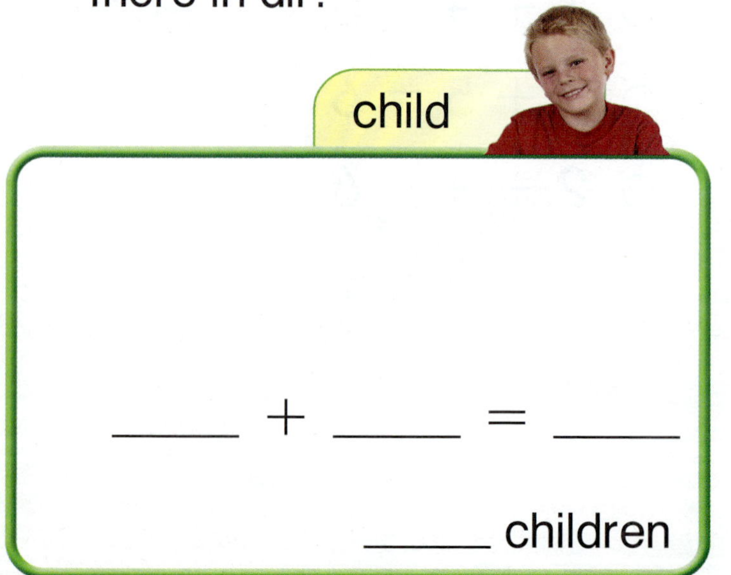

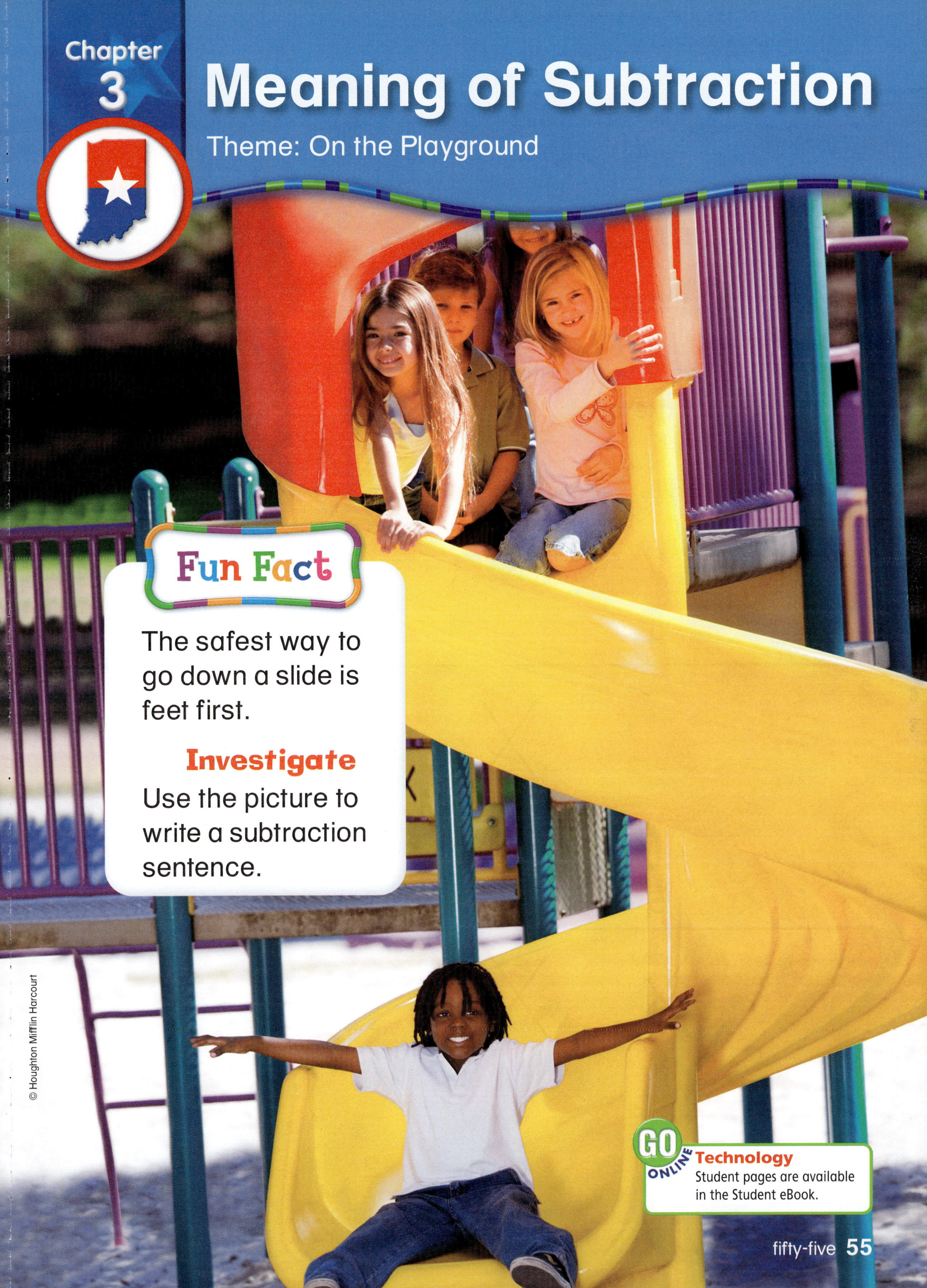

Chapter 3
Meaning of Subtraction
Theme: On the Playground

Fun Fact
The safest way to go down a slide is feet first.

Investigate
Use the picture to write a subtraction sentence.

© Houghton Mifflin Harcourt

GO ONLINE
Technology
Student pages are available in the Student eBook.

fifty-five 55

Show What You Know 

Use  to show the story.
Draw the .
Mark an X on the  you subtract.
Write how many are left.

1.

4   1   _____

2.

5   3   _____

3.

3   2   _____

At Home This page checks your child's understanding of important concepts and skills needed for success in Chapter 3.

Name ______________________________

Chapter 3 Lesson 1

Model Subtraction

Hands On

Essential Question

How do you model a take-away problem?

Vocabulary

take away
subtract
are left

Explore

Use 🔴 to show the subtraction story.

Draw the 🔴.

Cross out the ones you take away.

Subtract to find out how many are left.

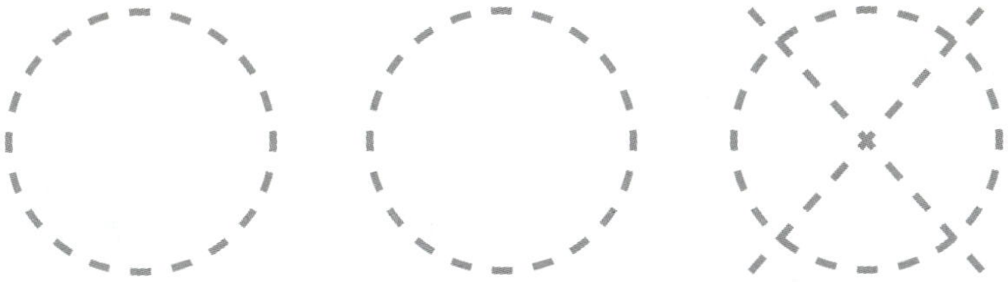

3 marbles   1 marble rolls away

2 marbles are left

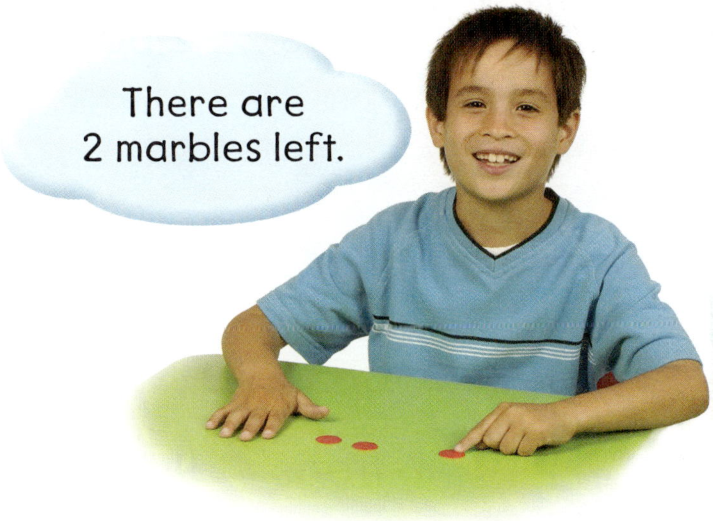

Connect

1. 2 girls   1 girl walks away   ____ girl is left

2. 4 kickballs   2 kickballs roll away   ____ kickballs are left

3. Math Talk How do you find how many are left? Explain.

1.1.5 Solve problems involving addition and subtraction by modeling addition of numbers to at least 100 and by modeling the inverse operation of subtraction using objects. *also* 1.1.6

Use ⬤ to show the subtraction story.
Draw the ⬤. Cross out the ones you take away. Write how many are left.

1.

5 boys   2 boys run away   _____ boys are left

2.

6 frogs   4 frogs hop away   _____ frogs are left

Math Board

Problem Solving: Real World

3. Look at the picture.
Complete the subtraction story.
Cross out the ones you take away.
Write how many are left.

4 bees   _____ bees fly away   _____ bees are left

Make up a subtraction story about 6 birds. Draw a picture. Cross out how many you take away. Write how many are left.

Chapter 3 Lesson 2

Use Symbols to Subtract

▶ **We Learn**

See    

Write __4__ (—) __3__ (=) __1__

Say 4 minus 3 is equal to 1.

The difference is 1.

▶ **Share and Show** | Math Board |

Use the picture. Write the subtraction sentence.

1.  

__2__ (—) __1__ (=) __1__

2.     

____ ( ) ____ ( ) ____

3.  

____ ( ) ____ ( ) ____

4.  

____ ( ) ____ ( ) ____

✓5.   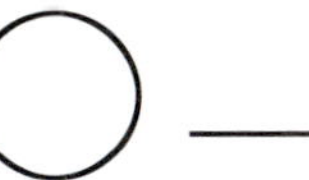

____ ( ) ____ ( ) ____

✓6.  

____ ( ) ____ ( ) ____

7. **Math Talk** How many objects do you cross out
   to solve 5 − 2 = ____? Explain.

⭐ **1.1.6** Demonstrate fluency with addition facts and the corresponding subtraction facts for totals to at least 20. *also* **1.1.5**

Use the picture.
Write the subtraction sentence.

1. 

______ ◯ ______ ◯ ______

2. 

______ ◯ ______ ◯ ______

3. 

______ ◯ ______ ◯ ______

4. 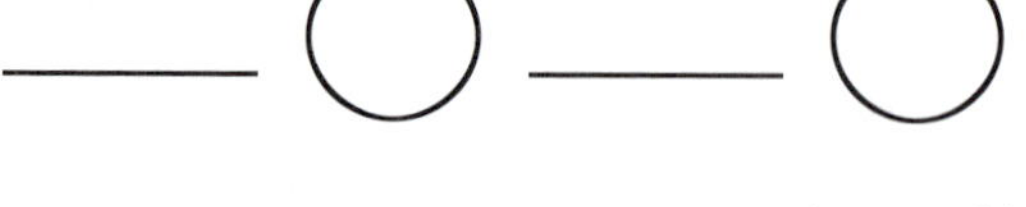

______ ◯ ______ ◯ ______

5. 

______ ◯ ______ ◯ ______

6. 

______ ◯ ______ ◯ ______

7. 

______ ◯ ______ ◯ ______

8. 

______ ◯ ______ ◯ ______

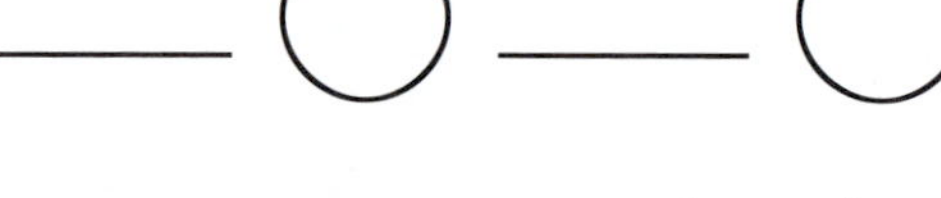

Problem Solving: Visual Thinking

9. Draw a picture to show the subtraction sentence.
Write the difference.

$6 - 3 = $ ______

Draw a picture to show subtraction. Write
the number sentence.

Chapter 3 Lesson 5

Vertical Subtraction Sentences

Essential Question
How do you subtract numbers vertically?

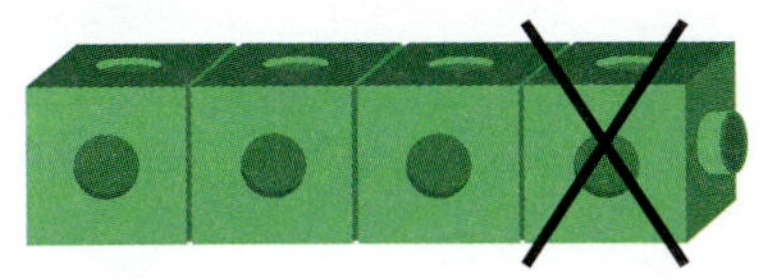

▶ We Learn

Subtract across.

$4 - 1 = \underline{}\,3$

Subtract down.

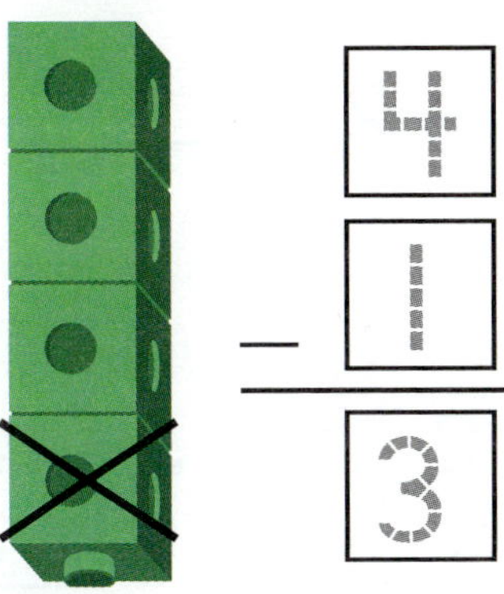

▶ Share and Show

Subtract across and down. Write the difference.

1.

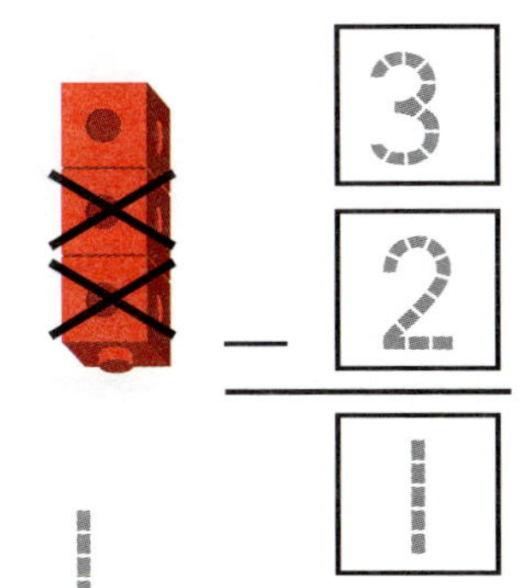

$3 - 2 = \underline{}$

2.

$2 - 2 = \underline{}$

☑ 3.

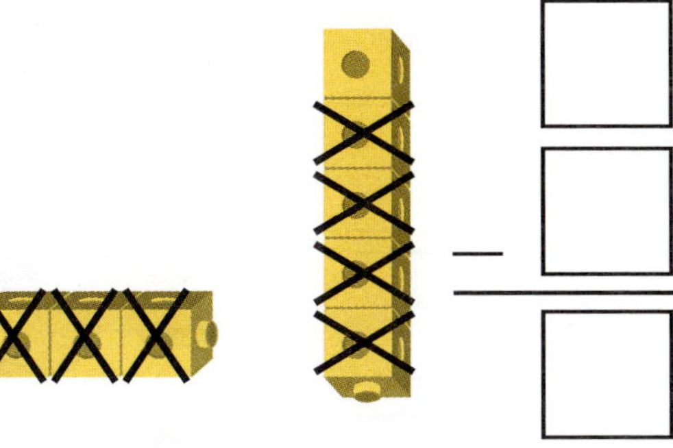

$5 - 4 = \underline{}$

☑ 4.

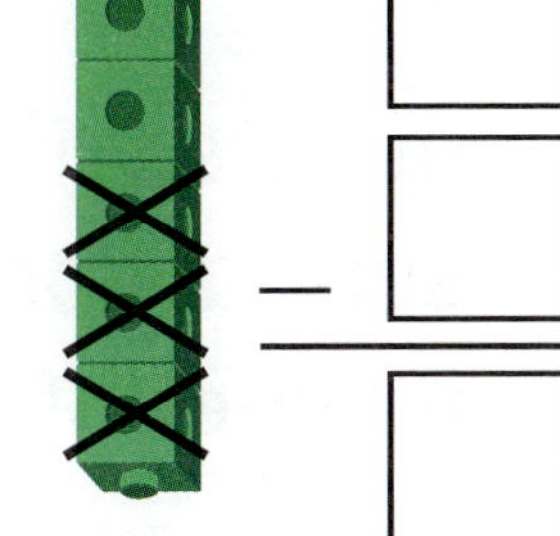

$6 - 3 = \underline{}$

5. (Math Talk) What is the error? Explain.

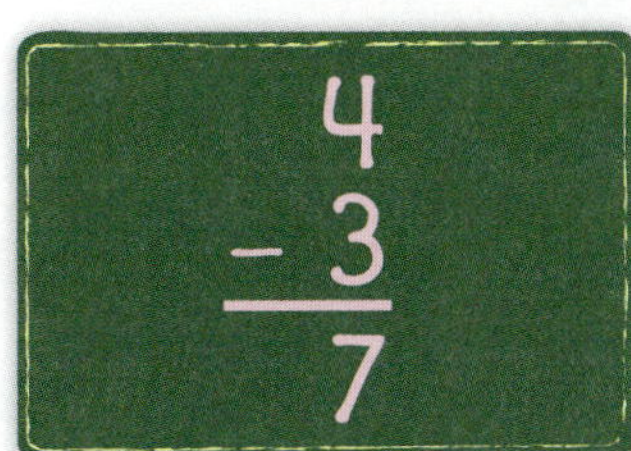

1.2.1 Write and solve equations involving addition. *also* **1.1.5; 1.1.6**

Write the difference.

1. 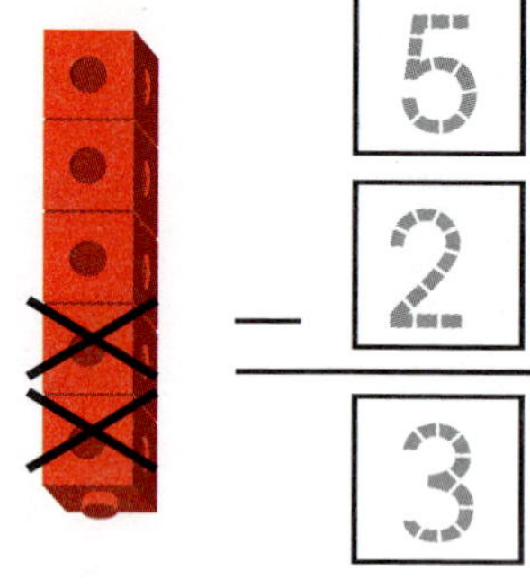

$5 - 2 = \underline{3}$

$\begin{array}{r} 5 \\ -\ 2 \\ \hline 3 \end{array}$

2. $\begin{array}{r} 2 \\ -1 \\ \hline \end{array}$
3. $\begin{array}{r} 3 \\ -3 \\ \hline \end{array}$
4. $\begin{array}{r} 5 \\ -4 \\ \hline \end{array}$
5. $\begin{array}{r} 1 \\ -1 \\ \hline \end{array}$
6. $\begin{array}{r} 6 \\ -2 \\ \hline \end{array}$

7. $\begin{array}{r} 7 \\ -7 \\ \hline \end{array}$
8. $\begin{array}{r} 8 \\ -2 \\ \hline \end{array}$
9. $\begin{array}{r} 7 \\ -2 \\ \hline \end{array}$
10. $\begin{array}{r} 6 \\ -3 \\ \hline \end{array}$
11. $\begin{array}{r} 8 \\ -0 \\ \hline \end{array}$

Math Board

Problem Solving: Visual Thinking

12. Use the picture. Write a subtraction sentence both ways.

There are 7 marbles. 2 of the marbles are blue. Write a subtraction sentence to find the number of yellow marbles.

____ – ____ = ____

____ yellow marbles

How does the picture help you write a subtraction sentence?

Chapter 3 Lesson 6

Understand Equality

$$10 - 4 = 6 \qquad\qquad 9 - 3 = 6$$

$$10 - 4 \qquad \text{is equal to} \qquad 9 - 3$$

$$10 - 4 \qquad\qquad = \qquad\qquad 9 - 3$$

Subtract each side.

Write $=$ inside the $\bigcirc$ if both sides are equal.

1. $7 - 1 \bigcirc 4 - 3$

2. $7 - 3 \bigcirc 9 - 5$

3. $8 - 2 \bigcirc 9 - 3$

4. $10 - 5 \bigcirc 6 - 1$

5. $6 - 5 \bigcirc 6 - 4$

6. $6 - 4 \bigcirc 10 - 1$

7. $8 - 3 \bigcirc 5 - 2$

8. $8 - 4 \bigcirc 6 - 2$

9. **Math Talk** Is the number sentence $5 - 1 = 3 - 3$ true? Explain.

Draw lines to match the facts that are equal.

1. 9 − 3		7 − 5
2. 8 − 1		9 − 1
3. 8 − 0		6 − 0
4. 5 − 2		10 − 3
5. 6 − 4		4 − 1

6. Write a number sentence that shows two equal subtraction facts.

Math Board Problem Solving: Real World

7. Mike planted 5  and 2 were picked.

Jen planted 4  and 1 was picked.

Write facts to show if Mike and Jen have an equal number of flowers that were not picked.

At Home Write three subtraction facts on a sheet of paper. Two of the facts should have an equal difference. Have your child find the answer for each fact. Then have him or her connect the two facts that are equal with an equal sign.

Model Part-Part-Whole

▶ **Explore**

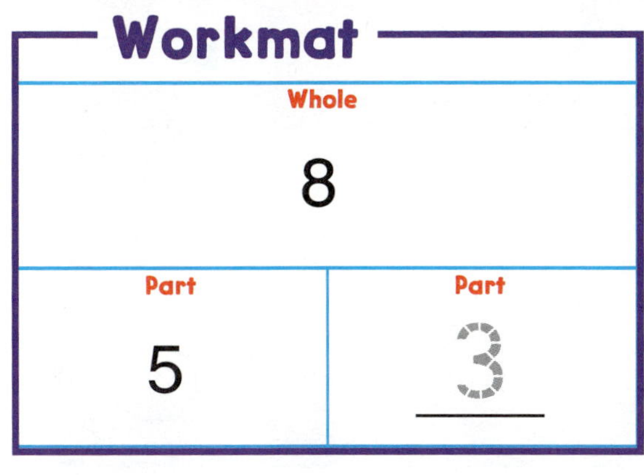

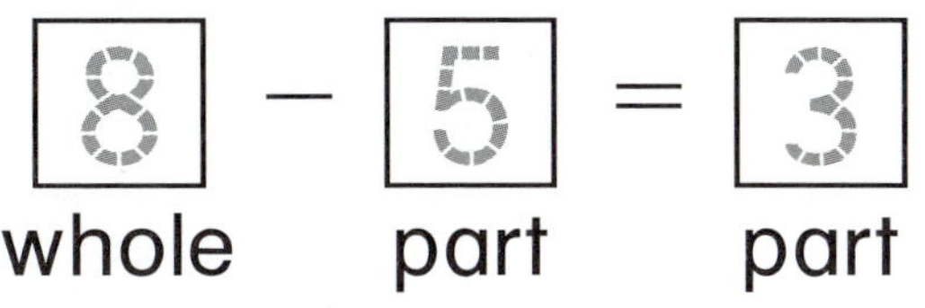

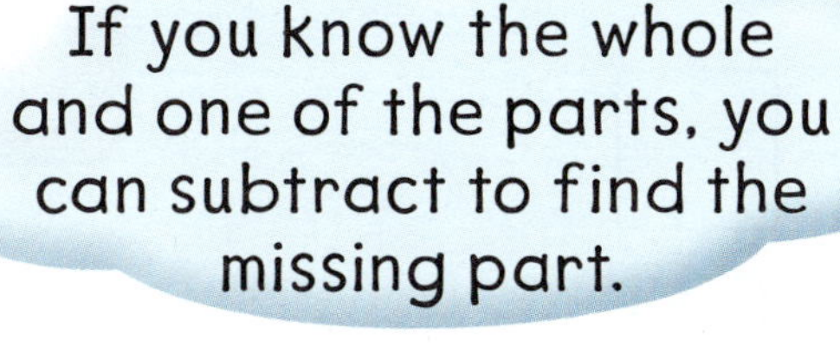

▶ **Connect**

Use Workmat 10 and ●.
Complete the subtraction sentence.

1.

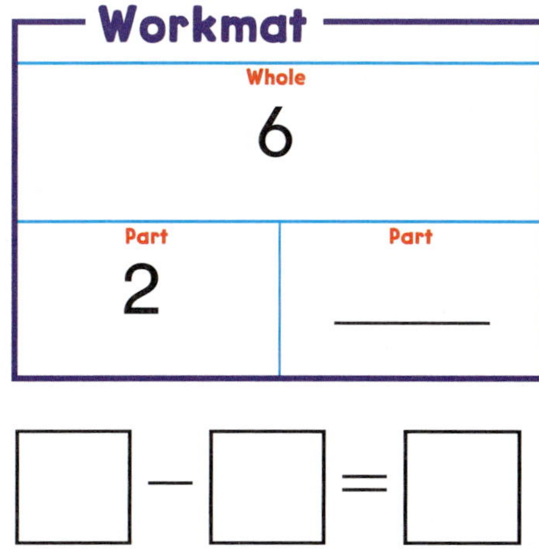

☑ 2.

☐ − ☐ = ☐
whole   part   part

☐ − ☐ = ☐
whole   part   part

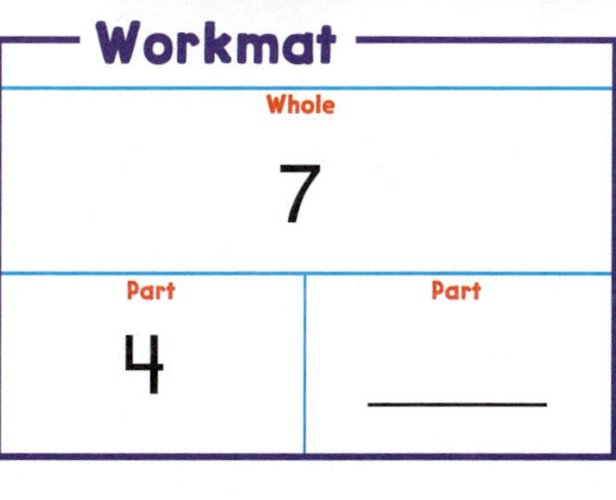

3. **Math Talk** How do you find the missing part? Explain.

Share and Show

Math Board

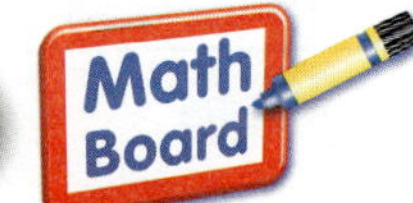

Use Workmat 10 and ●.

Complete the subtraction sentence.

1. **Workmat**

Whole	
6	
Part	Part
1	____

☐ − ☐ = ☐

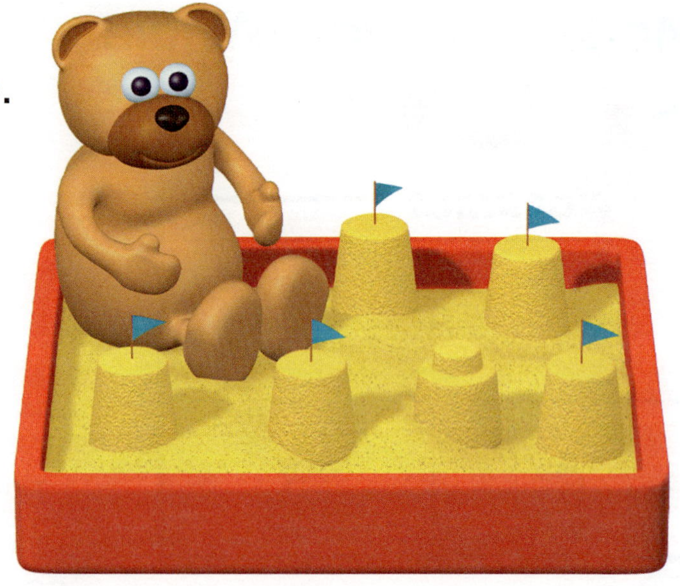

whole part part

2. 5 − 4 = ☐

whole part part

3. 7 − 3 = ☐

whole part part

4. 6 − 3 = ☐

whole part part

5. 8 − 5 = ☐

whole part part

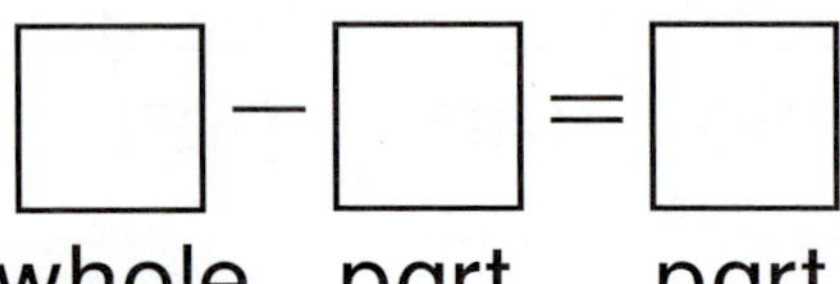

Math Board Problem Solving: Real World

6. Complete the sentence.

The park has 8 swings. 2 are baby swings.

The other swings are big swings.

How many swings are big swings?

☐ − ☐ = ☐

whole part part

____ big swings

Draw a picture to show how to solve the story problem.

At Home Have your child draw a story background, such as a playground scene. Then ask him or her to place a group of up to 8 small objects on the background as you make up part-part-whole subtraction stories. Have your child explain how to use the part-part-whole concept to solve the problems.

Subtract to Compare

Essential Question
How do you compare groups to subtract?

Vocabulary
compare
more
fewer

Subtract to compare groups.

$5 - 4 =$ ____

____ more 

$7 - 2 =$ ____

____ fewer

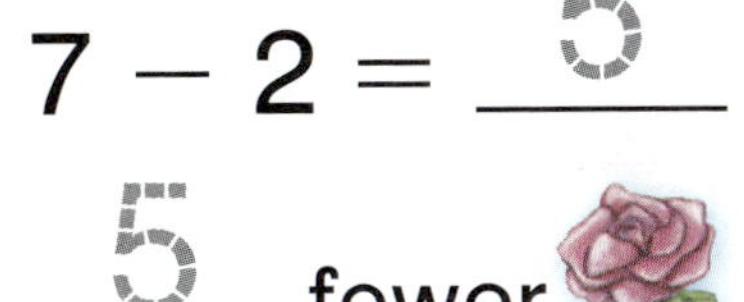

Draw lines to match. Subtract to compare.

1. 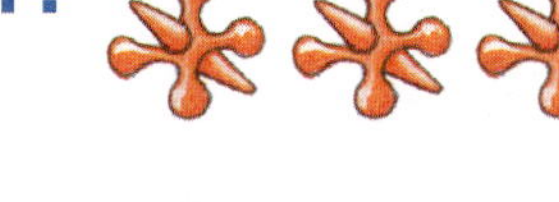

$4 - 1 =$ ____

____ fewer

2. 

$3 - 2 =$ ____

____ more

☑ 3. 

$7 - 6 =$ ____

____ more

☑ 4. 

$8 - 4 =$ ____

____ fewer

5. **Math Talk** What do you have to do when you subtract to compare? Explain.

▶ On Your Own

Draw lines to match.
Subtract to compare.

1. 

$5 - 1 =$ ____

____ more 

2. 

$5 - 3 =$ ____

____ fewer 

3. 

$4 - 2 =$ ____

____ more 

4. 

$6 - 1 =$ ____

____ more

5. 
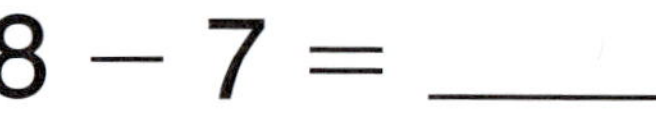

$8 - 7 =$ ____

____ fewer

6. 

$7 - 5 =$ ____

____ fewer

Problem Solving: Reasoning

Solve. Write the number.

7. I am 2 less than 5. What number am I?

____

8. I am 3 less than 7. What number am I?

____

9. I am 6 less than 8. What number am I?

____

How do you use subtraction to find each number? Explain.

Problem Solving Workshop
Strategy: Make a Model 

Problem Solving

Essential Question

How does making a model help you solve a problem?

There are 8 birds and 5 worms. How many fewer worms are there than birds?

🔑 Unlock the Problem

What do I need to find?

how many fewer
worms there are than
birds

What information do I need to use?

___8___ birds

___5___ worms

Show how to solve the problem.

Make a model. Use 🟦 for birds. Use 🟥 for worms. Draw the 🟦 🟥. Draw lines to match.

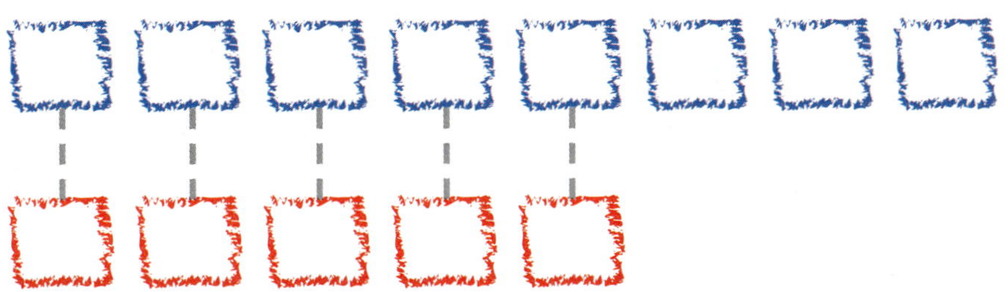

So, there are ____ fewer worms.

Math Talk How did making a model help you solve the problem? Explain.

1.1.6 Demonstrate fluency with addition facts and the corresponding subtraction facts for totals to at least 20. *also* **1.1.5**

Problem Solving Strategy Practice

Make a model to solve. Draw the 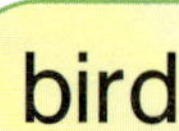.
Match or cross out to subtract.

1. There are 2 red slides and
4 blue slides. How many more
blue slides are there than
red slides?

slide

________ slides

2. 6 birds are in the tree.
6 birds fly away.
How many birds are left?

bird

________ birds

3. Pat has 8 leaves in all.
6 leaves are orange.
The other leaves are red.
How many leaves are red?

leaf

________ leaves

Try Your Own Problem

4. There are ________ ladybugs.
________ ladybugs fly away.
How many ladybugs are left?

ladybug

________ ladybugs

At Home Change the numbers in Exercise 1. Have your
child use pennies to make a model to solve the problem.

Name _______________________

Extra Practice

Use the picture to write the subtraction sentence.

1. 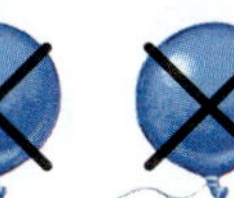
2. 

___ ◯ ___ ◯ ___   ___ ◯ ___ ◯ ___

Use  to show two ways to subtract from 7.
Complete the subtraction sentences.

3. $7 - \underline{\hspace{1cm}} = \underline{\hspace{1cm}}$ 4. $7 - \underline{\hspace{1cm}} = \underline{\hspace{1cm}}$

Write the difference.

5.	6.	7.	8.	9.	10.
3 -0	7 -7	5 -2	8 -4	7 -6	6 -3

Draw lines to match. Subtract to compare.

11. 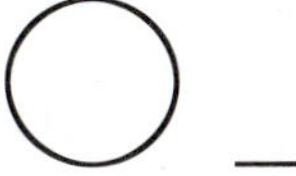
12. 

$8 - 5 = \underline{\hspace{1cm}}$ $4 - 3 = \underline{\hspace{1cm}}$

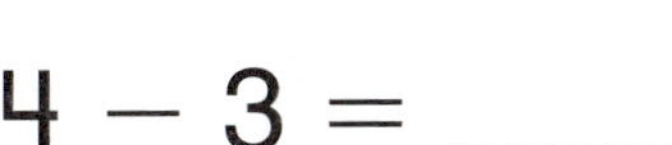

___ more   ___ fewer

Problem Solving

Make a model to solve. Draw the ◼.
Match or cross out to subtract.

13. Lee has 5 pens. 3 pens are red.
The rest are blue. How many
are blue?

___ blue pens

Technology
Use Mega Math CD-ROM, Country
Countdown, *Block Busters*, Level F.

Multistep Problems 
Chapter 3

1. Sally has 6 chickens.

1.1.5

- Circle the chickens that are outside the pen.

- How many chickens are inside the pen?

- Write a subtraction sentence to show how many chickens are left.

2. Use the picture clues to write a subtraction story. Write the subtraction sentence.

1.1.5

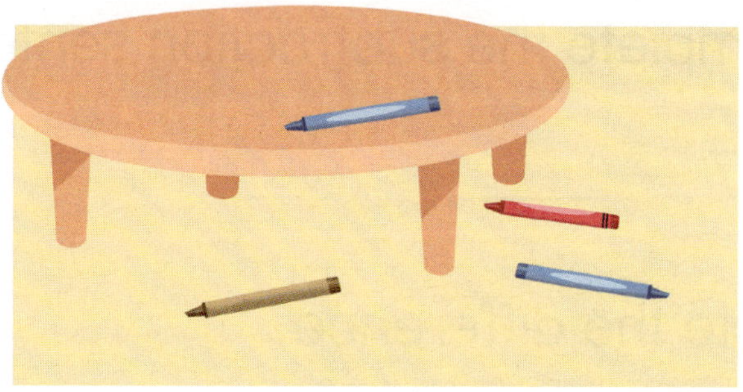

- Write a subtraction story.

- Write a subtraction sentence to match your story.

_____ − _____ = _____

 # Standards Quick Check

Cross out to subtract. Solve.

1. 

6 − 4 = _____

2.

5 − 2 = _____

Subtract to find the missing part.
Write the number sentence.

3.
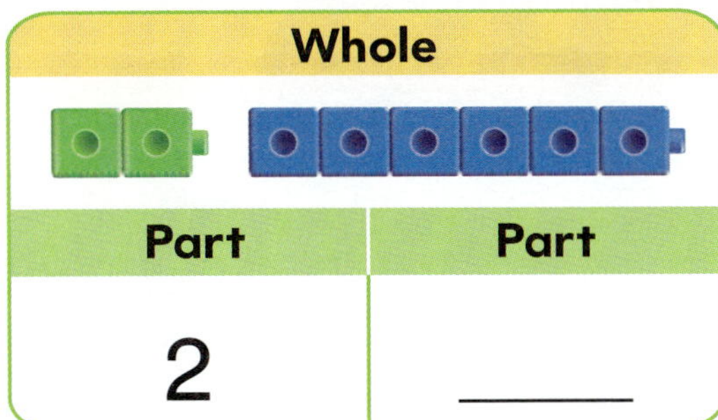

Whole	
Part	Part
2	_____

4.

Whole	
Part	Part
3	_____

_____ − _____ = _____

_____ − _____ = _____

Challenge 

Draw 10 ladybugs.
Color some .
Color some .

Write the missing numbers.

1.
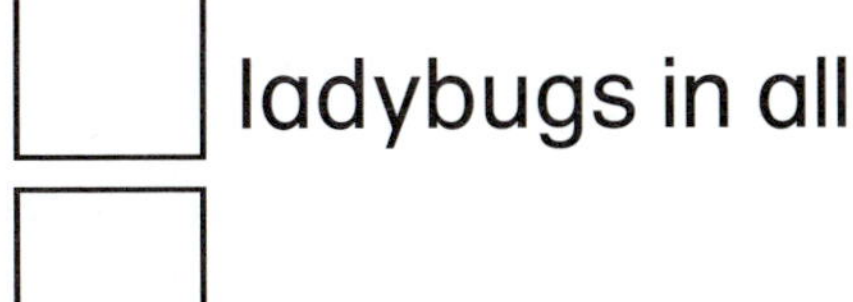

☐ ladybugs in all

− ☐

☐ blue ladybugs

2.

☐ ladybugs in all

− ☐

☐ red ladybugs

You can tell an animal's diet by its teeth. Animals that eat meat have sharp teeth. Animals that eat plants have flat teeth. Horses have flat teeth. Horses eat grass and hay. For treats, they eat carrots or apples.

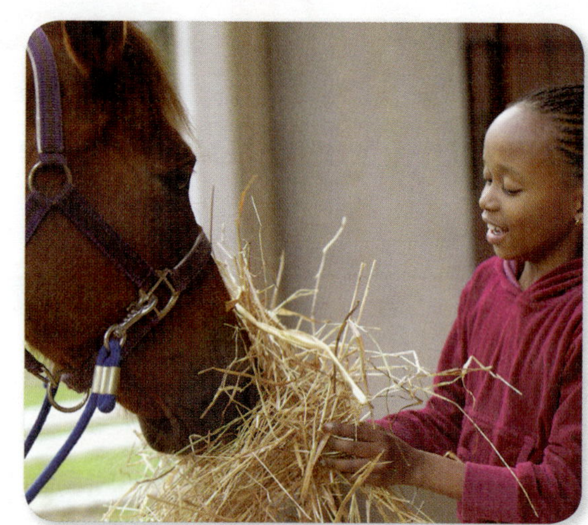

Draw to solve.
Write the subtraction sentence.

1. Ella brings 6 apples to the stable. The horses eat 4 apples. How many apples are left?

_____ ◯ _____ ◯ _____

_____ apples

2. Pedro has 8 carrots. He eats 4. He gives the rest to his horse. How many carrots does his horse eat?

_____ ◯ _____ ◯ _____

_____ carrots

 # Looking Ahead to the ISTEP+
Chapter 3

Mark the best answer for questions 1–4.

1. What is the difference? 1.1.6; 1.2.3

$$3 - 0 = \underline{\quad}$$

○ 0
○ 3
○ 4
○ 6

2. Which subtraction sentence tells about the picture? 1.1.5

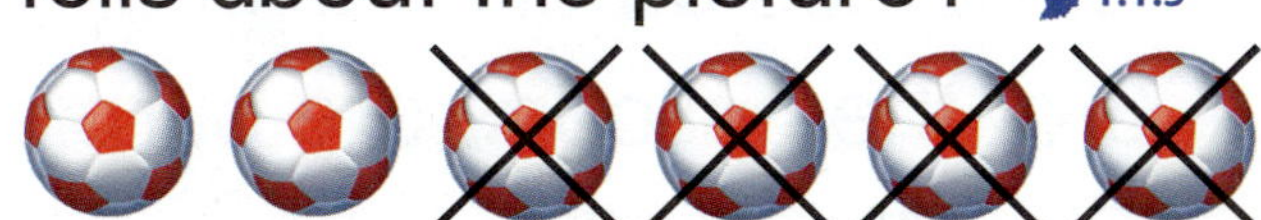

○ $2 - 0 = 2$
○ $4 - 2 = 2$
○ $6 - 4 = 2$
○ $6 - 3 = 3$

3. Which sentence shows a way to subtract from 6? 1.1.6

○ $9 - 3 = 6$
○ $8 - 6 = 2$
○ $7 - 1 = 6$
○ $6 - 5 = 1$

4. How many fewer basketballs are there than nets? 1.1.5

○ 0 fewer
○ 1 fewer
○ 4 fewer
○ 5 fewer

Mark the best answer for questions 5–6.

5. How many are left? **1.1.5**

- ○ 2
- ○ 4
- ○ 6
- ○ 8

6. What is the difference?

1.2.1

$$5 - 3$$

- ○ 1
- ○ 2
- ○ 5
- ○ 8

Open Ended

Draw ● to make a model. Write a number sentence. Solve. **1.1.5**

7. Ethan has 7 marbles. 3 of the marbles are red. How many marbles are not red?

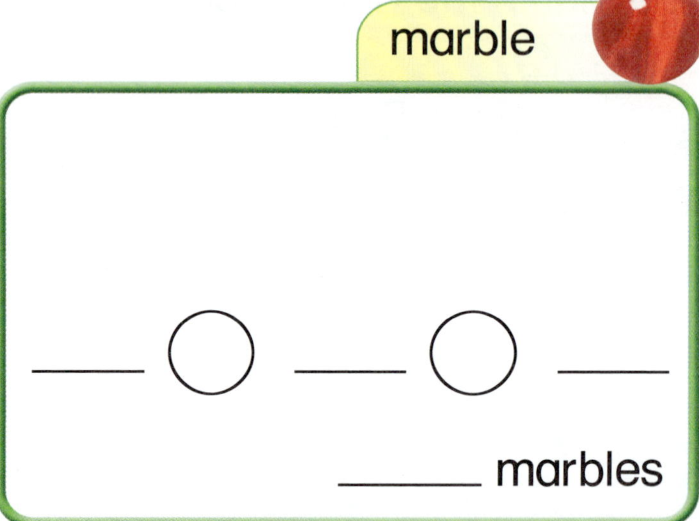

Draw ▨ to make a model. Match or cross out to subtract. **1.1.5**

8. Olivia has 8 balloons in all. 3 of the balloons are purple. The other balloons are pink. How many balloons are pink?

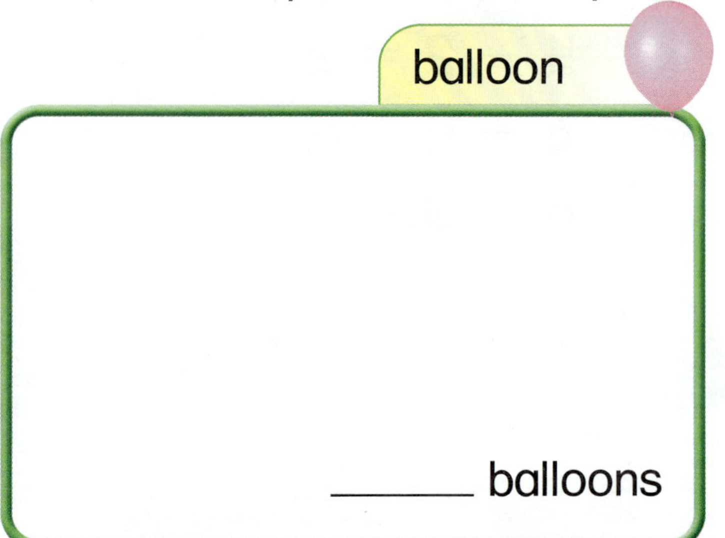

Reading and Writing Math

Sue has 4 apples.
Liam has 5 apples.
How many apples do they have in all?
You know the parts. Find the whole.

Whole	
?	
Part	**Part**
4	5

1. Draw a picture to help you add.

2. Write the number sentence.

3. Change the order of the addends.
Write the new number sentence.

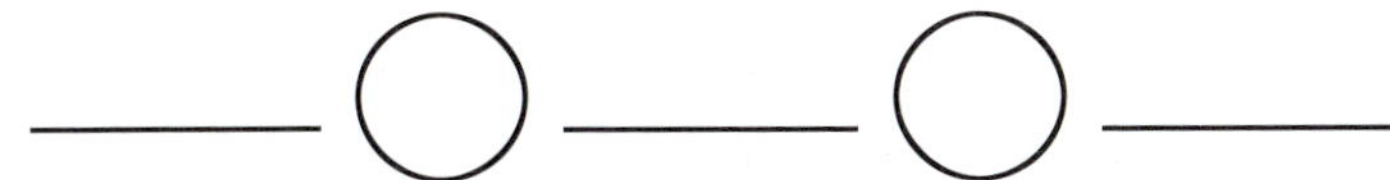

4. How many apples are there in all?

________ apples

5. Writing Math What else could you have
done to solve the problem?

____

____

Algebra

What Is Missing?

The same number is missing from both figures.

$8 - 2 = \boxed{6} \rightarrow \boxed{6} - 2 = \underline{4}$

Reasoning

Subtract. Use the missing number to subtract again.

1. $5 - 1 = \bigcirc \rightarrow \bigcirc - 1 = \underline{\quad}$

2. $7 - 3 = \pentagon \rightarrow \pentagon - 3 = \underline{\quad}$

3. $8 - 4 = \square \rightarrow \square - 4 = \underline{\quad}$

4. $6 - 0 = \hexagon \rightarrow \hexagon - 0 = \underline{\quad}$

On Your Own

Complete the subtraction sentences.
Write the same number in the matching figures.

5. $8 - 1 = \triangle \rightarrow \triangle - \underline{\quad} = \underline{\quad}$

Math Talk Look at Exercise 1. What is
the subtraction pattern? Explain.

The World Almanac for Kids

Crayon Colors

You can find many colors in a crayon box today. There are now colors called Purple Mountain's Majesty and Cotton Candy. What crayon colors do you like?

The first box of 8 crayons had the colors black, brown, green, blue, orange, red, violet, and yellow.

FACT·ACTIVITY

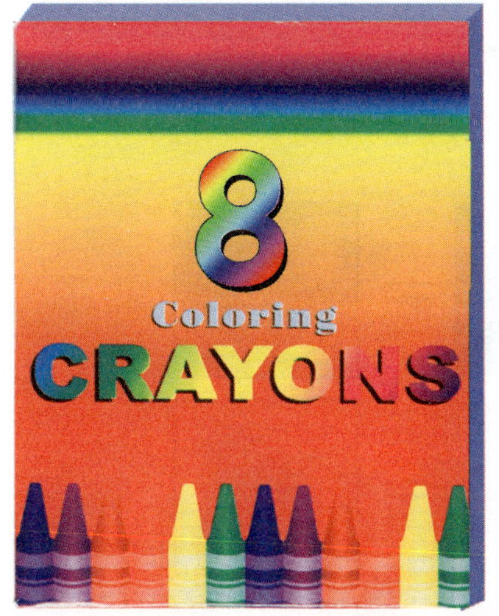

red

black

blue

orange

green

brown

yellow

violet

Color the crayon to answer each question.

1 I am the third crayon from the top.

2 I am the fourth crayon from the bottom.

3 The red is first. I am just before the eighth crayon.

4 The violet is first. I am between the fourth and sixth crayon.

Math Talk How many of these colors are in your state flag? Explain.

Color Codes

Have you ever used a code? Codes use pictures, letters, numbers, or colors to stand for things. The code below uses colors to stand for numbers. Use the code to solve the problems.

People in ancient Egypt used pictures to stand for words, sounds, and numbers. These pictures are called hieroglyphics.

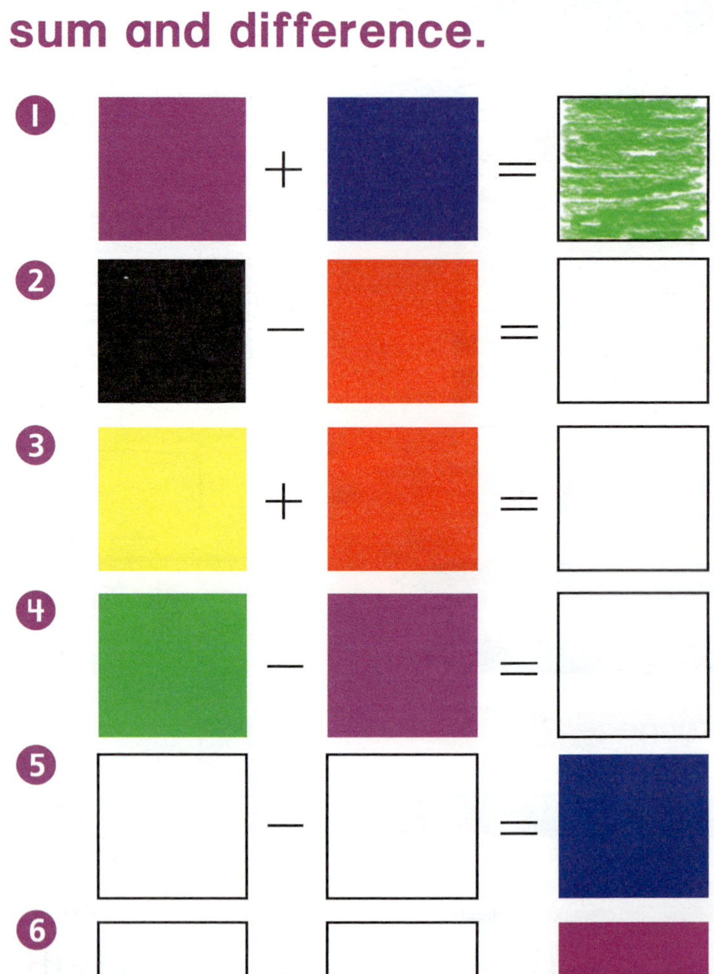

1 = (blue)
2 = (brown)
3 = (yellow)
4 = (red)
5 = (magenta)
6 = (green)
7 = (orange)
8 = (black)

Math Talk Use the code to make (magenta) in a different way. Explain.

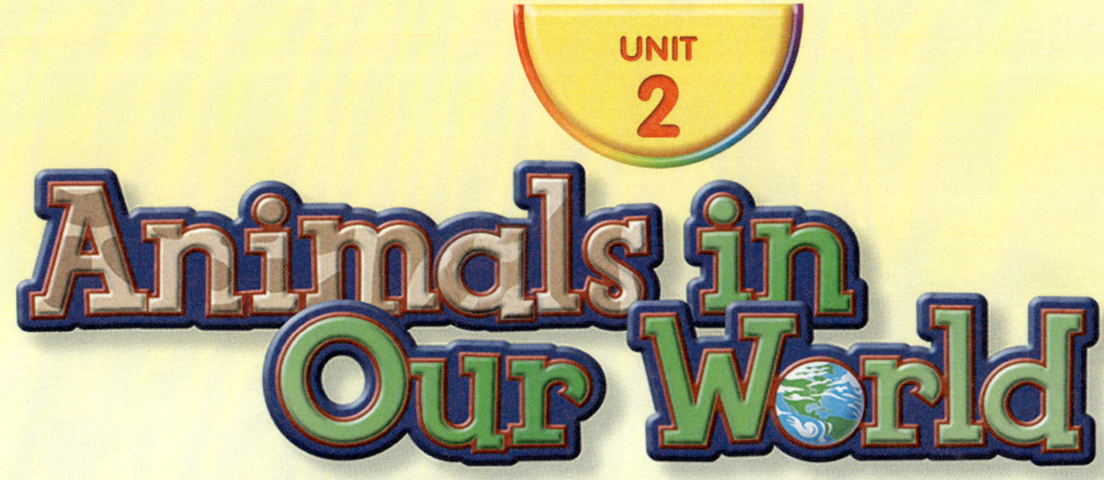

Animals in Our World

written by Martha Sibert

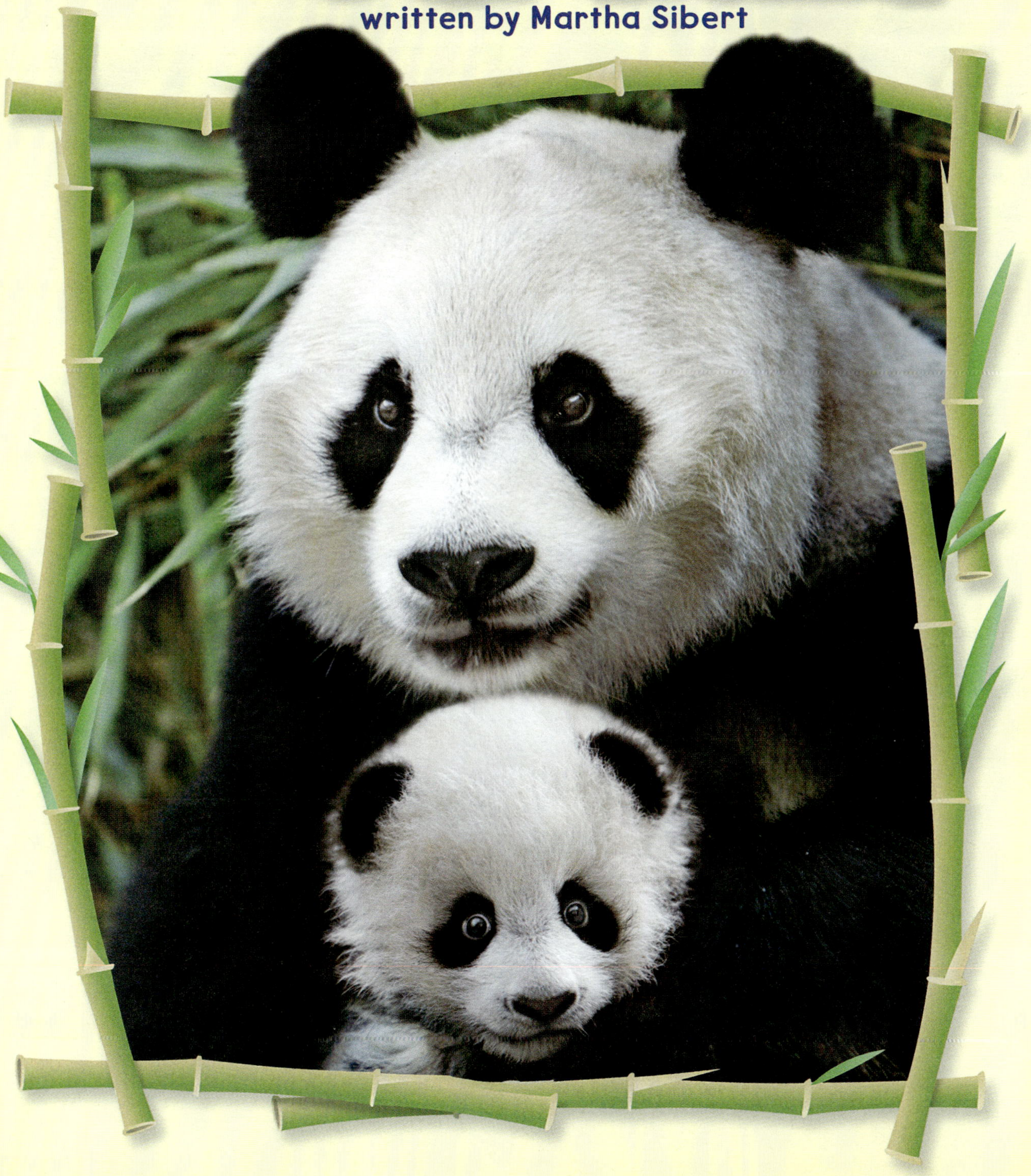

In this story you will also  and .

At Home This story will help your child review counting.

A

Two parrots sit on the branch of a tree.

How many beaks do you see? _____

B

Where do parrots live?

Four elephants walk. They are all the same kind.

How many trunks can you find? _____

Where do elephants live?

Three penguins stand. One is very small.

Each has two feet. How many feet in all? _____

D

Where do penguins live?

Four lions rest happy as can be.

Look at their ears. How many do you see? _____

Where do lions live?

E

Five giraffes stand straight and tall.

How many small horns do they have in all? ______

F

Where do giraffes live?

Look at the picture of the polar bears.
Draw or write an addition
or subtraction story.

Vocabulary Review

add	subtract
plus	minus
in all	are left

polar bears

Write Math

Write the number sentence. 

G

Name _______________________________

How Many Ears?

pandas

Look at the picture of the pandas.
What if there were five pandas?
How many ears would there be in all?

Fill in the chart.

Number of Pandas	Number of Ears	Draw to explain.
1	2	
2	4	
3		
4		
5		

Five pandas would have _______ ears in all.

Write Math ▸ Make up a question about another animal in the story. Make a new chart to answer your question. Have a classmate complete your chart.

H

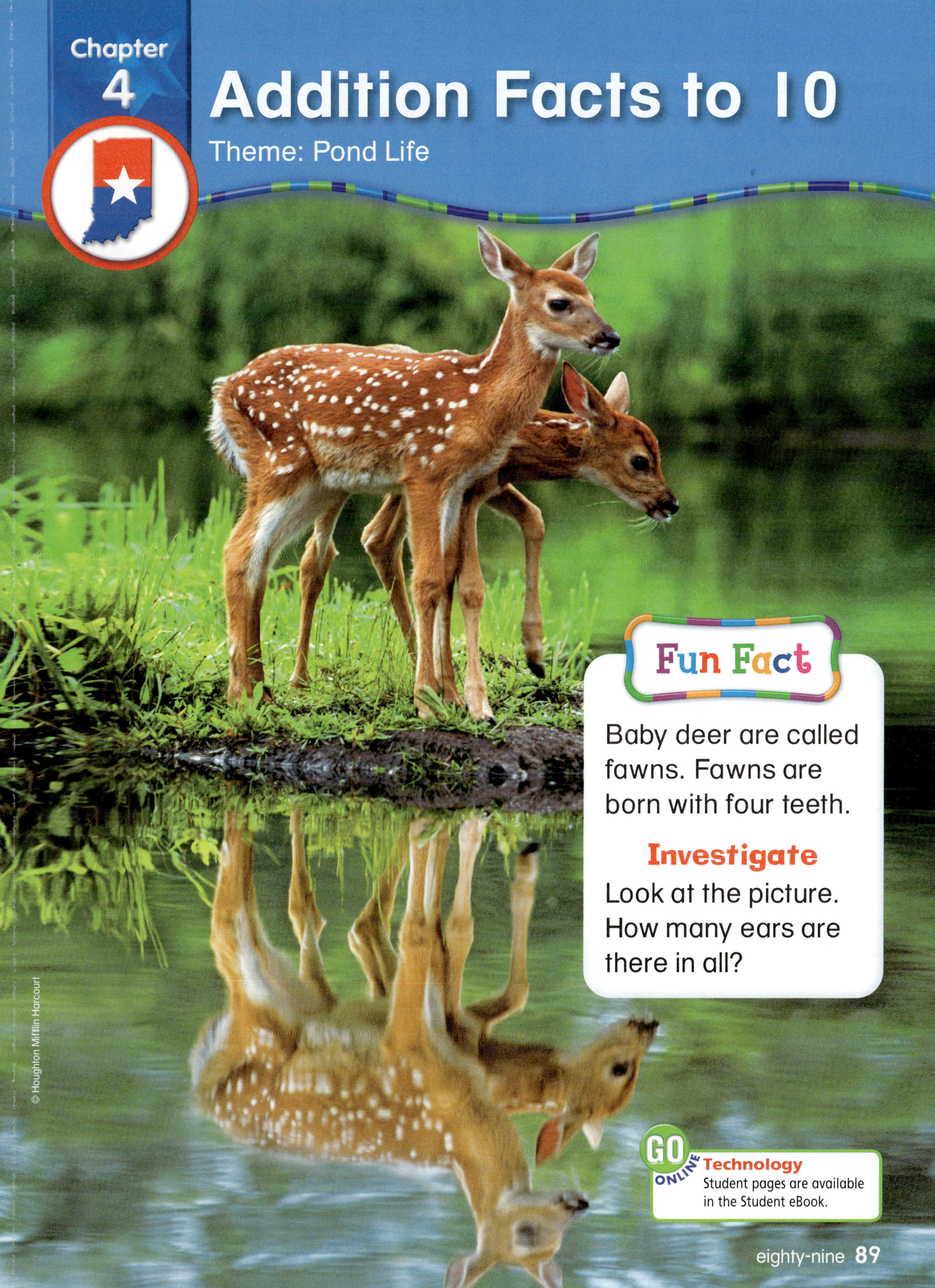

Chapter
4
Addition Facts to 10
Theme: Pond Life
Fun Fact
Baby deer are called fawns. Fawns are born with four teeth.
Investigate
Look at the picture. How many ears are there in all?
© Houghton Mifflin Harcourt
GO ONLINE Technology
Student pages are available in the Student eBook.
eighty-nine 89

Show What You Know 

Draw 1 more balloon.
Write the number of balloons in all.

1.

1   +   1   = _______

2.

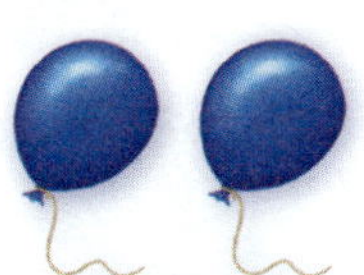

2   +   1   = _______

3.

3   +   1   = _______

4.

4   +   1   = _______

5.

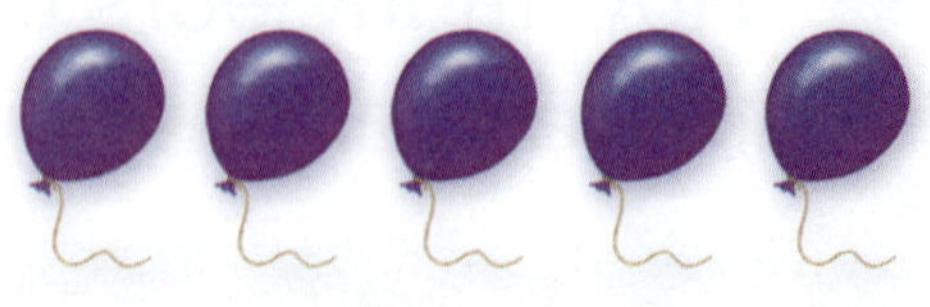

5   +   1   = _______

6.

6   +   1   = _______

At Home This page checks your child's understanding of important concepts and skills needed for success in Chapter 4.

Count On 1 or 2

Explore

 4  5 6

4 + 2 = ___6___

Hands On

Essential Question
How can you count on 1 or 2 to find a sum?

Vocabulary
count on

Connect

Use . Count on to find each sum.

1.

2 + 1 = _____

2.

2 + 2 = _____

3.

3 + 1 = _____

4.

3 + 2 = _____

5. **Math Talk** What is the sum of 0 + 2? Explain.

Count on to find each sum.

1.

$$5 + 1 = \underline{6}$$

2.

$$5 + 2 = \underline{}$$

3. $7 + 1 = \underline{}$

4. $7 + 2 = \underline{}$

5. $8 + 1 = \underline{}$

6. $8 + 2 = \underline{}$

7. $3 + 2 = \underline{}$

8. $4 + 2 = \underline{}$

9. $2 + 1 = \underline{}$

10. $5 + 2 = \underline{}$

11. $6 + 1 = \underline{}$

12. $4 + 1 = \underline{}$

13. $3 + 1 = \underline{}$

14. $6 + 2 = \underline{}$

15. $7 + 2 = \underline{}$

16. $9 + 1 = \underline{}$

17. $5 + 1 = \underline{}$

Math Board

Problem Solving: Reasoning

Write the number you count on from to
get each sum.

18.

$$\underline{} ¢ + 2¢ = 9¢$$

19.

$$\underline{} ¢ + 1¢ = 9¢$$

Explain how the pennies help you count on.

At Home Have your child choose a number between 1 and 8. Then have him or her count on 2. Have your child tell the sum.

Chapter 4 Lesson 2

Use a Number Line to Count On

▶ **We Learn**

You can use a number line to count on.

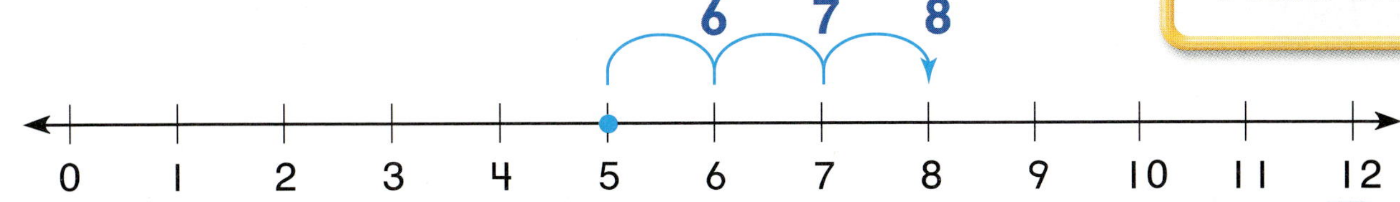

$$5 + 3 = \underline{}$$

▶ **Share and Show**

Put your finger on the first number.
Move your finger to the right to count on.
Write the sum.

1. $7 + 1 = \underline{}$	**2.** $9 + 1 = \underline{}$	**3.** $5 + 2 = \underline{}$
4. $3 + 3 = \underline{}$	**5.** $5 + 1 = \underline{}$	**6.** $6 + 1 = \underline{}$
7. $6 + 2 = \underline{}$	**8.** $4 + 3 = \underline{}$	**9.** $4 + 2 = \underline{}$
10. $7 + 3 = \underline{}$	**11.** $5 + 3 = \underline{}$	**12.** $8 + 1 = \underline{}$
13. $8 + 2 = \underline{}$	**14.** $4 + 3 = \underline{}$	**15.** $6 + 3 = \underline{}$

16. **Math Talk** Why do you move your finger to the right to count on? Explain.

1.1.6 Demonstrate fluency with addition facts and the corresponding subtraction facts for totals to at least 20. *also* **1.1.1**

Write each sum.

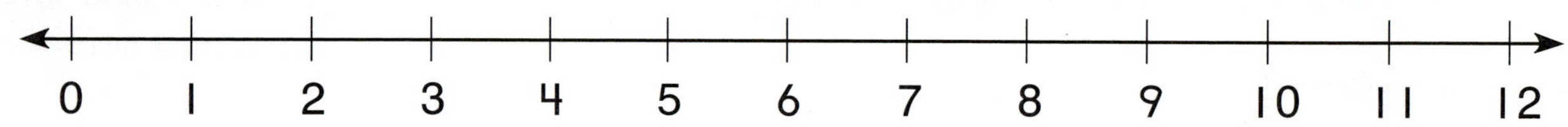

1. $\begin{aligned} 9 \\ +1 \\ \hline 10 \end{aligned}$	**2.** $\begin{aligned} 6 \\ +3 \\ \hline \end{aligned}$	**3.** $\begin{aligned} 8 \\ +1 \\ \hline \end{aligned}$

1. 9 +1 = 10 **2.** 6 +3 **3.** 8 +1 **4.** 6 +1 **5.** 3 +3 **6.** 7 +2

7. 6 +2 **8.** 5 +3 **9.** 7 +1 **10.** 7 +3 **11.** 9 +1 **12.** 4 +3

13. 4 +1 **14.** 8 +2 **15.** 4 +2 **16.** 5 +2 **17.** 6 +3 **18.** 5 +1

19. 7 +3 **20.** 7 +2 **21.** 6 +2 **22.** 4 +3 **23.** 8 +1 **24.** 5 +3

Problem Solving: Real World

25. Solve in your head.

Dylan has 6 fish in the bowl.
Hailey puts 3 more fish in the bowl.
How many fish are there in the bowl?   _______ fish

How can counting on help you
find the sum? Explain.

At Home Have your child tell you how to use the
number line to count on to find the sum for 5 + 3.

Chapter 4 Lesson 3

Count On Practice

▶ **We Learn**

Circle the greater number.
Then count on.

Count On 1 $\quad$ (4) + 1 = $\underline{5}$

Count On 2 $\quad$ 2 + (4) = $\underline{6}$

Count On 3 $\quad$ 3 + (4) = $\underline{7}$

▶ **Share and Show** 

Circle the greater number.
Count on. Write the sum.

1. (6) + 3 = $\underline{9}$ | 2. 8 + 1 = ____ | 3. 3 + 7 = ____

4. 2 + 5 = ____ | 5. 4 + 3 = ____ | 6. 3 + 5 = ____

7. 7 + 1 = ____ | 8. 8 + 2 = ____ | 9. 1 + 6 = ____

10. 7 + 2 = ____ | 11. 2 + 6 = ____ | 12. 9 + 1 = ____

13. **Math Talk** Why does it help to count on from the greater number? Use 🎲 and 🎲 to prove your answer.

1.1.6 Demonstrate fluency with addition facts and the corresponding subtraction facts for totals to at least 20. also **1.1.1**

Count on 1, 2, or 3.
Use the key to color.

Key

Count On 1	 GREEN
Count On 2	 BROWN
Count On 3	 BLUE

At Home Have your child get out his or her flash cards. Ask him or her to sort to show Count On 1, Count On 2, or Count On 3 facts.

Name ___________________

Chapter 4 Lesson 4
Add Doubles

▶ **Explore**

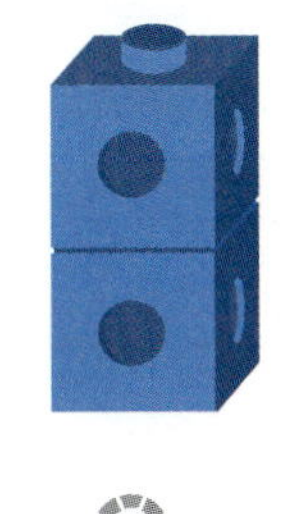 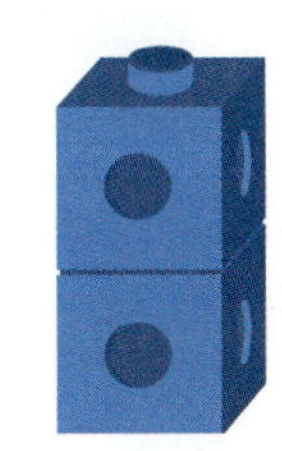

2 ⊕ 2 ⊜ 4

▶ **Connect**

Use  and .
Write the doubles fact.

1.  

___ ◯ ___ ◯ ___

2.  

___ ◯ ___ ◯ ___

✓**3.**  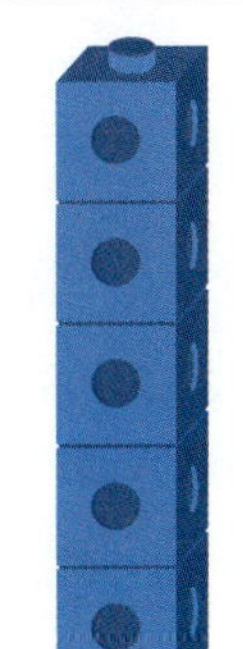

___ ◯ ___ ◯ ___

✓**4.** 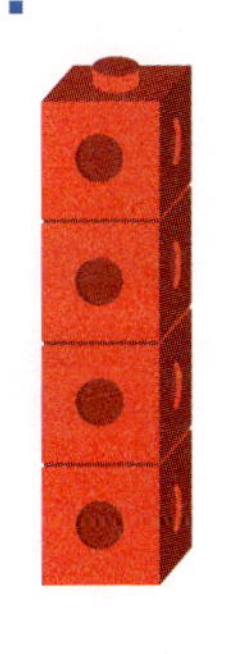 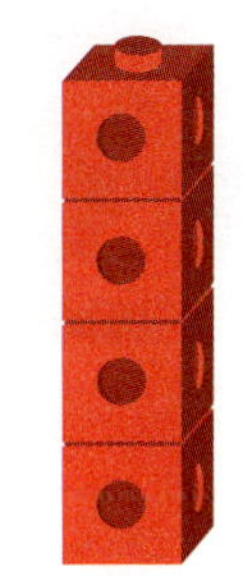

___ ◯ ___ ◯ ___

5. **Math Talk** Why is $5 + 5 = 10$ a doubles fact?

★ **1.2.1** Write and solve equations involving addition.

Write the doubles fact.

1.

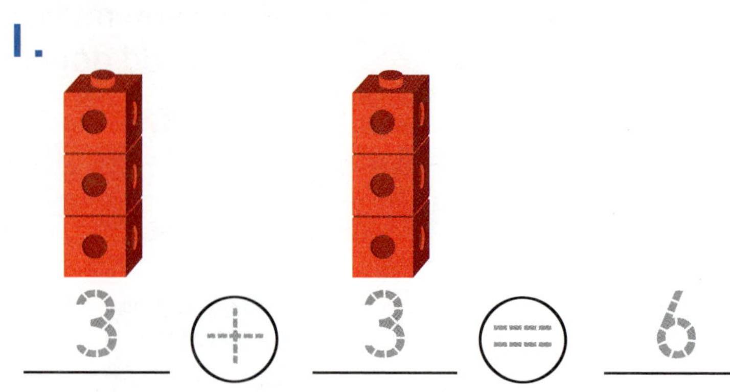

___3___ (+) ___3___ (=) ___6___

2.

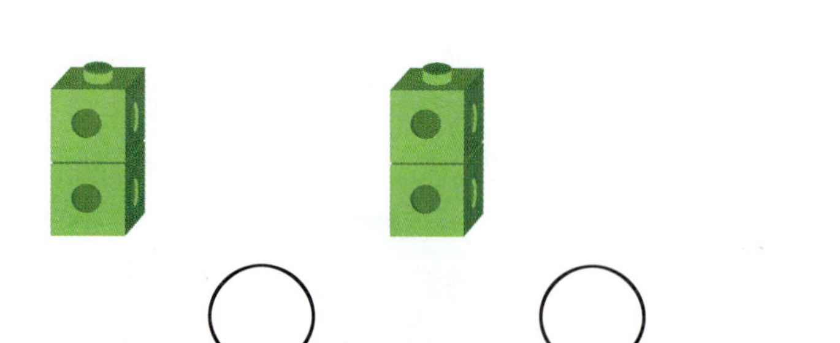

______ ( ) ______ ( ) ______

3.

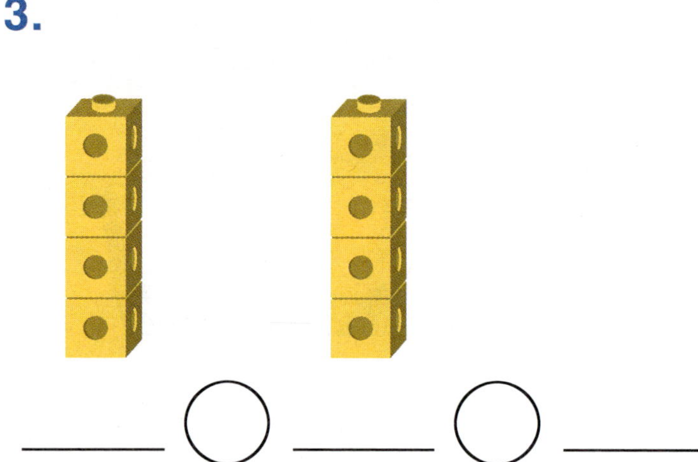

______ ( ) ______ ( ) ______

4.

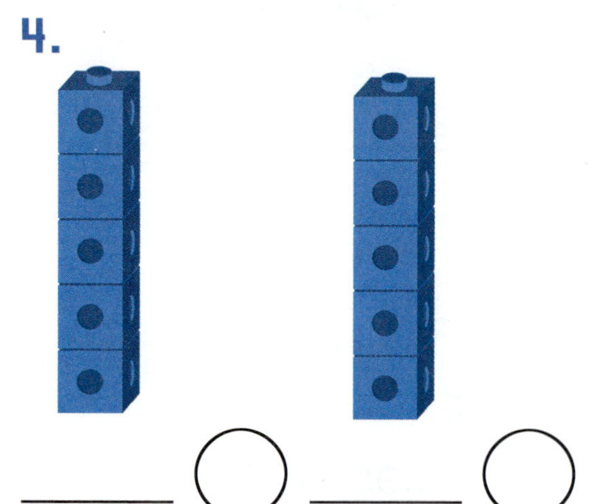

______ ( ) ______ ( ) ______

 Math Board

Problem Solving: Visual Thinking

Write a doubles fact for each picture.

5.

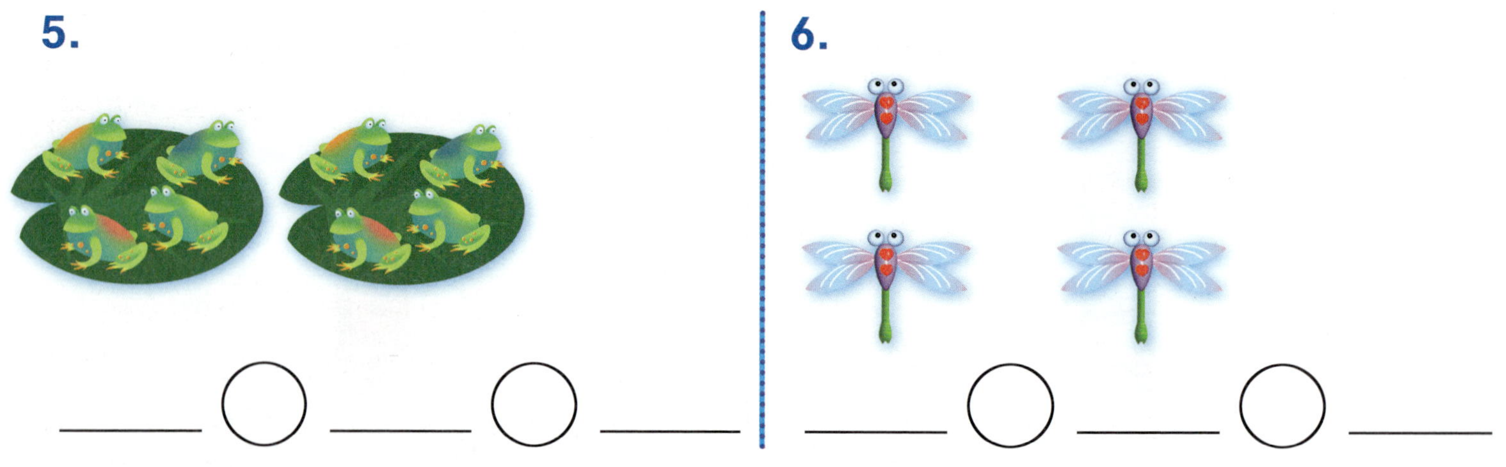

______ ( ) ______ ( ) ______

6.

______ ( ) ______ ( ) ______

Draw a picture that shows a doubles fact.
Write the doubles fact.

Chapter 4 Lesson 5

Doubles and Near Doubles

 **Explore**

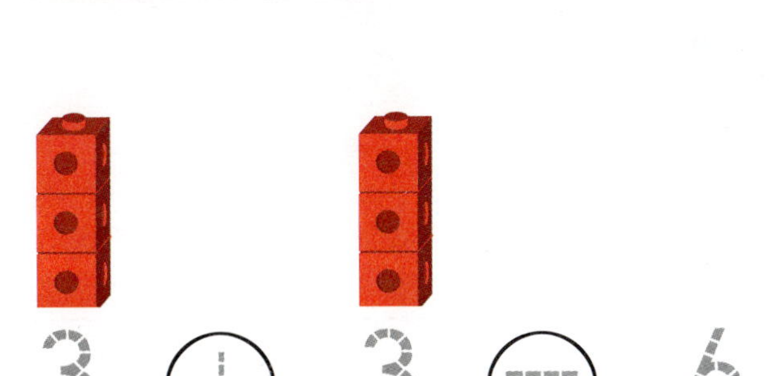

___ 3 $+$ ___ 3 $=$ ___ 6

doubles fact

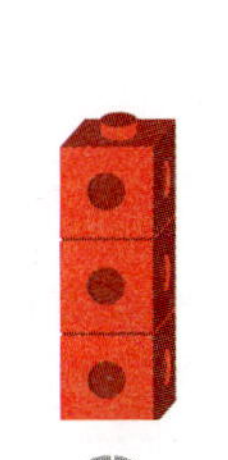 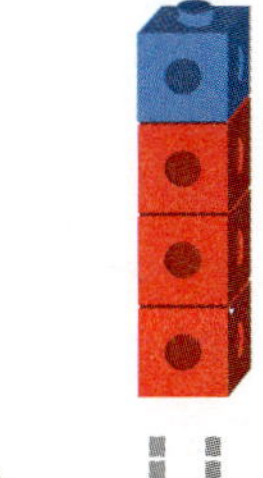

___ 3 $+$ ___ 4 $=$ ___ 7

doubles plus one fact

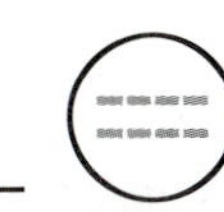  **Connect**

Use  and .

Write the addition sentences.

1.

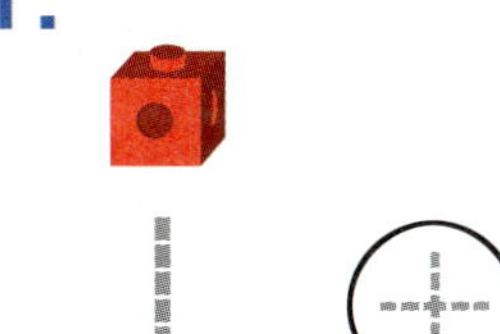 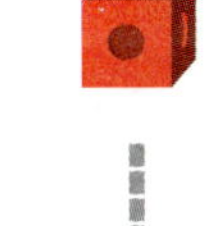 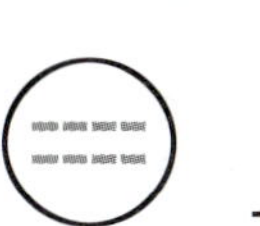 

___ 1 $+$ ___ 1 $=$ ___ 2

  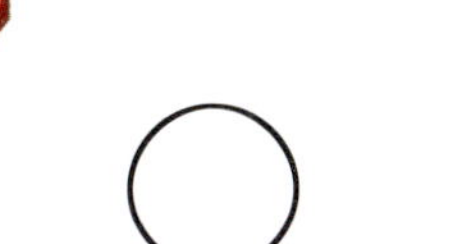

___ ◯ ___ ◯ ___

2.

___ ◯ ___ ◯ ___

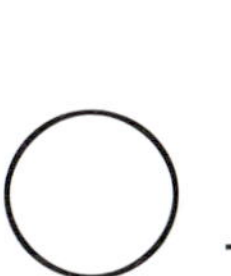 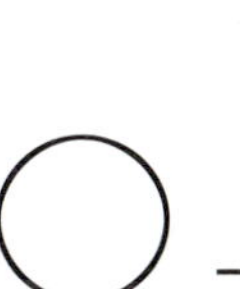

___ ◯ ___ ◯ ___

3.

  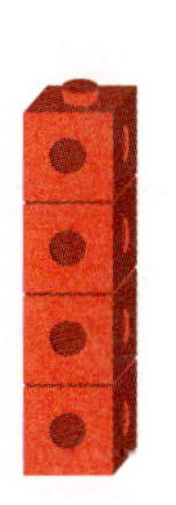

___ ◯ ___ ◯ ___

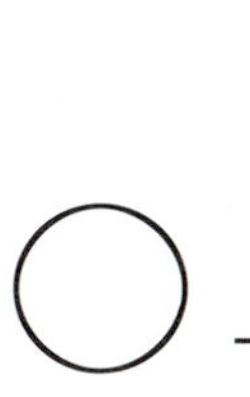 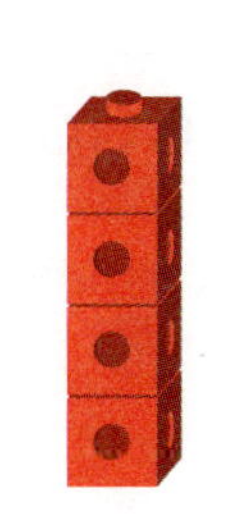  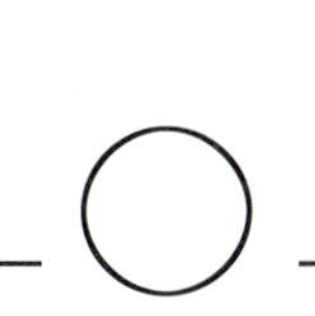

___ ◯ ___ ◯ ___

4. **Math Talk** How does 3 + 3 = 6 help you find the sum for 3 + 4? Explain.

1.2.1 Write and solve equations involving addition.

Use  and .
Write the addition sentences.

1.

  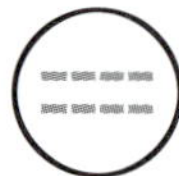 

___ 2 ⊕ + ___ 3 ⊜ = ___ 5   ___ ◯ ___ ◯ ___

2.

___ ◯ ___ ◯ ___   ___ ◯ ___ ◯ ___

3.

___ ◯ ___ ◯ ___   ___ ◯ ___ ◯ ___

 **Problem Solving: Reasoning**

Use  and . Complete each near doubles fact.

4. ___ + 2 = 3   ___ + 1 = 3

5. ___ + 4 = 9   ___ + 5 = 9

Explain how you found the missing numbers.

At Home Have your child choose a number between 1 and 5 and use it to write a near doubles fact.

Chapter 4 Lesson 6

Use the Strategies

▶ We Learn

These are the ways you have learned to find sums to 10.

$$7 + 1 = 8$$
$$7 + 2 = 9$$
$$7 + 3 = 10$$

$$4 + 4 = 8$$
$$4 + 5 = 9$$

▶ Share and Show

Add. Write the sums.

1. Count On 1

$$4 + 1 = \underline{5}$$
$$5 + 1 = \underline{}$$
$$6 + 1 = \underline{}$$
$$7 + 1 = \underline{}$$

2. Count On 2

$$5 + 2 = \underline{}$$
$$6 + 2 = \underline{}$$
$$7 + 2 = \underline{}$$
$$8 + 2 = \underline{}$$

✓3. Count On 3

$$4 + 3 = \underline{}$$
$$5 + 3 = \underline{}$$
$$6 + 3 = \underline{}$$
$$7 + 3 = \underline{}$$

✓4. Doubles

$$1 + 1 = \underline{}$$
$$2 + 2 = \underline{}$$
$$3 + 3 = \underline{}$$
$$4 + 4 = \underline{}$$

5. Near Doubles

$$1 + 2 = \underline{}$$
$$2 + 3 = \underline{}$$
$$3 + 4 = \underline{}$$
$$4 + 5 = \underline{}$$

6. **Math Talk** Which way can you use to add $4 + 3$? Explain.

1.2.2 Create, extend, and give a rule for number patterns using addition.

Add.

1. $3 + 3 = \underline{6}$ 　 2. $5 + 1 = \underline{\hspace{2em}}$ 　 3. $2 + 3 = \underline{\hspace{2em}}$

4. $2 + 8 = \underline{\hspace{2em}}$ 　 5. $7 + 3 = \underline{\hspace{2em}}$ 　 6. $4 + 4 = \underline{\hspace{2em}}$

7. $4 + 3 = \underline{\hspace{2em}}$ 　 8. $1 + 4 = \underline{\hspace{2em}}$ 　 9. $1 + 8 = \underline{\hspace{2em}}$

10. $7 + 2 = \underline{\hspace{2em}}$ 　 11. $2 + 6 = \underline{\hspace{2em}}$ 　 12. $5 + 5 = \underline{\hspace{2em}}$

13. $2 + 1 = \underline{\hspace{2em}}$ 　 14. $6 + 3 = \underline{\hspace{2em}}$ 　 15. $5 + 4 = \underline{\hspace{2em}}$

16. $3 + 5 = \underline{\hspace{2em}}$ 　 17. $2 + 2 = \underline{\hspace{2em}}$ 　 18. $1 + 9 = \underline{\hspace{2em}}$

Math Board

Problem Solving: Real World

19. Solve.

Count how many legs one puppy has.
How many legs would 2 puppies have?

_____ legs

Which way did you use to find your
answer? Explain.

puppy

Problem Solving Workshop
Strategy: Draw a Picture

Essential Question
How does drawing a picture help you solve a problem?

You know how to draw a picture.
Pictures can tell about math.
This picture can be used to show
$2 + 7 = 9$.

Draw Your Math Picture

Follow the directions to find out
how many orange fish there are.

Draw 8 fish.
Color 3 fish blue.
Color the other fish orange.

Math Talk How many fish are orange? Explain.

1.1.6 Demonstrate fluency with addition facts and the corresponding subtraction facts for totals to at least 20.

There are 8 turtles altogether.
6 are brown.
The other turtles are green.
How many turtles are green?

Unlock the Problem

What do I need to find?

how many turtles
are green

What information do I need to use?

8 turtles altogether

6 turtles are brown

Show how to solve the problem.

There are _____ green turtles.

Math Talk — Does your answer make sense? Explain.

Problem Solving Strategy Practice

Draw a picture to solve.

1. There are 9 frogs altogether.
3 are brown.
The other frogs are green.
How many frogs are green?

______ green frogs

2. There are 7 snakes in all.
5 are gray.
The other snakes are red.
How many snakes are red?

______ red snakes

3. There are 10 birds altogether.
3 are red.
The other birds are blue.
How many birds are blue?

______ blue birds

Try Your Own Problem

4. There are ______ fish in all.
______ are yellow.
The other fish are orange.
How many fish are orange?

______ orange fish

At Home Change the numbers in one of the problems. Have your
child draw a picture to solve the problem.

Mixed Strategy Practice

Draw a picture to solve.

1. There are 7 birds
in the tree.
Then 2 birds join them.
How many birds
are there in all?

bird

_____ birds

2. Pat and Jim saw the same
number of flowers. The sum
of the two numbers was 8.
How many flowers did
they each see?

flower

_____ flowers

3. Sam has 6 tadpoles.
He gives 2 tadpoles to his
friend. How many tadpoles
does Sam have left?

tadpole 

_____ tadpoles

4. Tal saw 9 ducklings.
Sue did not see any.
How many ducklings did
Tal and Sue see in all?

duckling

_____ ducklings

Name ________________________

Extra Practice

Use the number line to count on.
Write each sum.

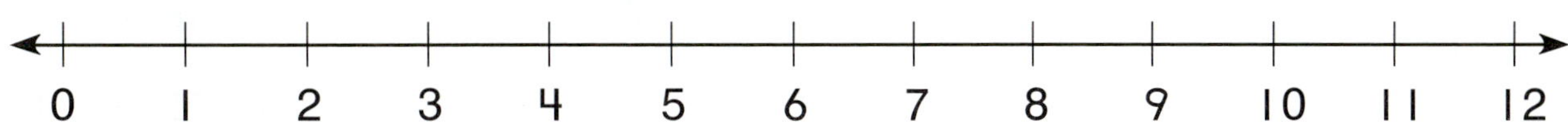

1. 5
   +3

2. 8
   +2

3. 4
   +1

4. 5
   +2

5. 8
   +1

6. 7
   +1

7. 7
   +3

8. 6
   +1

9. 7
   +2

10. 9
    +1

11. 6
    +2

12. 4
    +3

Write the doubles fact.

13.
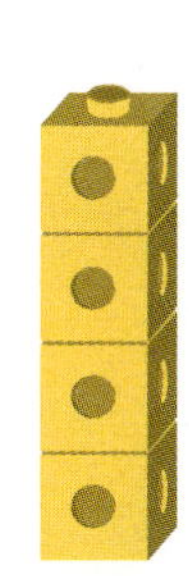

____ ◯ ____ ____

14.
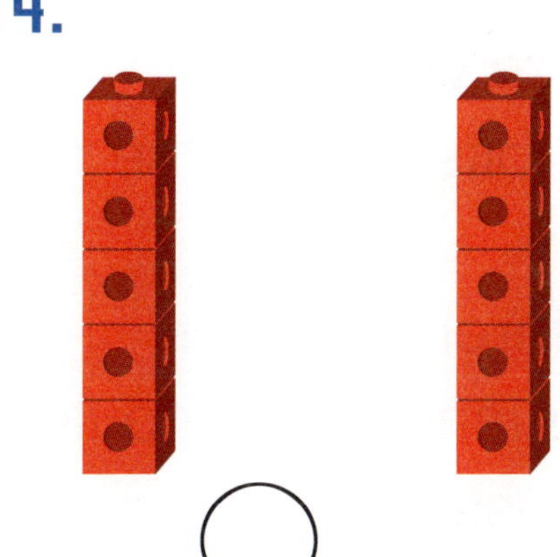

____ ◯ ____ ____

Problem Solving

Draw a picture to solve.

15. There are 9 birds in all.
3 are blue. The other birds
are red. How many birds
are red?

____ birds

Multistep Problems 
Chapter 4

1. Eric was counting rabbits in a barnyard. 1.2.1

- He counted some rabbits on one side of the barnyard.
- He counted the same number of rabbits on the other side of the barnyard.
- After Eric counted, he noticed there were fewer than 11 rabbits in all in the barnyard.
- Write 2 different addition number sentences that could fit this math story.

2. Stacy has some pennies. Alan has one more penny than Stacy. Together, they have fewer than 10 pennies.

1.2.1

- Draw how many pennies Stacy and Alan could have.
- Then write an addition sentence to go with the story.

 # Standards Quick Check

Count on to add.

1. $4 + 1 =$ _____   **2.** $7 + 2 =$ _____   **3.** $2 + 6 =$ _____

Write each sum.

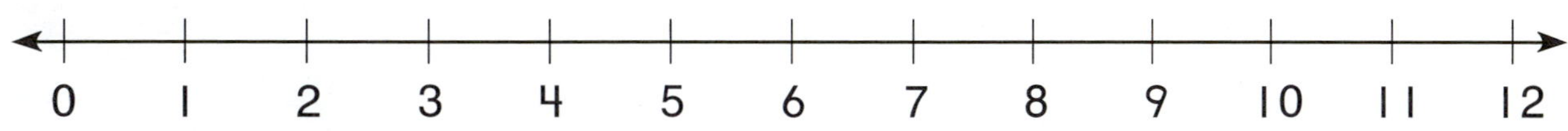

4. $5 + 3 =$ _____   **5.** $7 + 3 =$ _____   **6.** $8 + 2 =$ _____

Use doubles or doubles plus one. Add.

7.	**8.**	**9.**	**10.**	**11.**
4 + 4	5 + 4	3 + 3	5 + 5	3 + 4

Use the clue. Write the number on the sign.

Clue: If the number is doubled, it is more than 8 and less than 12.

Adding Doubles

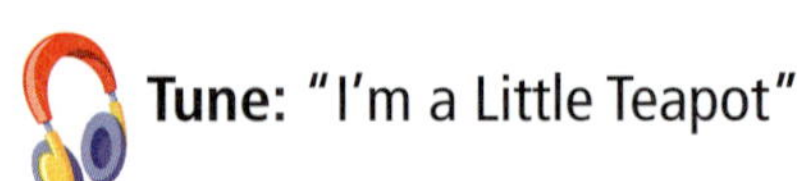
Tune: "I'm a Little Teapot"

I see 2 bananas on the tree.
I see 2 more. Do you agree?
Can you add these doubles?
Time to learn.
2 plus 2 is 4. It's your turn!

I see 3 potatoes on the ground.
Please find 3 more. Just look around.
Can you add these doubles?
Time to learn.
3 plus 3 is 6. It's your turn!

I see 4 red apples. They look great.
I see 4 more in one big crate.
Can you add these doubles?
Time to learn.
4 plus 4 is 8. It's your turn!

I see 5 tomatoes on a vine.
I picked 5 more and they are mine.
Can you add these doubles?
Time to learn.
5 plus 5 is 10. It's your turn!

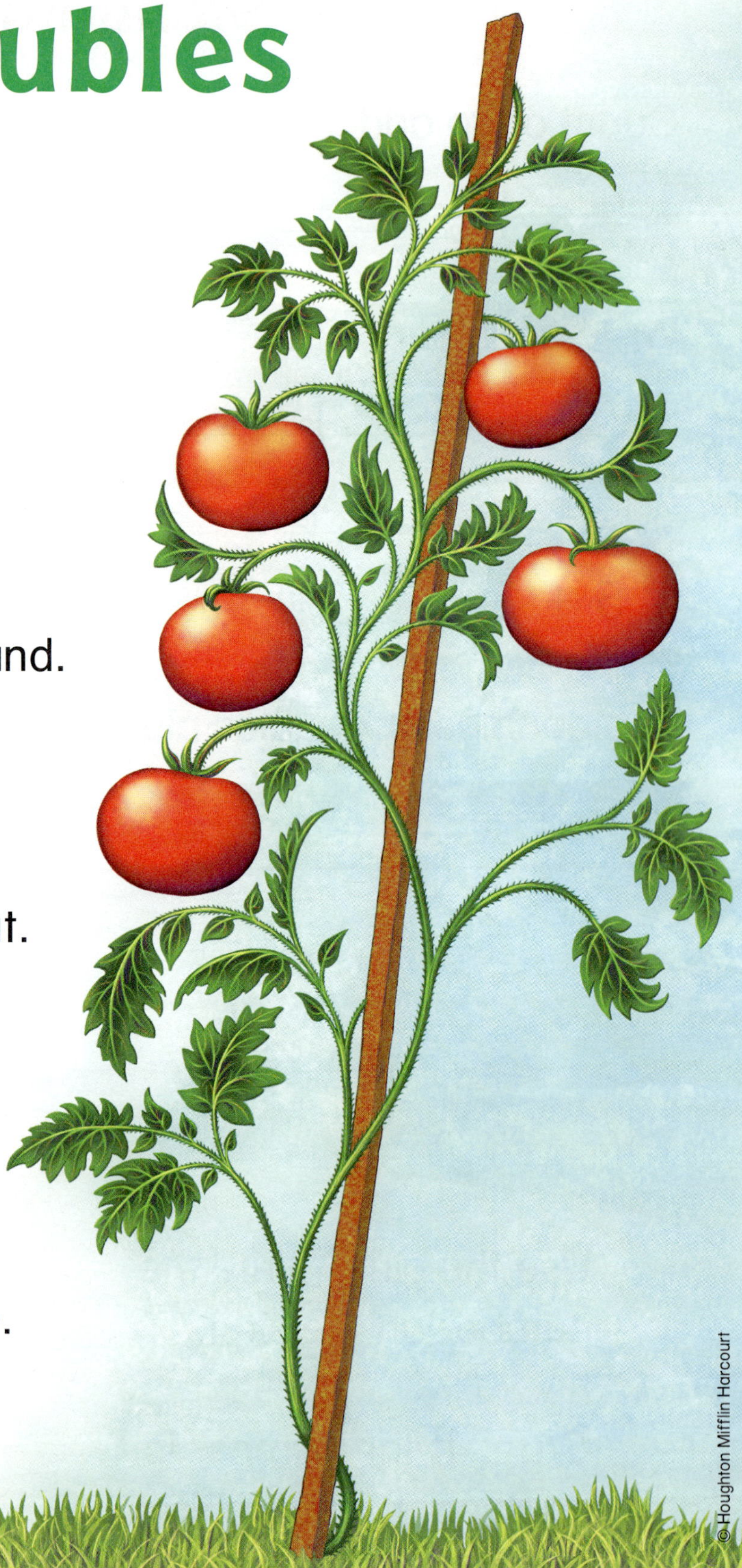

Looking Ahead to the ISTEP+
Chapter 4

Mark the best answer for questions 1–4.

1. Which addition sentence matches the picture? ▮ 1.2.1

- ○ $2 + 2 = 4$
- ○ $3 + 3 = 6$
- ○ $4 + 4 = 8$
- ○ $5 + 5 = 10$

2. What is the sum? ▮ 1.1.6

$3 + 4 = \underline{\quad}$

- ○ 1
- ○ 4
- ○ 7
- ○ 8

3. Which number sentence does the number line show? ▮ 1.1.6

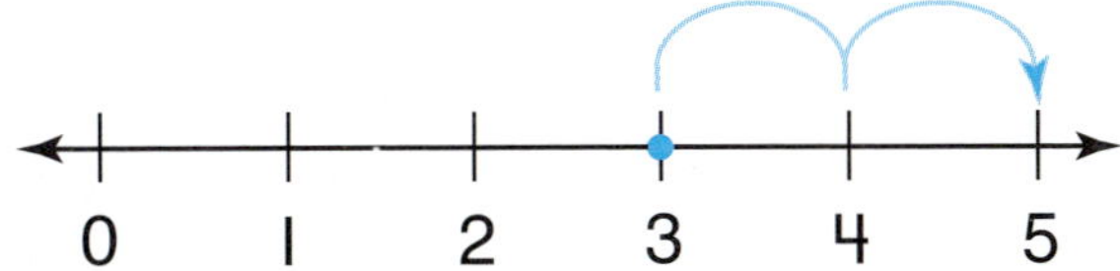

- ○ $5 + 2 = 7$
- ○ $3 + 2 = 5$
- ○ $5 - 2 = 3$
- ○ $3 - 2 = 1$

4. What is the sum? ▮ 1.2.1

$4 + 5 = \underline{\quad}$

- ○ 1
- ○ 3
- ○ 9
- ○ 10

Mark the best answer for questions 5–7.

5. What is the sum of $5 + 2$?

1.2.2

- ○ 0
- ○ 3
- ○ 7
- ○ 11

6. Which addition sentence uses near doubles? 1.2.1

- ○ $4 + 3 = 7$
- ○ $2 + 4 = 6$
- ○ $5 + 3 = 8$
- ○ $4 + 1 = 5$

7. What is the sum? 1.2.2

$3 + 6 = \underline{\hspace{1cm}}$

- ○ 7
- ○ 8
- ○ 9
- ○ 10

Open Ended

8. There are 9 fish altogether. 3 are blue. The other fish are yellow. How many fish are yellow? Draw a picture to solve.

1.1.6

_____ yellow fish

9. There are 7 turtles in all. 4 are green. The other turtles are brown. How many turtles are brown? Draw a picture to solve.

1.1.6

_____ brown turtles

Subtraction Facts to 10

Theme: Ocean Life

Fun Fact

Penguins cannot fly. They use their wings like flippers to swim in the sea.

Investigate

What subtraction sentence describes this picture?

Technology
Student pages are available in the Student eBook.

Show What You Know 

Use ▢ to show all the ways to subtract from 7.
Complete the subtraction sentences.

1. 7 − ____ = ____   2. 7 − ____ = ____

3. 7 − ____ = ____   4. 7 − ____ = ____

5. 7 − ____ = ____   6. 7 − ____ = ____

7. 7 − ____ = ____   8. 7 − ____ = ____

Cross out the frog that is going away.
Complete the subtraction sentence.

9.

3   −   1   =   ____

10.

4   −   1   =   ____

11.

5   −   1   =   ____

At Home This page checks your child's understanding
of important concepts and skills needed for success in
Chapter 5.

Chapter 5 Lesson 1

Use a Number Line to Count Back 1 and 2

You can **count back** on a number line to subtract.

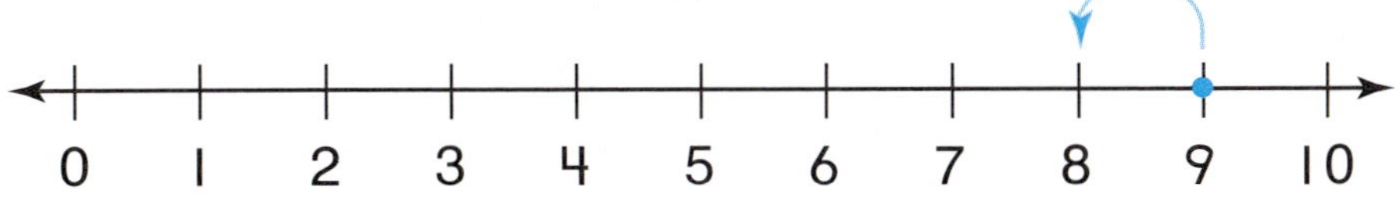

$$9 - 1 = \underline{8}$$

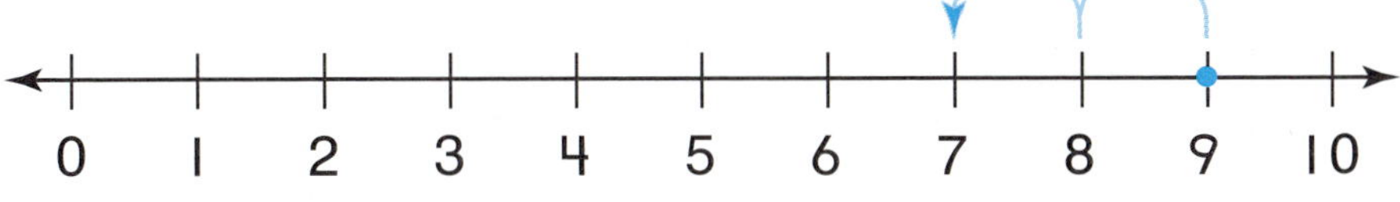

$$\underline{7} = 9 - 2$$

Put your finger on the first number.
Move your finger to the left to count back.
Write the difference.

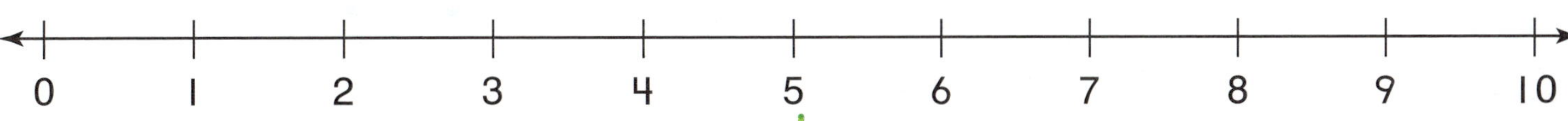

1. $8 - 1 = \underline{}$

2. $\underline{} = 5 - 2$

3. $\underline{} = 6 - 1$

4. $7 - 2 = \underline{}$

5. $\underline{} = 10 - 2$

6. $8 - 2 = \underline{}$

7. $10 - 1 = \underline{}$

8. $\underline{} = 6 - 2$

9. **Math Talk** Why do you move your finger to the left to count back? Explain.

Use the number line to subtract.
Write each difference.

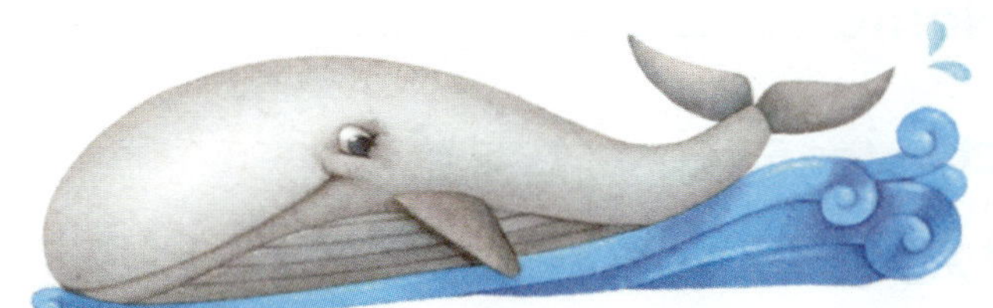

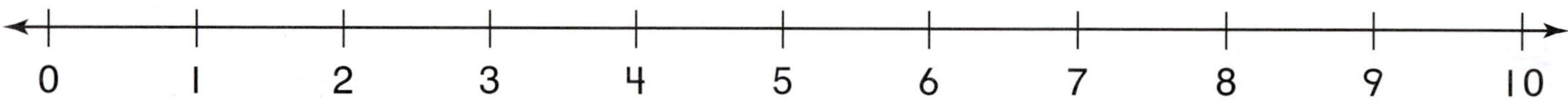

0 1 2 3 4 5 6 7 8 9 10

1. 8
   − 2
   6

2. 5
   − 1

3. 3
   − 2

4. 9
   − 2

5. 4
   − 1

6. 7
   − 1

7. 5
   − 2

8. 10
   − 1

9. 2
   − 2

10. 4
    − 2

11. 9
    − 1

12. 6
    − 1

13. 8
    − 1

14. 7
    − 2

15. 10
    − 2

16. 2
    − 1

17. 6
    − 2

18. 1
    − 1

Problem Solving: Real World

19. Solve. Use the number line.

0 1 2 3 4 5 6 7 8 9 10

There are 8 whales. 2 whales swim away. How many whales are left?

_____ whales

How does the number line help you find the difference?

At Home Have your child show how to use a number line to find the difference of 7 − 2. Repeat with other problems to count back 1 or 2 from 10 or less.

Use a Number Line to Count Back 3

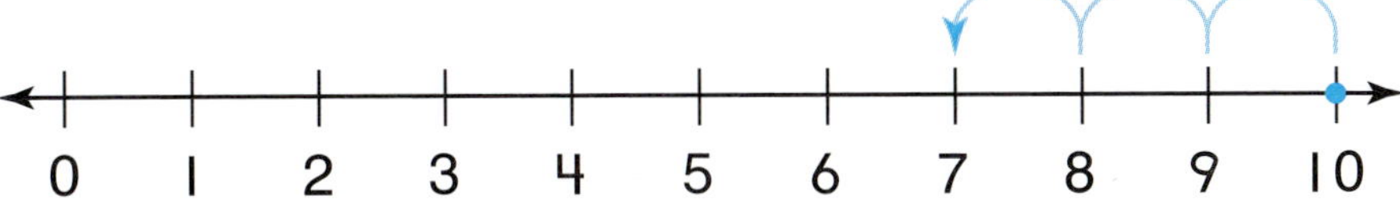

$$10 - 3 = \underline{7}$$

Put your finger on the first number.
Move your finger to the left to
count back. Write the difference.

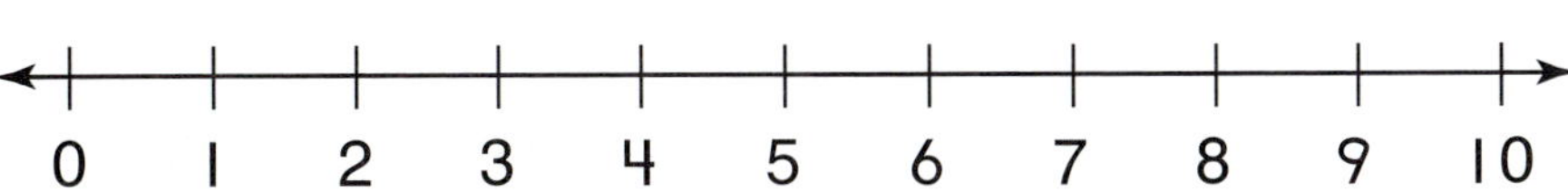

1. $\underline{} = 7 - 3$

2. $4 - 3 = \underline{}$

3. $\underline{} = 6 - 3$

4. $8 - 3 = \underline{}$

5. $5 - 3 = \underline{}$

6. $\underline{} = 3 - 3$

7. $\underline{} = 8 - 3$

8. $9 - 3 = \underline{}$

9. $10 - 3 = \underline{}$

10. $\underline{} = 5 - 3$

Math Talk What is the error? Use the
number line above to show the
correct answer.

$$10 - 3 = 8$$

Use the number line to subtract.
Write each difference.

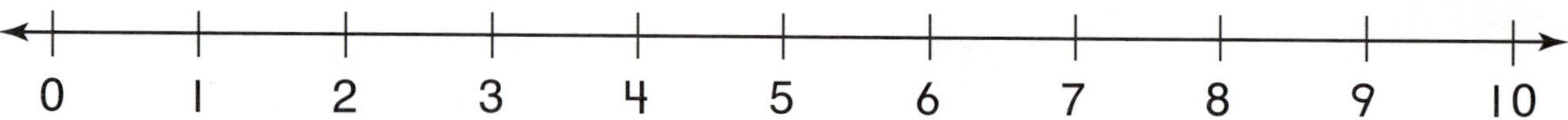

0 1 2 3 4 5 6 7 8 9 10

1. $9 - 3 = \underline{6}$

2. $\underline{} = 4 - 1$

3. $5 - 3 = \underline{}$

4. $7 - 2 = \underline{}$

5. $\underline{} = 2 - 2$

6. $6 - 1 = \underline{}$

7. $4 - 3 = \underline{}$

8. $\underline{} = 8 - 2$

9. $8 - 3 = \underline{}$

10. $5 - 2 = \underline{}$

11. $\underline{} = 7 - 3$

12. $7 - 1 = \underline{}$

13. $6 - 3 = \underline{}$

14. $\underline{} = 5 - 1$

15. $10 - 2 = \underline{}$

16. $8 - 1 = \underline{}$

17. $\underline{} = 3 - 3$

18. $9 - 1 = \underline{}$

19. $9 - 2 = \underline{}$

20. $\underline{} = 10 - 3$

21. $10 - 1 = \underline{}$

22. $9 - 3 = \underline{}$

23. $\underline{} = 7 - 2$

24. $8 - 3 = \underline{}$

Problem Solving: Algebra

Write the missing number.

25. $9 - \boxed{} = 7$

26. $4 = 7 - \boxed{}$

27. $10 - \boxed{} = 7$

28. $9 = 10 - \boxed{}$

Look at Exercise 27. How did you find the missing
number? Explain.

Chapter 5 Lesson 3

Think Addition to Subtract

Explore

You can use addition to help you subtract.

$5 + 4 = 9$
$9 - 4 = 5$

Think $5 + 4 = \underline{9}$ | So $9 - 4 = \underline{5}$

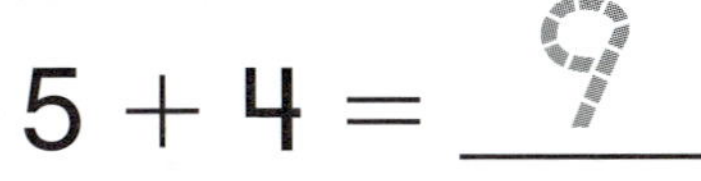
Connect

Use  and ▮ to add and to subtract.

1. Think $3 + 1 = \underline{4}$
   So $4 - 1 = \underline{3}$

2. Think $2 + 6 = \underline{}$
   So $8 - 6 = \underline{}$

3. Think $2 + 5 = \underline{}$
   So $7 - 5 = \underline{}$

4. Think $4 + 3 = \underline{}$
   So $7 - 3 = \underline{}$

5. Think $4 + 5 = \underline{}$
   So $9 - 5 = \underline{}$

6. Think $4 + 4 = \underline{}$
   So $8 - 4 = \underline{}$

7. **Math Talk** How does knowing addition help you subtract? Explain.

1.1.6 Demonstrate fluency with addition facts and the corresponding subtraction facts for totals to at least 20.

Use  and to add and to subtract.

1.

$$5 + 3 = 8$$

$$8 - 3 = 5$$

2.

$$1 + 1$$ $$2 - 1$$

3.

$$3 + 4$$ $$7 - 4$$

4.

$$0 + 5$$ $$5 - 5$$

5.

$$3 + 3$$ $$6 - 3$$

6.

$$4 + 6$$ $$10 - 6$$

7.

$$7 + 2$$ $$9 - 2$$

Problem Solving: Real World

Solve.

8. Carol has some books. She gives 3 away. She has 4 left. How many books did she start with?

_____ books

9. Charles has some toy cars. He gives 5 away. He has 5 left. How many toy cars did he start with?

_____ toy cars

Look at Exercise 9. How did you find how many toy cars Charles started with?

At Home Write 5 + 4 = ____ and ask your child to write the sum. Have him or her explain how to use 5 + 4 = 9 to solve ____ − 4 = 5 and then write the answer.

Chapter 5 Lesson 4

Practice Differences from 10

▶ **We Learn**

You have learned different strategies to subtract.

Count Back

Count Back 1 $9 - 1 = \underline{8}$

Count Back 2 $9 - 2 = \underline{7}$

Count Back 3 $9 - 3 = \underline{6}$

Think Addition to Subtract

Think $4 + 5 = \underline{9}$

So $9 - 5 = \underline{4}$

▶ **Share and Show**

Write the difference.

1. $6 - 1 = \underline{}$

2. $5 - 3 = \underline{}$

3. $8 - 4 = \underline{}$

4. $8 - 2 = \underline{}$

5. $6 - 3 = \underline{}$

6. $10 - 1 = \underline{}$

7. $\underline{} = 8 - 3$

8. $\underline{} = 10 - 3$

9. $\underline{} = 7 - 2$

10. $\underline{} = 9 - 3$

11. $\underline{} = 9 - 2$

12. $\underline{} = 10 - 2$

13. **Math Talk** How can you solve this problem? Explain two ways.

$7 - 3 = \underline{}$

1.1.6 Demonstrate fluency with addition facts and the corresponding subtraction facts for totals to at least 20.

Write the difference.

1. $\begin{array}{r} 4 \\ -\ 2 \\ \hline 2 \end{array}$	**2.** $\begin{array}{r} 5 \\ -\ 1 \\ \hline \end{array}$	**3.** $\begin{array}{r} 6 \\ -\ 2 \\ \hline \end{array}$	**4.** $\begin{array}{r} 4 \\ -\ 3 \\ \hline \end{array}$
5. $\begin{array}{r} 7 \\ -\ 1 \\ \hline \end{array}$	**6.** $\begin{array}{r} 7 \\ -\ 3 \\ \hline \end{array}$	**7.** $\begin{array}{r} 2 \\ -\ 1 \\ \hline \end{array}$	**8.** $\begin{array}{r} 2 \\ -\ 2 \\ \hline \end{array}$
9. $\begin{array}{r} 9 \\ -\ 2 \\ \hline \end{array}$	**10.** $\begin{array}{r} 8 \\ -\ 1 \\ \hline \end{array}$	**11.** $\begin{array}{r} 3 \\ -\ 3 \\ \hline \end{array}$	**12.** $\begin{array}{r} 6 \\ -\ 3 \\ \hline \end{array}$
13. $\begin{array}{r} 8 \\ -\ 4 \\ \hline \end{array}$	**14.** $\begin{array}{r} 8 \\ -\ 2 \\ \hline \end{array}$	**15.** $\begin{array}{r} 10 \\ -\ 2 \\ \hline \end{array}$	**16.** $\begin{array}{r} 10 \\ -\ 5 \\ \hline \end{array}$

Math Board

Problem Solving: Real World

Solve.

17. There are 7 fish in the tank. How many fish are behind the rock?

_____ fish

How did you find the number of fish behind the rock?

Problem Solving Workshop
Strategy: Write a Number Sentence

Problem Solving

Essential Question

How can you figure out what number sentence to write to solve a problem?

You can write a number sentence to solve a problem.

It helps to draw a picture before you write a number sentence.

There are 6 seashells.
2 seashells are washed away.

Write a number sentence to find how many seashells are left.

6  2  4

Write how many you start with.	Use a minus sign to show that some are washed away.	Write how many are washed away.	Use an equal sign to write a number sentence.	Write how many are left.

Try Your Own Number Sentence

Draw a picture. Write a number sentence.

There are 8 seashells.
3 seashells are washed away.
How many seashells are there now?

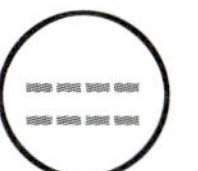 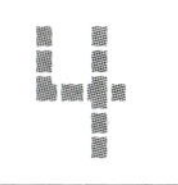

8  3  5 seashells

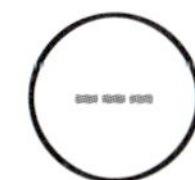 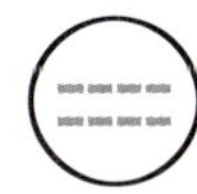 

 How does the picture help you write a number sentence? Explain.

Use the Strategy • Write a Number Sentence

There are 7 fish.
1 fish swims away.
How many fish are there now?

 Unlock the Problem

What do I need to find?

how many fish there
are now

What information do I need to use?

7 fish

1 fish swims away

Show how to solve the problem.

Write a number sentence: ____ ◯ ____ ◯ ____

There are now _____ fish.

Math Talk Does your answer make sense? Explain.

Problem Solving Strategy Practice

Draw a picture. Use the picture to write a number sentence.

1. There are 4 seals.
3 seals swim away.
How many are
there now?

seal

____ ◯ ____ ◯ ____

______ seal

2. There are 9 fish. 2 fish
are blue. The other fish
are yellow. How many
fish are yellow?

fish

____ ◯ ____ ◯ ____

______ fish are yellow

3. There are 7 red crabs.
There are 5 blue crabs.
How many more red
crabs are there than
blue crabs?

crab

____ ◯ ____ ◯ ____

______ more red crabs

Try Your Own Problem

4. There are ______ clams.
______ clams move away.
How many are there now?

clam

____ ◯ ____ ◯ ____

______ clams

At Home Tell your child a subtraction story. Ask your child to draw a picture and write a number sentence to solve it.

Mixed Strategy Practice

Choose a way to solve each problem.
Show your work.

1. There is 1 fish.
5 more fish join it.
How many fish are there in all?

_____ fish

2. 8 otters are on a rock.
3 otters go in the water.
How many are
left on the rock?

_____ otters

3. There are 9 sponges.
None float away.
How many are there now?

_____ sponges

4. There are 7 dolphins in all.
4 are large dolphins.
The others are small dolphins.
How many small
dolphins are there?

_____ small dolphins

Name _______________________________

Extra Practice

Use the number line to subtract. Write each difference.

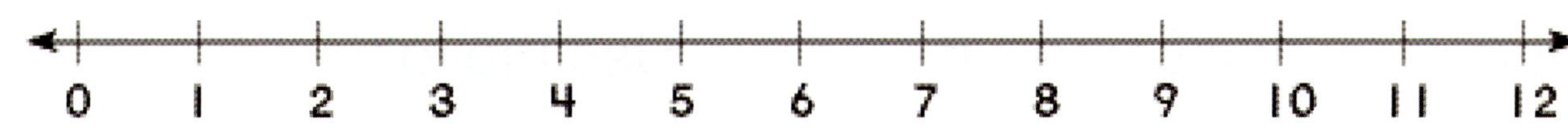

1. $5 - 3 =$ _____   2. $7 - 2 =$ _____   3. $9 - 1 =$ _____

4. $8 - 1 =$ _____   5. $9 - 2 =$ _____   6. $6 - 2 =$ _____

7. $6 - 3 =$ _____   8. $8 - 2 =$ _____   9. $8 - 3 =$ _____

10. $10 - 2 =$ _____   11. $10 - 3 =$ _____   12. $9 - 3 =$ _____

Use 🔴 and 🔵 to add and to subtract.

13. $\begin{array}{r} 4 \\ +3 \\ \hline \end{array}$ $\begin{array}{r} 7 \\ -3 \\ \hline \end{array}$ 14. $\begin{array}{r} 2 \\ +8 \\ \hline \end{array}$ $\begin{array}{r} 10 \\ -8 \\ \hline \end{array}$ 15. $\begin{array}{r} 4 \\ +5 \\ \hline \end{array}$ $\begin{array}{r} 9 \\ -5 \\ \hline \end{array}$

Write the difference.

16. $\begin{array}{r} 6 \\ -6 \\ \hline \end{array}$ 17. $\begin{array}{r} 8 \\ -0 \\ \hline \end{array}$ 18. $\begin{array}{r} 10 \\ -4 \\ \hline \end{array}$ 19. $\begin{array}{r} 9 \\ -4 \\ \hline \end{array}$ 20. $\begin{array}{r} 7 \\ -3 \\ \hline \end{array}$ 21. $\begin{array}{r} 10 \\ -7 \\ \hline \end{array}$

Problem Solving

Draw a picture. Use the picture
to write a number sentence.

22. There are 10 fish.
4 fish swim away.
How many fish are
there now?

_____ ◯ _____ ◯ _____

_____ fish

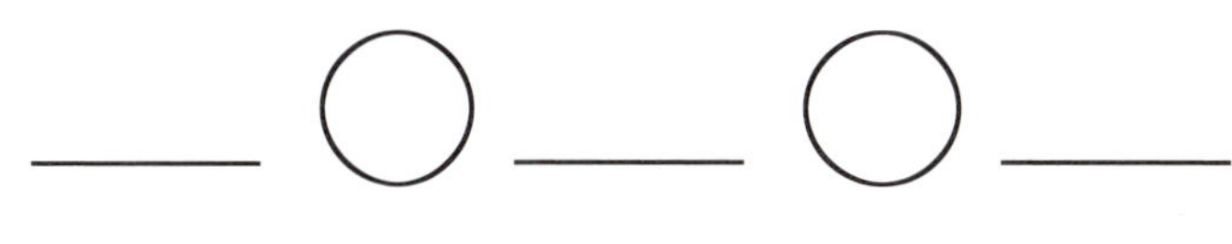

Technology
Use HMH Mega Math, Numberopolis,
Cross Town Number Line, Level E.

Multistep Problems
Chapter 5

1. Adam's cat had some kittens. There were less than 10 kittens. Adam gave 3 kittens to his neighbor.

1.1.1, 1.1.5, 1.1.6

- Write a subtraction sentence to show how many kittens Adam could have left.

____ ◯ ____ ◯ ____

- Write an addition sentence that could help Adam check his answer.

____ ◯ ____ ◯ ____

- Show the subtraction on the number line.

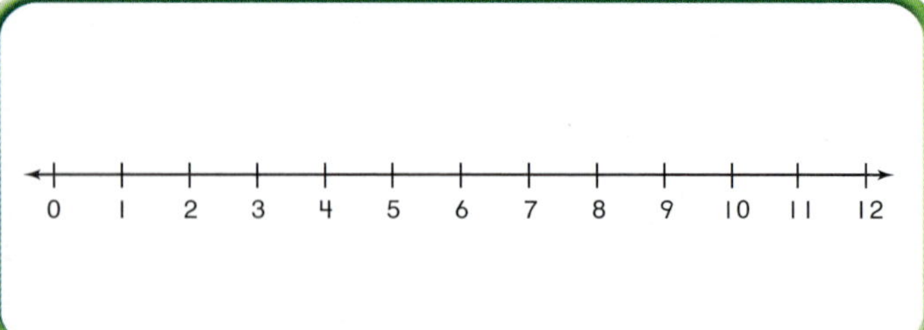

2. Use the table.

1.1.1, 1.1.5, 1.1.6

Books Read	
Roger	3
William	3
Elizabeth	10

How many books did Roger and William read in all?

- Write a subtraction sentence to show how many more books Elizabeth read than Roger and William altogether.

____ ◯ ____ ◯ ____

- Write an addition sentence that could help you check you answer.

____ ◯ ____ ◯ ____

- Show your subtraction on the number line.

Roger and William read ______ books altogether.

Standards Quick Check

Find the difference.

1. $8 - 5 =$ _____   2. $8 - 8 =$ _____   3. $7 - 4 =$ _____

4. $9 - 4 =$ _____   5. $10 - 5 =$ _____   6. $7 - 1 =$ _____

7. $\begin{array}{r} 7 \\ -7 \\ \hline \end{array}$ 8. $\begin{array}{r} 10 \\ -7 \\ \hline \end{array}$ 9. $\begin{array}{r} 5 \\ -0 \\ \hline \end{array}$ 10. $\begin{array}{r} 7 \\ -5 \\ \hline \end{array}$ 11. $\begin{array}{r} 9 \\ -6 \\ \hline \end{array}$

Challenge

Write the different ways to subtract from 6.

1. ___ ◯ ___ ◯ ___   2. ___ ◯ ___ ◯ ___

3. ___ ◯ ___ ◯ ___   4. ___ ◯ ___ ◯ ___

5. ___ ◯ ___ ◯ ___   6. ___ ◯ ___ ◯ ___

7. ___ ◯ ___ ◯ ___

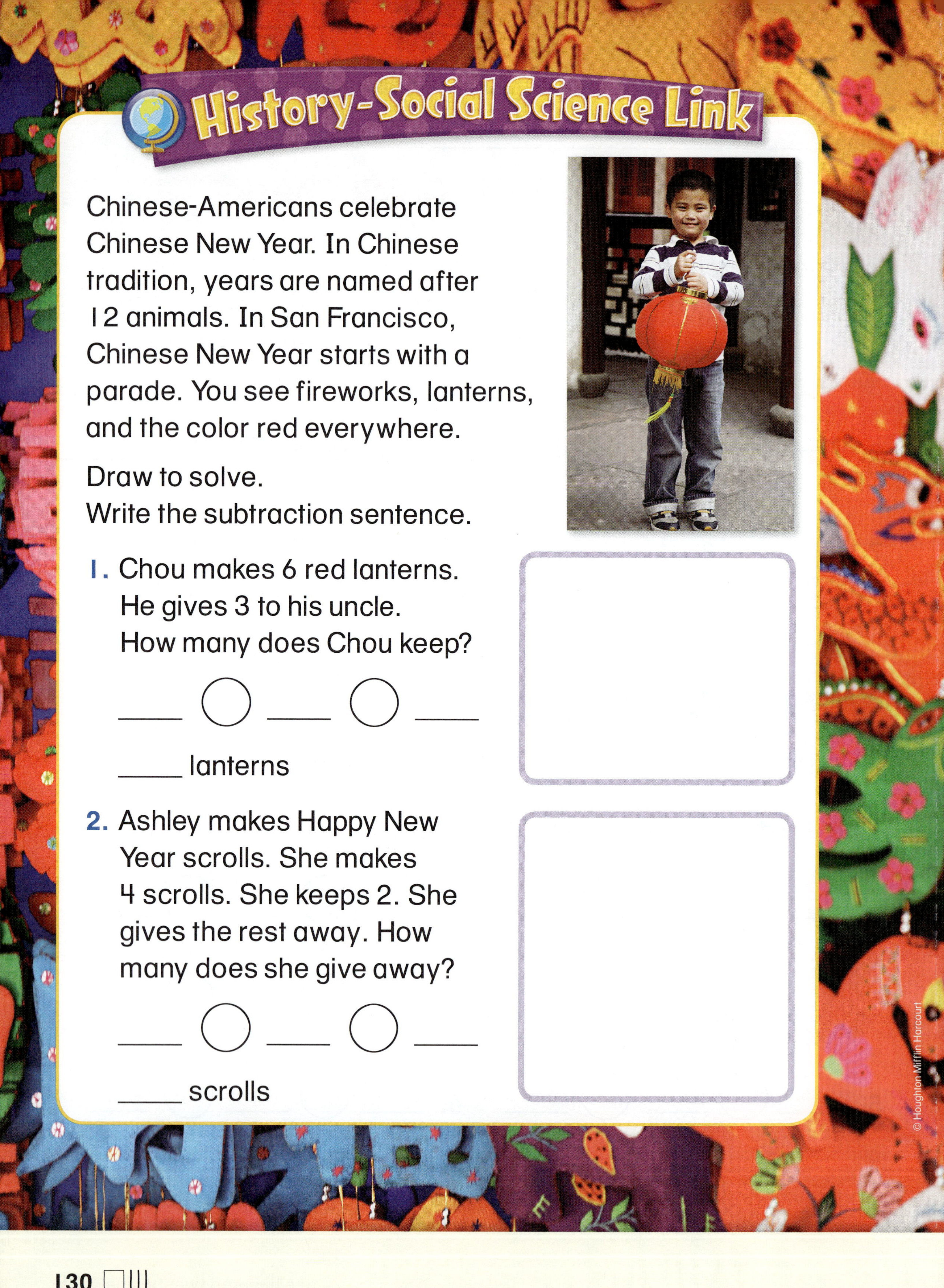

Chinese-Americans celebrate Chinese New Year. In Chinese tradition, years are named after 12 animals. In San Francisco, Chinese New Year starts with a parade. You see fireworks, lanterns, and the color red everywhere.

Draw to solve.
Write the subtraction sentence.

1. Chou makes 6 red lanterns. He gives 3 to his uncle. How many does Chou keep?

   ____ ◯ ____ ◯ ____

   ____ lanterns

2. Ashley makes Happy New Year scrolls. She makes 4 scrolls. She keeps 2. She gives the rest away. How many does she give away?

   ____ ◯ ____ ◯ ____

   ____ scrolls

Looking Ahead to the ISTEP+
Chapter 5

Mark the best answer for questions 1–4.

1. Which number sentence does the number line show? ▮ 1.1.1, 1.1.5

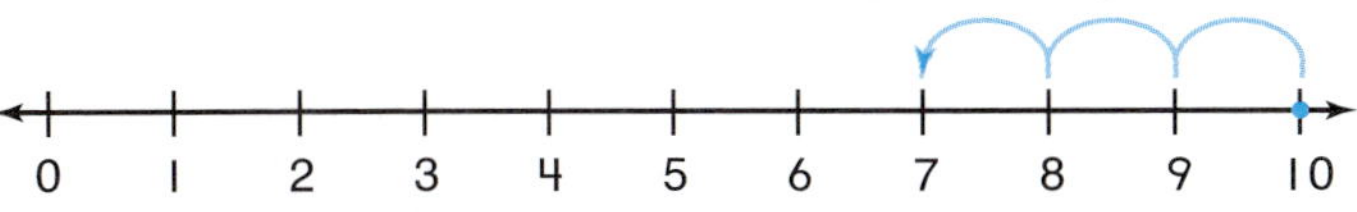

- ○ $9 - 2 = 7$
- ○ $10 - 3 = 7$
- ○ $10 - 2 = 8$
- ○ $11 - 3 = 8$

2. What is the difference? ▮ 1.1.6

$$\begin{array}{r} 8 \\ -3 \\ \hline \end{array}$$

- ○ 5
- ○ 8
- ○ 9
- ○ 10

3. What is the difference of $7 - 2$? ▮ 1.1.6

- ○ 4
- ○ 5
- ○ 9
- ○ 10

4. Which subtraction sentence matches the story? ▮ 1.2.1

There are 10 penguins. 8 penguins swim away. How many penguins are there now?

- ○ $2 + 8 = 10$
- ○ $10 - 3 = 7$
- ○ $10 - 8 = 2$
- ○ $8 - 2 = 6$

Mark the best answer for questions 5–6.

5. Which addition sentence can help solve $7 - 5 = \underline{\hspace{1cm}}$?

1.1.6

- ○ $5 + 0 = 5$
- ○ $5 + 2 = 7$
- ○ $2 + 7 = 9$
- ○ $7 + 5 = 12$

6. Which number sentence matches the story? 1.2.1

There are 6 cats in all. 2 are striped. The other cats are not striped. How many cats are not striped?

- ○ $6 + 2 = 8$
- ○ $6 - 2 = 4$
- ○ $2 + 0 = 0$
- ○ $6 - 0 = 6$

Open Ended

7. There are 8 jellyfish. 3 jellyfish move away. How many jellyfish are left?

1.2.1

$\underline{\hspace{1cm}} \bigcirc \underline{\hspace{1cm}} \bigcirc \underline{\hspace{1cm}}$

$\underline{\hspace{1cm}}$ jellyfish

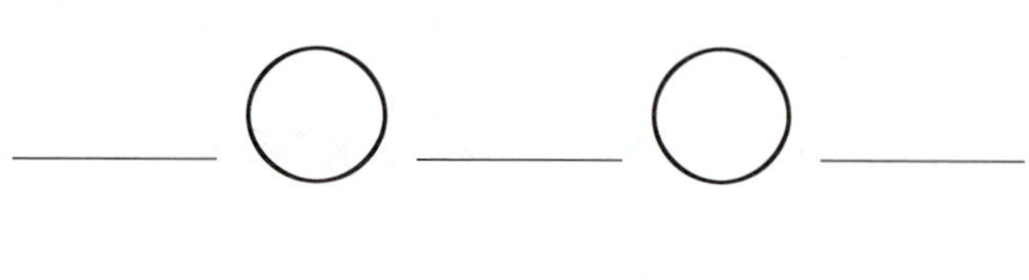

8. There are 9 baby seals. There are 2 adult seals. How many more baby seals are there than adult seals?

1.2.1

$\underline{\hspace{1cm}} \bigcirc \underline{\hspace{1cm}} \bigcirc \underline{\hspace{1cm}}$

$\underline{\hspace{1cm}}$ more baby seals

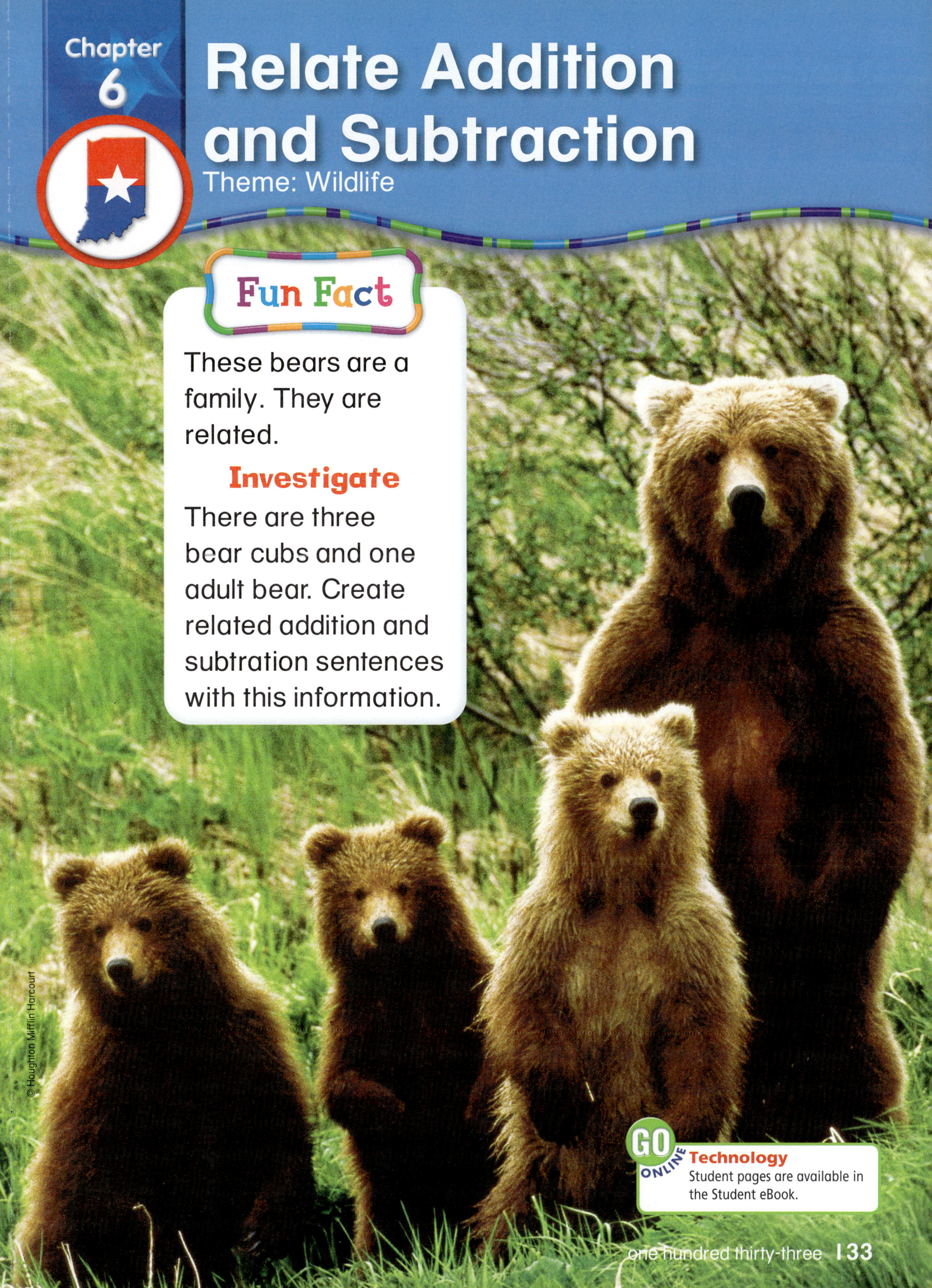

Relate Addition and Subtraction

Theme: Wildlife

© Houghton Mifflin Harcourt

Name _______________________________

Show What You Know

Write the sum. Circle the addition sentences
in each row that use the same addends.

1. $1 + 3 = $ _____   **2.** $2 + 2 = $ _____   **3.** $3 + 1 = $ _____

4. $5 + 2 = $ _____   **5.** $2 + 5 = $ _____   **6.** $5 + 1 = $ _____

Use the number line. Count on.
Write each sum.

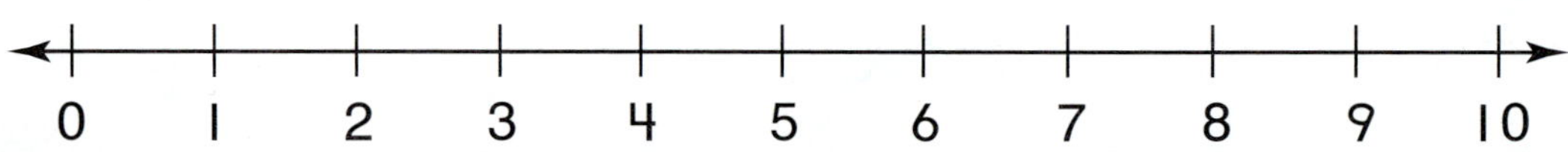

7. $9 + 1 = $ _____   **8.** $7 + 2 = $ _____

Use the number line. Count back.
Write each difference.

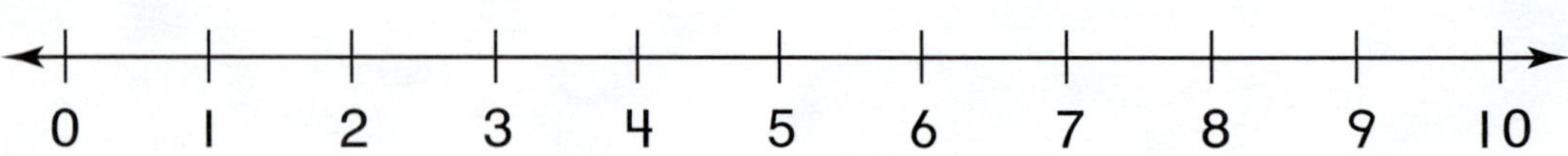

9. $10 - 1 = $ _____   **10.** $8 - 2 = $ _____

  □|||°°°°

At Home This page checks your child's understanding
of important concepts and skills needed for success in
Chapter 6.

Related Addition Facts

Related addition facts use the same numbers.

$$\begin{array}{r} 5 \\ + 4 \\ \hline 9 \end{array} \qquad \begin{array}{r} 4 \\ + 5 \\ \hline 9 \end{array}$$

Essential Question

How can you find related addition facts?

Vocabulary

related addition facts

sum

If you know the sum of 5 + 4, you know the sum of 4 + 5.

Write the sum.

Write the related addition fact.

1.
$$\begin{array}{r} 7 \\ + 3 \\ \hline \square \end{array} \qquad \begin{array}{r} \square \\ + \square \\ \hline \square \end{array}$$

2.
$$\begin{array}{r} 4 \\ + 3 \\ \hline \square \end{array} \qquad \begin{array}{r} \square \\ + \square \\ \hline \square \end{array}$$

3.
$$\begin{array}{r} 3 \\ + 6 \\ \hline \square \end{array} \qquad \begin{array}{r} \square \\ + \square \\ \hline \square \end{array}$$

4.
$$\begin{array}{r} 9 \\ + 1 \\ \hline \square \end{array} \qquad \begin{array}{r} \square \\ + \square \\ \hline \square \end{array}$$

5.
$$\begin{array}{r} 2 \\ + 8 \\ \hline \square \end{array} \qquad \begin{array}{r} \square \\ + \square \\ \hline \square \end{array}$$

6.
$$\begin{array}{r} 2 \\ + 4 \\ \hline \square \end{array} \qquad \begin{array}{r} \square \\ + \square \\ \hline \square \end{array}$$

7. **Math Talk** Is this true or false? Explain.

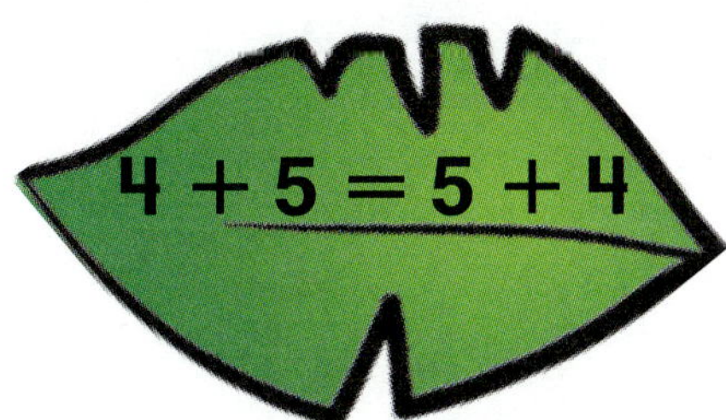

1.1.6 Demonstrate fluency with addition facts and the corresponding subtraction facts for totals to at least 20.

Write the sum.
Write the related addition fact.

1. 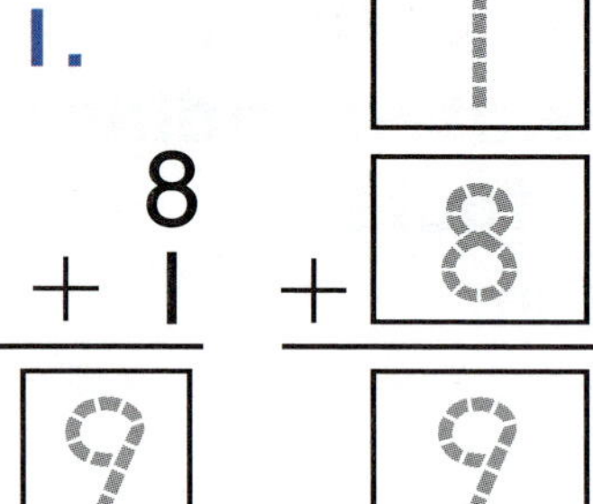

$$\begin{array}{r} 8 \\ + 1 \\ \hline 9 \end{array} \qquad \begin{array}{r} \\ + 8 \\ \hline 9 \end{array}$$

2. 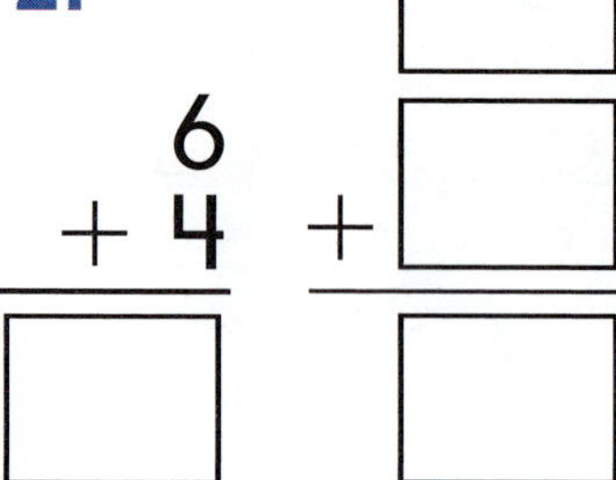

$$\begin{array}{r} 6 \\ + 4 \\ \hline \end{array} \qquad \begin{array}{r} \\ + \\ \hline \end{array}$$

3. 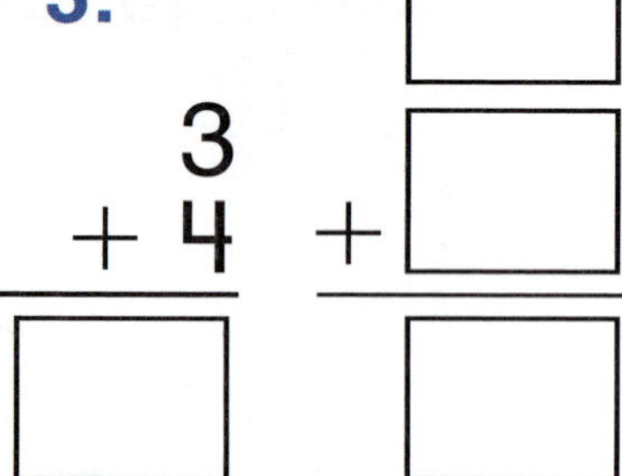

$$\begin{array}{r} 3 \\ + 4 \\ \hline \end{array} \qquad \begin{array}{r} \\ + \\ \hline \end{array}$$

Write the missing number.
Write the related addition fact.

4. 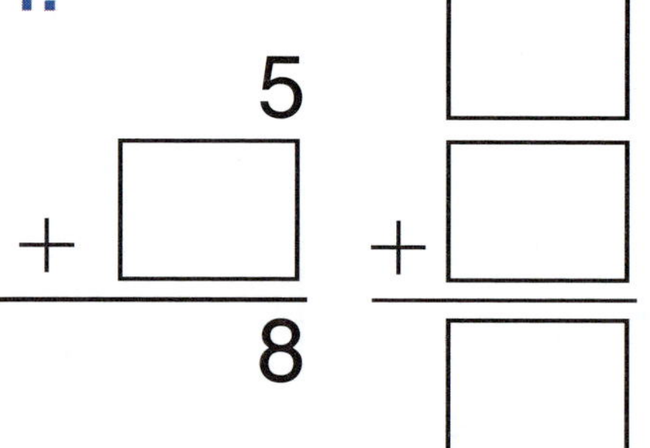

$$\begin{array}{r} 5 \\ + \square \\ \hline 8 \end{array} \qquad \begin{array}{r} \\ + \\ \hline \end{array}$$

5. 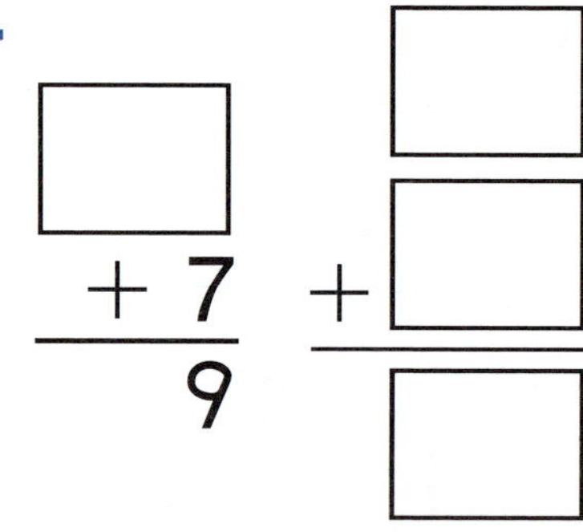

$$\begin{array}{r} \square \\ + 7 \\ \hline 9 \end{array} \qquad \begin{array}{r} \\ + \\ \hline \end{array}$$

6.

$$\begin{array}{r} 10 \\ + \square \\ \hline 10 \end{array} \qquad \begin{array}{r} \\ + \\ \hline \end{array}$$

Math Board — **Problem Solving: Algebra**

Use the picture. Write a number or word
to make each sentence true.

7. $7 + \underline{\quad} = 2 + 7$

8. red birds + blue birds = blue birds + \underline{\qquad} birds

Draw a picture and use words to show $5 + 3 = 3 + 5$.

Related Subtraction Facts

Related subtraction facts use the same numbers.

$$10 - 3 = 7$$

$$10 - 7 = 3$$

Subtract.
Circle the pairs of related subtraction facts.

1. $10 - 6 = \underline{4}$
   $10 - 4 = \underline{6}$

2. $9 - 5 = \underline{\hphantom{0}}$
   $9 - 4 = \underline{\hphantom{0}}$

3. $8 - 7 = \underline{\hphantom{0}}$
   $8 - 6 = \underline{\hphantom{0}}$

4. $8 - 5 = \underline{\hphantom{0}}$
   $8 - 3 = \underline{\hphantom{0}}$

5. $9 - 2 = \underline{\hphantom{0}}$
   $10 - 2 = \underline{\hphantom{0}}$

6. $5 - 4 = \underline{\hphantom{0}}$
   $5 - 2 = \underline{\hphantom{0}}$

7. $10 - 9 = \underline{\hphantom{0}}$
   $10 - 8 = \underline{\hphantom{0}}$

8. $7 - 2 = \underline{\hphantom{0}}$
   $7 - 5 = \underline{\hphantom{0}}$

9. $9 - 0 = \underline{\hphantom{0}}$
   $9 - 9 = \underline{\hphantom{0}}$

10. **Math Talk** $9 - 1 = 8$. What is the related subtraction fact? Explain.

1.1.6 Demonstrate fluency with addition facts and the
corresponding subtraction facts for totals to at least 20.

Subtract. Color the leaves  that have pairs of related subtraction facts.

$$\begin{array}{cc} 9 & 9 \\ -7 & -1 \\ \hline 2 & \end{array}$$

$$\begin{array}{cc} 8 & 8 \\ -8 & -0 \\ \hline & \end{array}$$

$$\begin{array}{cc} 10 & 10 \\ -6 & -7 \\ \hline & \end{array}$$

$$\begin{array}{cc} 9 & 9 \\ -4 & -5 \\ \hline & \end{array}$$

$$\begin{array}{cc} 10 & 10 \\ -8 & -2 \\ \hline & \end{array}$$

$$\begin{array}{cc} 9 & 9 \\ -6 & -3 \\ \hline & \end{array}$$

$$\begin{array}{cc} 10 & 9 \\ -5 & -5 \\ \hline & \end{array}$$

$$\begin{array}{cc} 8 & 8 \\ -2 & -6 \\ \hline & \end{array}$$

$$\begin{array}{cc} 10 & 10 \\ -7 & -3 \\ \hline & \end{array}$$

At Home Write 3, 7, 10, −, and = on separate index cards. Have your child use the cards to show a subtraction fact and then rearrange them to show the related subtraction fact.

Chapter 6 Lesson 3
Build Fact Families

▶ **Explore**

A **fact family** uses the same numbers to make addition and subtraction sentences.

Hands On

Essential Question
What models can you make to show a fact family?

Vocabulary
fact family

$$4 + 5 = 9$$

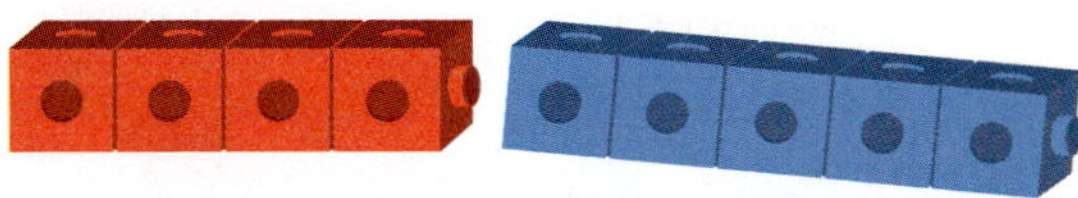

$$9 - 5 = 4$$

$$5 + 4 = 9$$

$$9 - 4 = 5$$

▶ **Connect**

Use  and . Add or subtract.
Write the numbers in the fact family.

1. $3 + 6 = \underline{9}$ $9 - 6 = \underline{3}$ [3] [6] [9]
   $6 + 3 = \underline{9}$ $9 - 3 = \underline{6}$

2. $8 + 2 = \underline{\quad}$ $10 - 2 = \underline{\quad}$ ☐ ☐ ☐
   $2 + 8 = \underline{\quad}$ $10 - 8 = \underline{\quad}$

3. $3 + 5 = \underline{\quad}$ $8 - 5 = \underline{\quad}$ ☐ ☐ ☐
   $5 + 3 = \underline{\quad}$ $8 - 3 = \underline{\quad}$

4. **Math Talk** Which does not belong in the fact family? Explain.

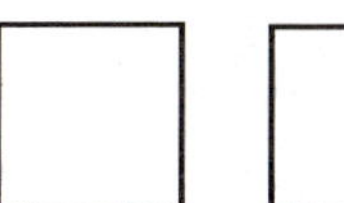

1.1.6 Demonstrate fluency with addition facts and the corresponding subtraction facts for totals to at least 20.

Add or subtract. Write the numbers in the fact family. Use 🎲 and 🎲 if you need to.

1. $3 + 7 = \underline{10}$ $10 - 7 = \underline{3}$

$7 + 3 = \underline{10}$ $10 - 3 = \underline{7}$

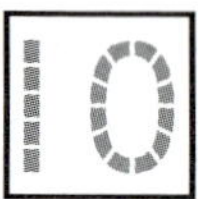

2. $8 + 1 = \underline{\hphantom{00}}$ $9 - 1 = \underline{\hphantom{00}}$

$1 + 8 = \underline{\hphantom{00}}$ $9 - 8 = \underline{\hphantom{00}}$

3. $5 + 4 = \underline{\hphantom{00}}$ $9 - 4 = \underline{\hphantom{00}}$

$4 + 5 = \underline{\hphantom{00}}$ $9 - 5 = \underline{\hphantom{00}}$

4. $3 + 4 = \underline{\hphantom{00}}$ $7 - 4 = \underline{\hphantom{00}}$

$4 + 3 = \underline{\hphantom{00}}$ $7 - 3 = \underline{\hphantom{00}}$

Math Board **Problem Solving: Visual Thinking**

5. Use the pictures to write a fact family.

$\square + \square = \square \mid \square - \square = \square$

$\square + \square = \square \mid \square - \square = \square$

Write the numbers in the fact family.
Explain how you found them.

Chapter 6 Lesson 7

Algebra: Ways to Make Numbers to 20

Essential Question
How can you add and subtract to make the same number?

▶ **Explore**

You can make the number 10 in different ways.

10
6 + 4
5 + 2 + 3
20 − 10

▶ **Connect**

Use 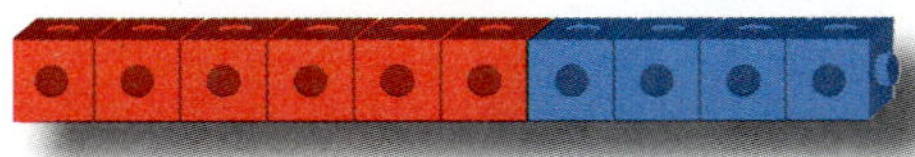 . Write ways to make the number at the top.

1.

12
____ + ____
____ − ____
____ + ____ + ____
____ + ____
____ ◯ ____

✓2.

9
____ − ____
____ + ____
____ − ____
____ + ____ + ____
____ ◯ ____

3. **Math Talk** What are some ways to make 18?

Use 🎲 🎲 🎲. Write ways to make
the number at the top.

1.

7
$\underline{3} + \underline{3} + \underline{1}$
$\underline{} + \underline{}$
$\underline{} - \underline{}$
$\underline{} \bigcirc \underline{}$

2.

14
$\underline{} + \underline{}$
$\underline{} + \underline{} + \underline{}$
$\underline{} - \underline{}$
$\underline{} \bigcirc \underline{}$

3.

11
$\underline{} + \underline{}$
$\underline{} + \underline{} + \underline{}$
$\underline{} - \underline{}$
$\underline{} \bigcirc \underline{}$

4.

8
$\underline{} + \underline{}$
$\underline{} + \underline{} + \underline{}$
$\underline{} - \underline{}$
$\underline{} \bigcirc \underline{}$

Problem Solving: Reasoning

5. Circle the ways that show 13.

thirteen 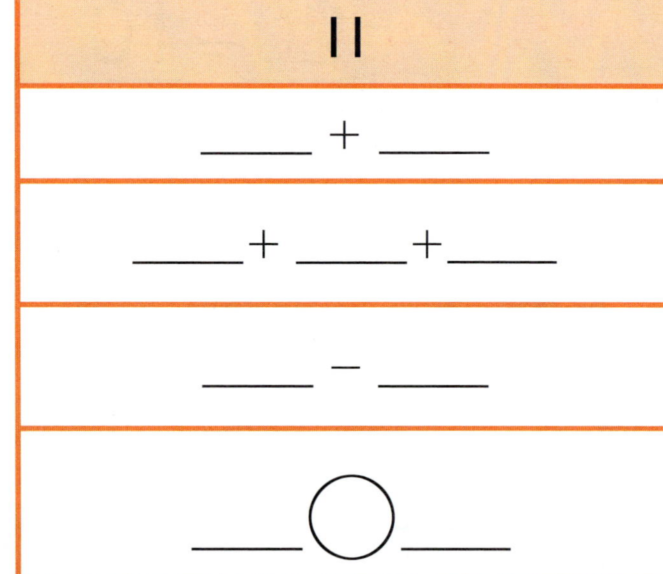 $9 + 5$ 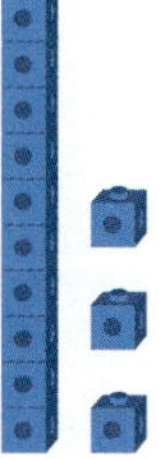

Use words, numbers, or pictures
to show 13 another way.

Chapter 6 Lesson 8

Create Addition and Subtraction Problems

Essential Question
What models can you make to show sums and differences?

Hands On

▶ Explore

____5____ brown rabbits

____4____ gray rabbits

____9____ rabbits altogether

____4____ gray rabbits

How many rabbits are there?

__5__ (+) __4__ (=) __9__
rabbits

How many rabbits are brown?

__9__ (−) __4__ (=) __5__
rabbits

▶ Connect

Use  to show the picture. Write the numbers and the number sentence.

1. ______ green frogs

______ yellow frogs

______ frogs altogether

______ green frogs

How many frogs are there?

____ ◯ ____ ◯ ____
frogs

How many frogs are yellow?

____ ◯ ____ ◯ ____
frogs

2. **Math Talk** Create a story problem that has $3 + 7 = 10$ as the answer.

Write the numbers and the number sentence.
Use  if you need to.

1. _____ green lizards

_____ blue lizards

_____ lizards altogether

_____ blue lizards

How many lizards are there?

____ ◯ ____ ◯ _____
lizards

How many lizards are green?

____ ◯ ____ ◯ _____
lizards

2. _____ blue fish

_____ red fish

_____ fish altogether

_____ blue fish

How many fish are there?

____ ◯ ____ ◯ _____
fish

How many fish are red?

____ ◯ ____ ◯ _____
fish

Problem Solving: Reasoning

3. Choose your own numbers. Draw your story.
Write the number sentence.

_____ yellow birds

_____ orange birds

_____ birds altogether

____ ◯ ____ ◯ _____
birds

Did you write an addition sentence or
a subtraction sentence? Explain.

At Home Place 3 pennies next to 2 dimes. Have your child write
an addition sentence to find how many coins in all. Have him or
her write a subtraction sentence to find the number of dimes.

Problem Solving Workshop
Strategy: Draw a Picture

Essential Question

How does drawing a picture help you solve a problem?

There are 10 rabbits.
Some rabbits run away.
There are 8 rabbits left.
How many rabbits ran away?

Unlock the Problem

What do I need to find?

how many rabbits ran away

What information do I need to use?

10 rabbits to start

8 rabbits are left

Show how to solve the problem.

Draw 10 rabbits. Count 8 rabbits.
Cross out the other rabbits.

How many rabbits ran away?
_______ rabbits

Math Talk Tell an addition fact that will help check your answer. Explain.

© Houghton Mifflin Harcourt

1.1.5 Solve problems involving addition and subtraction by modeling addition of numbers to at least 100 and by modeling the inverse operation of subtraction using objects.

Problem Solving Strategy Practice 

Draw a picture to solve.

1. There are 7 beavers. Some beavers run away. There are 3 beavers left. How many beavers ran away?

beaver

_____ beavers

2. There are 10 hawks. Some hawks fly away. There are 4 hawks left. How many hawks flew away?

hawk

_____ hawks

3. There are 9 skunks. Some skunks walk away. There are 6 skunks left. How many skunks walked away?

skunk

_____ skunks

4. Try Your Own Problem

There are _____ turtles.
Some turtles swim away.
There are _____ turtles left.
How many turtles swam away?

turtle

_____ turtles

At Home In the first problem, change the number 7 to 10. Have your child draw a picture to show how to solve the new problem.

Name _______________________

Extra Practice

Write the sum. Write the related addition fact.

1. $7 + 3 = \boxed{}$

$\boxed{} + \boxed{} = \boxed{}$

2. $4 + 5 = \boxed{}$

$\boxed{} + \boxed{} = \boxed{}$

Subtract. Circle the pairs of related subtraction facts.

3. $10 - 4 = \underline{}$ **4.** $8 - 2 = \underline{}$ **5.** $9 - 1 = \underline{}$

$10 - 6 = \underline{}$ $8 - 5 = \underline{}$ $9 - 8 = \underline{}$

Complete the fact family.

6. $6 + \boxed{} = 8$ $\boxed{} - 2 = 6$

$2 + \boxed{} = 8$ $\boxed{} - \boxed{} = 2$

Follow a rule to complete the table.

7.

Subtract 3	
3	
7	
9	

8.

Add 4	
1	
5	
6	

9.

Subtract 2	
9	
6	
4	

Problem Solving

Draw a picture to solve.

10. There are 10 birds. Some birds
fly away. There are 3 birds left.
How many birds fly away?

_______ birds

Technology
Use HMH Mega Math, Country
Countdown, *Counting Critters,* Level I.

Multistep Problems
Chapter 6

1. Marta went inside the barn. There were lambs in 2 stalls.

1.1.6

- Marta counted 3 lambs in one stall.

- She counted some more lambs in the other stall.

- Marta counted fewer than 7 lambs in all.

- Write a number sentence that fits this math story.

- Write the other number sentences in that fact family.

Show your work.

2. Steve and Joy are playing a math game. The game is called Follow the Rule.

1.2.2

- Steve's rule is to add 4. Fill in the missing numbers in Steve's table.

Add 4	
0	
2	
	8
	10

- Joy's rule is to subtract 3. Fill in the missing numbers in Joy's table.

Subtract 3	
5	
6	
	4
	5

Standards Quick Check

Subtract. Check by adding.

1.
$$\begin{array}{r} 9 \\ -\ 6 \\ \hline \end{array}$$

$$\begin{array}{r} \square \\ +\ \square \\ \hline \square \end{array}$$

2.
$$\begin{array}{r} 7 \\ -\ 5 \\ \hline \end{array}$$

$$\begin{array}{r} \square \\ +\ \square \\ \hline \square \end{array}$$

Complete the fact family.

3. 

$4 + \square = 6$ $\qquad$ $6 - 2 = \square$

$2 + 4 = \square$ $\qquad$ $\square - \square = \square$

4.

$3 + \square = 9$ $\qquad$ $9 - 6 = \square$

$6 + 3 = \square$ $\qquad$ $\square - \square = \square$

Challenge — H.O.T.

Write your own subtraction story.
Write a subtraction sentence to solve.

____

____

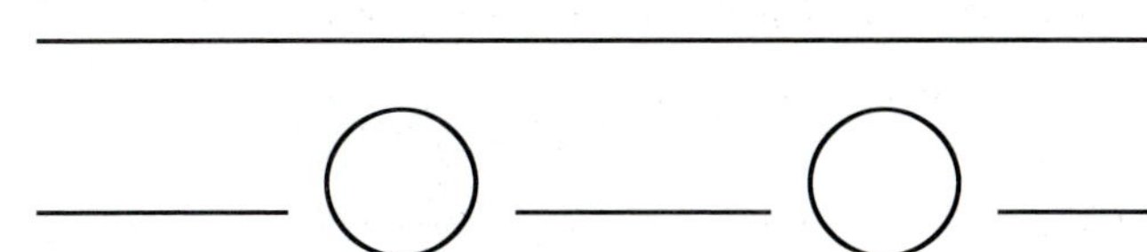

Fact Family Bugs

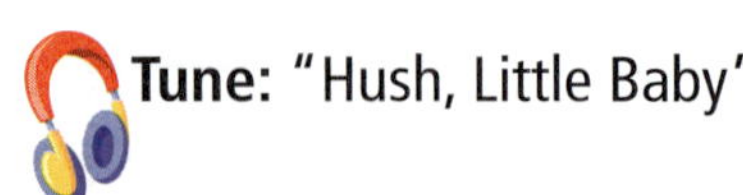

Tune: "Hush, Little Baby"

Read these numbers: 9, 6, 3.
They are all part of a fact family.

3 little bumblebees start to dine.
6 more join them. Now there are 9.

6 little ants crawl up a vine.
3 more join them. Now there are 9.

9 little spiders spin in a tree.
6 creep away and now there are 3.

9 little butterflies sit on some sticks.
3 fly away and now there are 6.

Write the number sentence for each fact.
Try your best to be exact!

156

Looking Ahead to the ISTEP+
Chapter 6

Mark the best answer for questions 1–4.

1. Which is the related subtraction fact? 1.1.6

$$8 - 3 = 5$$

- ○ $5 + 3 = 8$
- ○ $5 - 3 = 2$
- ○ $8 - 8 = 0$
- ○ $8 - 5 = 3$

2. Which is the related addition fact? 1.1.6

$$5 + 4 = 9$$

- ○ $2 + 3 = 5$
- ○ $2 + 2 = 4$
- ○ $4 + 5 = 9$
- ○ $9 - 5 = 4$

3. Which numbers make up the fact family for this number sentence? 1.1.6

$$6 - 1 = 5$$

- ○ 1, 6, 7
- ○ 1, 6, 11
- ○ 1, 5, 11
- ○ 1, 5, 6

4. Which fact completes the fact family? 1.1.6

$$3 + 6 = 9 \qquad 9 - 6 = 3$$
$$6 + 3 = 9 \qquad \boxed{}$$

- ○ $9 + 3 = 12$
- ○ $3 + 9 = 12$
- ○ $9 - 3 = 6$
- ○ $9 - 6 = 3$

Mark the best answer for questions 5–6.

5. Which is the related subtraction fact? 1.1.6

$$10 - 4 = 6$$

- ○ $10 - 6 = 4$
- ○ $10 - 2 = 8$
- ○ $4 + 6 = 10$
- ○ $6 + 4 = 10$

6. What is the missing number? 1.2.2

Add 3	
2	5
4	7
6	

- ○ 3
- ○ 5
- ○ 6
- ○ 9

Open Ended

Draw a picture to solve.

7. There are 5 toucans. 3 toucans fly away. How many toucans are there now?

1.2.1

_______ toucans

Draw a picture to solve.

8. There are 9 dolphins. Some dolphins swim away. There are 6 dolphins left. How many dolphins swam away? 1.2.1

_______ dolphins

Reading and Writing Math

Jon has 10 animal stickers.
He gives away 6 of them.
How many stickers does he have left?

You know the whole and one of the parts.
Subtract to find the other part.

Whole	
10	
Part	**Part**
6	?

1. Draw a picture to help you find the difference.

2. Write the number sentence.

______ ◯ ______ ◯ ______

3. Use a related addition fact to check your subtraction.

______ ◯ ______ ◯ ______

4. How many stickers are left?

______ stickers

5. Writing Math Write the fact family for the numbers you used above.

______ + ______ = ______   ______ − ______ = ______

______ + ______ = ______   ______ − ______ = ______

Which Number is Missing?

$5 = 7 - \underline{2}$ $5 = \underline{7} - 2$

Reasoning

Subtract.
Write the missing numbers.

1.
  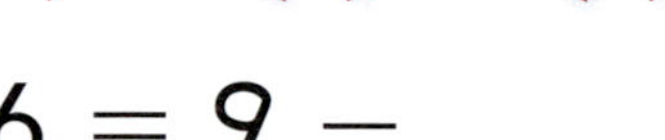       

$6 = 9 - \underline{}$ $6 = \underline{} - 3$

2.
  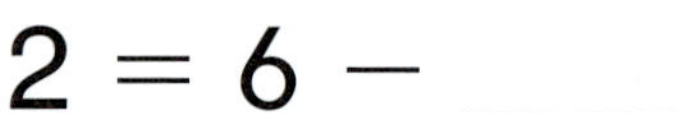 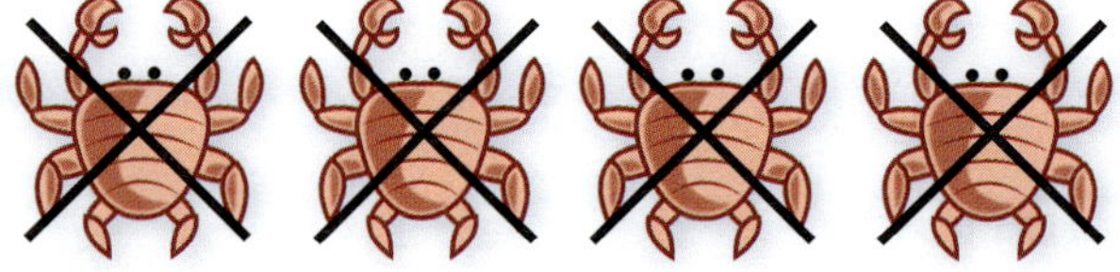

$2 = 6 - \underline{}$ $2 = \underline{} - 4$

3.

$8 = 10 - \underline{}$ $8 = \underline{} - 2$

On Your Own

Cross off some of the fish. Write the missing numbers.

4.

$\underline{} = 8 - \underline{}$

Math Talk Look at the picture in Exercise 4.
How did it help you find each missing number?

Baby Animals

Baby animals have different names. Baby cows are calves. Baby goats are kids. Baby sheep are lambs. Baby ducks are ducklings. What groups of baby animals do you see in the picture?

Baby tigers and baby bears are both called cubs.

tiger cubs

bear cubs

FACT·ACTIVITY

Circle each group of baby animals.

Write each number.

❶ Count on 2 from the number of  . _______________

❷ Double the number of  . _______________

❸ Double the number of  . Count back 2. _______________

Math Talk Which group has the same number as 1 more than the number of calves? Explain.

Panda Twins

Two baby animals born at the
same time are called twins.
People can also have twins.
Do you know any twins?

In a Chinese zoo, 5 sets of panda twins were born in the same year!

panda twins

FACT·ACTIVITY

Write each sum.
Draw a line to show which addition path leads to the panda twin.

START

$2 + 2 = \boxed{}$

$\begin{array}{r} 3 \\ +5 \\ \hline \boxed{} \end{array}$

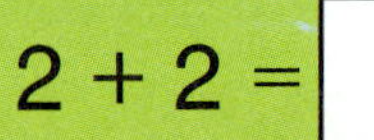

$9 + 1 = \boxed{}$

$\begin{array}{r} 1 \\ +1 \\ \hline \boxed{} \end{array}$

$\begin{array}{r} 7 \\ +2 \\ \hline \boxed{} \end{array}$

$\begin{array}{r} 3 \\ +3 \\ \hline \boxed{} \end{array}$

$4 + 4 = \boxed{}$

$5 + 5 = \boxed{}$

$4 + 6 = \boxed{}$

Math Talk What is the same about all of the number
sentences on the correct path?

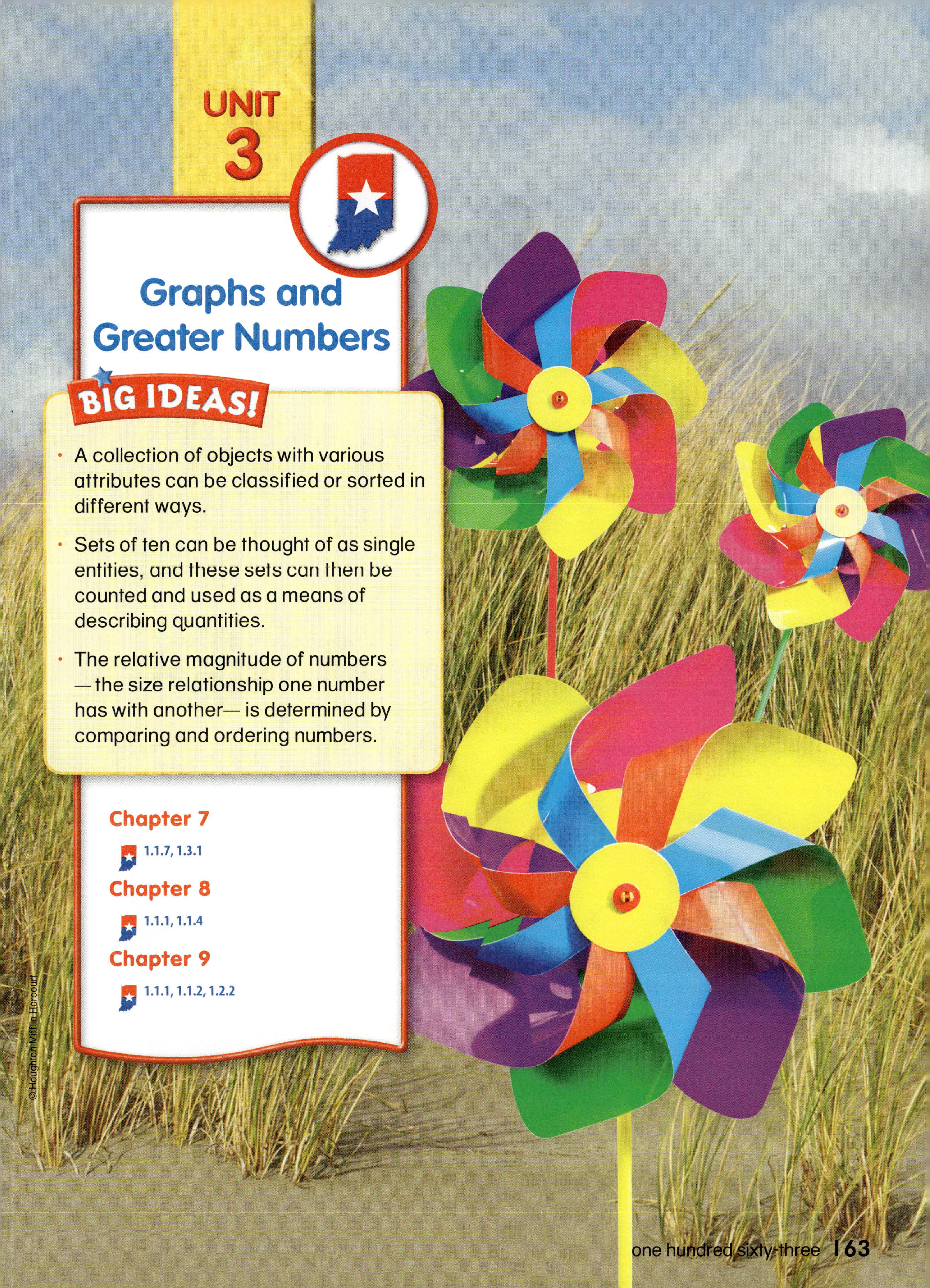

UNIT
3

Graphs and
Greater Numbers

BIG IDEAS!

· A collection of objects with various
attributes can be classified or sorted in
different ways.

· Sets of ten can be thought of as single
entities, and these sets can then be
counted and used as a means of
describing quantities.

· The relative magnitude of numbers
—the size relationship one number
has with another— is determined by
comparing and ordering numbers.

Chapter 7
1.1.7, 1.3.1
Chapter 8
1.1.1, 1.1.4
Chapter 9
1.1.1, 1.1.2, 1.2.2

Get Ready Game

Build a Graph

1. Choose a color—red, green, or blue.
2. Take turns tossing the cube.
3. The player with that color can color a box on the graph.
4. The winner is the first player to color all 10 boxes in his or her row.

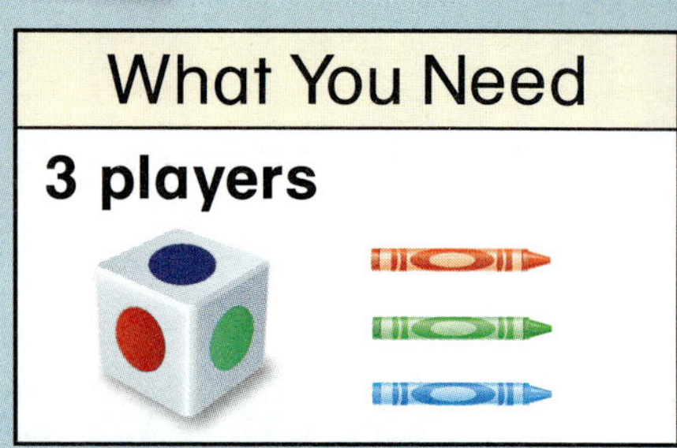

What You Need
3 players

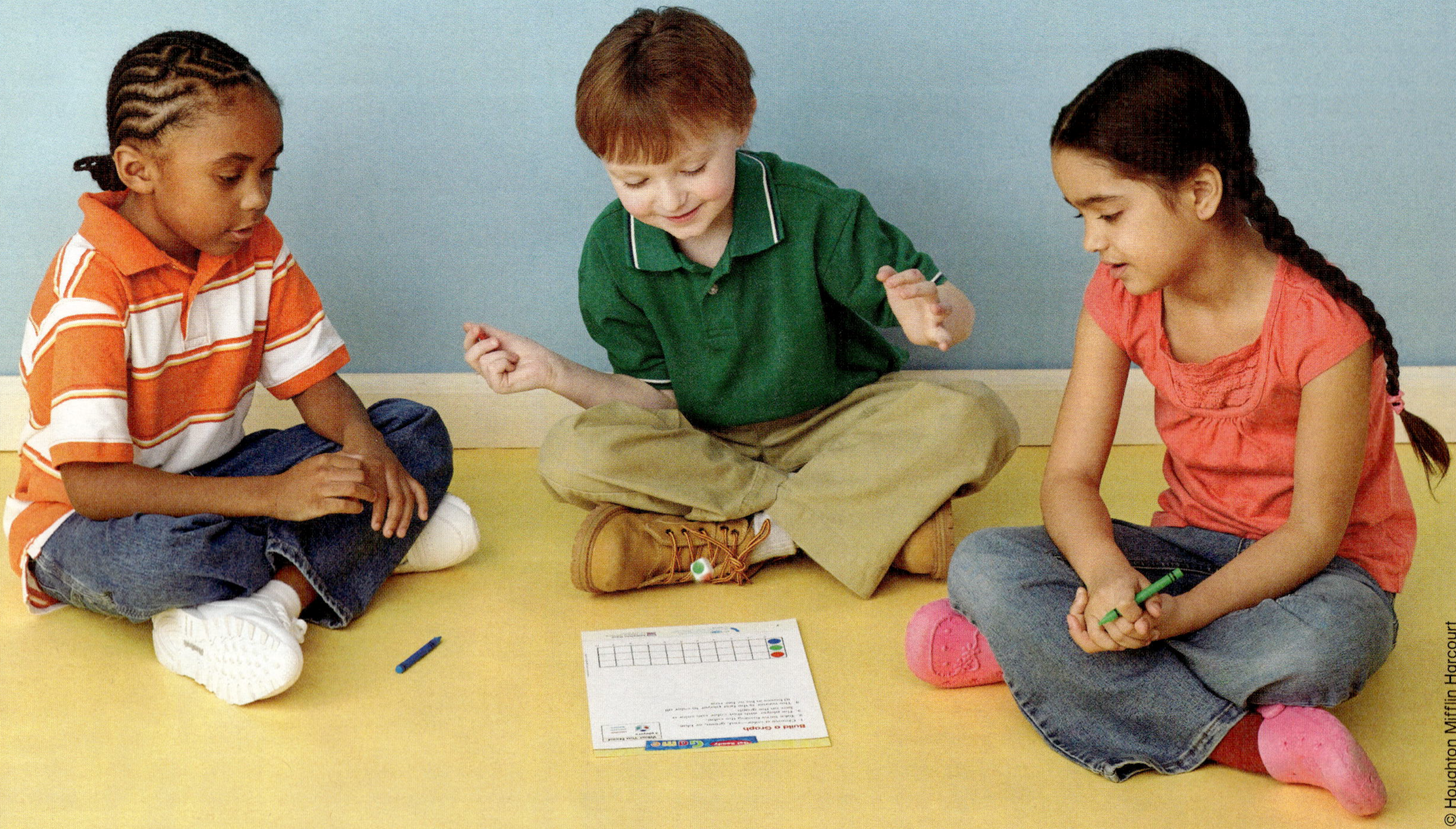

Math at Home

Dear Family,

My class started Unit 3 today. In the next few chapters, I will learn about numbers to 100, graphing data, and number patterns. Here are some vocabulary words and activities for us to share.

From,

____

Vocabulary

picture graph A graph in which pictures show data.

33 has 3 **tens** and 3 **ones**.
28 has 2 **tens** and 8 **ones**.

33 **is greater than** 28.
$$33 > 28$$

28 **is less than** 33.
$$28 < 33$$

Family Math Activity

Let your child put chunks of fruit in small groups on a plate. Arrange the fruit in a pattern, for example: 2 strawberries, 4 strawberries, 6 strawberries, 8 strawberries. Discuss how this shows the number pattern of counting by twos.

Try different number patterns. Talk about the patterns as you work together with your child.

Literature

These books link to the math in this unit. Look for them at the library.

- **Lemonade for Sale**
  by Stuart J. Murphy
  Illustrated by Tricia Tusa
  (HarperCollins, 1998)
- **Making Graphs**
  by Michelle Wagner Nechaev
  Illustrated by Michael Jarrett
- **What's Next, Nina?**
  by Sue Kassirer
  Illustrated by Paige Eastburn O'Rourke

Math at Home

Chapter 7

Have your child create a picture graph using a handful of jelly beans that are only three colors. Sort the jelly beans according to color, then place them into a graph. Draw a jelly bean next to the real jelly bean in each square.

Jelly Bean Colors			
red			
purple			
orange			

Chapter 8

Go on a nature or architecture walk. Have your child estimate and then count the number of bricks in a walkway, the number of leaves on a branch, or the number of windows in a building.

Chapter 9

Use a calendar. If the number for today's date is 2, what will it be in 2 days? If the number for today's date is 4, what will it be in 4 days? If the number for today's date is 5, what will it be in 5 days? If the number for today's date is 6, what will it be in 6 days?

At Home These activities are designed for you to work with your child at home.

written by Margie Sigman

In this story you will also Math Talk and Write Math.

At Home This story will help your child review counting.

A

B

Draw to complete the picture graph.

How many raincoats? _____

How many umbrellas? _____

Describe rainy weather.

D

Draw to complete the graph.

How many sunglasses? _____

How many sun hats? _____

Describe sunny weather.

F

Describe the weather shown here.

Name ______________________________

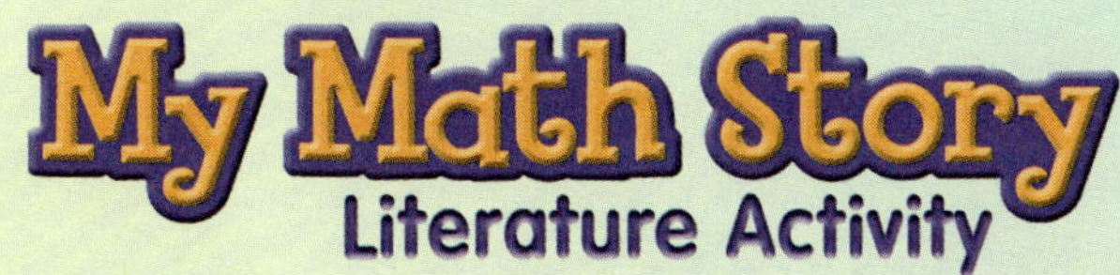

My Math Story
Literature Activity

Draw some sun hats and sunglasses in the graph.

Vocabulary Review
picture graph

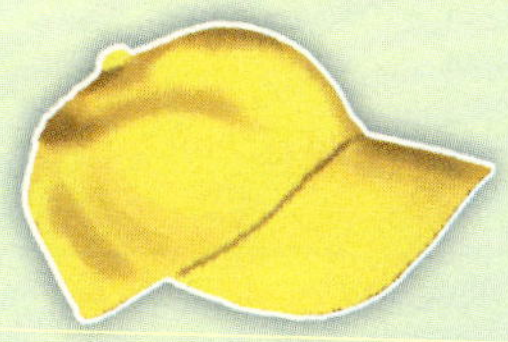					
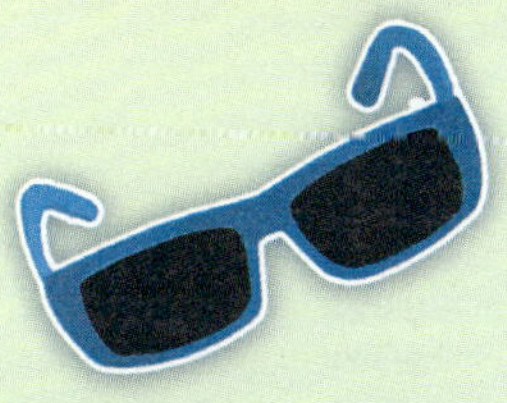					

Write Math Write a sentence telling how many sunglasses. Write a sentence telling how many sun hats.

____

____

____

Name _______________________________

More or Fewer?

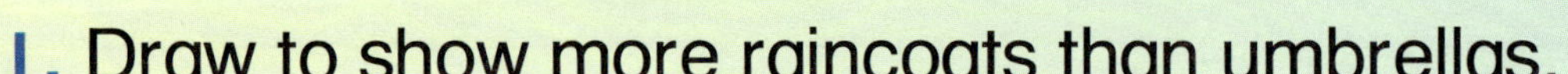

1. Draw to show more raincoats than umbrellas.

2. Draw to show fewer raincoats than umbrellas.

Write Math ▶ Write a story problem about raincoats and umbrellas.

H

Data and Graphs

Theme: Beach Days

Fun Fact

This girl is wearing sunglasses to protect her eyes from the sun.

Investigate

Ask 5 classmates if they have been to a beach. Sort their answers. Then make a graph.

Show What You Know 

Use the picture graph.

Fruit We Like

1. Write how many. ______    ______ 

Use the picture graph.

Snacks We Like

2. Write how many.

______     ______    ______

3. Circle which has the least number.

4. Circle which has the greatest number.

 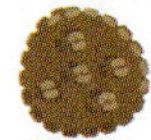 

At Home This page checks your child's understanding of important concepts and skills needed for success in Chapter 7.

Chapter 7 Lesson 1

Algebra: Sort and Classify

Explore

How can you **sort** these bears?

Essential Question
How can you sort figures into groups?

Vocabulary
sort

Connect

Sort the bears a different way.
Draw each group.

 **1.**

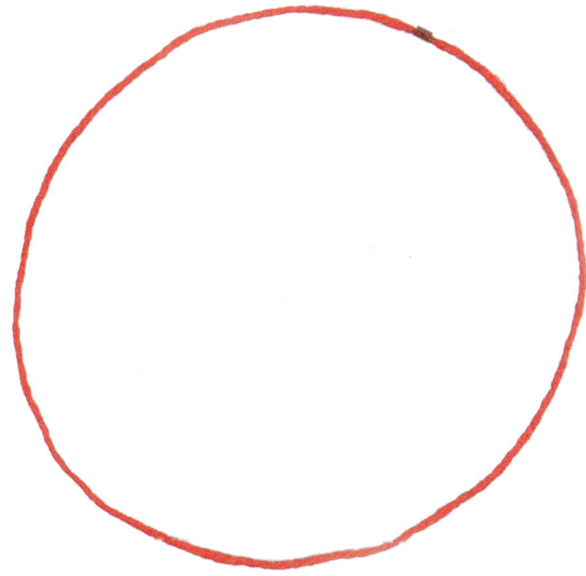

2. (Math Talk) Look at Exercise 1. What is the same and
different in the two groups?

1.3.1 Identify, describe, compare, sort and draw triangles,
rectangles, squares and circles in terms of their attributes.
Use simple plane shapes to compose a given shape.

Circle which belongs in each group.

1.

2.

3.

4.

Math Board

Problem Solving: Reasoning

5. Sort the figures by color and shape.
   Draw the figures in each group.

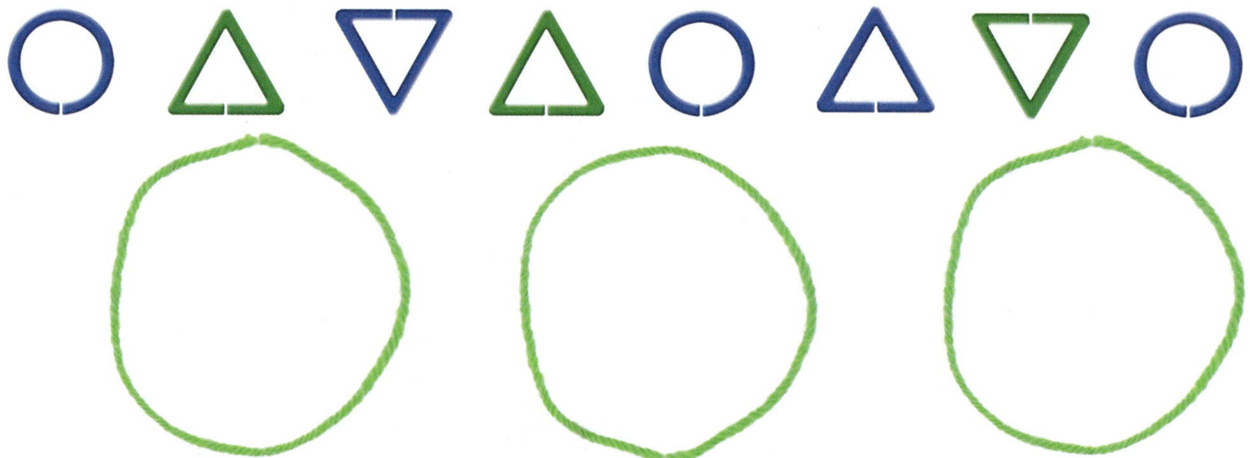

Why are there three groups? Explain.

At Home Make a collection of large and small objects such as pencils, crayons, and paper clips. Lay out 3 pieces of paper and have your child sort the objects into 3 groups. Ask your child to explain how the groups are sorted.

Venn Diagrams

Explore

A Venn Diagram shows how things are alike and how things are different.

You can sort these shapes with a Venn Diagram.

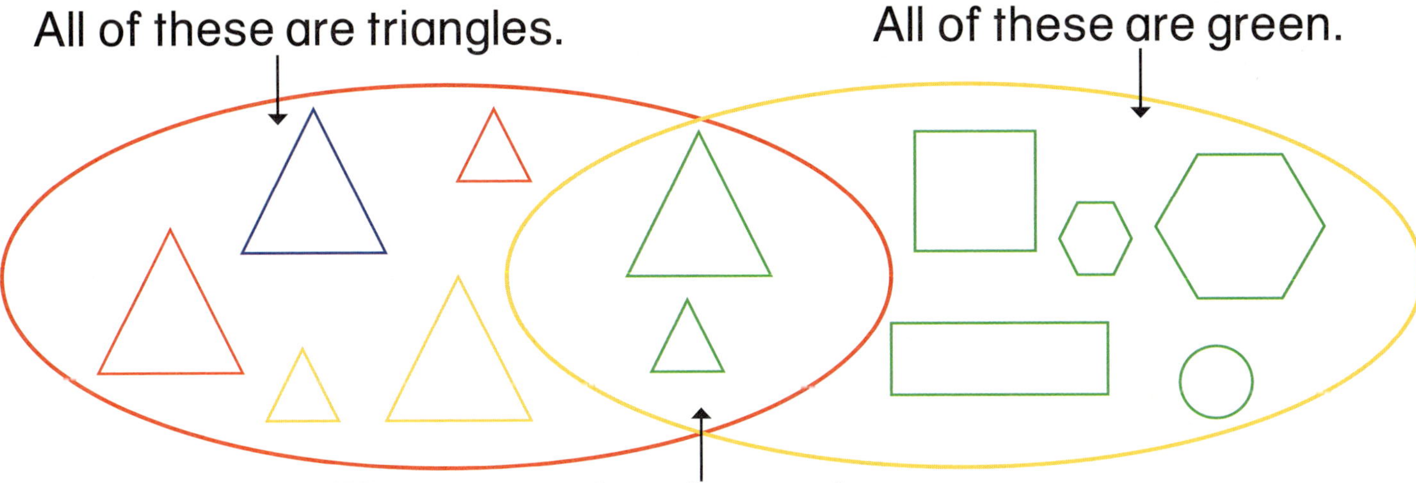

Connect

1. Sort your shapes in a different way.
   Draw each group. Tell how you sorted.

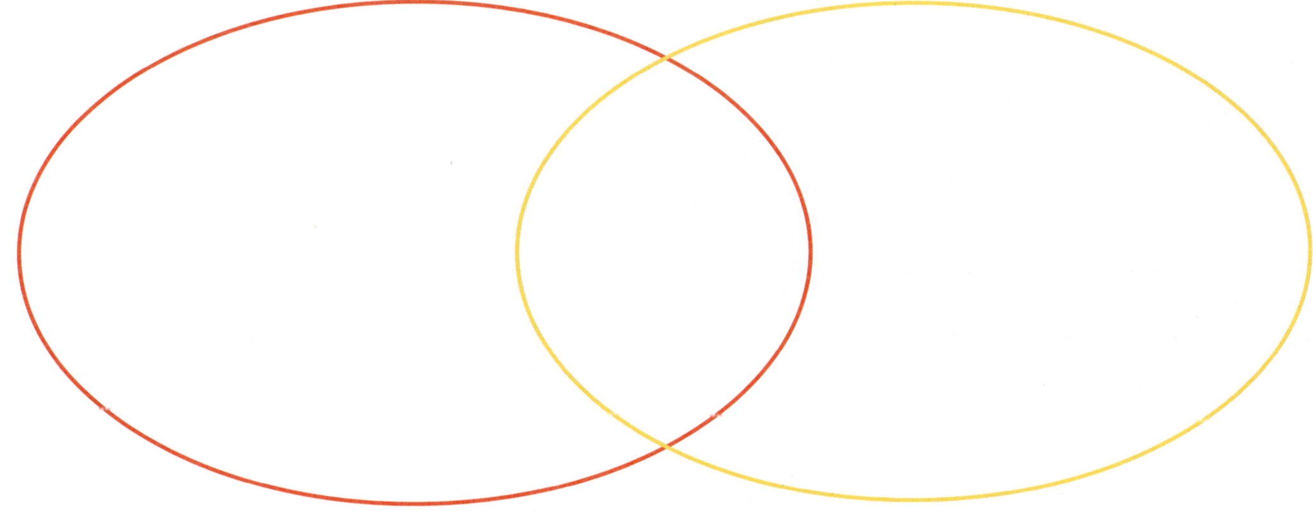

2. **Math Talk** How could you sort your shapes into four different groups? Show one way.

1.1.7 Pose a question and collect and represent data using pictures or picture graphs to answer the question posed.

Draw a line from each shape to the group where it belongs.

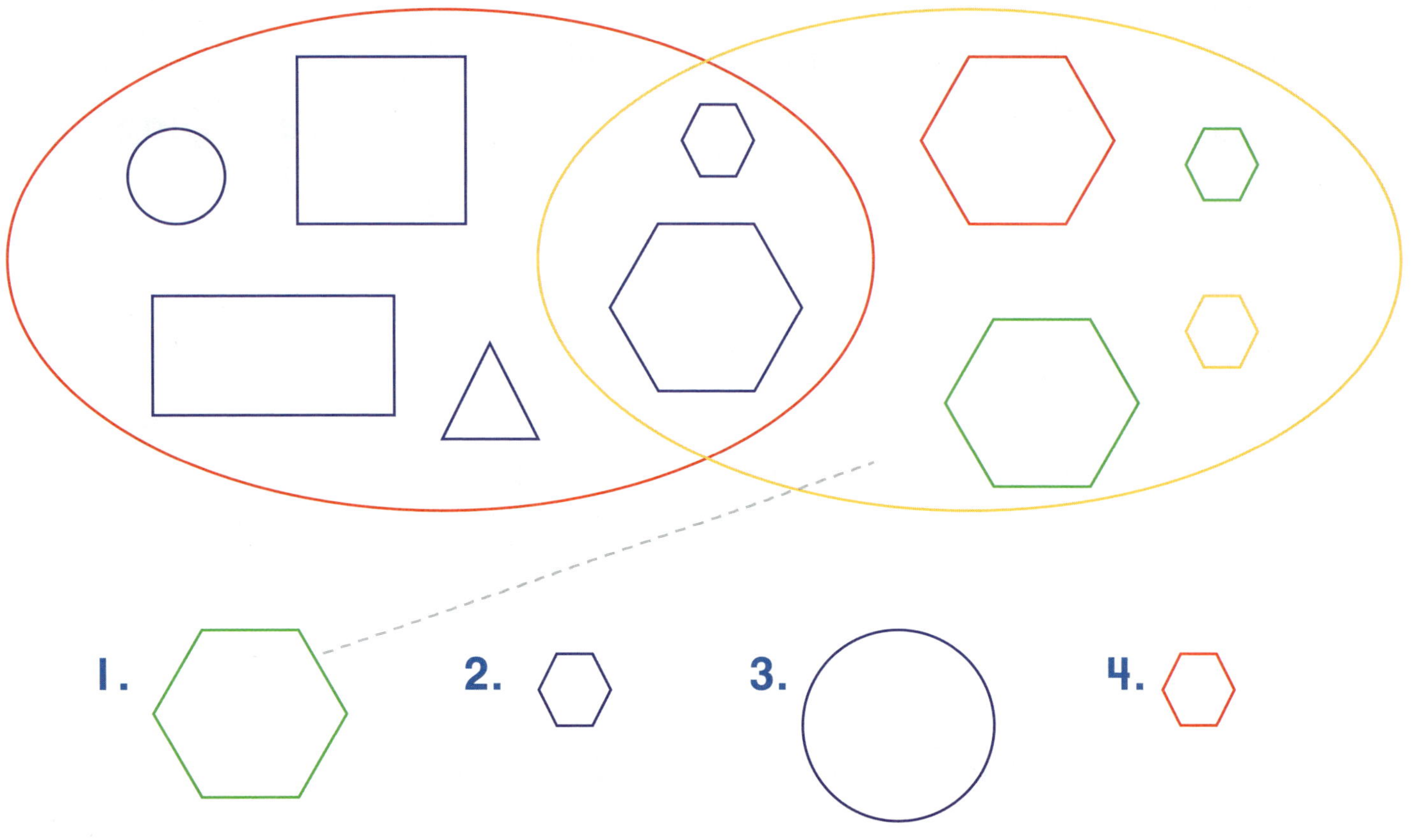

1. 2. 3. 4.

Problem Solving: Application

5. Draw how you could sort these buttons.

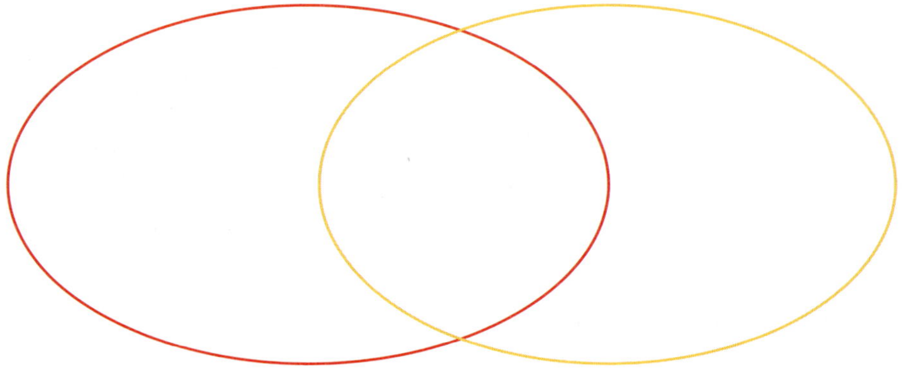

Why is sorting important?

Chapter 7 Lesson 3

Concrete Graphs

A concrete graph uses real objects to compare information.

Essential Question
How do you use objects and pictures to show data?

Vocabulary
concrete graph

Connect

Sort 🟥 , 🟨 , and 🟩 . Make a concrete graph.

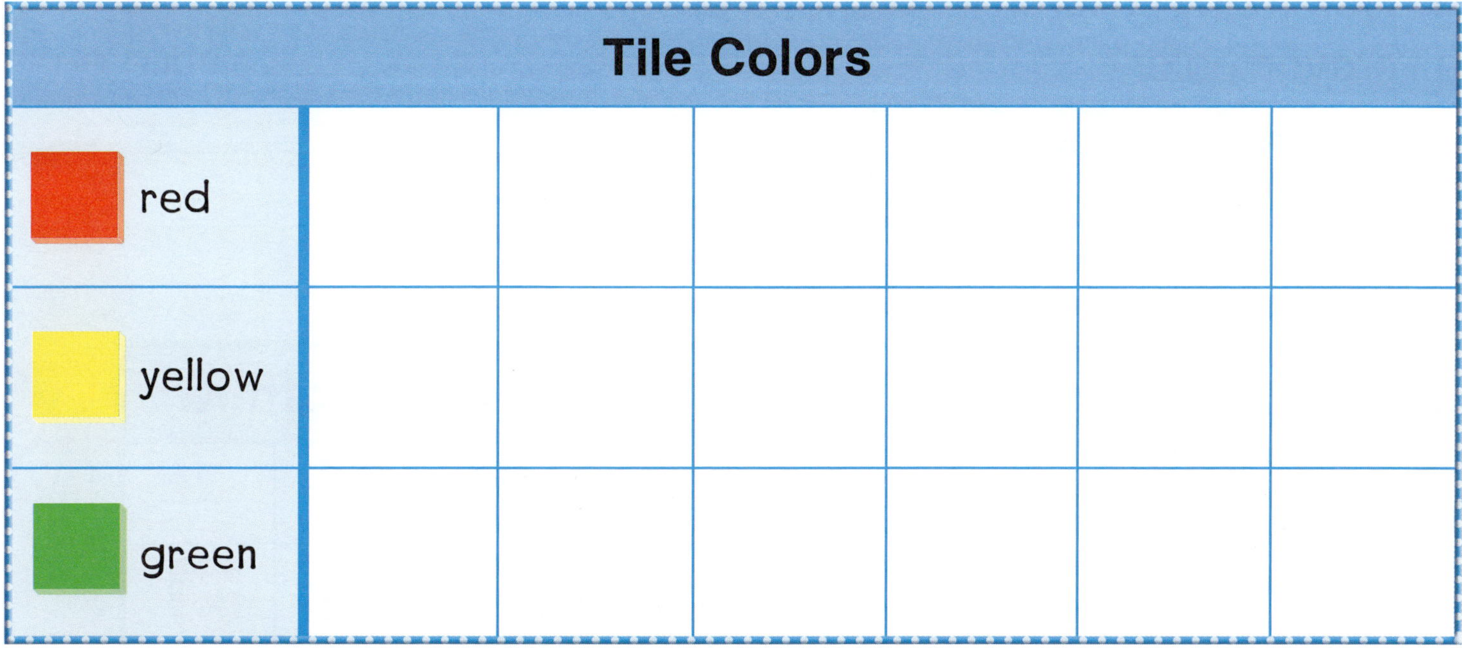

How many of each color?

1. 🟥 _______   ✓2. 🟨 _______   ✓3. 🟩 _______

4. **Math Talk** Which color tile shows the fewest? Explain.

1.3.1 Identify, describe, compare, sort and draw . . . in terms of their attributes. Use simple plane shapes to compose a given shape. **1.1.7** Pose a question and collect and represent data using pictures to picture graphs to answer the question posed.

Use the graph to answer the questions.

Crayon Colors We Like

1. How many children chose yellow? _______ children

2. Which color did fewer children choose? Circle. 

3. How many children chose blue? _______ children

4. How many children in all chose a
   crayon color? _______ children

Problem Solving: Reasoning

Use the graph. Circle the true statements.

5. There are 3 yellow cubes.

6. There are more blue cubes
   than red cubes.

7. There are 6 cubes in all.

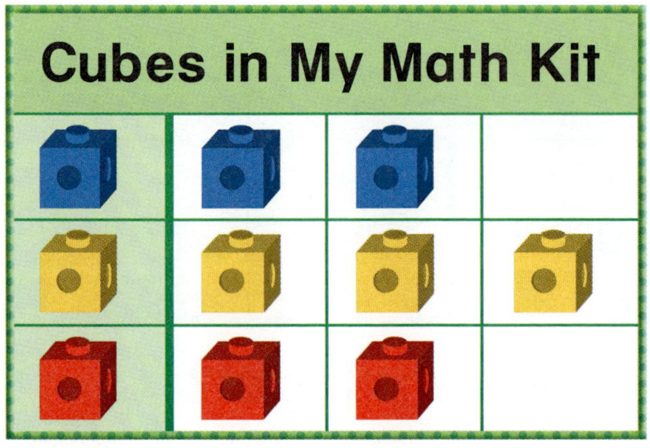

How do you know which statement
is not true? Explain.

Chapter 7 Lesson 4

Use Pictures to Show Data

We Learn

You can sort pictures to compare information.

Share and Show Math Board

Use the pictures to answer the questions.

1. How many  are there in all? ________ 

2. Are there more  or ? Circle. 

✓3. Are there fewer  or ? Circle. 

✓4. Which 2 groups have the same number of toys? Circle.

5. **Math Talk** Which toy is there the most of? Explain how the picture helps you decide.

1.1.7 Pose a question and collect and represent data using pictures or picture graphs to answer the question posed. *also* **1.1.1**

Essential Question
How can you use pictures to sort and compare data?

Vocabulary
sort

Use the picture to answer the questions.

1. How many ![shovel] are there in all? _____ 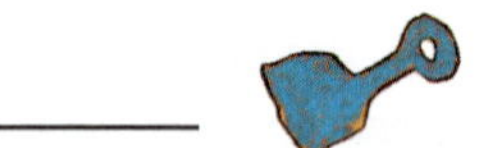

2. How many more ![truck] are there than ![rake] ? _____ 

3. How many fewer ![rake] are there than ![ball] ? _____ 

4. How many fewer ![shovel] are there than ![truck] and ![ball] ? _____ 

5. Which object is there the fewest of? Circle. 

6. Which 2 groups have the same number? Circle.

At Home Make a group of your child's toys, such as stuffed animals, stickers, or toy cars. Have your child sort the toys into two groups and explain how he or she sorted. Challenge your child to sort the toys a different way and explain the new rule.

Chapter 7 Lesson 5

Read Picture Graphs

A picture graph uses pictures to show information.

Fruits We Like					
oranges	🍊	🍊			
grapes	🍇	🍇	🍇	🍇	🍇
peaches	🍑	🍑	🍑		

More children chose grapes than oranges or peaches.

Share and Show Math Board

Vegetables We Like					
carrots	🥕	🥕	🥕	🥕	🥕
peppers	🫑	🫑			
celery	🥬	🥬	🥬		

Use the picture graph to answer the questions.

1. Which vegetable did the fewest children choose? Circle.

2. Is there one vegetable that was chosen equally to  and  altogether? What is it? ________________

3. How many more children chose  than  ? ________ more children

4. **Math Talk** How does the picture graph show the most chosen and the least chosen? Explain.

1.1.7 Pose a question and collect and represent data using pictures or picture graphs to answer the question posed. *also* **1.1.1**

Juices We Like									
apple									
grape									
orange									

Use the picture graph to answer the questions.

1. Which juice did the most children choose? Circle.

2. How many children chose ? _______ children

3. How many more children chose than ? _______ more children

4. How many fewer children chose than ? _______ fewer children

 **Problem Solving: Real World**

5. Complete the picture graph.

Tina asked 10 children to tell their favorite fruits. 6 children chose orange. 2 children chose apple. Draw to show how many children chose peach.

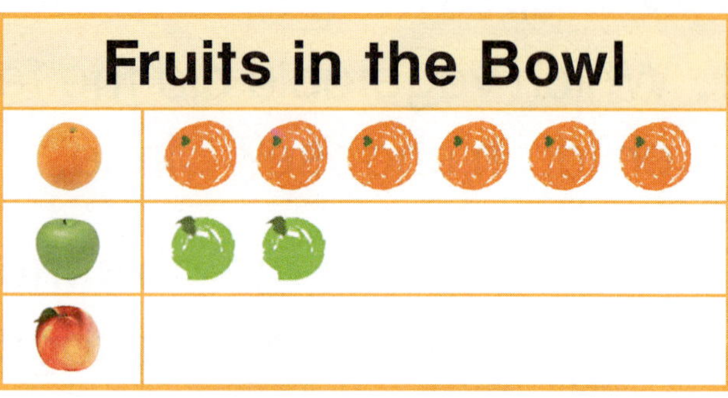

Fruits in the Bowl

Explain how you found the number of children who chose peach.

Make Picture Graphs

▶ Explore

You can make a picture graph to show the favorite subjects of your class.

Subjects We Like

🟩 math	☐	☐	☐	☐	☐	
📖 reading	☐	☐				
🌡 science	▯	▯	▯			

Hands On 🖐

Essential Question
How do you make a picture graph?

Vocabulary
picture graph

▶ Connect

1. Ask each of 10 classmates to choose the art activity he or she likes the best. Draw a picture to show each choice.

Our Favorite Art Activities

painting									
drawing									
poster									

2. How many children chose painting? _______ children

3. Did more children choose drawing or poster? Circle.  

4. Which activity did most children choose? Circle.   

5. **Math Talk** How does the picture graph make it easier to compare the groups in Exercise 4? Explain.

1.1.7 Pose a question and collect and represent data using pictures or picture graphs to answer the question posed.

Count each figure. Draw the figures in the graph.
Use your graph to answer the questions.

Figures in the Picture

□ square							
○ circle							
▭ rectangle							
△ triangle							

1. How many circles are there? _______ circles

2. Are there fewer squares or triangles?
Circle your answer.

3. Which group has the most figures?
Circle your answer.

4. How many more rectangles are there
than triangles? _______ rectangles

At Home Have your child sort red, blue, yellow, and green crayons by color. Work together to show the information as a picture graph.

Problem Solving Workshop

Skill: Make and Use a Graph 

Which group of figures has the most?

Step 1: Sort the figures by shape.

Step 2: Make a picture graph to find the answer.

Draw one picture for each figure.

Plane Figures

squares										
triangles										
circles										

Use the graph to answer the questions.

1. How many circles are there?   ______circles

2. Which group has the fewest figures? Circle your answer.

3. How many more triangles are needed to make the number of triangles equal to the number of squares?   ______more triangle

Math Talk Look at Exercise 3. How does the picture graph help you answer the question?

Problem Solving Skill Practice 

Make a picture graph of the ribbons.
Use the graph to answer the questions.

Ribbon Colors

red															
blue															
yellow															
green															

1. How many green ribbons are there? _______green ribbons

2. Which color has the fewest ribbons? Circle your answer.

3. How many more blue ribbons are there than red ribbons? _______blue ribbons

4. How many more blue ribbons are there than red and yellow ribbons? _______blue ribbons

5. How many fewer red ribbons are there than green ribbons? _______red ribbon

Take a Survey

You can take a **survey** to get information. Jane took a survey of how her friends came to school today. The tally chart shows the results.

Essential Question

How can a survey help you get information?

Vocabulary

survey

1. Take a survey. Ask ten children which season is their favorite. Fill in the tally chart to show their answers.

✓2. Which season did the most children choose as their favorite?

____

3. Did more children choose winter or summer? _______________________________

Our Favorite Seasons	
Season	**Tally**
winter	
spring	
summer	
fall	

4. Which season did the fewest children choose as their favorite? _______________________________

5. **Math Talk** Can you tell how many boys like summer the best? Explain.

1.1.7 Pose a question and collect and represent data using pictures or picture graphs to answer the question posed.

1. Take a survey. Ask ten children which of these snacks is their favorite. Fill in the tally chart to show their answers.

Our Favorite Snacks	
Snack	**Tally**
apples	
raisins	
crackers	
popcorn	

2. Which snack did most children choose as their favorite?

____

3. Did more children in your class choose apples or popcorn?

____

4. Did more children in your class choose raisins or crackers?

____

5. Which snack did the fewest children choose as their favorite?

____

Math Board Problem Solving: Real World

6. How many more children would have to choose blue to make it the favorite color of the most children?

Our Favorite Colors	
Color	**Tally**
blue	卌 ‖
red	‖‖‖
green	卌 卌 ‖

_______ more children

Explain how you found the answer.

Bar Graphs

Read the bar graph to find how many children chose each kind of food.

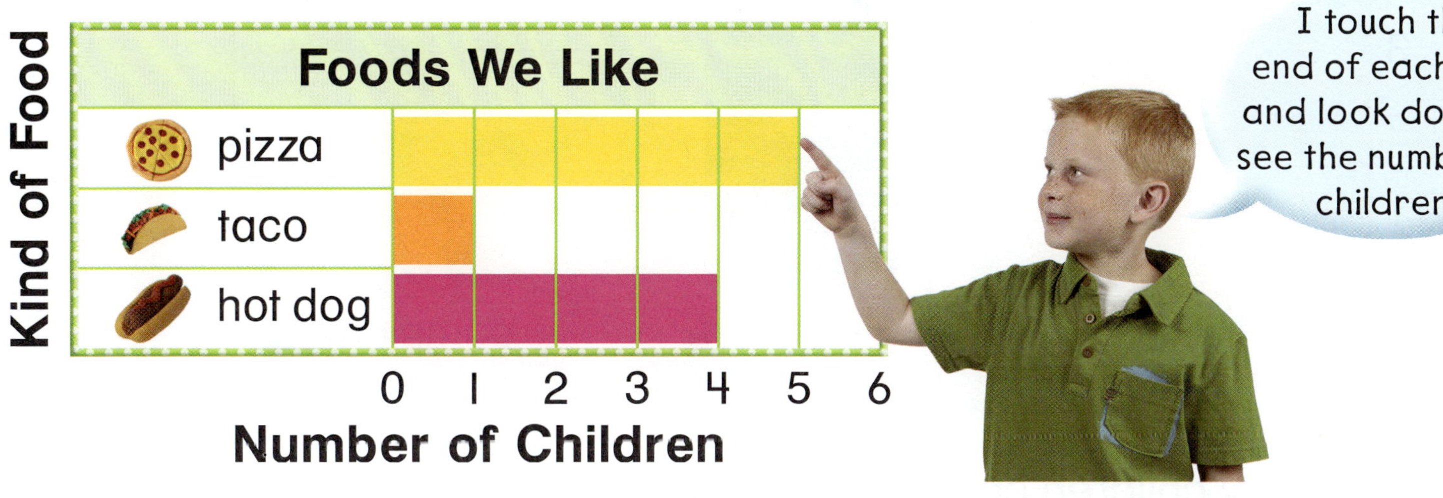

Read the bar graph to answer the questions.

1. How many children chose 🍕?

   _____ children

2. How many children chose 🌭?

   _____ children

3. Which food did the most children choose? Circle.

4. Which food did the fewest children choose? Circle.

5. **Math Talk** Predict which food the fewest children would choose if you asked ten more children which food they like. Explain.

Read the bar graph to answer the questions.

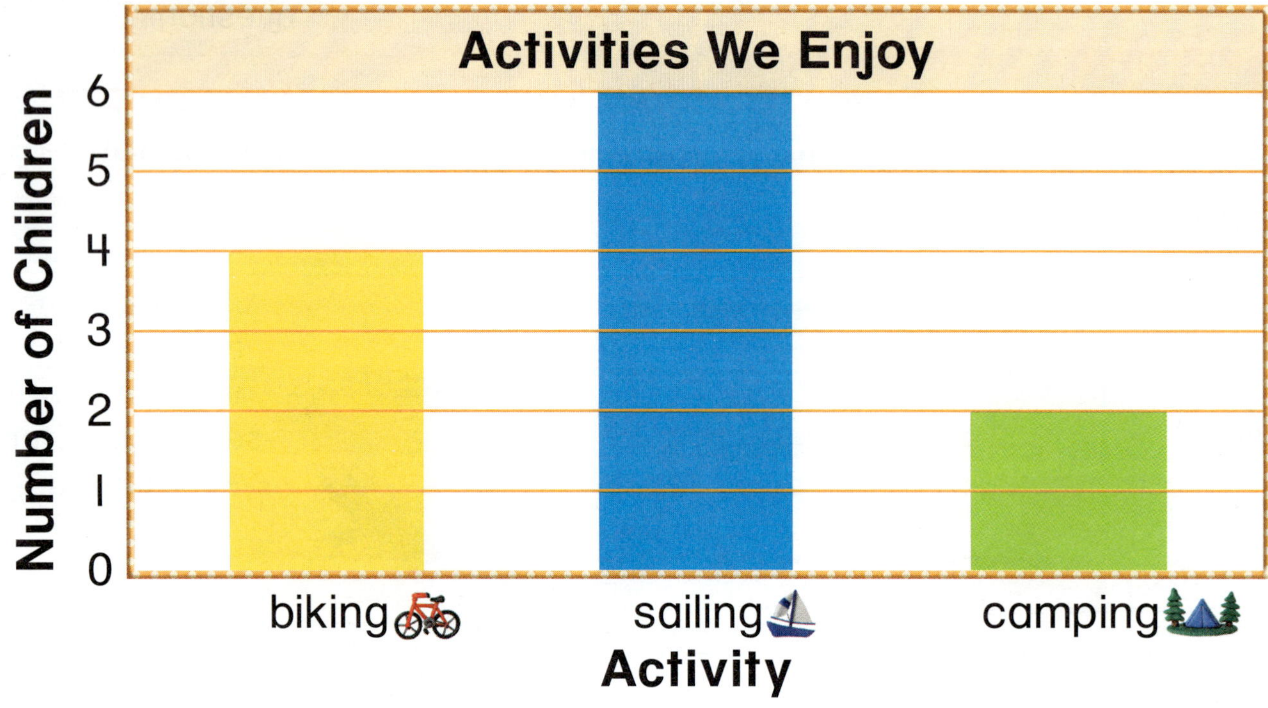

1. How many children chose  ?

______ children

2. How many children chose 🛥️ ?

______ children

3. Which activity do the most children like? Circle.

4. How many more children chose 🛥️ than 🏕️ ?

______ more children

 **Problem Solving: Real World**

5. Use the "Activities We Enjoy" graph. Order **biking**, **sailing**, and **camping** from the most children to the fewest.

______________   ______________   ______________

most   fewest

How is a bar graph like a picture graph? How is it different? Explain.

At Home Use the graph on this page. You and your child choose between biking and camping, and then show how those bars would change with your choices.

Problem Solving Workshop
Strategy: Predict and Test

Essential Question

How can you solve problems by using the strategy *predict and test*?

You can predict an event and then test your prediction.

Predict and Test

Sharon pulls five cubes. Predict the color she is more likely to pull. Circle your prediction. Then use ■, ■, and a bowl to test. Record your test using tally marks.

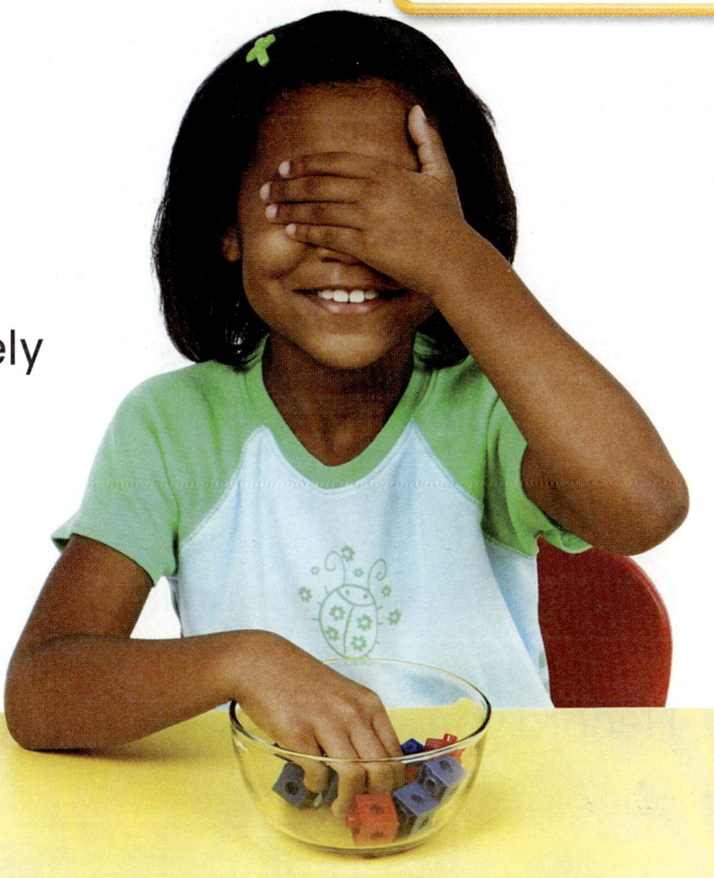

	Predict	**Test**		**Tally**
3 ■	■	■	■	
6 ■	■	■	■	

Math Talk Look at the chart. Predict which color cube Sharon is more likely to pull if she pulls five more cubes.

1.1.7 Pose a question and collect and represent data using pictures or picture graphs to answer the question posed.

Jason pulls five cubes.
Which color is he
more likely to pull?

🔑 Unlock the Problem

What do I need to find?

which color is more
likely to be pulled

What information do I need to use?

_____3_____ green cubes

_____7_____ yellow cubes

Show how to solve the problem.

Predict the color Jason is more likely to pull.
Then use , and a bowl. Circle your prediction.
Record your test using tally marks.

	Predict	Test	Tally	
7				
3				

 Look at your tally marks. Was your
prediction reasonable? Explain.

Name ______________________

Problem Solving Strategy Practice

Technology
Use HMH Mega Math, Numberopolis, *Wash 'n Spin*, Level I.

Predict the color that you are more likely to pull. Circle your prediction. Then use cubes and a bowl to test. Pull five cubes. Record your test using tally marks.

		Predict	Test	Tally	
1.	3				
	6				
2.	9				
	1				
3.	4				
	7				
4.	8				
	5				
5.	**Try Your Own Problem**				
	______				
	______				

At Home Put 8 pennies and 2 nickels in a bowl. Ask your child to predict which coin he or she is more likely to pull and to explain why. Then have your child pull a coin to test the prediction.

Mixed Strategy Practice

Choose a way to solve each problem.
Show your work.

Choose a Strategy
- Draw a Picture
- Make a Model
- Predict and Test
- Write a Number Sentence

1. There are 2 wheels on each bike. How many wheels are on 5 bikes?

_____ wheels

2. There are 4 birds in a tree. There are 4 birds on the ground. How many birds are there in all?

_____ birds

3. Casey has 7 apples. Some apples are red, and 2 of the apples are green. How many apples are red?

_____ red apples

4. Vic has 5 pens. He gets some more. Now he has 8 pens. How many more pens did he get?

_____ more pens

Name _______________________________

Extra Practice

Write A, B, or C to show the group each object belongs in.

A

B

C

1. _____

2. _____

3. _____

4. _____

Use the picture graph to answer the questions.

Bike or Scooter									
 bike									
scooter									

5. How many  are there? _____ bikes

6. How many fewer  than are there? _____ fewer

Problem Solving

Make a picture graph of the sport balls.
Use the graph to answer the questions.

Kinds of Sport Balls						
soccer ball						
basketball						
kickball						

7. Which group has the fewest sport balls? Circle.

Multistep Problems
Chapter 7

1. Ellen wants to know how her classmates got to school. ♩ 1.1.7

- What question can she ask them to find out?

  ____

- Ask 10 classmates the question.

- Make a graph to match your classmates' answers.

How We Get to School										
on a bus										
on a bike										
walking										
in a car										

0 1 2 3 4 5 6 7 8 9 10

- Explain what you found out.

2. Use the clues to make a graph. ♩ 1.1.7

____

- The graph is about favorite games.

- The games are baseball, soccer, and football.

- 3 people chose football.

- 2 more people chose soccer than football.

- 9 people in all were asked to choose.

⬤ Standards Quick Check

Use the graph to answer the questions.

1. How many children chose apple as
   their favorite fruit?   _______ children

2. How many children chose banana as
   their favorite fruit?   _______ children

3. How many more children picked banana
   than grapes?   _______ more children

Use the "Favorite Fruits" graph to answer the questions.

1. 20 children in all were asked to name their favorite fruits.
   How many children liked orange the best?   _______
   Draw to show how many children chose orange.

2. How many children in all chose banana or orange?   _______

3. How many children in all chose apple or banana?   _______

Energy from the sun warms the air. When the air is warm, you do not need a jacket. When the air is cold, a jacket feels good.

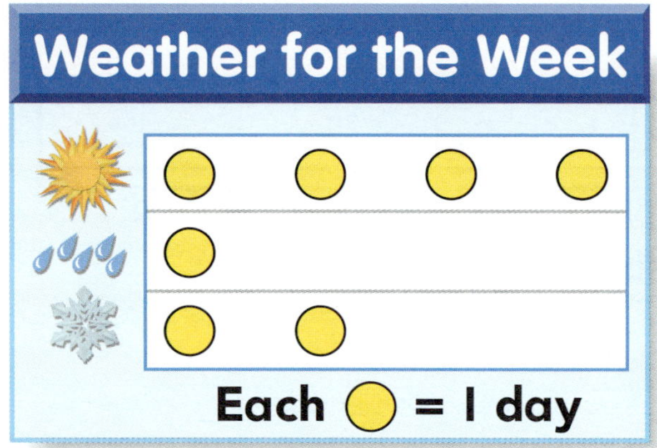

Weather for the Week

Each ○ = 1 day

Use the graph to solve.

1. Which weather happened the most? Circle.

2. Which weather happened the least?

3. How many more days have ☀ than ❄ ?

_______ more days

Name _______________________________

 # Looking Ahead to the ISTEP+
Chapter 7

Mark the best answer for questions 1–4.

1. Which figure belongs to this group? 1.3.1

○ (yellow circle)

○ (blue triangle)

○ (red triangle)

○ (green rectangle)

2. Look at the group above. How many  are there? 1.1.7

○ 1

○ 2

○ 3

○ 4

Use the graph to answer questions 3 and 4.

3. How many were found? 1.1.7

○ 1

○ 2

○ 3

○ 4

4. How many shells were found in all? 1.1.7

○ 7

○ 8

○ 9

○ 10

Mark the best answer for questions 5–6.

Use the graph to answer questions 5 and 6.

Flowers We Like

daisy	*	*	*	*
rose	🌹	🌹	🌹	
tulip	🌷	🌷		

5. How many children chose 🌹?

1.1.7

- ○ 2
- ○ 3
- ○ 4
- ○ 5

6. How many more children chose ✿ than 🌷? 1.1.7

- ○ 0
- ○ I
- ○ 2
- ○ 3

Make a picture graph of the fruits in the box. Use the graph to answer the questions. 1.1.7

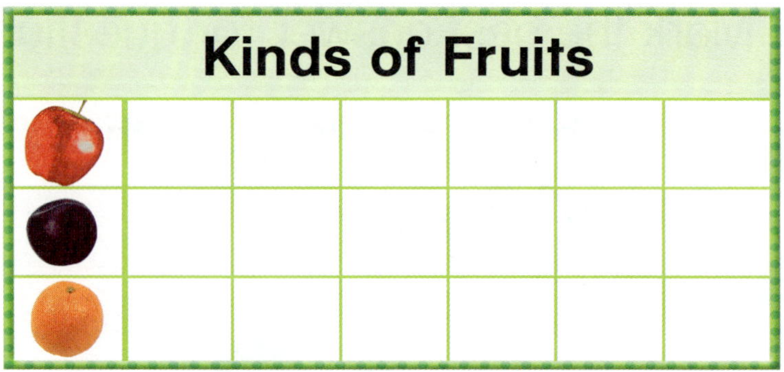

Kinds of Fruits

7. Which group has the fewest fruits? Circle.

8. How many fewer 🍎 are there than 🍒?

______ fewer

Numbers to 100

Theme: Autumn Days

Fun Fact

The first day of autumn comes in September. On that day, the daytime and nighttime hours are equal.

Investigate

How many days are in September? Which other months have the same number of days?

GO ONLINE
Technology
Student pages are available in the Student eBook.

Show What You Know

Count the ●. Write the number.

1. _______

2. _______

3. _______

4. _______

5. _______

6. _______

At Home This page checks your child's understanding of important concepts and skills needed for success in Chapter 8.

Chapter 8 Lesson 1
Model Ten and More

You can group 10 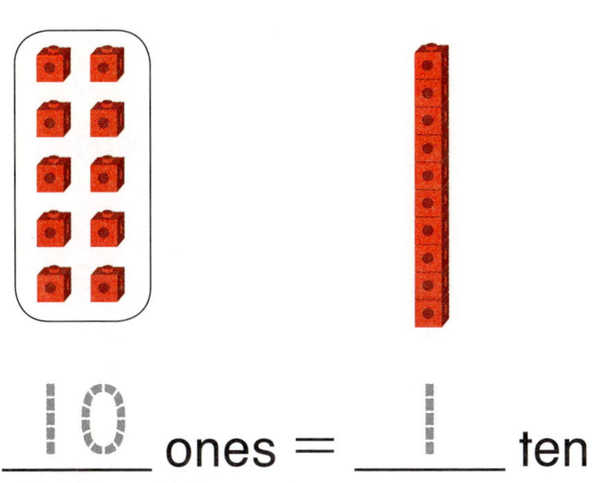 to make 1 ten.

Essential Question
How can you show a number as ten and some more?

Vocabulary
ten
ones

Workmat

Tens	Ones

_______ ones = _______ ten

1 ten   0 ones

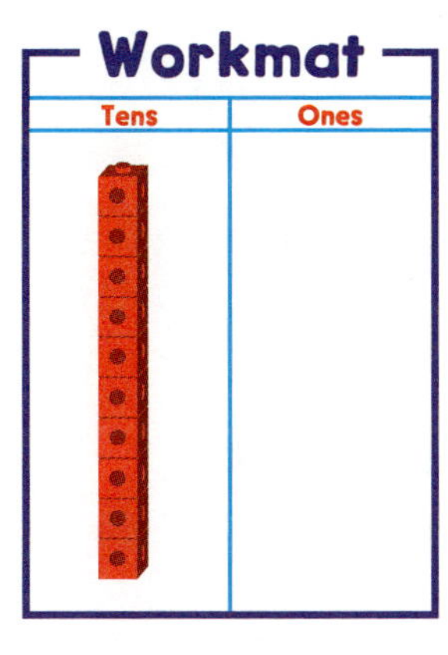

Use Workmat 3 and 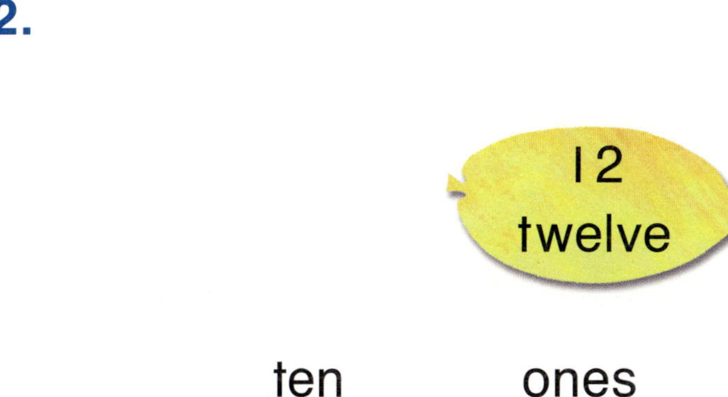. Make groups of ten and ones. Draw your work. Write how many.

1.

_______ ten _______ one

2.

_______ ten _______ ones

3.

_______ ten _______ ones

4.

_______ ten _______ ones

5. **Math Talk** Why is 1 ten the same as 10 ones?

1.1.4 Show equivalent forms of whole numbers to at least 100 as groups of tens and ones.

one hundred ninety-nine **199**

Use Workmat 3 and .
Make groups of ten and ones.
Draw your work. Write how many.

1. 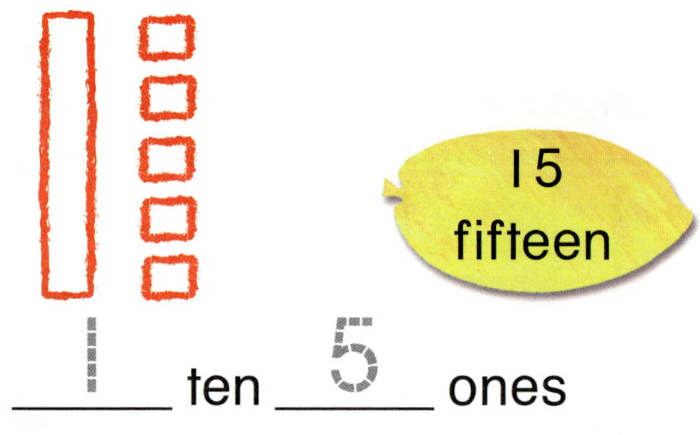

_______ ten _______ ones

2.

_______ ten _______ ones

3. 

_______ ten _______ ones

4. 

_______ ten _______ ones

5. 

_______ ten _______ ones

6. 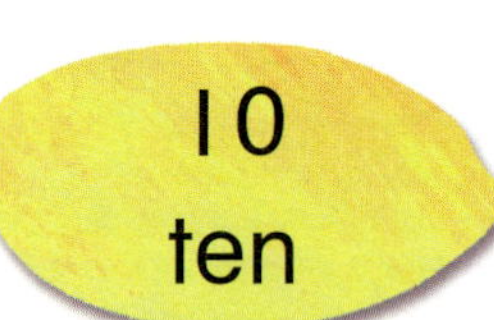

_______ ten _______ ones

Problem Solving: Reasoning

Write each number.

7. 3 ones 1 ten = _______

8. 1 ten 8 ones = _______

Draw to show each number you wrote for
Exercises 7 and 8.

At Home Name numbers from 11–19 with your child. Have
your child work with pennies to show a group of ten pennies
and a group of ones for each number.

Chapter 8 Lesson 2

Read and Record Numbers to 20

Essential Question
How can you show a number as 10 and some more?

Vocabulary
ten
ones

▶ **Explore**

Model   Write   Say

_____ ten _____ one = _____

▶ **Connect**

Use  to model. Write how many tens and ones. Write the number. Say the number.

	Model	Write	Say
1.		_____ ten __2__ ones = __12__	twelve
2.		_____ ten _____ ones = _____	thirteen
3.		_____ ten _____ ones = _____	fourteen
4.		_____ ten _____ ones = _____	fifteen

5. **Math Talk** Look at the chart. What pattern do you see? Explain.

1.1.4 Show equivalent forms of whole numbers to at least 100 as groups of tens and ones. *also* **1.1.2**

Use ▨ to model. Write how many tens and ones. Write the number. Say the number.

	Model	Write	Say
1.		_____1_____ ten _____7_____ ones = _____17_____	seventeen
2.		_________ ten _________ ones = _________	nineteen
3.		_________ ten _________ ones = _________	eighteen
4.		_________ ten _________ ones = _________	sixteen

Problem Solving: Real World

5. Draw a picture. Solve.

Sandy has 10 stickers on one page and 5 on another page. How many stickers does she have?

________ stickers

What does the 1 in 14 stand for?

At Home Show your child one group of ten pennies and one group of eight pennies. Ask your child to tell how many tens and ones are there and say the number. Repeat with other numbers from 11–19.

Chapter 8 Lesson 3

Tens

Explore

You can group 20 ones
to make 2 tens.

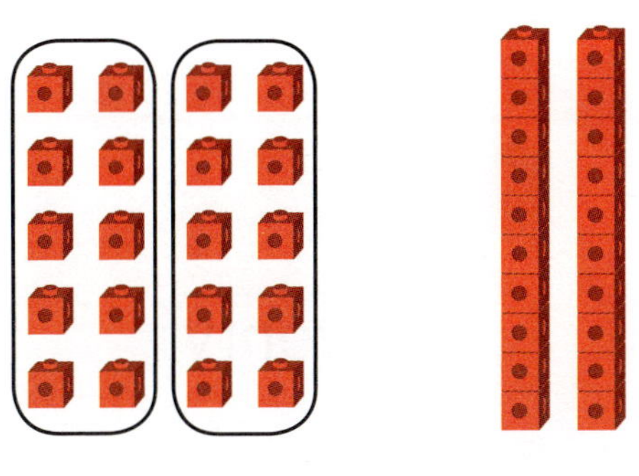

20 ones $=$ 2 tens

Hands On

Essential Question
How can you group cubes to make tens?

Vocabulary
tens
ones

2 tens is the same as 20.

Connect

Use . Make groups of ten. Draw the tens.
Count by tens. Write the number.

1. 3 tens

$\dfrac{30}{\text{thirty}}$

2. 4 tens

$\dfrac{\rule{2em}{0.4pt}}{\text{forty}}$

3. 5 tens

$\dfrac{\rule{2em}{0.4pt}}{\text{fifty}}$

4. **Math Talk** How many ones are the same as 100?
Explain.

1.1.4 Show equivalent forms of whole numbers to at least 100
as groups of tens and ones.

Use ⬛. Make groups of ten. Draw the tens.
Count by tens. Write the number.

1. 6 tens

______
sixty

2. 7 tens

______
seventy

3. 8 tens

______
eighty

4. 9 tens

______
ninety

Problem Solving: Real World

5. Act out the story with ▭▭▭ ▭.
Write the answer.

Lee picks apples from 4 trees.
He picks 10 apples from each tree.
How many apples does he pick in all?

______ apples

Explain your answer.

At Home Have your child count out small objects into groups
of 10, tell how many tens in all, and then say the number word.

Name _______________________

Chapter 8 Lesson 4

Tens and Ones to 50

The **3** in **34**
means **3** tens.

The **3** in **43**
means **3** ones.

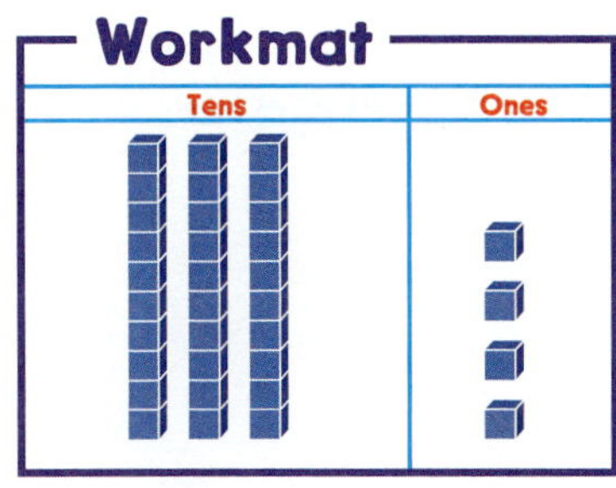

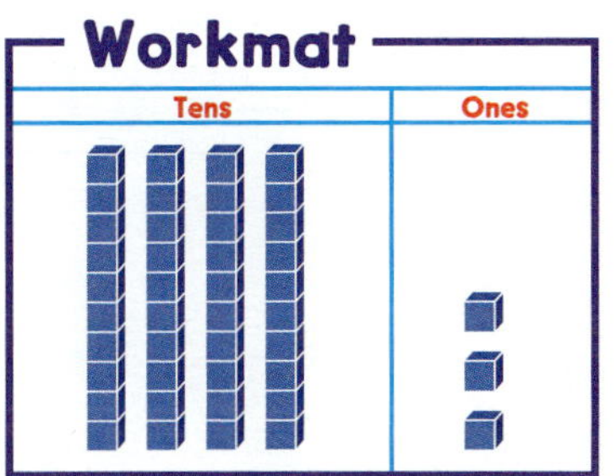

___3___ tens ___4___ ones = ___34___ | ___4___ tens ___3___ ones = ___43___

Use Workmat 3 and .
Show the tens and ones. Write how many
tens and ones. Write the number.

1. 

_______ tens _______ ones = _______

2. 

_______ tens _______ ones = _______

3. 

_______ tens _______ ones = _______

4. 

_______ tens _______ ones = _______

5. **Math Talk** How can you show that 45 is
different from 54?

Write how many tens and ones.
Write the number.

1. 

_______ ten _______ one = _______

2. 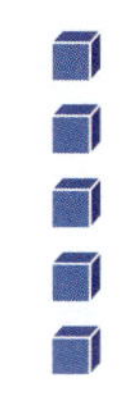

_______ tens _______ ones = _______

3.  

_______ tens _______ ones = _______

4. 

_______ tens _______ ones = _______

5. 

_______ tens _______ ones = _______

6. 

_______ tens _______ ones = _______

Problem Solving: Reasoning

Write the answer to each riddle.

7. I am a number less than 35.
I have 3 tens and some ones.
What numbers could I be?

____

8. I am a number less than 50.
I have 8 ones and some
tens. What numbers could I
be?

____

What if the number in Exercise 8 was less than
18 and had no tens? What could the number be?

Chapter 8 Lesson 5

Tens and Ones to 100

▶ **Explore**

The number just after 99 is 100. | 10 tens is the same as 1 hundred.

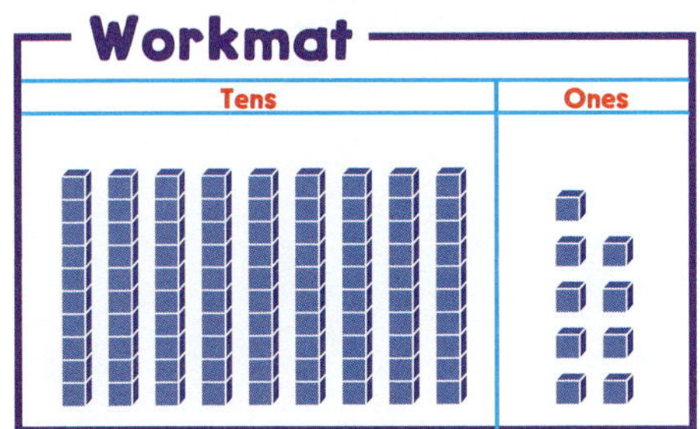

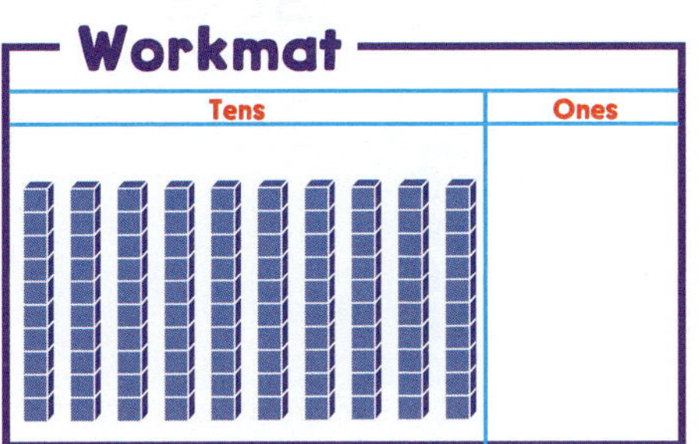

__9__ tens __9__ ones = __99__ | __10__ tens __0__ ones = __100__

▶ **Connect**

Use Workmat 3 and .
Write how many tens and ones.
Write the number.

1. 

______ tens ______ ones = ______

2. 

______ tens ______ ones = ______

 **3.** 

______ tens ______ ones = ______

4. 

______ tens ______ ones = ______

5. **Math Talk** What does the number 9 represent in each of these numbers? Which number is greater?

1.1.4 Show equivalent forms of whole numbers to at least 100 as groups of tens and ones. also **1.1.2**

Write how many tens and ones.
Write the number.

1. 

__6__ tens __8__ ones = __68__

2. 

______ tens ______ ones = ______

3. 

______ tens ______ ones = ______

4. 

______ tens ______ ones = ______

5. 

______ tens ______ ones = ______

6. 

______ tens ______ ones = ______

Problem Solving: Reasoning

Write how many tens and ones.
Write the number.

7. 

______ tens ______ ones = ______

8. 

______ tens ______ ones = ______

Explain how you found the answer to Exercise 7.

At Home Tell your child numbers from 50 to 99. Ask your child to draw a picture to show the tens and the ones in each number and then write the number.

Chapter 8 Lesson 6

Algebra: Ways to Expand Numbers

► **We Learn**

There are different ways
to think about a number.

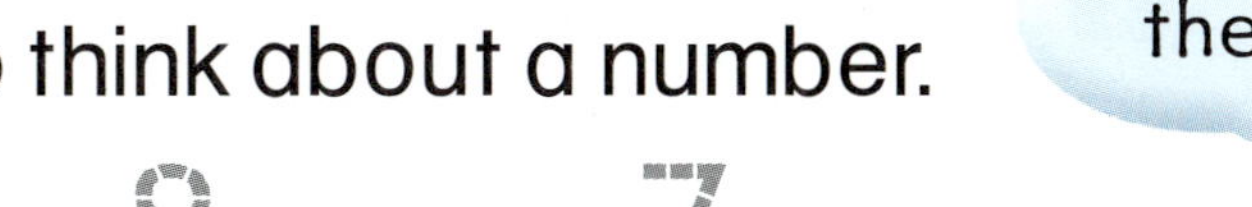

_____ tens _____ ones

_____ + _____

_____

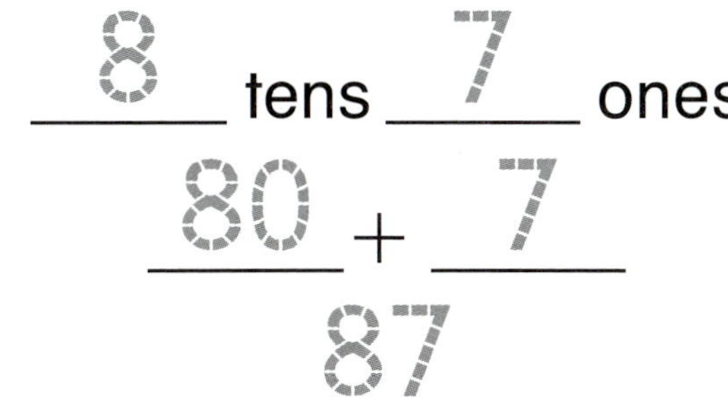

► **Share and Show**  

Write how many tens and ones.
Write the number in two different ways.

1. 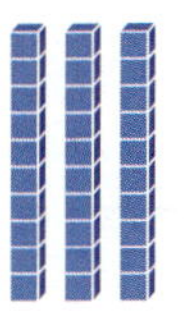

_____ tens _____ ones

_____ + _____

_____

2.

_____ tens _____ ones

_____ + _____

_____

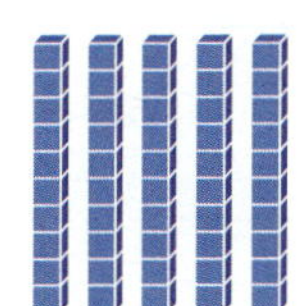

☑ 3. 

_____ tens _____ ones

_____ + _____

_____

☑ 4.

_____ tens _____ ones

_____ + _____

_____

5. **Math Talk** Does the 7 in this number represent 7 or
70? Explain.

1.1.4 Show equivalent forms of whole numbers to at least
100 as groups of tens and ones. *also* **1.1.2**

Write how many tens and ones.
Write the number in two different ways.

1. 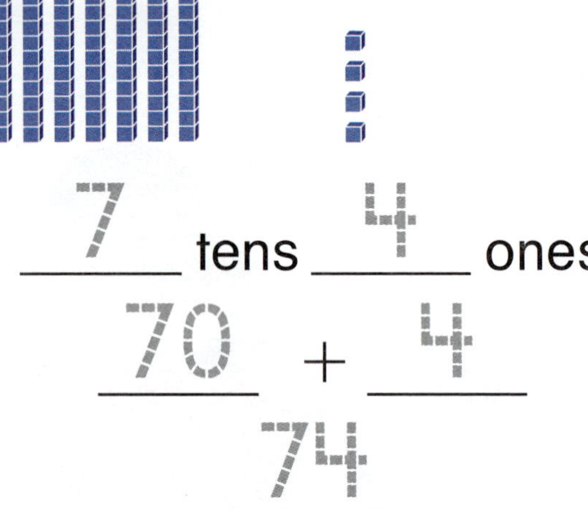

___7___ tens ___4___ ones

___70___ + ___4___

___74___

2. 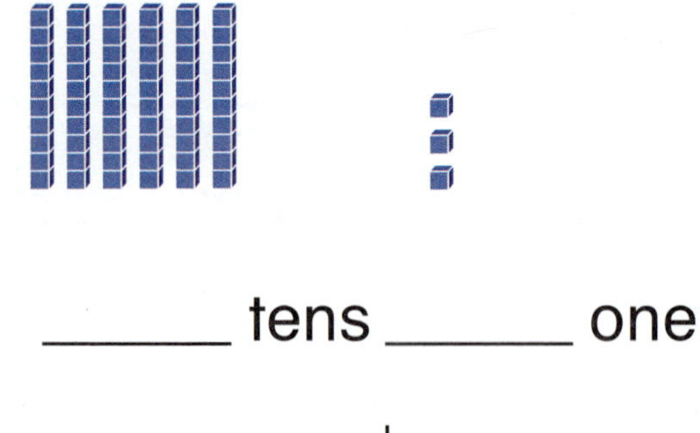

______ tens ______ ones

_____ + _____

______

3. 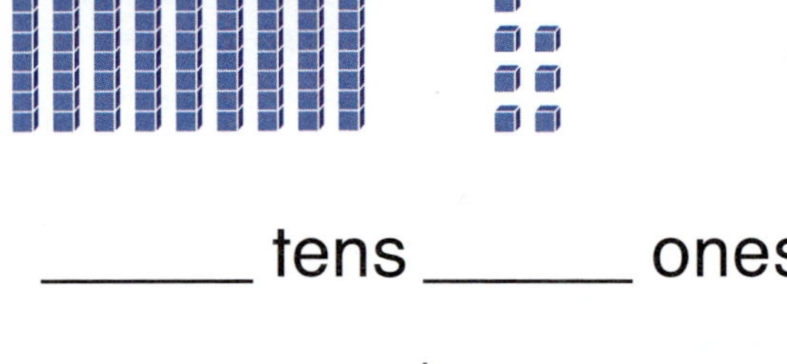

______ tens ______ ones

_____ + _____

______

4. 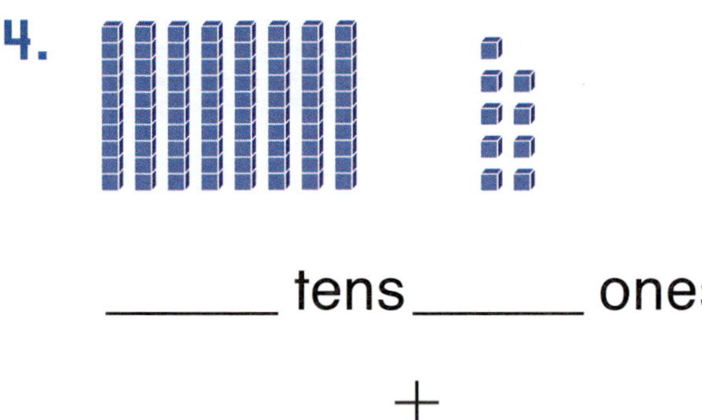

______ tens ______ ones

_____ + _____

______

 **Problem Solving: Visual Thinking**

5. Draw the same number using only tens.
Write how many tens and ones.
Write the number in two different ways.

______ tens ______ ones

_____ + _____

______

| ______ tens ______ ones

_____ + _____

______

How are the two ways different?

Problem Solving Workshop
Skill: Make Reasonable Estimates

Essential Question

How can you find about how many are in a group?

About how many apples can you hold in one hand?

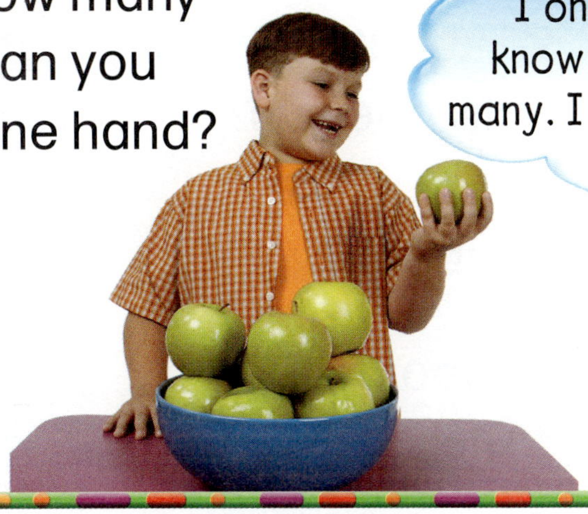

about 1
about 10
about 100

Circle the closest estimate.

1. About how many  can you hold in one hand?

about 6 

about 60 

about 600

2. About how many would fit in one backpack?

about 1

about 10

about 100

✓3. About how many Math are in your classroom?

about 3 Math

about 30 Math

about 300 Math

✓4. About how many ______ can you hold in one hand?

about 7

about 70

about 700

Math Talk Look at Exercise 4. How could you find out exactly how many ______? Explain.

Problem Solving Skill Practice 

Circle the closest estimate.

THINK Which answer makes the most sense?

1. About how many ▪ would cover your desk?

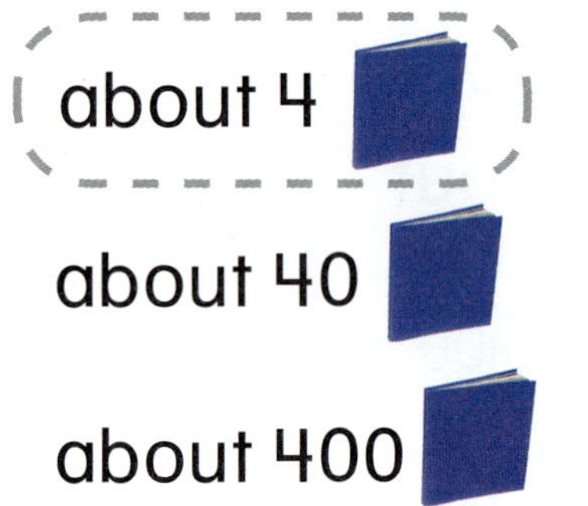

(about 4)

about 40

about 400

2. About how many ⌒ would fill one cup?

about 2

about 20

about 200

3. About how many ▬ can you hold in two hands?

about 1

about 10

about 100

4. About how many ● would fill two cups?

about 3

about 30

about 300

5. About how many ▪ would fill one cup?

about 2

about 20

about 200

6. About how many ● can you hold in one hand?

about 8

about 80

about 800

At Home Ask your child to choose the closest estimate for the number of dimes he or she could hold in two hands, 2 or 20. Then have him or her check.

Extra Practice

Use 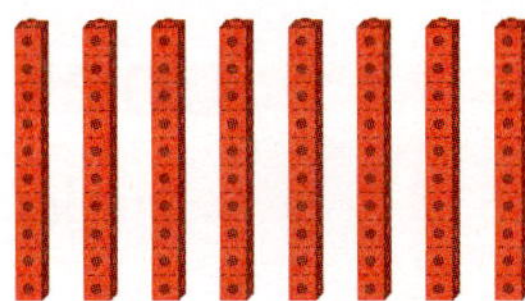. Make groups of ten.
Count by tens. Write the number.

1. 8 tens

____
eighty

Write how many tens and ones. Write the number.

2.

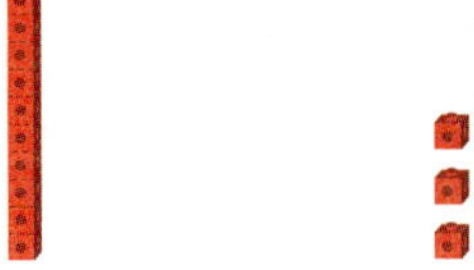

_______ ten _______ ones = _______

3.

_______ tens _______ ones = _______

4.

_______ tens _______ ones = _______

5.

_______ tens _______ ones = _______

Problem Solving

Circle the closest estimate.

6. About how many  are in your classroom?

about 3 

about 30 

about 300

7. About how many ___ can you hold in one hand?

about 5

about 50

about 500

GO ONLINE
Technology
Use HMH Mega Math, Country Countdown,
Block Busters, Level I.

Multistep Problems
Chapter 8

1. Count the number of cubes. 1.1.4

- How many cubes are there?

- If you made groups of tens, how many tens would there be?

- If you made groups of tens, how many ones would be left over?

- What is another way to write the number?

2. Rita put 97 stickers in her book. Each page holds 10 stickers. 1.1.4

book

- How many tens and ones are in the number 97?

  ______ tens ______ ones

- How many pages does Rita fill?

- How many stickers are left over to start a new page?

Standards Quick Check

Write the tens and ones.
Write the number.

1.

Tens	Ones

_______ tens _______ ones

____

forty-two

2.

Tens	Ones

_______ tens _______ ones

____

thirty-seven

There are 29 pumpkins in all. 10 are on
the vines. 10 are in a shed. The rest are
in a wagon. How many are in the wagon?   _______

Food changes form when it is baked. Mix eggs, milk, flour, oil, and sugar. You have muffin batter. You can pour the batter into a muffin tray and bake it in an oven. Then you can eat yummy muffins!

Use Workmat 3 and 🔲 to solve.

1. Enrico pours batter into a muffin pan.
   He fills 11 spaces.
   What is 1 more than 11?

   ____

2. Van makes 36 muffins.
   What is 10 less than 36?

   ____

3. Chang makes 48 muffins.
   Write the tens and the ones.

   _______ tens _______ ones

# Looking Ahead to the ISTEP+
Chapter 8

Mark the best answer for questions 1–4.

1. Which number is equal to 1 ten 4 ones? **1.1.4**

○ 11
○ 14
○ 41
○ 49

2. Which number tells how many? **1.1.4**

○ 5
○ 6
○ 50
○ 60

3. Which is another way to write 5 tens 9 ones? **1.1.4**

○ 50
○ 59
○ 90
○ 95

4. Which number tells how many? **1.1.4**

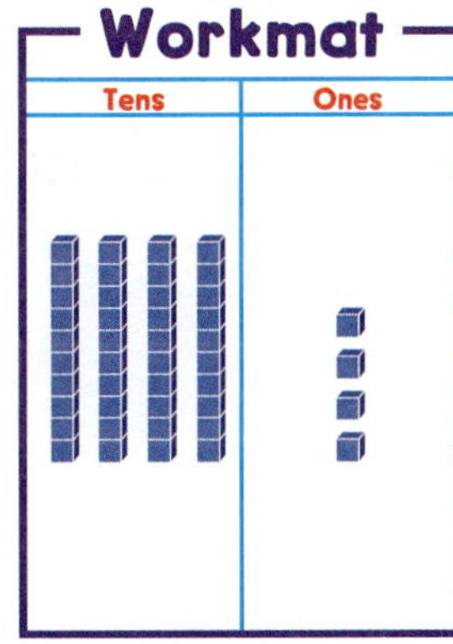

○ 4 tens 3 ones
○ 0 tens 8 ones
○ 4 tens 4 ones
○ 8 tens 4 ones

Mark the best answer for questions 5–7.

5. Which number is equal to
2 tens 6 ones? 1.1.4

○ 6

○ 20

○ 26

○ 62

6. About how many 🍓 can you
hold in one hand? 1.1.1

○ about 5

○ about 25

○ about 50

○ about 100

7. About how many 🐻 can you
hold in two hands? 1.1.1

○ about 1

○ about 10

○ about 50

○ about 100

Open Ended

8. Write how many tens and
ones. Write the number in
two different ways. 1.1.4

______ tens ______ ones

______ + ______

______

Circle the closest estimate.

9. About how many ⬭ can
you hold in one hand?

1.1.1

about 3 ⬭

about 30 ⬭

about 300 ⬭

218

Chapter 9

Compare, Order, and Number Patterns

Theme: Rainy Days

Fun Fact

Small raindrops are shaped like circles. Larger raindrops are round on top and flatter on the bottom.

Investigate
Use the word **more**, **less**, or **equal** to compare two colors on the umbrella.

© Houghton Mifflin Harcourt

GO ONLINE
Technology
Student pages are available in the Student eBook.

two hundred nineteen 219

Show What You Know 

1. Use cubes to show a group of more cubes.
Draw the cubes.

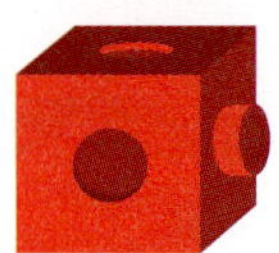  

2. Use cubes to show a group of fewer cubes.
Draw the cubes.

3. Use cubes to show an equal group.
Draw the cubes.

At Home This page checks your child's understanding of important concepts and skills needed for success in Chapter 9.

Name ____________________

Chapter 9 Lesson 1

Algebra: Greater Than

▶ **Explore**

Compare numbers to find which is greater.

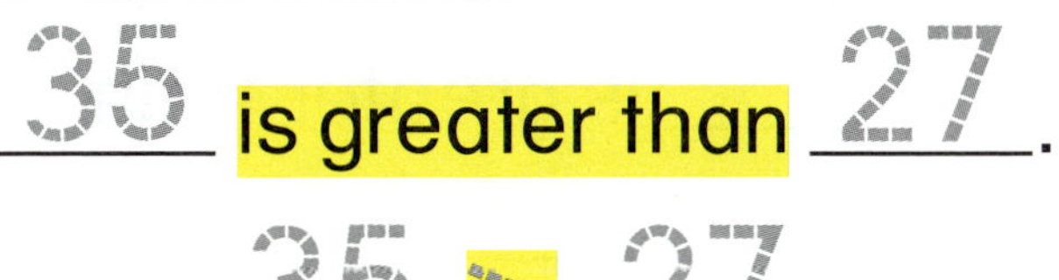

____35____ is greater than ____27____.

35 > 27

▶ **Connect**

Use Workmat 3 and  to show each number. Circle the greater number. Write the numbers.

1.

____48____ is greater than ____21____.

48 > 21

2.
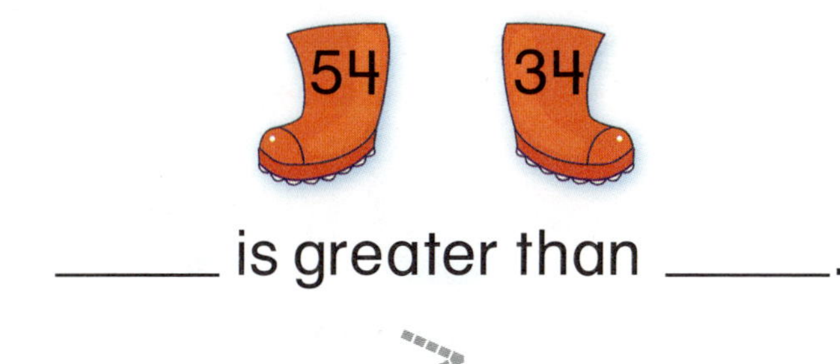

______ is greater than ______.

______ > ______

3.

______ is greater than ______.

______ > ______

4.

______ is greater than ______.

______ > ______

5. Math Talk Why do you compare the tens before you compare the ones? Explain.

 **1.1.1** Count, read, write, order, rename and compare whole numbers to at least 100. *also* **1.1.2**

Share and Show

Circle the greater number.
Write the numbers.

REMEMBER!
Compare the tens first.

1. 

32 is greater than 27 .

32 > 27

2. 

_____ is greater than _____ .

_____ > _____

3. 

_____ is greater than _____ .

_____ > _____

4. 

_____ is greater than _____ .

_____ > _____

5. 

_____ is greater than _____ .

_____ > _____

6. 

_____ is greater than _____ .

_____ > _____

7. 

_____ is greater than _____ .

_____ > _____

8. 

_____ is greater than _____ .

_____ > _____

Problem Solving: Application

9. Circle the numbers that are greater than 56.

50   65   52   80   46   59

Compare 59 and 56. Draw tens and ones to show which number is greater.

Chapter 9 Lesson 2

Algebra: Less Than

Compare numbers to find which is less.

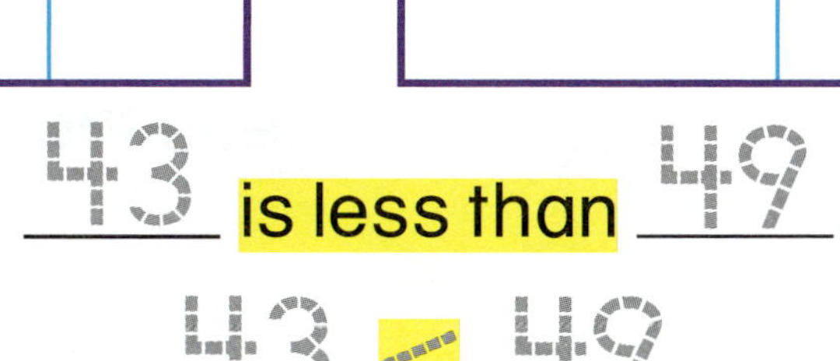

__43__ **is less than** __49__.

__43__ < __49__

Hands On

Essential Question
How can you make a model to show which number is less?

Vocabulary
is less than <

▶ **Connect**

Use Workmat 3 and ▭ ▫ to show each number.
Circle the number that is less. Write the numbers.

1.

__36__ is less than __39__.

__36__ < __39__

2.

_____ is less than _____.

_____ < _____

3.

_____ is less than _____.

_____ < _____

4.

_____ is less than _____.

_____ < _____

5. **Math Talk** Explain how you know that 41 is less than 45.

1.1.1 Count, read, write, order, rename and compare whole numbers to at least 100. *also* **1.1.2**

REMEMBER! If the tens are the same, compare the ones.

Circle the number that is less.
Write the numbers.

1. 

47 48

_47_ is less than _48_.

_47_ < _48_

2. 

75 82

______ is less than ______.

______ < ______

3.

53 35

______ is less than ______.

______ < ______

4.

58 70

______ is less than ______.

______ < ______

5.

84 88

______ is less than ______.

______ < ______

6.

62 61

______ is less than ______.

______ < ______

7.

76 67

______ is less than ______.

______ < ______

8.

94 90

______ is less than ______.

______ < ______

Math Board

Problem Solving: Application

9. Circle the numbers that are less than 63.

83 58 61 36 70 67

Explain how you know which numbers
are less than 63.

Name ______________________

Algebra: Greater Than, Less Than, and Equal To

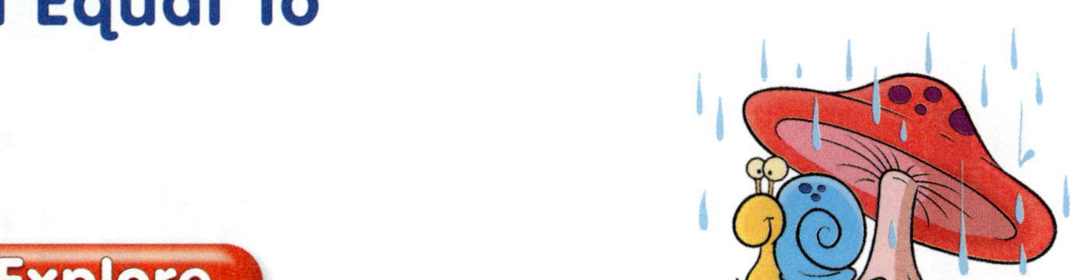

Essential Question
What symbols do you use to compare numbers?

Vocabulary
is equal to =
is greater than >
is less than <

▶ **Explore**

21 < 24
21 is less than 24.

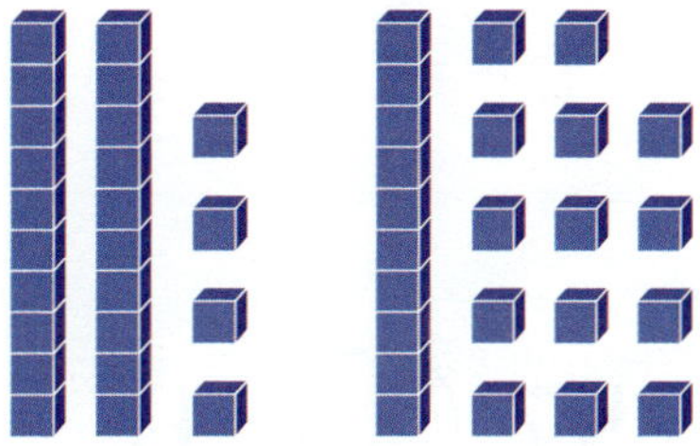

24 = 24
24 is equal to 24.

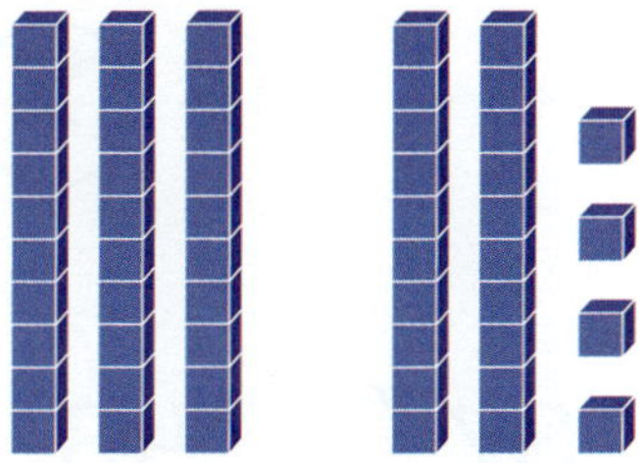

30 > 24
30 is greater than 24.

▶ **Connect**

Use and draw ▬ ▪ to show each number.
Write <, >, or =. Complete the sentence.

1.

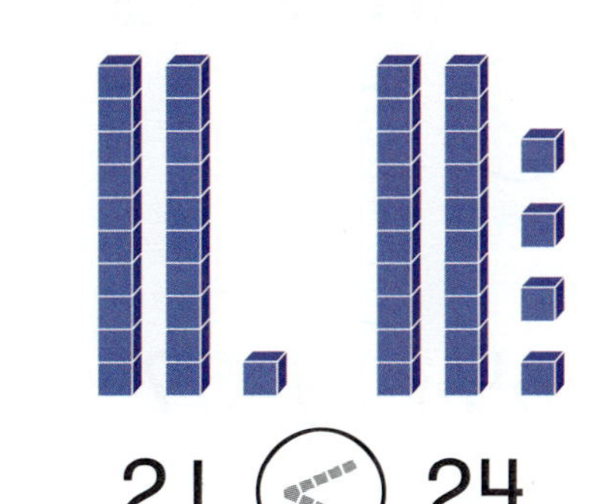

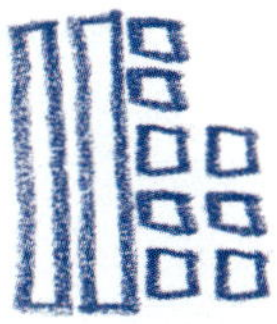

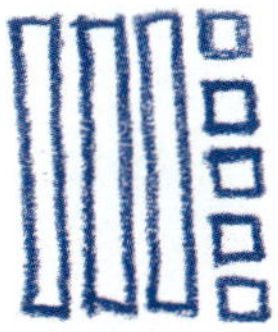

28 < 35

28 ___is less than___ 35.

2.

16 ◯ 16

16 ________________ 16.

3.

46 ◯ 31

46 ________________ 31.

4.

55 ◯ 58

55 ________________ 58.

5. **Math Talk** Compare 47 and 32 in two ways. Which symbols will you use?

 **1.1.1** Count, read, write, order, rename and compare whole numbers to at least 100. *also* **1.1.2**

Share and Show 

Write <, >, or =.
Use 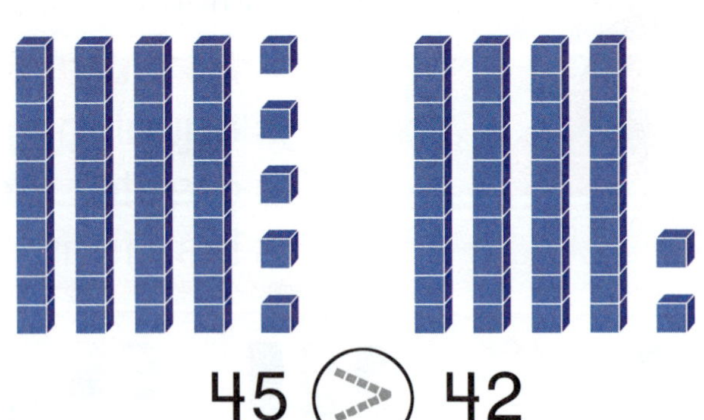 if you need to.

1.

$$45 \gtrdot 42$$

2.

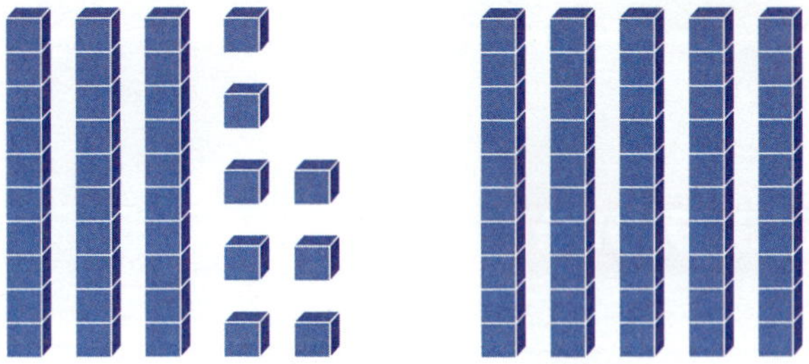

$$38 \bigcirc 50$$

3. $\quad 37 \bigcirc 43$

4. $\quad 47 \bigcirc 47$

5. $\quad 64 \bigcirc 59$

6. $\quad 56 \bigcirc 56$

7. $\quad 62 \bigcirc 72$

8. $\quad 70 \bigcirc 65$

9. $\quad 79 \bigcirc 84$

10. $\quad 90 \bigcirc 93$

11. $\quad 93 \bigcirc 90$

Problem Solving: Number Sense

Write each number. Compare.
Write <, >, or =.

12.

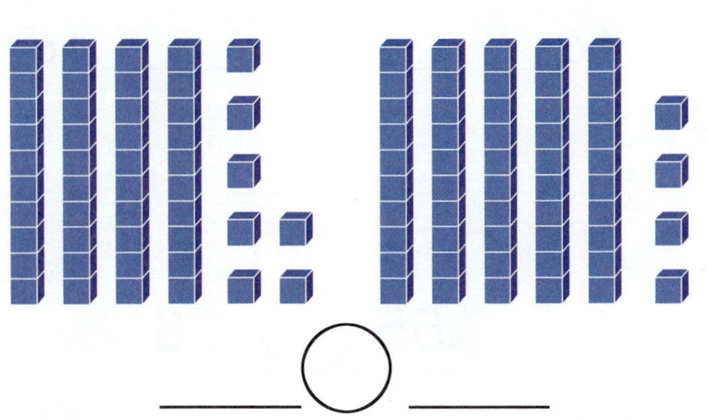

____ $\bigcirc$ ____

13.

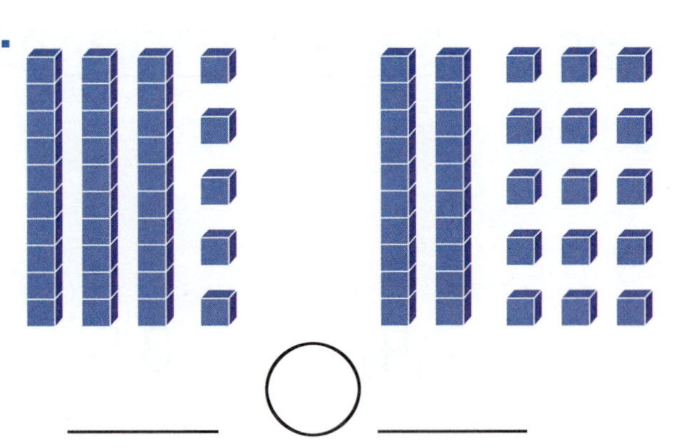

____ $\bigcirc$ ____

Choose two new numbers.
Compare them by using <, >, or =.

Chapter 9 Lesson 4

One More, One Less

Essential Question
How can you identify one more and one less than a given number?

Vocabulary
one less
one more

One less than 39 is ___38___.

39

One more than 39 is ___40___.

Connect

Use .

Write the numbers that are one less and one more.

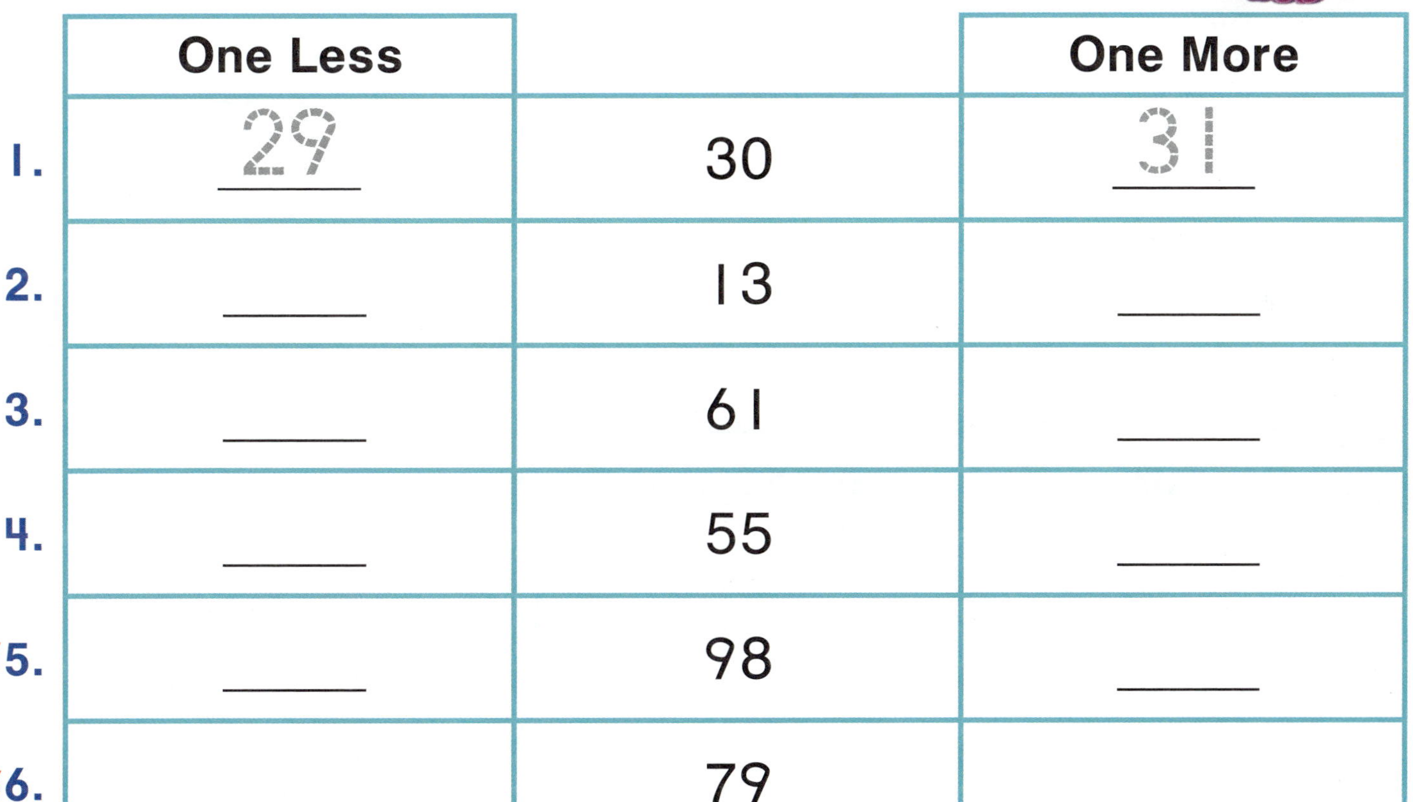

	One Less		One More
1.	29	30	31
2.	___	13	___
3.	___	61	___
4.	___	55	___
5.	___	98	___
6.	___	79	___

7. **Math Talk** Use the words **one less** and **one more** to describe these numbers.

1.1.2 Name the number that is one more than or one less than any number to at least 100. *also* **1.1.1; 1.1.3**

Use ▭ ▫.
Complete the chart.

	One Less		One More
1.	52	53	54
2.	____	36	____
3.	81	____	83
4.	____	70	____
5.	64	____	66
6.	____	59	____
7.	____	92	____
8.	49	____	51

Math Board

Problem Solving: Mental Math

Solve in your head.

9. Lisa has 60 crayons. Jim has 1 fewer crayon than Lisa. How many crayons does Jim have?

______ crayons

10. Bill has 19 markers. Mia has 1 more marker than Bill. How many markers does Mia have?

______ markers

Explain how you solved Exercise 9.

Chapter 9 Lesson 5

Ten More, Ten Less

Essential Question
How can you identify ten more and ten less than a given number?

Vocabulary
ten less
ten more

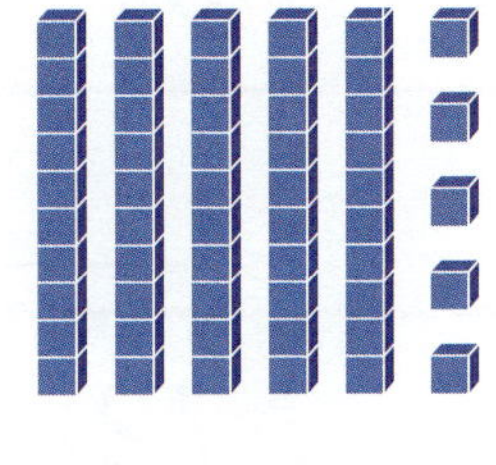

Ten less than 55 is __45__. | 55 | Ten more than 55 is __65__.

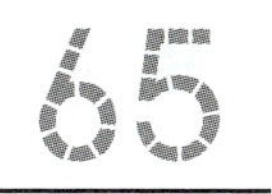

Use  .

Write the numbers that are ten less and ten more.

	Ten Less		Ten More
1.	70	80	90
2.	___	36	___
3.	___	41	___
4.	___	73	___
5.	___	65	___
6.	___	29	___

7. **Math Talk** Explain how you know that 84 is ten less than 94.

1.1.1 Count, read, write, order, rename and compare whole numbers to at least 100.

Use ▬▬▬▬ ▪.
Complete the chart.

	Ten Less		Ten More
1.	38	48	58
2.	____	61	____
3.	14	____	34
4.	____	72	____
5.	39	____	59
6.	____	56	____
7.	____	87	____
8.	50	____	70

Math Board

Problem Solving: Reasoning

Solve each riddle.

9. I am ten less than 50.
I am ten more than 30.
What number am I?

____

10. 92 is ten more than I am.
72 is ten less than I am.
What number am I?

____

Write a riddle for the number 25. Use the
words **ten more** and **ten less** in your riddle.

Chapter 9 Lesson 6

Order on a Number Line

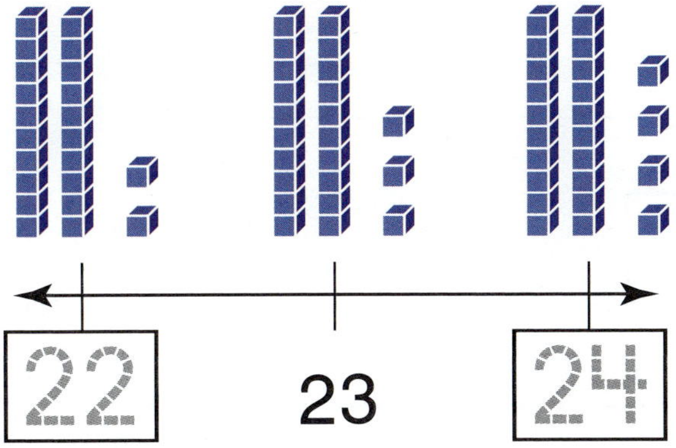

22   23   24

Essential Question
How can you use a number line to order numbers?

Vocabulary
before
between
after

Write the number that is just before, between, or just after.

1. 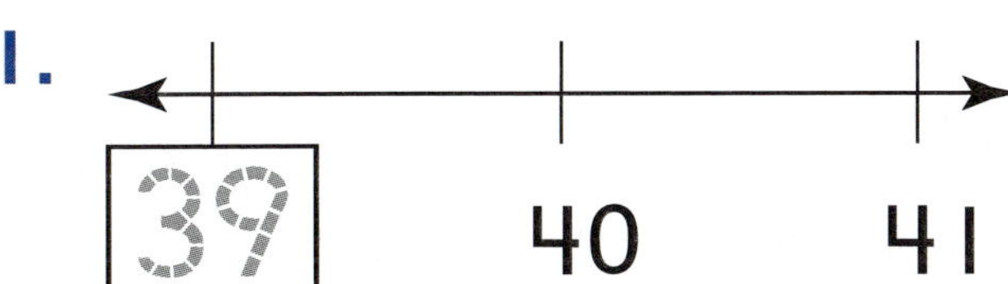

39   40   41

2. 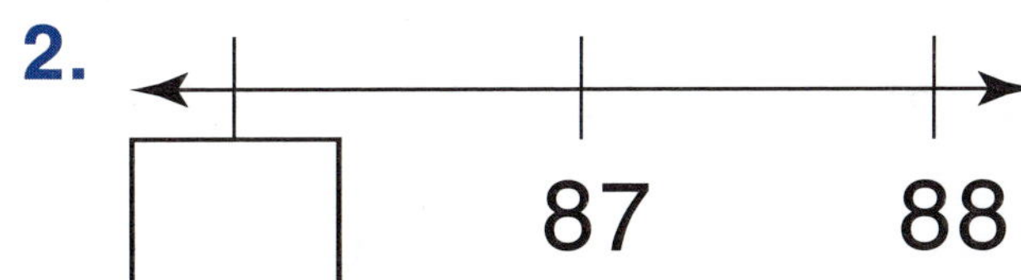

87   88

3. 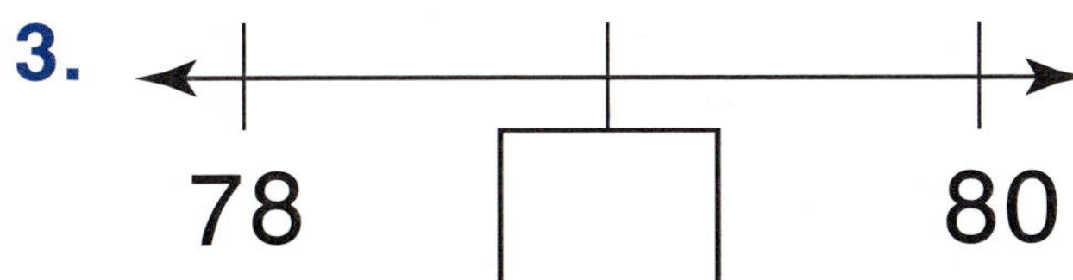

78   80

4. 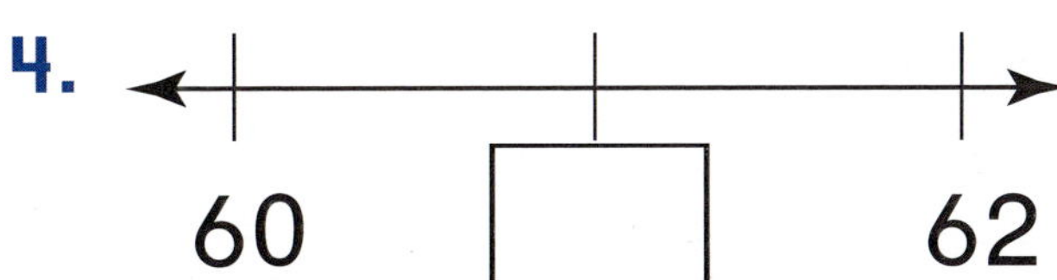

60   62

5. 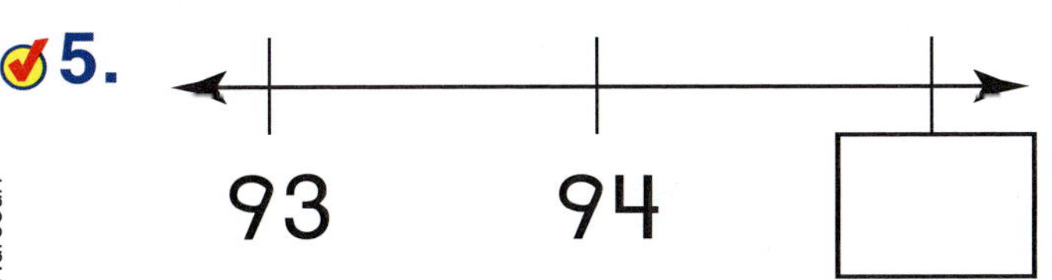

93   94

6. 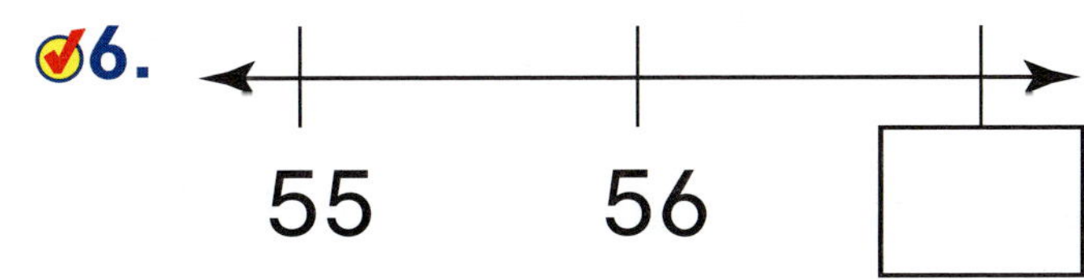

55   56

7. **Math Talk** What number is just after 100? Explain.

1.1.1 Count, read, write, order, rename and compare whole numbers to at least 100. **1.1.2** Name the number that is one more than or one less than any number to at least 100.

Write the numbers that are just before, between, or just after.

1. 27   28   29

27 is just before 28.
29 is just after 28.

2. ___   52   ___

3. ___   20   ___

4. ___   76   ___

5. ___   69   ___

6. 96   ___   ___   ___   100

Math Board

Problem Solving: Application

Write the numbers that are just before, just after, or between.

7. ___   43

8. 89   ___

9. 36   ___   ___   39

10. 70   ___

11. ___   30

12. 48   ___   ___   51

Use the words **before**, **after**, and **between** to describe the missing numbers in Exercise 9.

At Home Write a 2-digit number, such as 46 or 90. Have your child identify the number that is just before and just after. Write two numbers that skip a number in between, such as 54 and 56. Ask your child to name the number between.

Chapter 9 Lesson 7

Order 3 Numbers

Compare groups of numbers to put them in order.

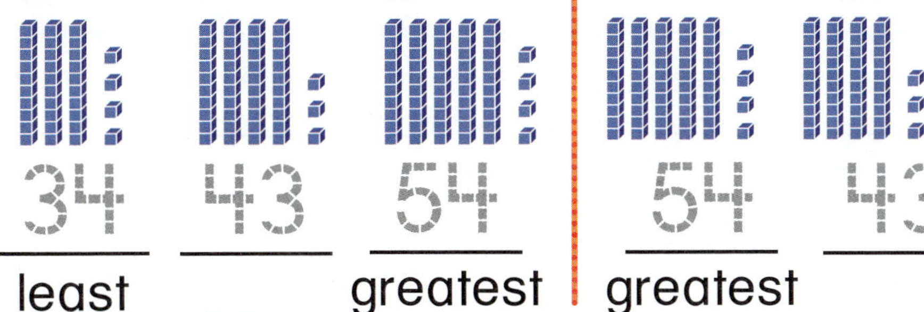

Write the numbers in order.

	Least to Greatest	Greatest to Least
62 26 46	1. 26 46 62	2. 62 46 26
45 64 51	3. ___ ___ ___	4. ___ ___ ___
38 43 36	5. ___ ___ ___	6. ___ ___ ___
80 90 85	7. ___ ___ ___	8. ___ ___ ___
74 47 57	9. ___ ___ ___	10. ___ ___ ___

11. **Math Talk** Which number is greatest? Explain.

1.1.1 Count, read, write, order, rename and compare whole numbers to at least 100.

Write the numbers in order.

	Least to Greatest	Greatest to Least
67 60 76	1. _60_ _67_ _76_	2. _76_ _67_ _60_
56 35 42	3. ____ ____ ____	4. ____ ____ ____
31 29 37	5. ____ ____ ____	6. ____ ____ ____
74 82 96	7. ____ ____ ____	8. ____ ____ ____
53 63 48	9. ____ ____ ____	10. ____ ____ ____
65 77 70	11. ____ ____ ____	12. ____ ____ ____
95 92 98	13. ____ ____ ____	14. ____ ____ ____

Math Board

Problem Solving: Real World

Use the clues to write the numbers in order.

15. Sue has the number between 77 and 79.
The number just after 86 belongs to Nell.
Ray has the number just before 100.
Ken has a number between 60 and 58.

87

78   59

99

____ ____ ____ ____
Ray   Nell   Sue   Ken

Describe how the numbers are ordered.

At Home Write three 2-digit numbers, such as 47, 28, and 63. Have your child write the numbers in order from least to greatest and then in order from greatest to least.

Count Forward and Backward

▶ We Learn

Count forward from 63.

63, _64_, _65_, _66_, _67_

Count backward from 63.

63, _62_, _61_, _60_, _59_

▶ Share and Show

Count forward. Write the numbers.

1. 78, _79_, _80_, _81_, _82_   2. 23, ____, ____, ____, ____

3. 47, ____, ____, ____, ____   4. 11, ____, ____, ____, ____

5. 30, ____, ____, ____, ____   ✓6. 96, ____, ____, ____, ____

Count backward. Write the numbers.

7. 22, _21_, _20_, _19_, _18_   8. 10, ____, ____, ____, ____

9. 86, ____, ____, ____, ____   10. 55, ____, ____, ____, ____

11. 41, ____, ____, ____, ____   ✓12. 74, ____, ____, ____, ____

13. **Math Talk** Explain how to find the number just before 30. What is the number?

Count forward or backward. Write the numbers.

1. 51, 50, <u>49</u>, <u>48</u>, <u>47</u>, <u>46</u>, <u>45</u>, <u>44</u>, <u>43</u>, <u>42</u>

2. 82, 83, ____, ____, ____, ____, ____, ____, ____, ____

3. 30, 29, ____, ____, ____, ____, ____, ____, ____, ____

4. 18, 17, ____, ____, ____, ____, ____, ____, ____, ____

5. 37, 38, ____, ____, ____, ____, ____, ____, ____, ____

6. 68, 69, ____, ____, ____, ____, ____, ____, ____, ____

7. 50, 51, ____, ____, ____, ____, ____, ____, ____, ____

8. 99, 98, ____, ____, ____, ____, ____, ____, ____, ____

Math Board

Problem Solving: Algebra

9. Find the missing numbers.
   Write the number on each boat.

How did you find the number on the first boat?

At Home Have your child count forward and backward four numbers from 31. Repeat for 69 and 93.

Chapter 9 Lesson 9

Skip Count by Twos, Fives, and Tens

Skip count the leaves by twos to find how many.

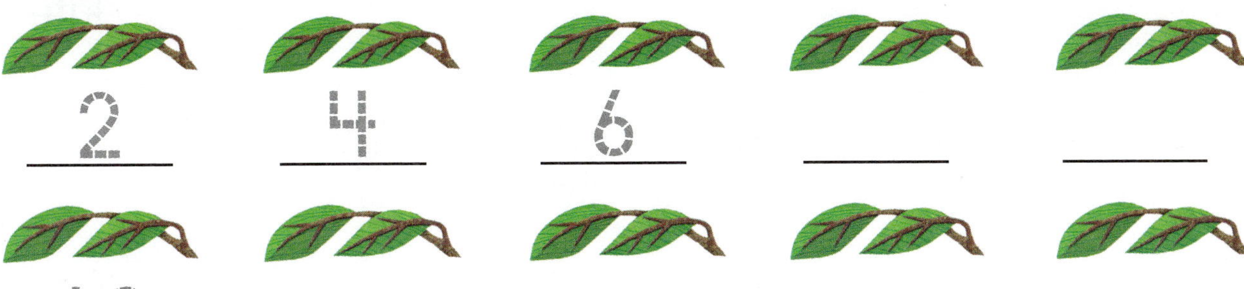

2   4   6   ____   ____

12   ____   ____   ____   ____ leaves

Skip count the petals by fives to find how many.

1.
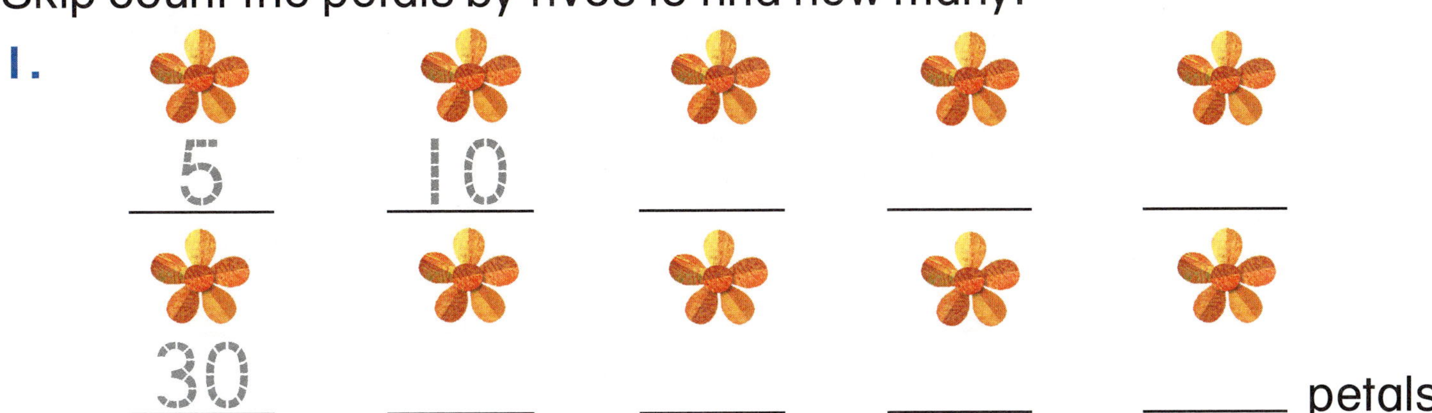

5   10   ____   ____   ____

30   ____   ____   ____   ____ petals

Skip count the fingers by tens to find how many.

2.
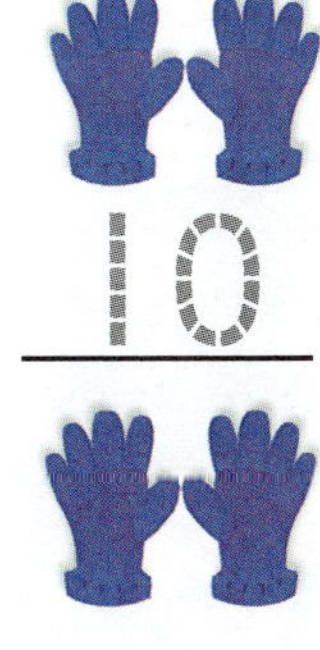 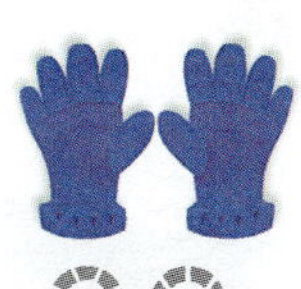  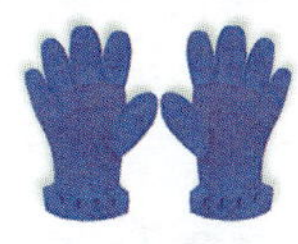 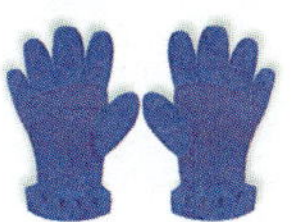

10   20   ____   ____   ____

 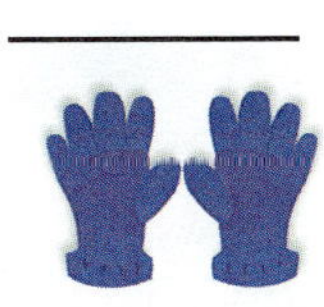 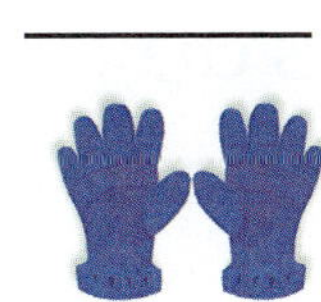 

____   ____   ____   ____   ____ fingers

3. **Math Talk** Look at Exercise 1. Describe the pattern that helps you count the petals.

1.1.1 Count, read, write, order, rename and compare whole numbers to at least 100. **1.2.2** Create, extend, and give a rule for number patterns using addition.

Skip count to find how many.

1.

2 ____ ____ ____ ____ ____ ____ ____ kites

2.

5 ____ ____ ____ ____ ____ ____ flowers

3.

10 ____ ____ ____ ____ ____ ____ toes

Skip count. Write the missing numbers.

4. 2, 4, ____, ____, ____, 12, 14, ____, 18

5. 5, ____, 15, 20, ____, ____, 35, ____, ____

6. ____, 20, 30, ____, ____, ____, 70, ____, 90

Math Board

Problem Solving: Application

7. Solve.

Each ladybug has 5 spots.
How many spots do
6 ladybugs have in all?

_____ spots

What skip counting pattern do you
notice when you count by fives?

Algebra: Skip Count on a Hundred Chart

Name _______________________

▶ **We Learn**

Write the missing numbers. Count by fives. Use  to color the numbers you say.

Start on 5. Count forward by fives.

1	2	3	4	5	6	7	8	9	
11	12	13	14		16	17	18	19	
21	22	23	24		26	27	28	29	
31	32	33	34		36	37	38	39	
41	42	43	44		46	47	48	49	
51	52	53	54		56	57	58	59	
61	62	63	64		66	67	68	69	
71	72	73	74		76	77	78	79	
81	82	83	84		86	87	88	89	
91	92	93	94		96	97	98	99	

▶ **Share and Show** **Math Board**

1. Count again. Count by tens.
   Use to circle the numbers you say.

2. **Math Talk** Describe a pattern you see in the chart.

1. Write the missing numbers. Count by twos.
Use ✏ to circle the numbers you say.

1		3		5		7		9	
11		13		15		17		19	
21		23		25		27		29	
31		33		35		37		39	
41		43		45		47		49	
51		53		55		57		59	
61		63		65		67		69	
71		73		75		77		79	
81		83		85		87		89	
91		93		95		97		99	

Math Board

Problem Solving: Reasoning

2. Write the missing numbers.

	10	15			30	

What pattern do you see in the numbers?

At Home Have your child explain how to use the hundred chart to count by twos and by tens.

Algebra: Identify Number Patterns

You can find a skip count pattern in these numbers.

20, 22, 24, _26_, _28_, _30_, _32_, _34_

Find the pattern. Write the numbers.

1. 46, 48, 50, ______, ______, ______, ______, ______

2. 15, 20, 25, ______, ______, ______, ______, ______

3. 30, 40, 50, ______, ______, ______, ______, ______

4. 8, 10, 12, ______, ______, ______, ______, ______

5. 60, 65, 70, ______, ______, ______, ______, ______

6. 74, 76, 78, ______, ______, ______, ______, ______

7. 25, 35, 45, ______, ______, ______, ______, ______

8. **Math Talk** What pattern helps you find the next number? What is the number?

64, 66, 68, ____

Find the pattern.
Write the missing numbers.

1. 18, 20, _22_, 24, 26, _28_, 30, _32_, _34_

2. 44, _____ 48, 50, _____, _____, 56, 58, _____

3. 30, 35, _____, 45, 50, _____, _____, 65, _____

4. 55, _____, _____, 70, 75, _____, 85, _____, 95

5. 20, _____, 40, 50, 60, _____, 80, _____, _____

6. 5, 15, 25, _____, _____, 55, 65, _____, _____

7. 66, 68, _____, _____, 74, _____, _____, 80, 82

8. _____, 50, 55, _____, _____, 70, 75, 80, _____

9. 74, _____, 78, 80, _____, 84, 86, _____, _____

10. _____, _____, 30, _____, 50, 60, _____, 80, 90

Problem Solving: Reasoning

Find the pattern. Write the numbers.

11. 12, 10, 8, _____, _____, _____

12. 25, 20, 15, _____, _____, _____

13. 50, 40, 30, _____, _____, _____

Describe the patterns in Exercises 11, 12, and 13.

At Home Write the number pattern 14, 16, 18. Have your child identify the pattern and then say or write the next three numbers. Repeat for 35, 40, 45 and 50, 60, 70.

Problem Solving Workshop

Strategy: Find a Pattern

You can solve a problem by finding a pattern. Complete a chart to find a number pattern.

Find a Pattern

There are 6 kites.
There are 5 bows on each kite.

Complete a chart to find out how many bows there are.

THINK The rule for this pattern is count by fives.

number of kites	1	2	3	4	5	6
number of bows	5	10	15	20	25	30

6 kites have ____30____ bows.

Math Talk What patterns do you see in the chart? Explain.

1.2.2 Create, extend, and give a rule for number patterns using addition.

Use the Strategy • Find a Pattern

There are 2 wheels on a bicycle.
How many wheels are there on 8 bicycles?

? Unlock the Problem

bicycle

What do I need to find?

how many wheels
are on 8 bicycles

What information do I need to use?

2 wheels on each bicycle

Show how to solve the problem.

Find a pattern rule.
Complete the chart.

number of bicycles	1	2	3	4	5	6	7	8
number of wheels	2	4	6					

How many wheels are there on 8 bicycles?

8 bicycles have _______ wheels.

 How does finding a pattern help you solve the
problem? Explain.

Problem Solving Strategy Practice

Find the pattern. Complete the chart to solve.

1. A starfish has 5 arms.
How many arms are on 7 starfish?

starfish

number of starfish	1	2	3	4	5	6	7
number of arms	5	10					

7 starfish have _______ arms.

2. Each box has 10 crayons.
How many crayons are in 8 boxes?

crayon box

number of boxes	1	2	3	4	5	6	7	8
number of crayons	10	20						

8 boxes have _______ crayons.

3. Try Your Own Problem

A rabbit has 2 ears.

How many ears do _______ rabbits have?

rabbit

number of rabbits						
number of ears						

_______ rabbits have _______ ears.

At Home Ask your child to look at Exercise 1, tell how many arms 10 starfish have, and explain the pattern.

Mixed Strategy Practice

Choose a way to solve each problem. Show your work.

Choose a Strategy
- Draw a Picture
- Find a Pattern
- Make a Model
- Write a Number Sentence

1. There are 9 red kites flying. There are 6 blue kites flying. How many more red kites than blue kites are flying?

kite

______ more red kites

2. Jan cut 4 figures out of paper. Matt cut out double that number of figures. How many figures did Matt cut out?

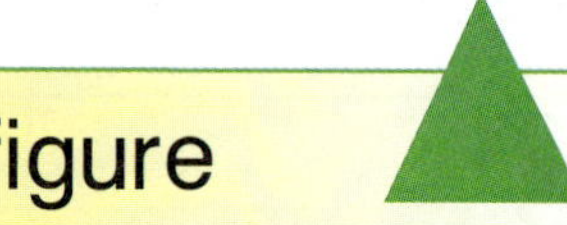

figure

______ figures

3. Dave had 10 pencils. He put some in his desk. He still has 1 pencil. How many pencils did Dave put in his desk?

pencil

______ pencils

4. Tia puts 2 muffins in each bag. How many muffins does she need for 5 bags?

muffin

______ muffins

Name ______________________________

Extra Practice

Write <, >, or =. Use 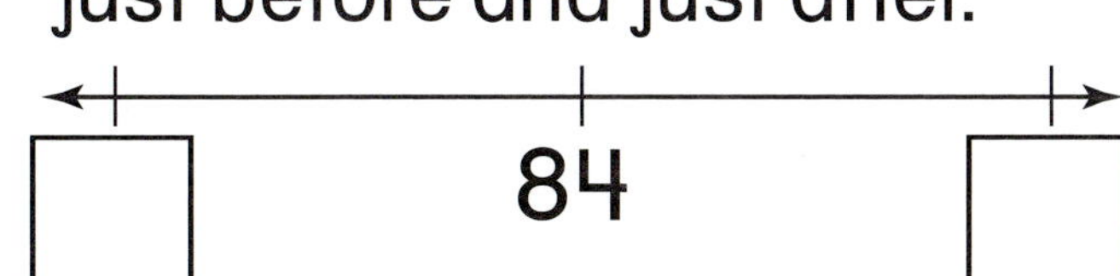 if you need to.

1. 76 ◯ 67   **2.** 94 ◯ 90   **3.** 81 ◯ 86

Find the pattern. Write the numbers.

4. 4, 6, _____, 10, 12, _____, 16, 18, _____

5. 20, _____, _____, 35, 40, _____, 50, _____, 60

6. 16, 26, _____, 46, 56, _____, _____, 86, _____

7. Write the numbers that are just before and just after.

☐   84   ☐

8. Write the number that is between.

74   ☐   76

Write the numbers in order.

	Least to Greatest	Greatest to Least
73 65 68	**9.** _____ _____ _____	**10.** _____ _____ _____

Problem Solving

Find the pattern. Complete the chart to solve.

11. A cat has 2 eyes. How many eyes do 8 cats have?

number of cats	1	2	3	4	5	6	7	8
number of eyes	2	4						

8 cats have _____ eyes.

Technology
Use HMH Mega Math, Numberopolis, *Cross Town Number Line*, Levels K, O, S, Q.

Multistep Problems
Chapter 9

1. Look at the numbers. 1.1.1

54 27 38 59 81 73

- Write the numbers in order from least to greatest.

- Circle the numbers that are less than 70.

- Compare the numbers you did not circle.
  Use $>$, $<$, or $=$.

Show your work.

2. Maria has 4 tomato plants. There are 5 tomatoes on each plant. How many tomatoes are on 4 plants?

1.2.2

- Draw a picture and complete the chart to solve.

Number of plants	1	2	3	4
Number of tomatoes	5	10		

# Standards Quick Check

Write the number that is 1 more.

1. | 64 | | **2.** | 29 | |

Write the number that is 1 less.

3. | | 45 | **4.** | | 87 |

Write the number that is 10 more.

5. 80 | (blank)   **6.** 72 | (blank)

Write the number that is 10 less.

7. (blank) | 45   **8.** (blank) | 26

Circle the number that matches the clue.

1. It is less than 90.
10 less is 73.

63   89   83

2. It has more than 6 tens.
1 more is 72.

75   71   61

3. It is less than 49.
10 less is 38.

49   48   58

4. It has 6 tens.
1 less is 59.

60   58   69

July 4 is Independence Day in the United States. People dress in red, white, and blue. They fly U.S. flags. Music bands march in rows at parades. At night, fireworks explode in bright colors.

Count by 2s, 5s, or 10s to solve.

1. Sue Jung colors 2 U.S. flags on each placemat. She makes 4 placemats. How many flags does she color?

————, ————, ————, ————

______ flags

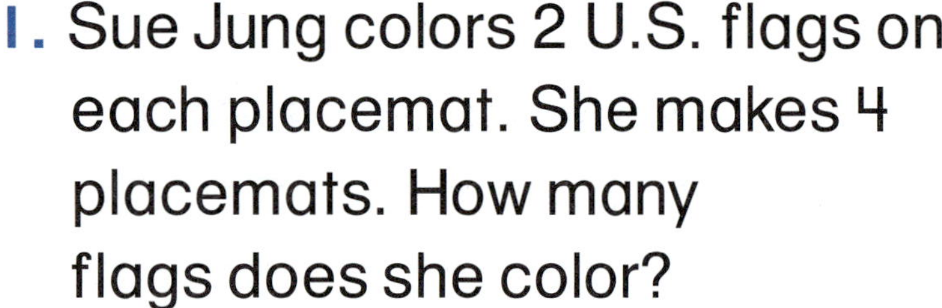

2. Conrad sees a marching band. 10 people march in each row. The band has 4 rows. How many people are marching?

————, ————, ————, ————

______ people

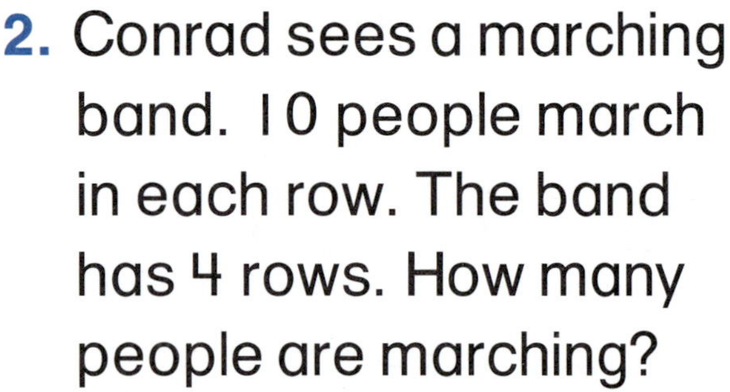

Looking Ahead to the ISTEP+
Chapter 9

Mark the best answer for questions 1–5.

1. Which is the missing number?

1.1.1

______ > 64

○ 14
○ 46
○ 63
○ 72

2. What symbol completes the sentence? *1.1.1*

17 ◯ 17

○ >
○ —
○ =
○ <

3. What number is just after 27?

1.1.1, 1.1.2

○ 26
○ 28
○ 29
○ 72

4. Which is the missing number?

1.1.1

______ < 23

○ 19
○ 24
○ 32
○ 33

5. Which number comes between? *1.1.1, 1.1.2*

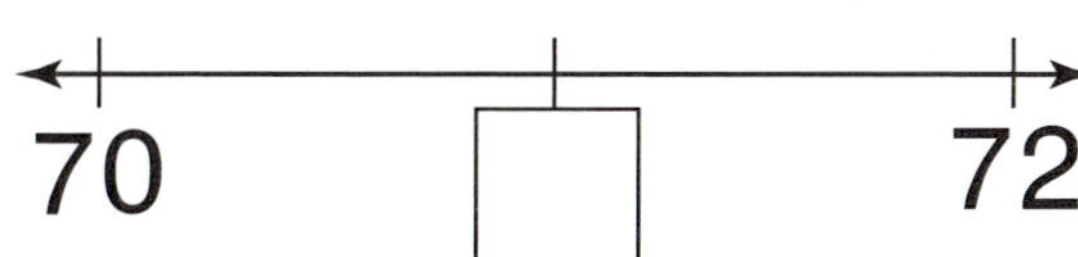

○ 74
○ 73
○ 71
○ 69

Mark the best answer for questions 6–8.

6. What number is just before 54? 1.1.1. 1.12

- ○ 44
- ○ 53
- ○ 55
- ○ 64

7. Count forward. Which number comes next? 1.1.1, 1.1.2

92, 93, 94, 95, _____

- ○ 90
- ○ 91
- ○ 94
- ○ 96

8. What are the missing numbers? 1.1.1, 1.2.2

2, 4, ___, ___, 10, ___

- ○ 5, 6, 11
- ○ 6, 7, 12
- ○ 6, 8, 11
- ○ 6, 8, 12

Open Ended

Use the table. Write each number.

Compare. Write >, <, or =. 1.1.1

Number of Rainy Days Each Month	
Month	**Rainy Days**
October	18
November	23
December	21

9. _____ ◯ _____

October   November

10. _____ ◯ _____

November   December

📖 Reading and Writing Math

Draw a quick picture to help you compare numbers. Circle the words that make the sentence true.

1. is greater than ($>$)

95 is less than ($<$) 85.

2. is less than ($<$)

65 is equal to ($=$) 68.

3. is greater than ($>$)

56 is equal to ($=$) 56.

4. Writing Math Choose three of the numbers that you compared. Order the numbers from least to greatest.

____

Identify Teen Numbers

Rainy Day Riddles

Answer this riddle.

I have 1 ten.
I have 9 ones.
What number am I?

I ten means the number is a teen number. The teen number with 9 ones is 19.

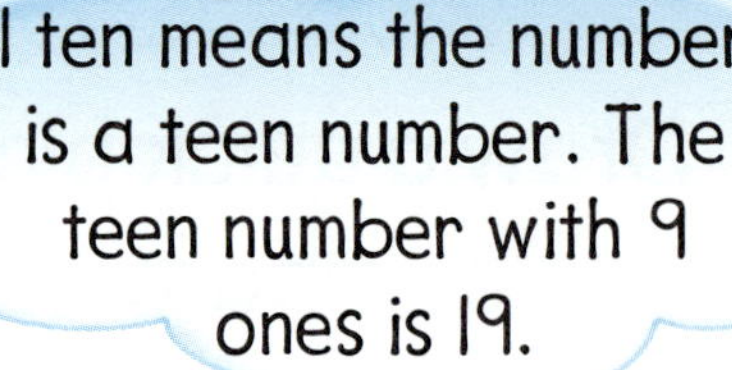

Reasoning

Write the number that answers each riddle.

1. I have 1 ten.
I have 2 ones.
What number am I? __12__

2. I have 1 ten.
I have 6 ones.
What number am I? ______

3. I am greater than 13.
I am less than 15.
What number am I? ______

4. I am less than 19.
I am greater than 17.
What number am I? ______

On Your Own

Write numbers to complete each riddle.
Then ask a partner to solve your riddles.

5. I am greater than ______.

I am less than ______. ______

What number am I?

6. I have ______ ten.

I have ______ ones. ______

What number am I?

Math Talk Look at Exercise 4. How do you use
each clue to solve the riddle? Explain.

THE WORLD ALMANAC FOR KIDS

Soccer Balls

Do you play soccer? Soccer is the most popular sport in the world. There are soccer teams for children 5 years old and older.

A soccer ball shows 32 figures. 20 figures have 6 sides. 12 figures have 5 sides.

FACT·ACTIVITY

Solve. Write the numbers.

1 start

0

end

10   Add 2.

2 start

0

end

15   Add 3.

3

end

16

Add 4.

start

0

4 Try Your Own

end

Add ☐.

start

0

Math Talk What would the end number be if the rule in Exercise 1 were Add 5? Explain.

Bounce Around

Not all bounces are the same.
Superballs have more bounce.
Baseballs have less bounce.
What does the picture below
show you?

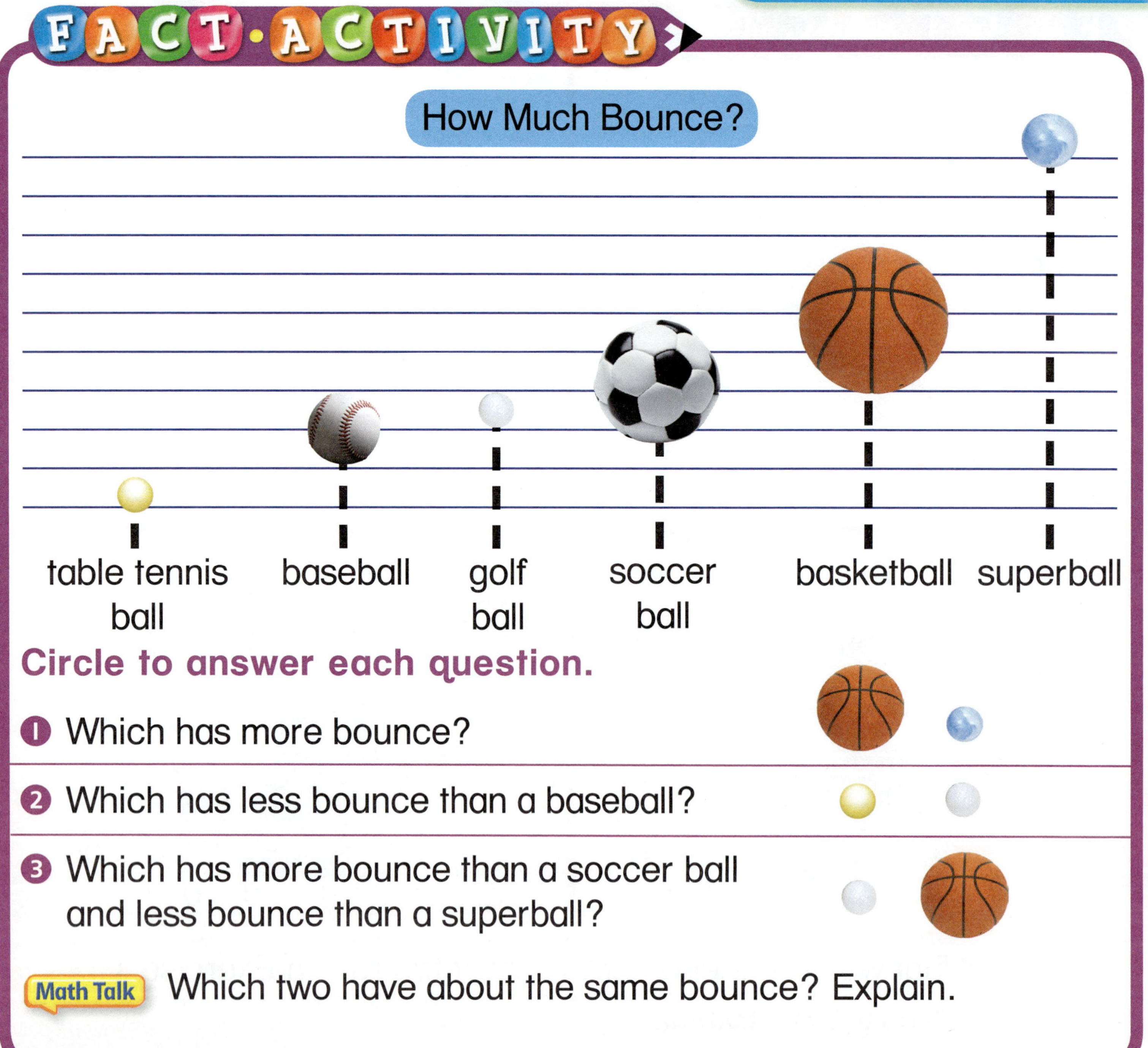

Circle to answer each question.

❶ Which has more bounce?

❷ Which has less bounce than a baseball?

❸ Which has more bounce than a soccer ball
and less bounce than a superball?

Math Talk Which two have about the same bounce? Explain.

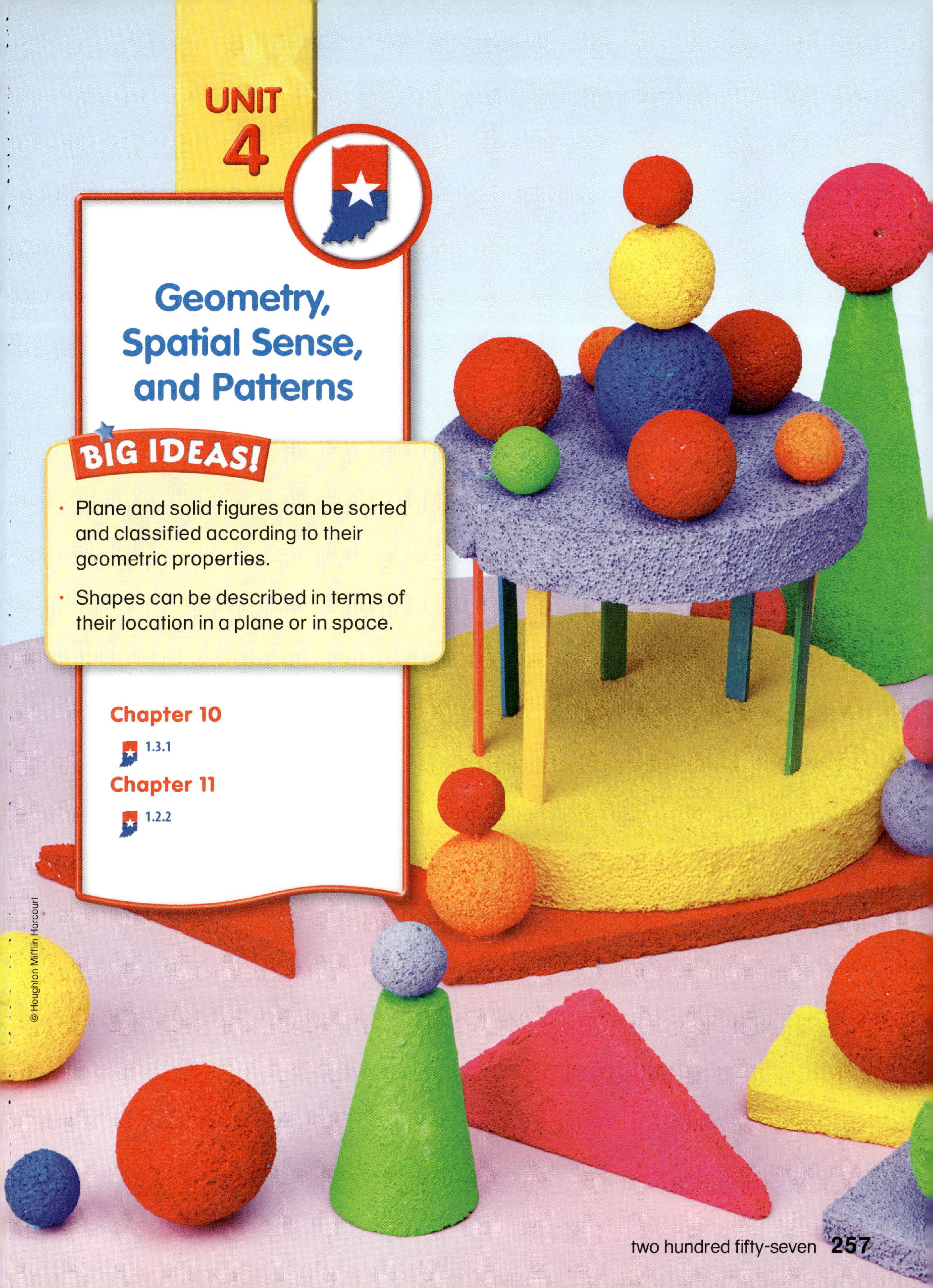

UNIT
4

Geometry,
Spatial Sense,
and Patterns

BIG IDEAS!

• Plane and solid figures can be sorted and classified according to their geometric properties.

• Shapes can be described in terms of their location in a plane or in space.

Chapter 10
1.3.1
Chapter 11
1.2.2

Figures and Colors

1. Put your counter on the big brush.

2. Take turns. Spin. Move your counter to that figure or color.

3. If your spin lands on the brush, skip a turn.

4. The first player to move his or her counter all the way around the palette wins.

What You Need
2 players 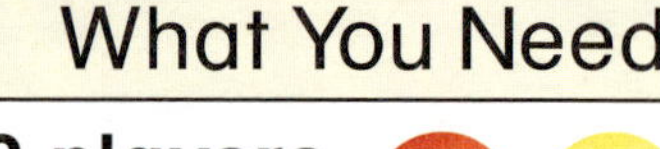  

Math at Home

Dear Family,

My class started Unit 4 today. In the next few chapters, I will learn about geometry, spatial sense, and patterns. Here are some vocabulary words and activities for us to share.

From,

____

Vocabulary

 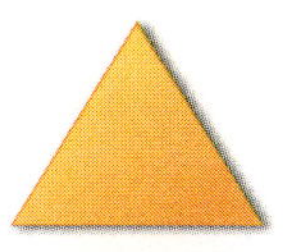 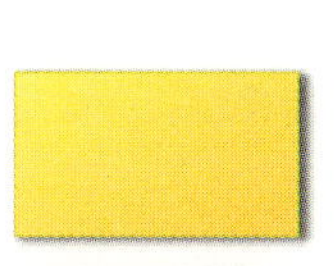 

circle   **triangle**   **rectangle**   **square**

These are all **plane figures**.

cube   **cone**   **cylinder**   **pyramid**

sphere   **rectangular prism**

These are all **solid figures**.

Family Math Activity

Play "I Spy" to help your child practice position words (above, behind, left, right, and so on) and figure names. Give clues until your child guesses the object you have in mind. Then switch roles and let your child give you clues.

Literature

These books link to the math in this unit. Look for them at the library.

- **All Sorts of Shapes**
  by Hannah Reidy
  Illustrated by Emma Dodd
  (*Picture Window Books, 2005*)

- **Bigger, Better, Best!**
  by Stuart J. Murphy
  Illustrated by Marsha Winborn

- **Super Sand Castle Saturday**
  by Stuart J. Murphy
  Illustrated by Julia Gorton

Math at Home

Chapter 10

Have your child invent and draw a friendly robot, using only designated geometric figures such as triangles, rectangles, and circles.

Discuss with your child what the world would be like if there were no round things. Have your child illustrate a story on this theme.

Chapter 11

Hide various objects in safe places around the house. Give your child directions on where to find the objects, such as "below the table" or "to the left of the bed." Stay with your child as he or she searches, and discuss how your directions were helpful. Then, hide objects with your child, and ask your child how he or she would give directions on where to find them.

At Home These activities are designed for you to work with your child at home.

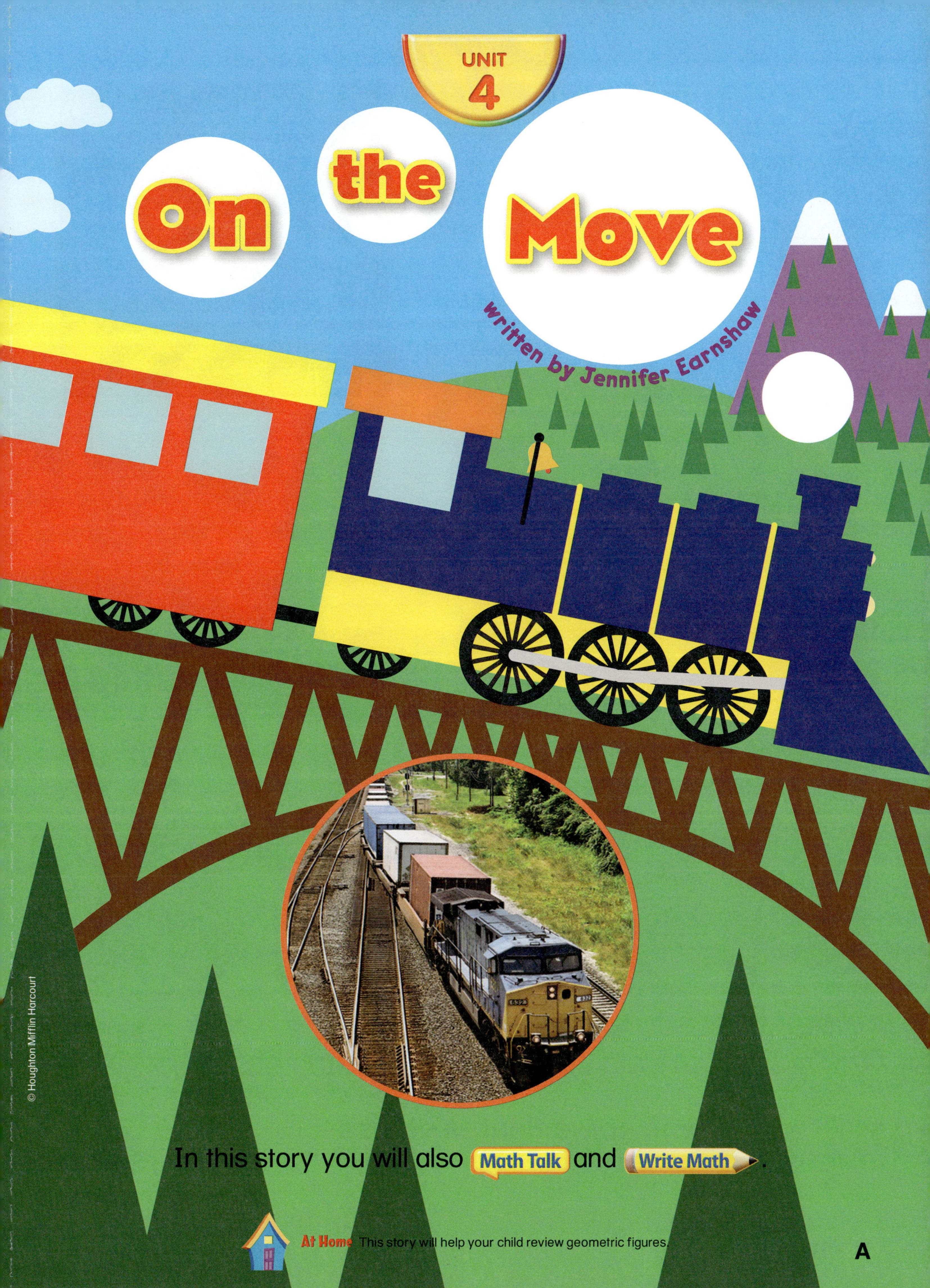

© Houghton Mifflin Harcourt

The train car waits for the engine.

Name some figures you see.

What will this train bring?

The big truck travels up the road.

Name some figures you see.

What will this truck bring?

The ship loads at the dock.

Name some figures you see.

D

What will this ship bring?

These trucks drive across town.

Name some figures you see.

What will these trucks bring?

E

The airplane arrives at the airport.

Name some figures you see.

What will this airplane bring?

My Math Story
Literature Activity

Think of another kind of truck that takes goods from one place to another. Draw a picture. Use circles, squares, triangles, or rectangles in your drawing.

Vocabulary Review

circle   triangle

square   rectangle

Write Math ▸ Write about your drawing.

Name _______________________________

Figure it Out

1. Draw an airplane.
Use some triangles and circles in your drawing.

2. Draw a train.
Use some rectangles and circles
in your drawing.

Write Math ➤ Choose 2 figures to use to draw
a ship. Draw the ship.

Solid and Plane Figures

Theme: In the Water

Fun Fact

Most of the water on Earth is salty or frozen.

Investigate

A beach ball has a curved surface. Name another curved object.

GO ONLINE Technology
Student pages are available in the Student eBook.

Show What You Know 

Sort by color.
Circle the figure that belongs in the group.

1.

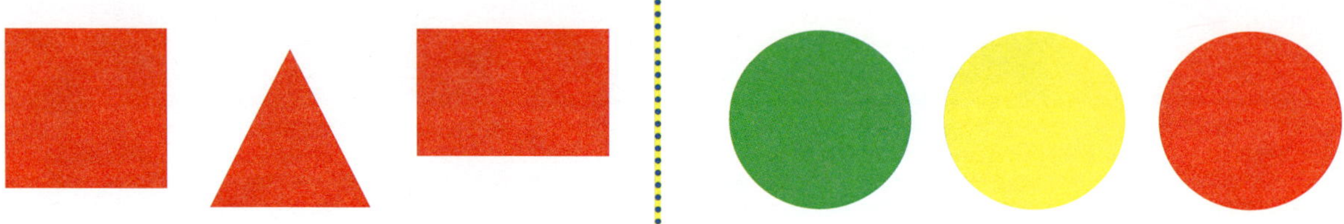

2.

Sort by size.
Mark an X on the object that does not belong.

3.

4.

 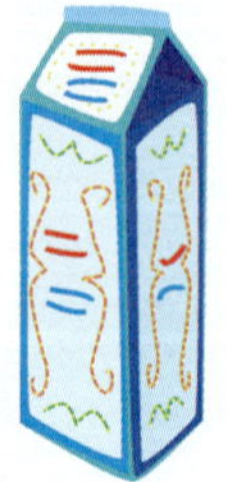  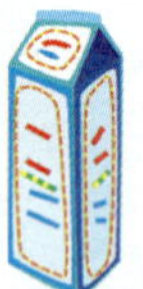

Chapter 10 Lesson 1
Solid Figures

These are some solid figures.

sphere	cone	cylinder
pyramid	rectangular prism	cube

Essential Question
How can you describe and classify solid figures?

Vocabulary
solid figure
sphere cylinder
cone   pyramid
cube
rectangular prism

Circle each cylinder.

1.

Circle each cone.

2.

Circle each rectangular prism.

3.
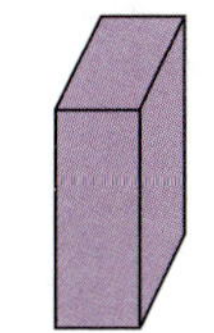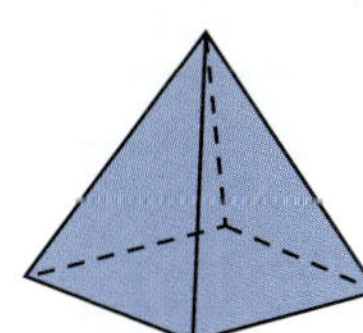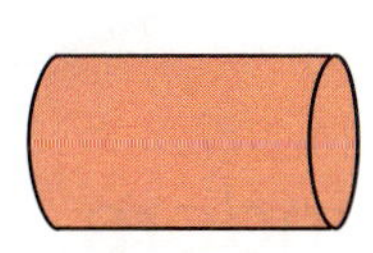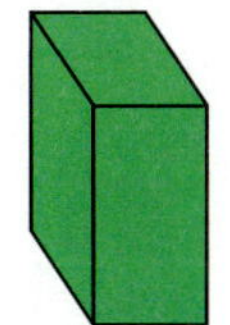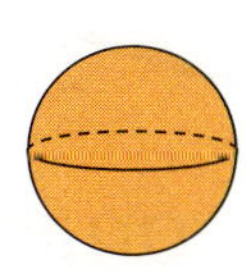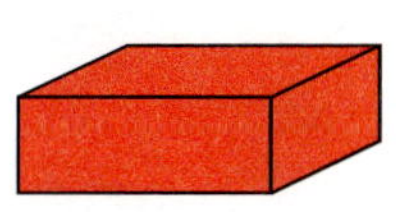

4. **Math Talk** How are all cylinders alike? Explain.

Circle each cube.

1.  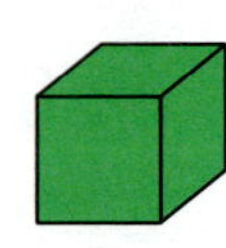 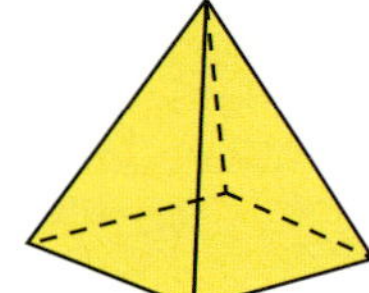 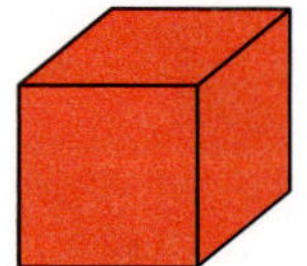 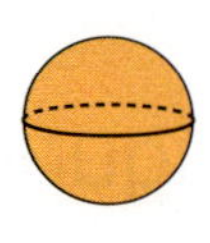 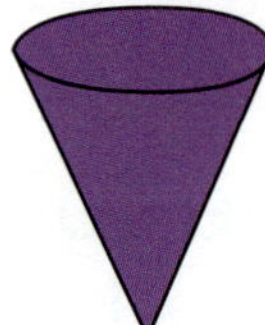 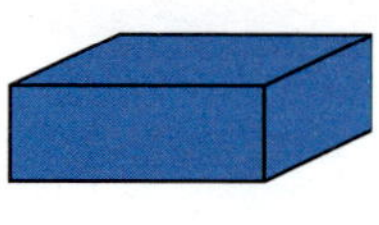

Circle each pyramid.

2. 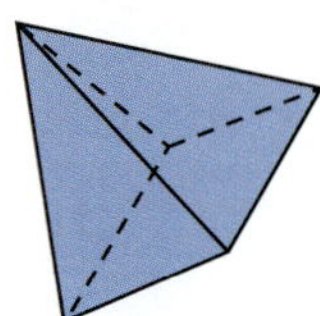 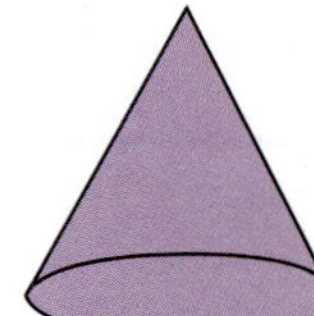 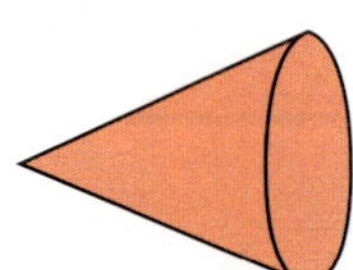 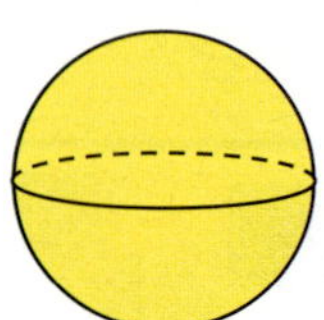 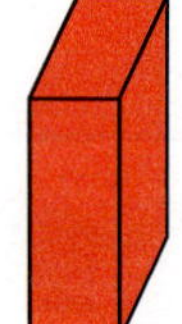 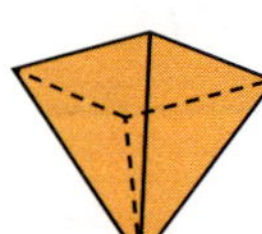 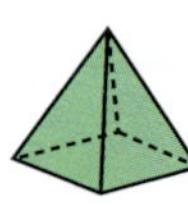

Circle each sphere.

3.  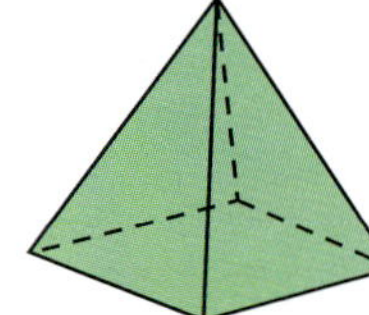 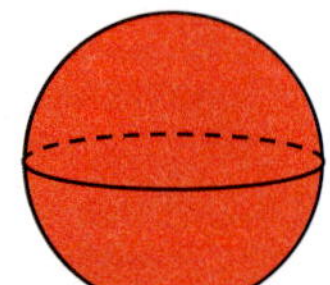 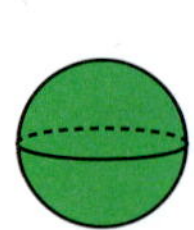 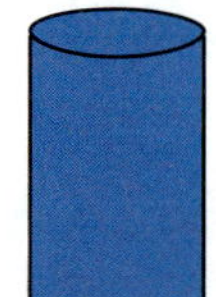  

Problem Solving: Reasoning

Circle the word to tell how these figures are sorted.

4. 

cones   pyramids

5. 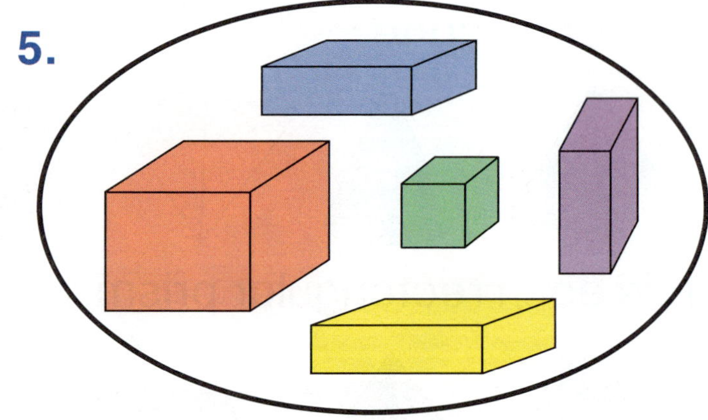

cylinders   rectangular prisms

Draw an object shaped like one of the solids on
this page. Write the name of the solid it shows.

Chapter 10 Lesson 2
Sort Solid Figures

 **Explore**

Some solids have a **curved surface**.

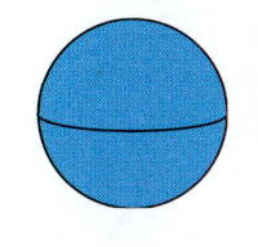

sphere

cone

cylinder

Some solids have **flat surfaces**.

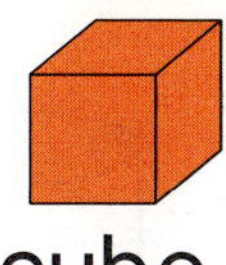

cube

pyramid

rectangular prism

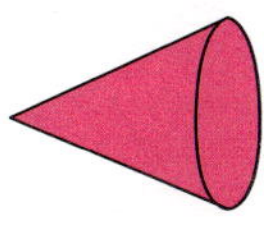

cone

cylinder

Some solids have both curved and flat surfaces.

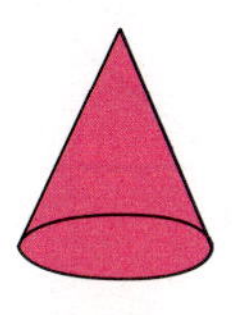

cone

cylinder

Connect

Use solids.

1. Circle each solid with only flat surfaces.

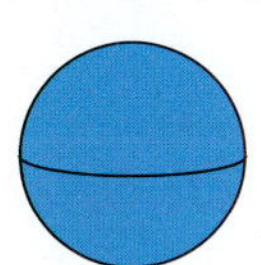 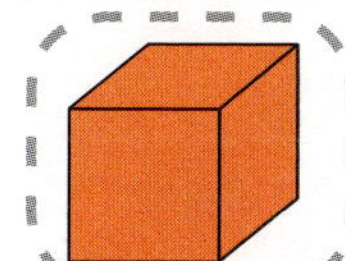  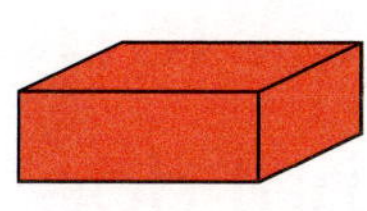 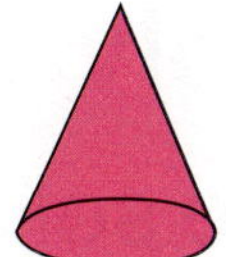 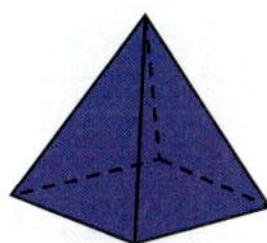

2. Circle each solid with only a curved surface.

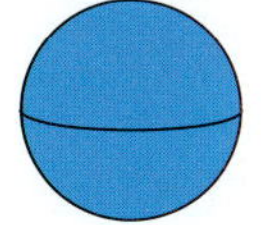   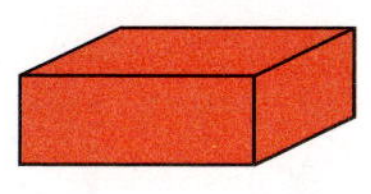 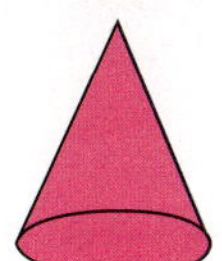 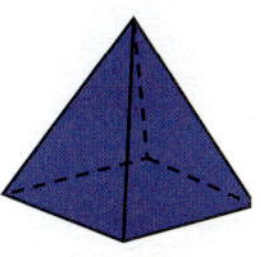

3. Circle each solid with both curved and flat surfaces.

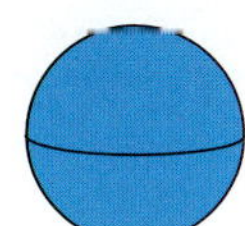 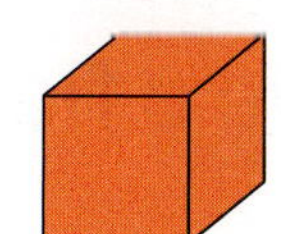 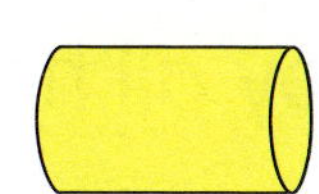 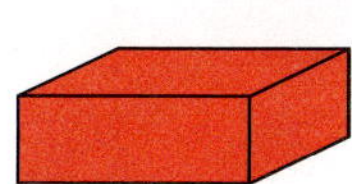 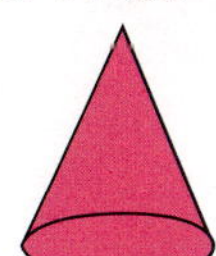 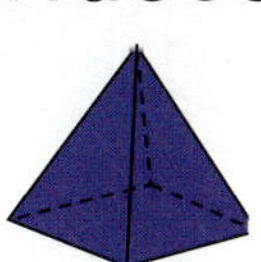

4. **Math Talk** How are a cone and a cylinder the same? How are they different?

Representation

Color the pictures. Use solids if you need.

1. I have only a curved surface.
2. I have only flat surfaces.
3. I have both curved and flat surfaces.

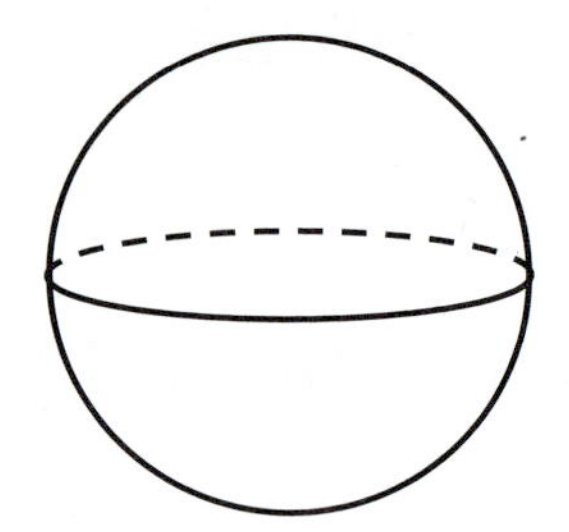 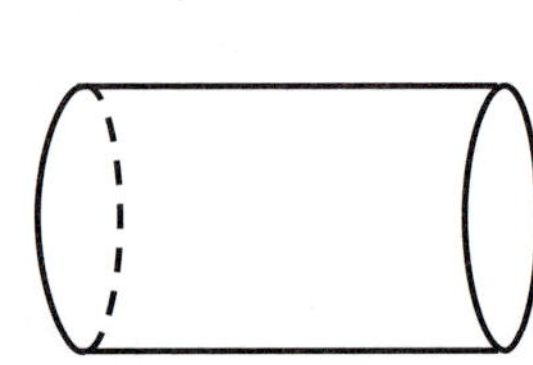 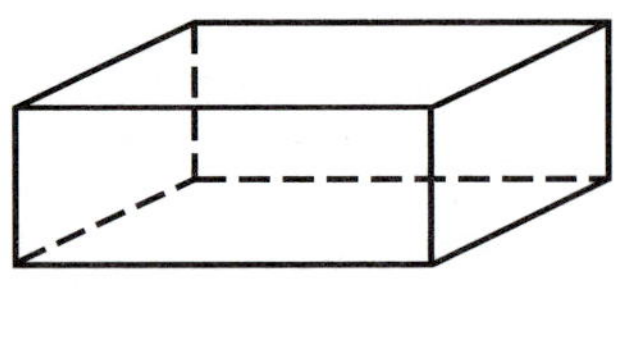 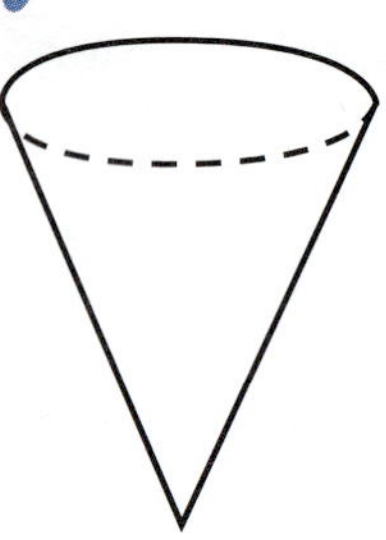

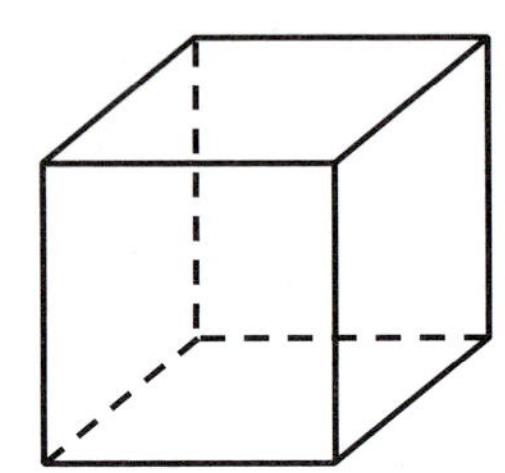 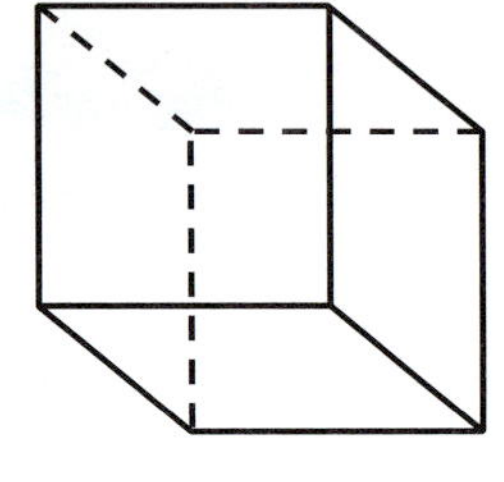 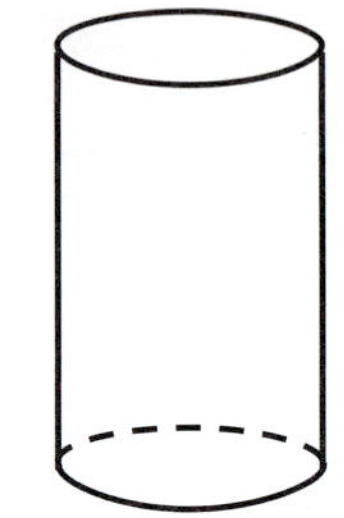 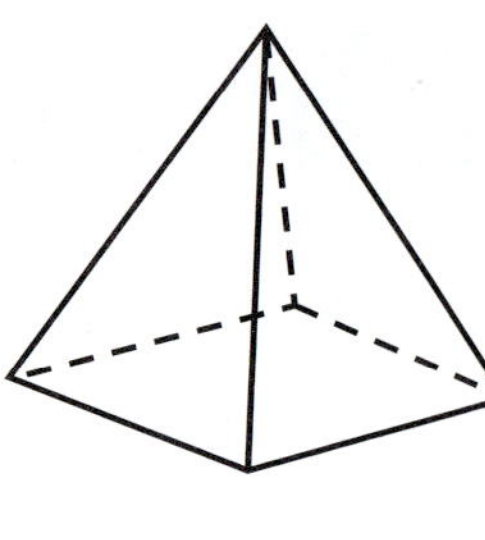

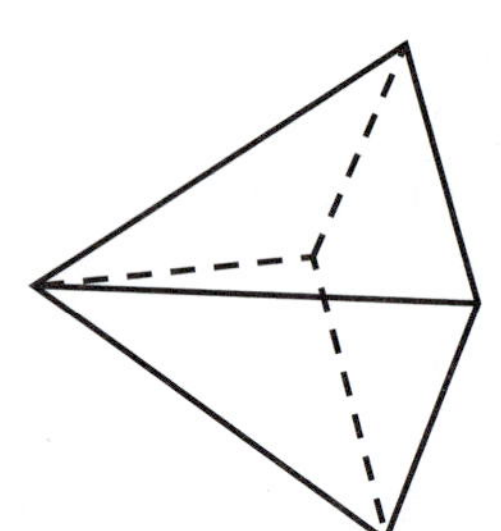 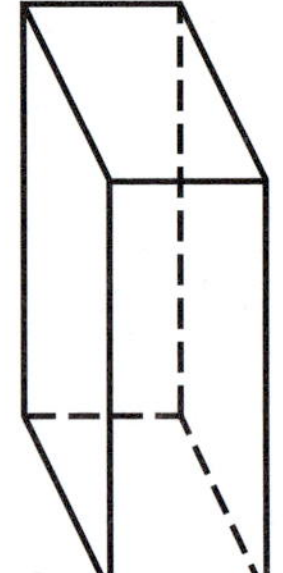 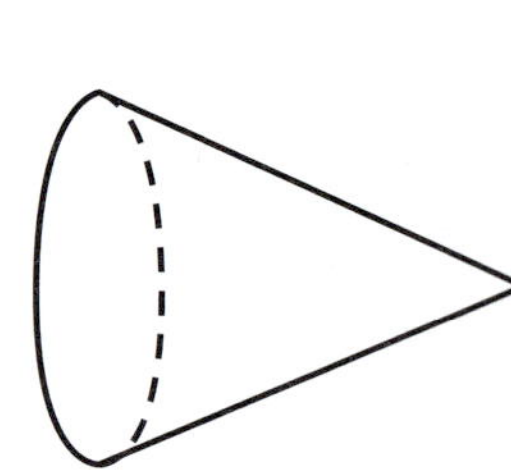 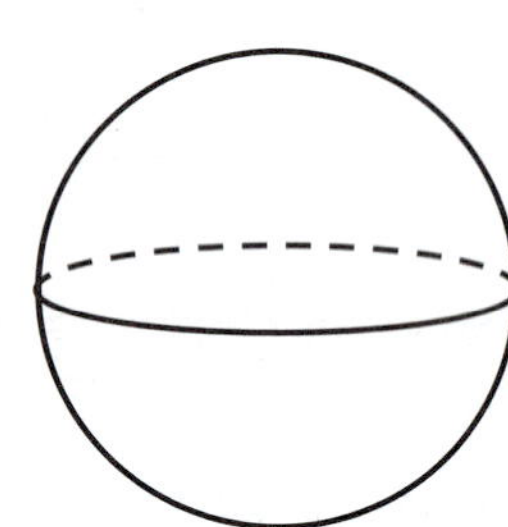

Problem Solving: Visual Thinking

4. Sort. Cross out one solid that does not belong.
   Circle the sentence that tells your sorting rule.

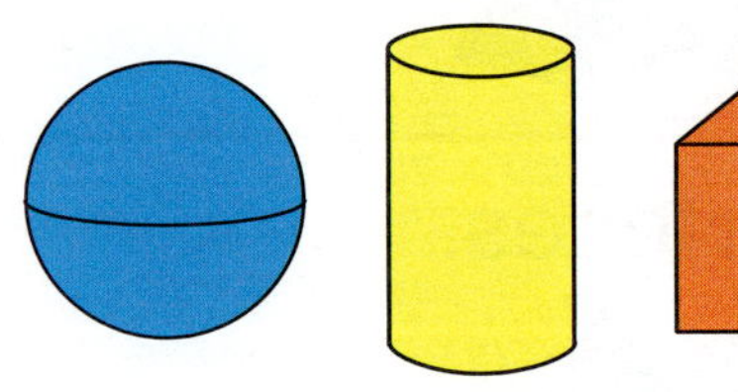

They all have a curved surface.

They all have a flat surface.

Use the other sorting rule to sort the four solids.
Which solid do you cross out? Explain.

Chapter 10 Lesson 3

Compare Solid Figures

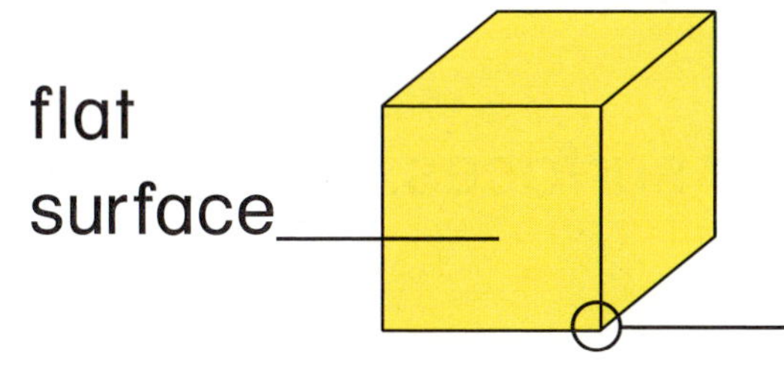

Use solids.

1. Circle each solid with 5 corners.

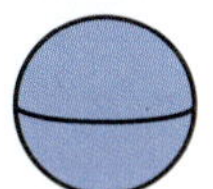  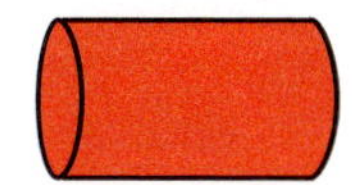 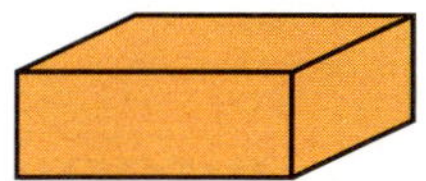  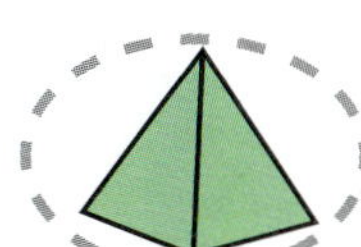

2. Circle each solid with 5 flat surfaces.

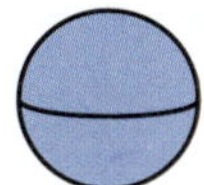 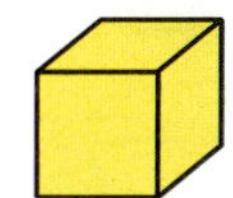    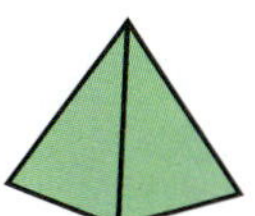

3. Circle each solid with 6 flat surfaces.

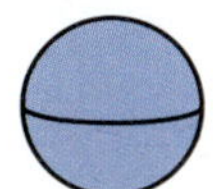 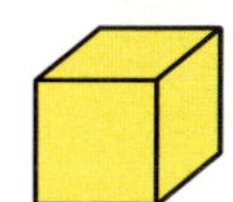 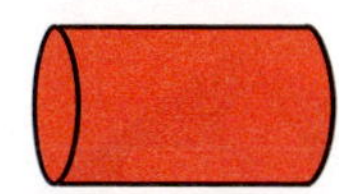 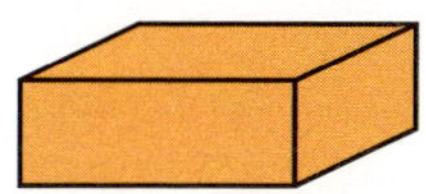 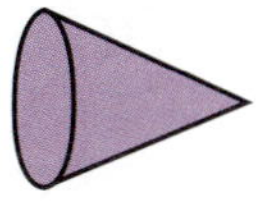 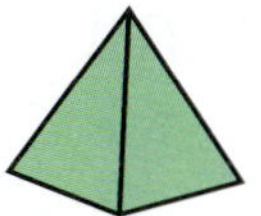

4. Circle each solid with 8 corners.

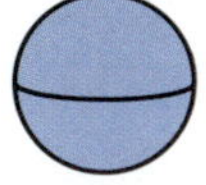 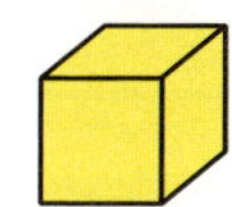 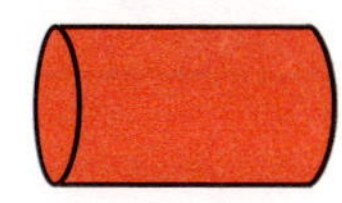 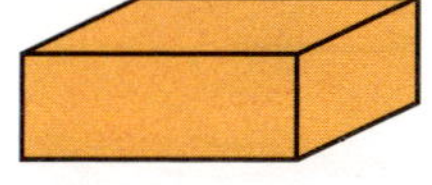  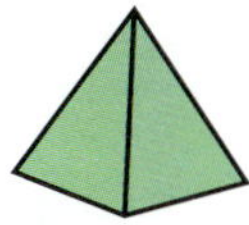

5. Circle each solid with 2 flat surfaces.

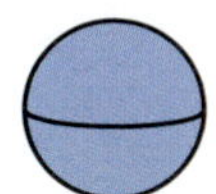 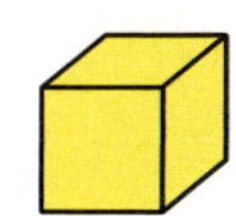 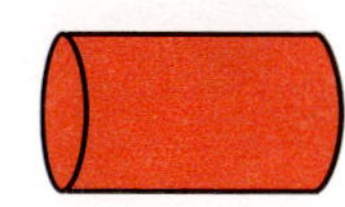   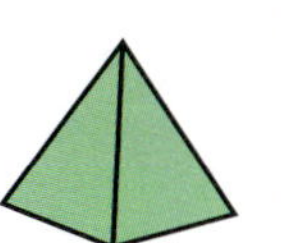

6. **Math Talk** How are a rectangular prism and a cube alike?

Representation

Use solids. Write the number of
flat surfaces and corners.

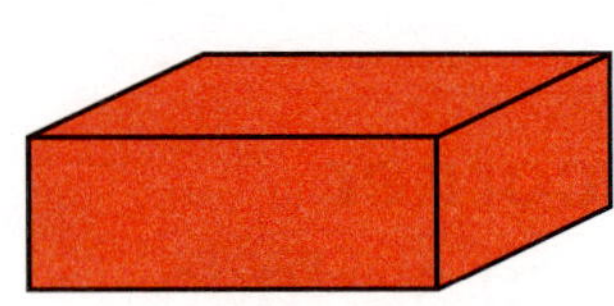

1. This rectangular prism has __6__ flat surfaces.

2. This rectangular prism has ______ corners.

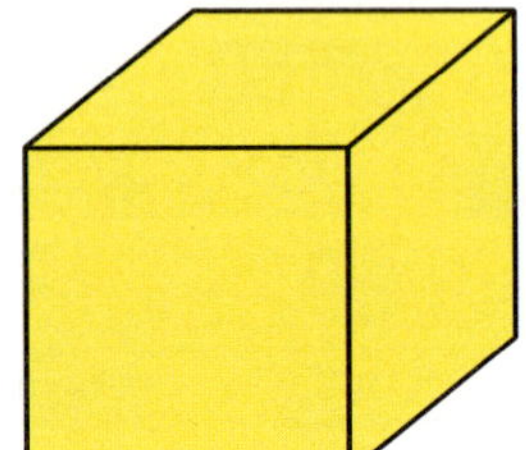

3. This cube has ______ flat surfaces.

4. This cube has ______ corners.

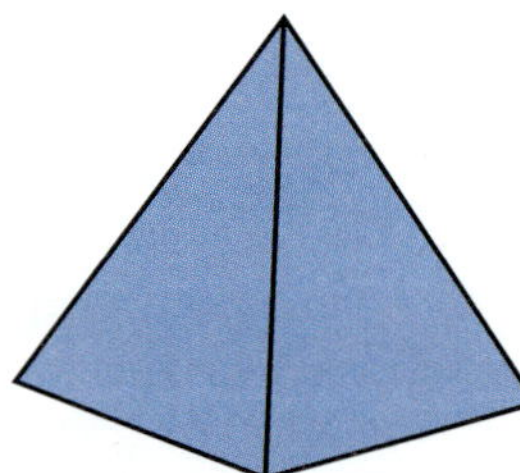

5. This pyramid has ______ flat surfaces.

6. This pyramid has ______ corners.

Problem Solving: Reasoning

Circle two objects that have the same
number of corners.

7.    

8.    

Draw something in your classroom that has
8 corners. Write the name of the solid it shows.

At Home Ask your child to count the corners and flat surfaces
on a tissue box. Have him or her tell the name of the solid it
shows.

Chapter 10 Lesson 4

Plane Figures on Solids

 **Explore**

Flat surfaces on solid figures are ==plane figures==.

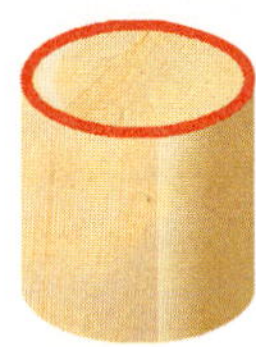
circle

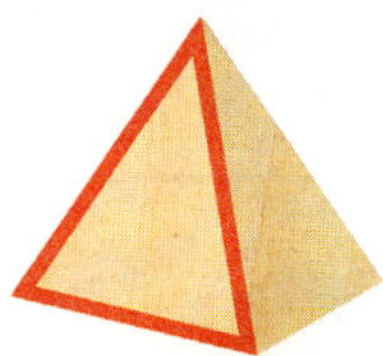
triangle

rectangle

square

Essential Question

What plane figures do you see on solid figures?

Vocabulary

==plane figure==
==circle==
==triangle==
==rectangle==
==square==

Connect

Trace around the solid.
Write the name of the figure you drew.

1. 

____
rectangle

2. 

____

✓3. 

____

✓4. 

____

5. **Math Talk** What figures can you trace
from a pyramid? Explain.

© Houghton Mifflin Harcourt

1.3.1 Identify, describe, compare, sort and draw triangles, rectangles, squares and circles in terms of their attributes. Use simple plane shapes to compose a given shape.

Circle the objects you could trace to make the figure.

1. 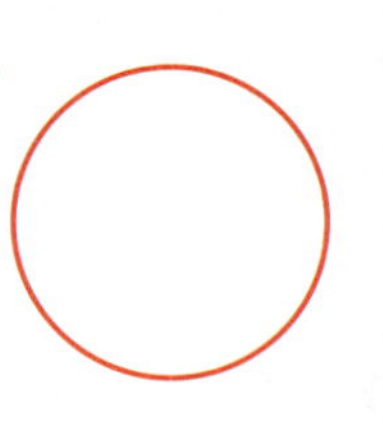     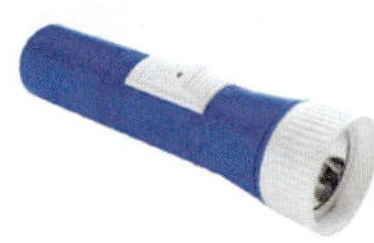

2. 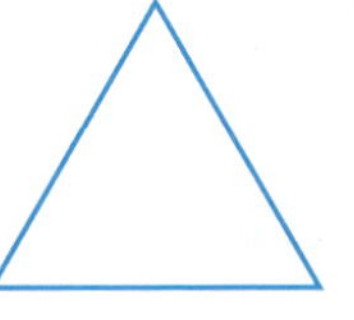     

3. 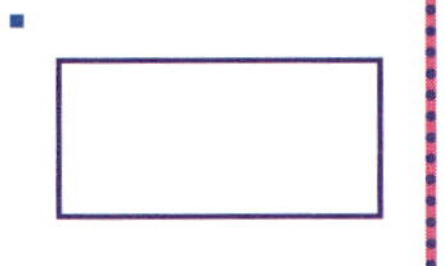   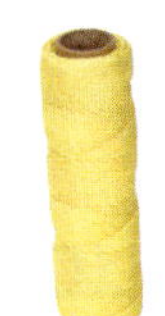  

4.      

Math Board **Problem Solving: Reasoning**

Connect the dots to draw each figure.
Color the square 🖍️. Color the triangle 🖍️.
Color the rectangle 🖍️.

5. 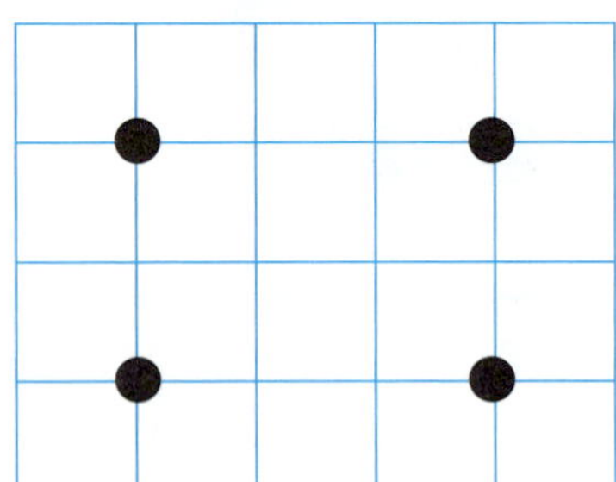 **6.** 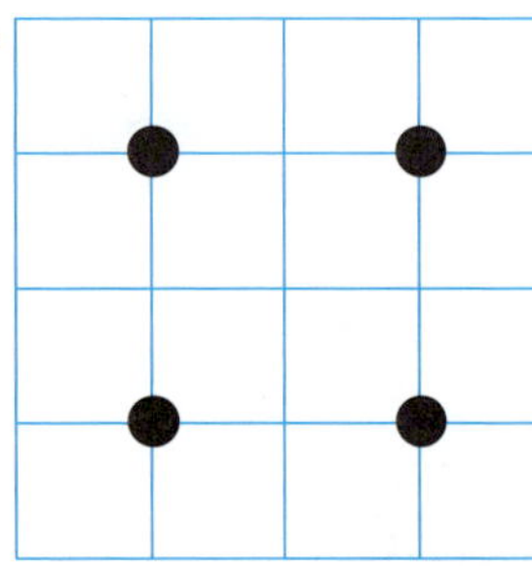 **7.** 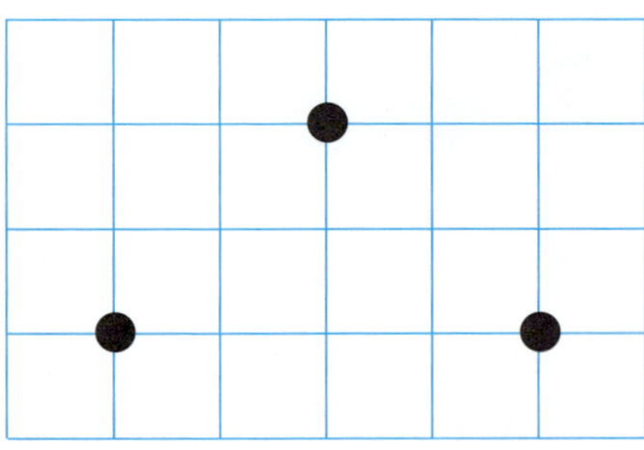

Describe what you notice about the square.

Chapter 10 Lesson 5

Open and Closed Figures

Essential Question
How can you identify open and closed figures?

Vocabulary
open
closed

See how the figures below are different.
Some figures are open and some are closed.

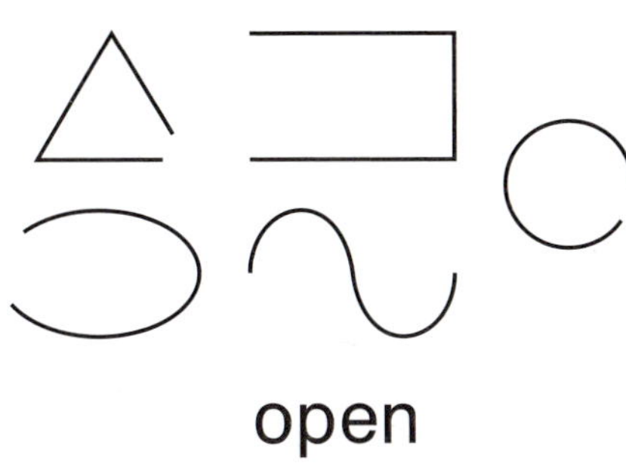

open

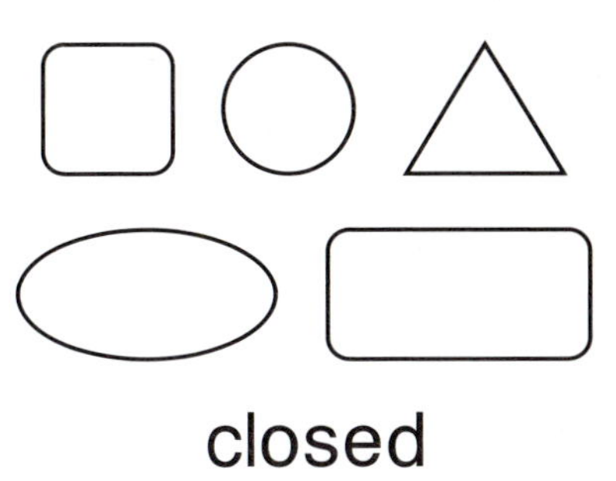

closed

Color each closed figure.
Circle each open figure.

1.  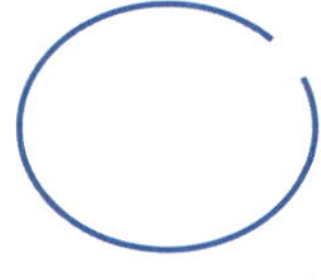 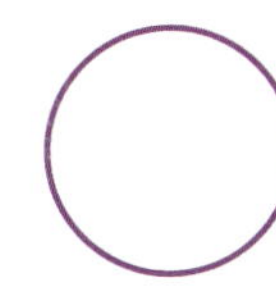

2.  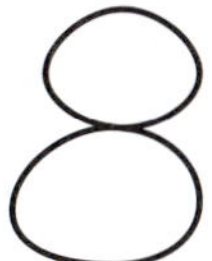  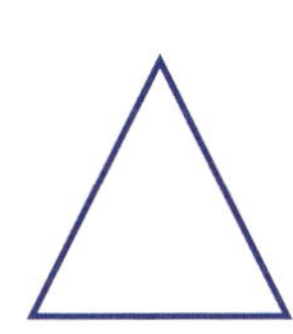

3.   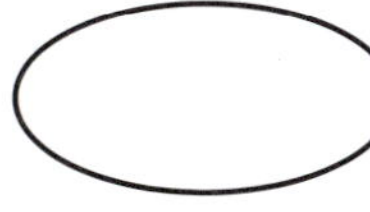 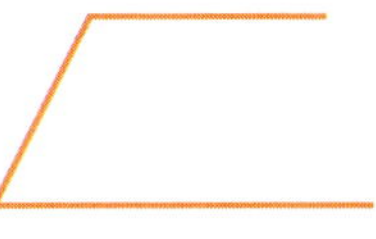

4. 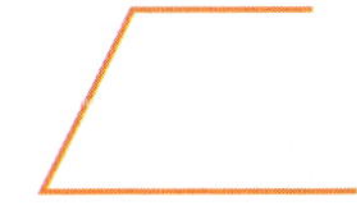   

5. **Math Talk** How can you tell if a figure is open or closed? Explain.

1.3.1 Identify, describe, compare, sort and draw triangles, rectangles, squares and circles in terms of their attributes. Use simple plane shapes to compose a given shape.

Color each closed figure.
Circle each open figure.

1.  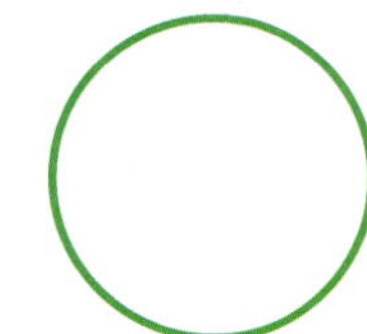  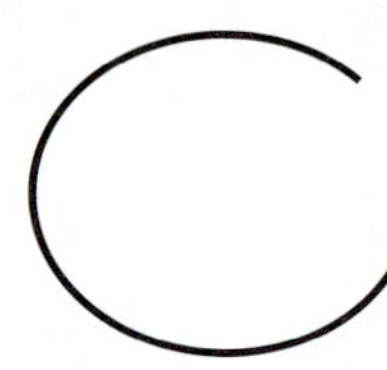

2. 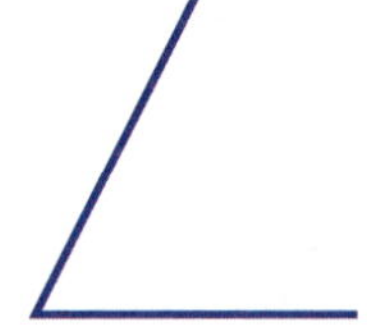  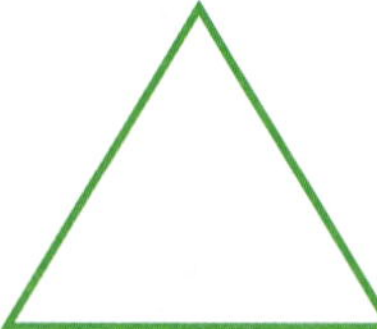 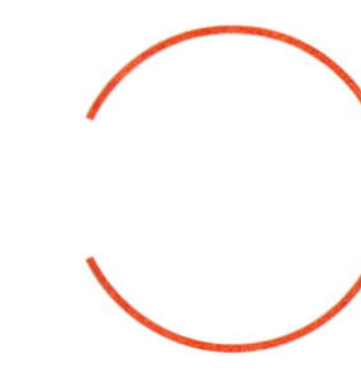

3.  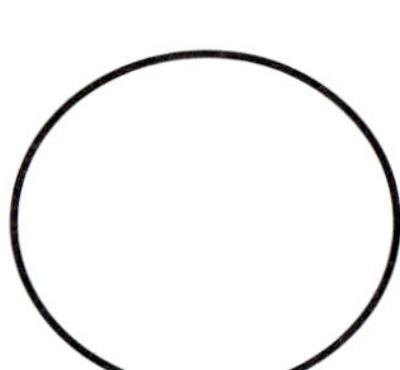 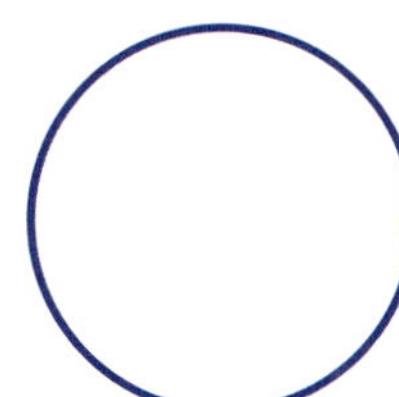 

Problem Solving: Reasoning

Circle the word that tells how these figures are sorted.

4. 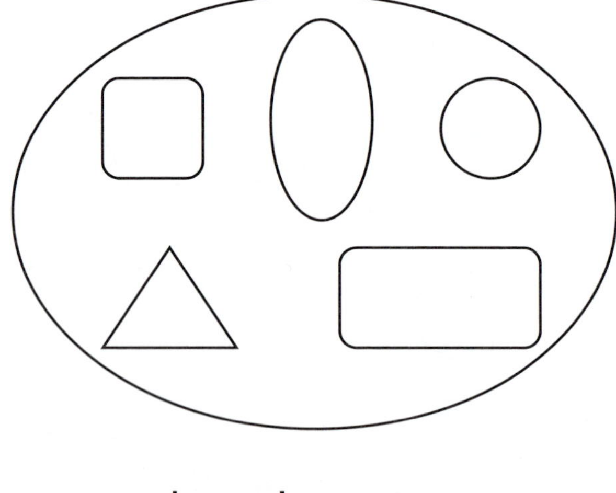

closed   open

5. 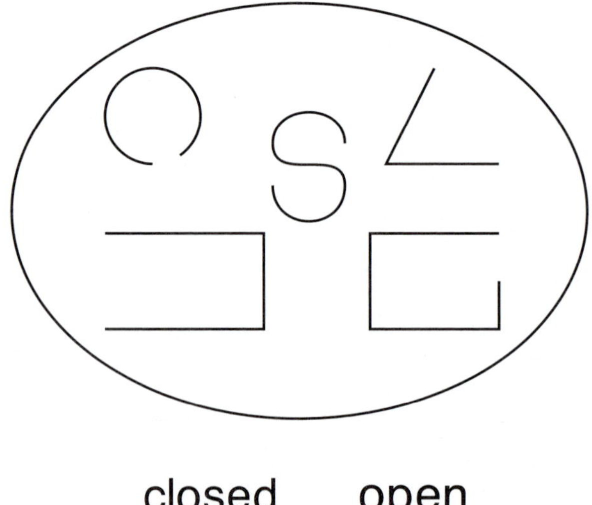

closed   open

Describe what you notice about the figures.

Chapter 10 Lesson 6

Sort Plane Figures

▶ **We Learn**

rectangle   square   circle   triangle

▶ **Share and Show** Math Board

1. Color each circle.

2. Color each square.

3. Color each rectangle.

4. **Math Talk** Which figures are triangles? Explain.

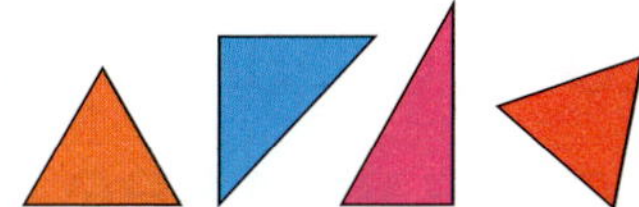

1.3.1 Identify, describe, compare, sort and draw triangles, rectangles, squares and circles in terms of their attributes. Use simple plane shapes to compose a given shape.

1. Color ◯ . **2.** Color ▢ . **3.** Color △ .

Math Board

Problem Solving: Reasoning

4. Draw a house. Use at least four different rectangles.

Look around your classroom. Write the name of a figure you see and draw a picture to show what it is.

Chapter 10 Lesson 7

Compare Plane Figures

▶ **Explore**

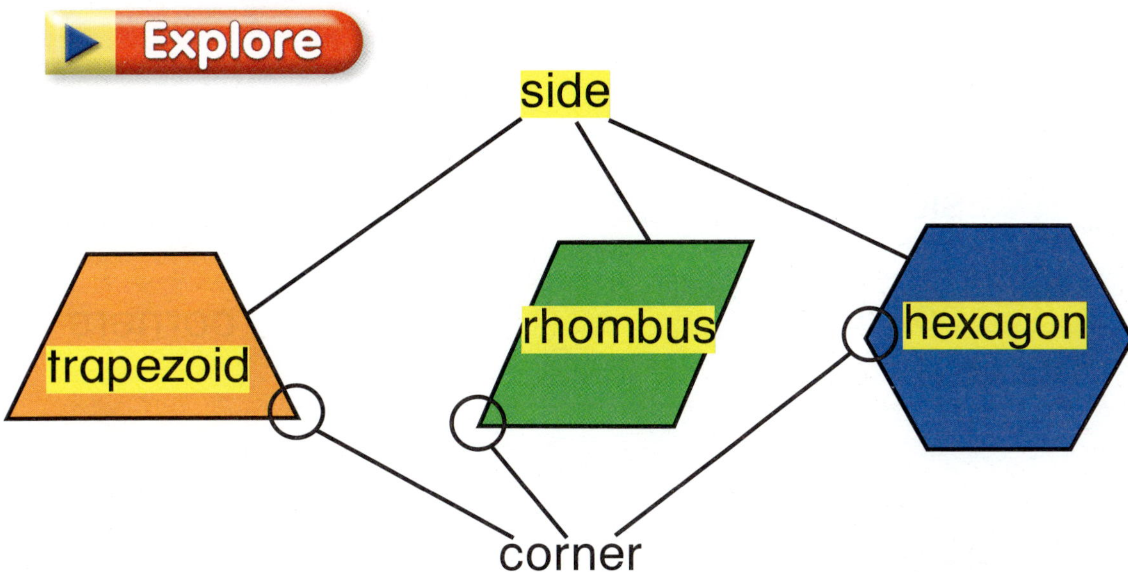

Essential Question
What attributes can you use to classify plane figures?

Vocabulary
trapezoid
rhombus
hexagon
side
corner

▶ **Connect**

Use pattern blocks to sort. Write the number of straight sides and corners.

	Plane Figure	Straight Sides	Corners
1.	hexagon		
2.	rhombus		
3.	square		
4.	trapezoid		
5.	triangle		

6. **Math Talk** Compare the figures in the chart. What is the same? Explain.

1.3.1 Identify, describe, compare, sort and draw triangles, rectangles, squares and circles in terms of their attributes. Use simple plane shapes to compose a given shape.

Use 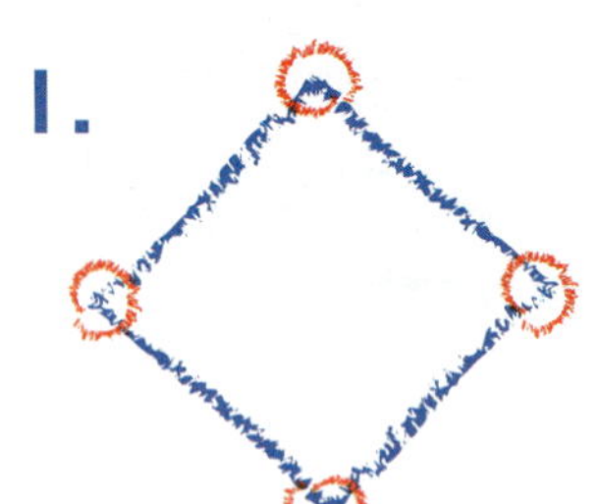 to trace each straight side.
Use 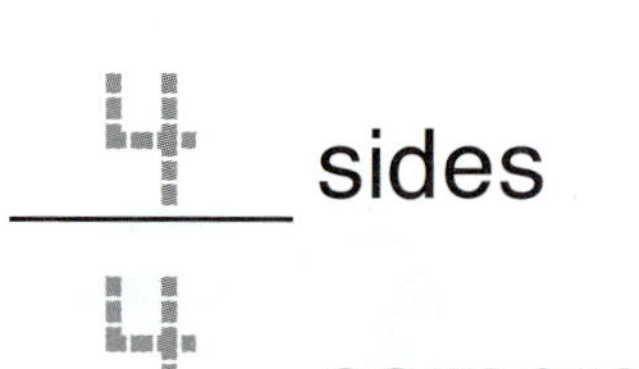 to circle each corner.
Write the number of sides and corners.

1. 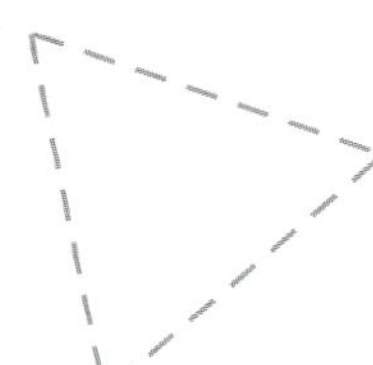

_____ 4 sides

_____ 4 corners

2.

_____ sides

_____ corners

3.

_____ sides

_____ corners

4.

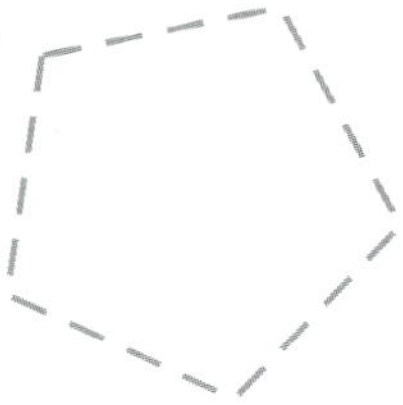

_____ sides

_____ corners

5.

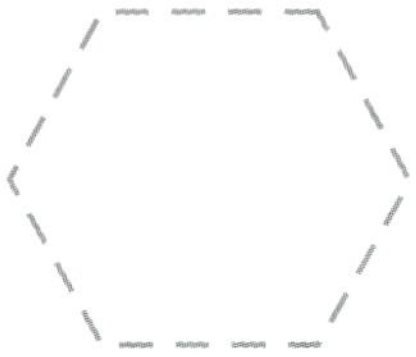

_____ sides

_____ corners

6.

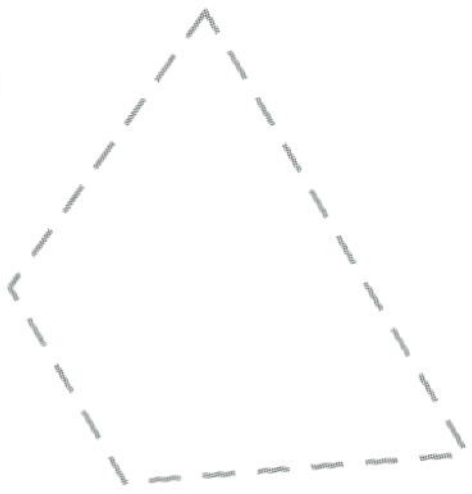

_____ sides

_____ corners

Problem Solving: Visual Thinking

Draw a picture to solve.

7. I am a figure with 3 straight sides and 3 corners.

8. I am a figure with 4 straight sides and 4 corners.

Look at Exercise 8. Draw a different figure to solve the problem. Explain.

At Home Have your child draw a square, rectangle, and triangle. For each figure, have him or her show you the sides and corners and tell how many of each there are.

Chapter 10 Lesson 8
Combine Plane Figures

▶ **Explore**

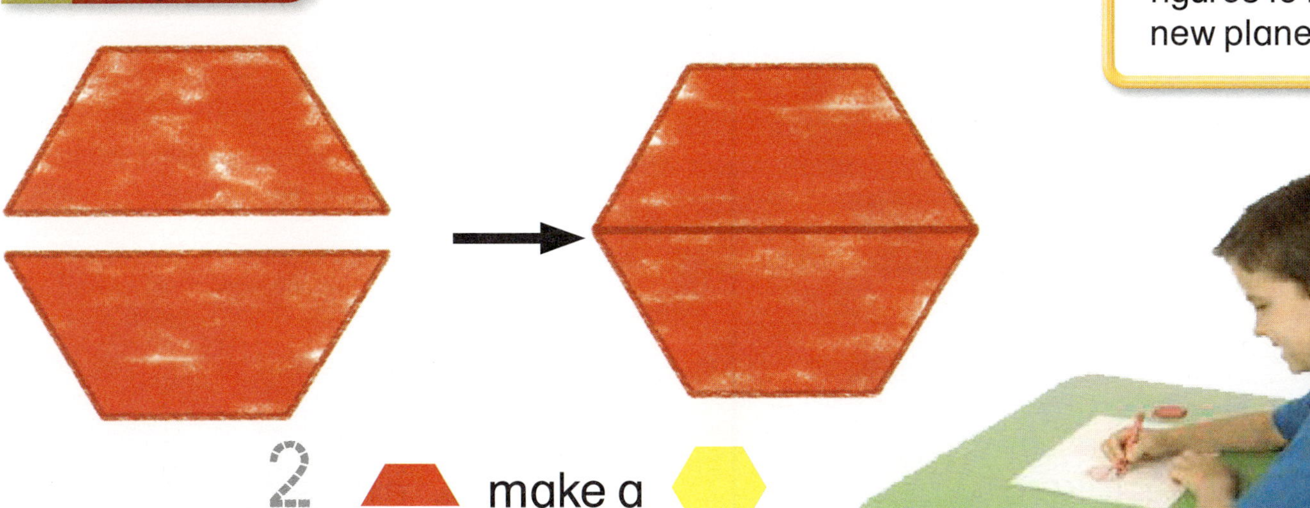

_2_  make a ⬡

▶ **Connect**

Use pattern blocks. Draw to show the blocks.
Write how many blocks you used.

1.

2.

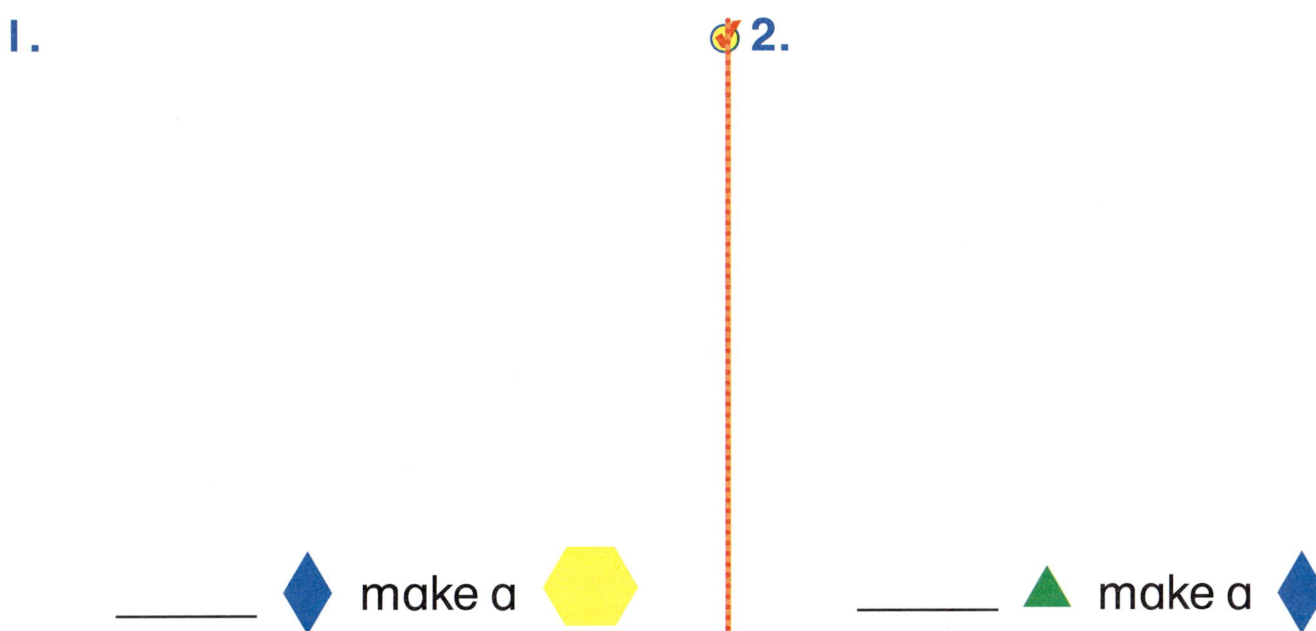

_______ ◆ make a ⬡

_______ ▲ make a ◆

3. **Math Talk** Tell how you found the answer to Exercise 2.

1.3.1 Identify, describe, compare, sort and draw triangles, rectangles, squares and circles in terms of their attributes. Use simple plane shapes to compose a given shape.

Use pattern blocks. Draw to show the blocks.
Write how many blocks you used.

1.

2.

_______ ▲ make a 🟡

_______ ▲ make a 🔴

Problem Solving: Reasoning

Solve. Circle a block to show your answer.

3. Use me two times to make this figure. Which block am I?

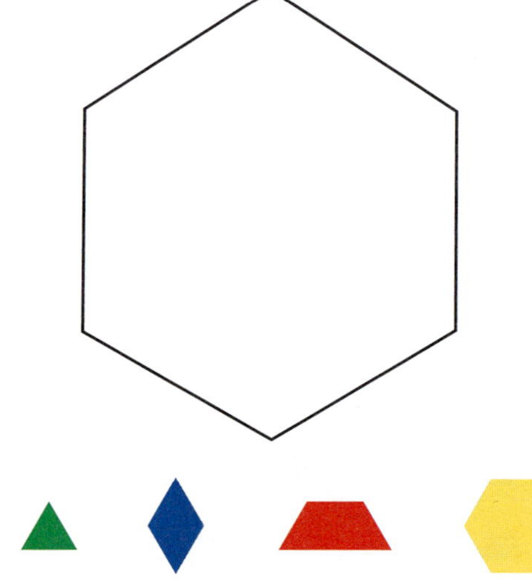

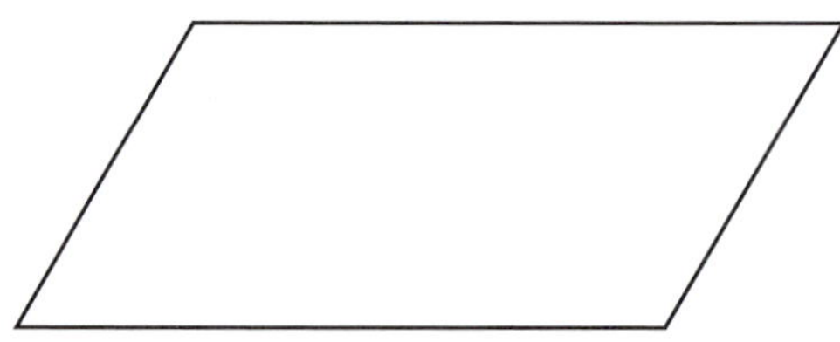

4. Use me two times to make this figure. Which block am I?

Draw to show how you solved Exercise 4.

At Home Have your child explain
how he or she solved Exercises 1 and 2.

Chapter 10 Lesson 9

Separate Plane Figures

Explore

You can take apart figures
to make new figures.

triangle   square   hexagon   trapezoid

circle   rectangle   rhombus

Essential Question
How can you take apart a figure to make two new figures?

Connect

Use paper figures. Fold to make two new figures.
Cut along the fold. Trace and name the new figures.

1.

____

✓2.

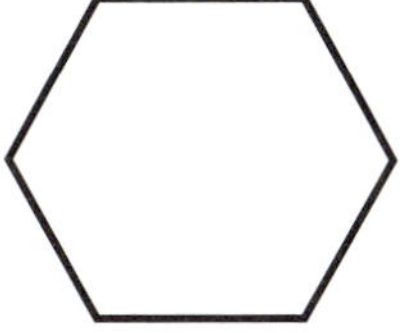

____

3. **Math Talk** Is there another way the figure in Exercise 1
   can be taken apart? Explain.

1.3.1 Identify, describe, compare, sort and draw triangles,
rectangles, squares and circles in terms of their attributes. Use
simple plane shapes to compose a given shape.

▶ Share and Show

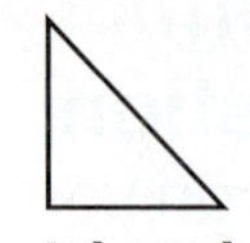 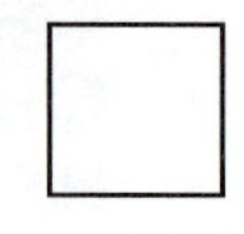 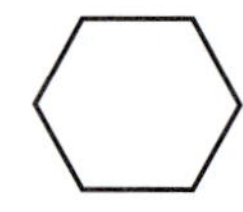 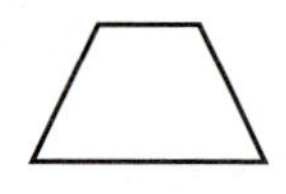 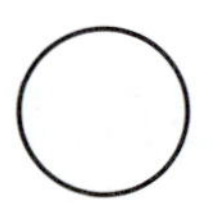 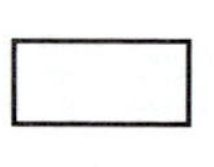 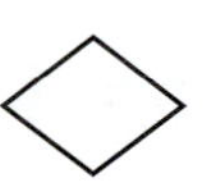

triangle   square   hexagon   trapezoid   circle   rectangle   rhombus

Use paper figures to make three new figures.
Cut along the folds. Trace and name the new figures.

1.

____

2.

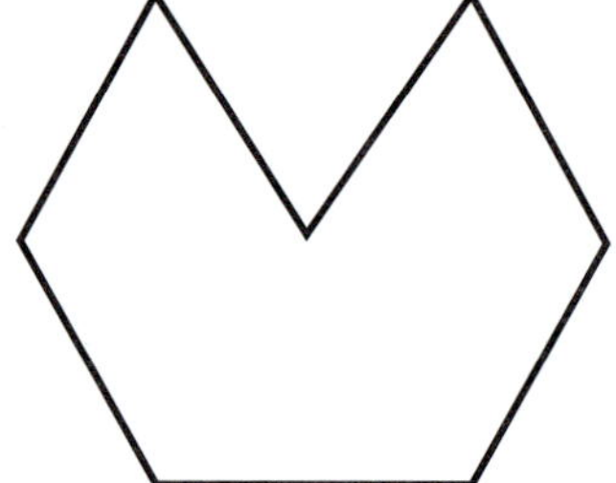

____

3.

____

Problem Solving: Real World

Draw a picture to solve.

4. Shelby wants to make a hexagon.
She uses 2 colors of pattern blocks.
Draw and color a hexagon that
Shelby could make.

Use pattern blocks. Find another way to make a hexagon.
Draw, color, and name the figures.

At Home Have your child tell you what two figures he or she
can make by taking apart each two-dimensional figure.

Problem Solving Workshop

Strategy: Use Logical Reasoning

You can think like a math detective to solve problems.

I have straight sides.
I have fewer than 5 sides.
I have only 3 corners.
Which figure am I?

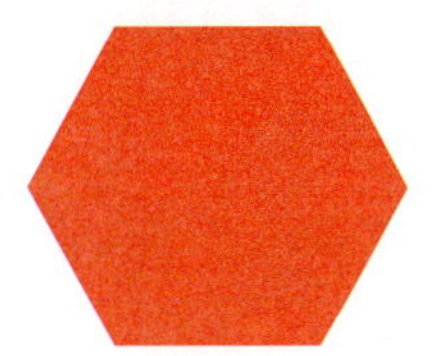  

Use Logical Reasoning

Use the clues. Cross off each figure that does not match. Circle the figure that is left.

Clue 1 I have straight sides.
The 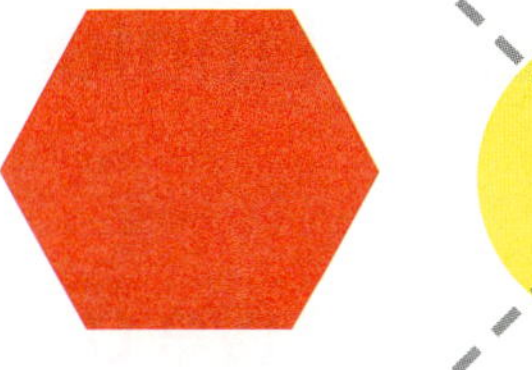 has no straight sides.

Clue 2 I have fewer than 5 sides.
The 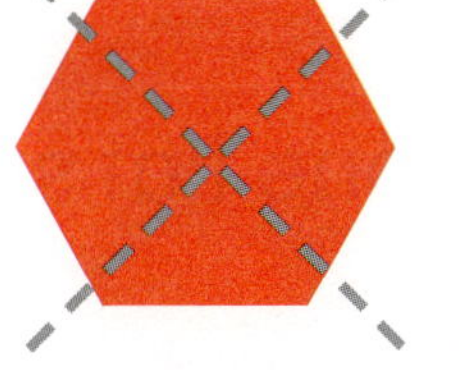 has more than 5 sides.

Clue 3 I have 3 corners.
A 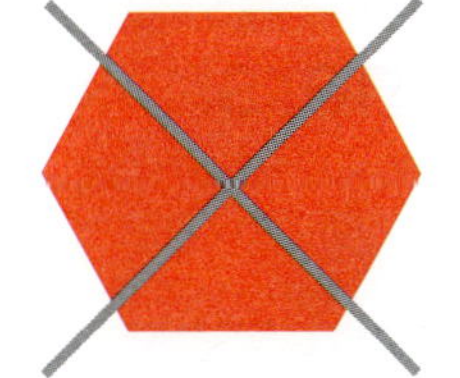 has 3 corners.

 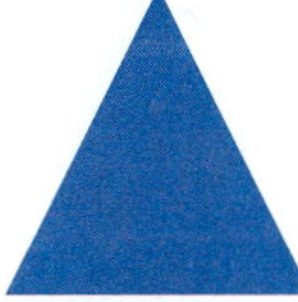    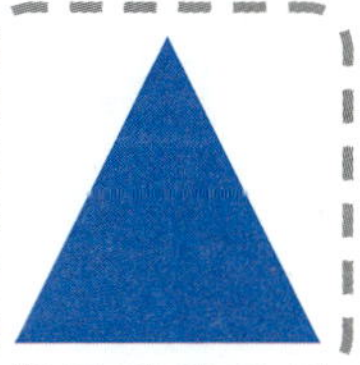

Math Talk Explain how your answer matches each clue.

1.3.1 Identify, describe, compare, sort and draw triangles, rectangles, squares and circles in terms of their attributes. Use simple plane shapes to compose a given shape.

I have a curved surface.
I have two flat surfaces.
I have no corners.
Which figure am I?

 **Unlock the Problem**

What do I need to find?

which figure
matches

What information do I need to use?

_____ 1 _____ curved surface

_____ 2 _____ flat surfaces

_____ 0 _____ corners

Show how to solve the problem.

Find the figure that matches all the clues.

The ▢ does not have a curved surface.

The △ has only one flat surface.

The ▮ has no corners.

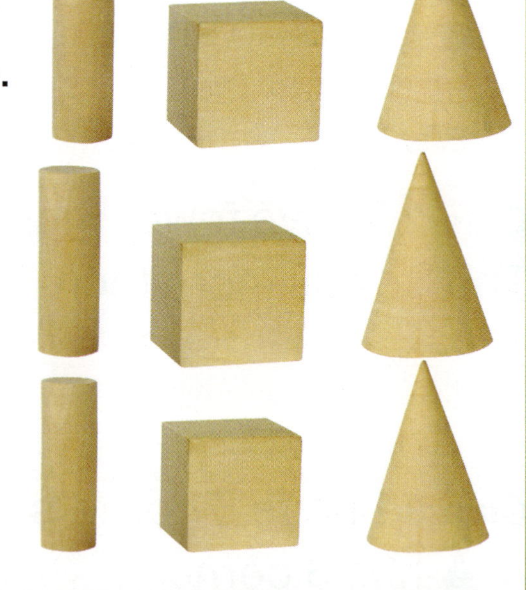

Math Talk Explain how your answer matches each clue.

Problem Solving Strategy Practice

Cross off figures that do not match the clues. Circle the figure that is left.

1. I have straight sides. I have more than 3 corners. My sides do not all have the same length. Which figure am I?

2. I have no curved surface. I have more than 5 flat surfaces. All of my flat surfaces are the same size. Which figure am I?

3. I have a curved surface. I have no flat surfaces. I have no corners. Which figure am I?

Try Your Own Problem

4. My sides all have the same length. I have more than _____ sides.
I have _____ corners.
Which figure am I?

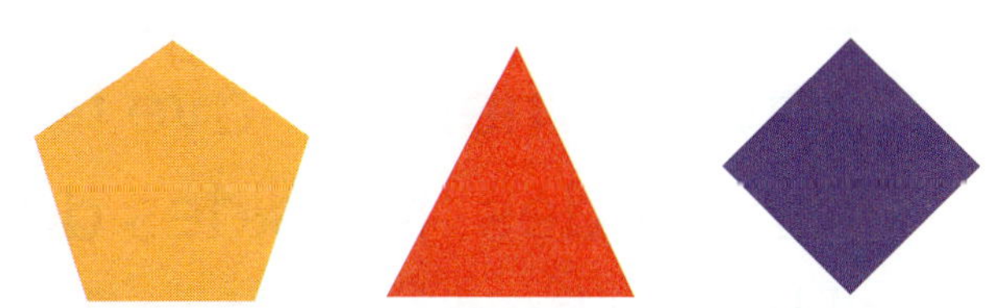

At Home Draw and cut out a rectangle, a circle, and a triangle. Give your child clues, and ask him or her to identify the figure that matches the clues.

Mixed Strategy Practice

Choose a way to solve each problem. Show your work.

1. Jeremy sees 9 ducks. Paula sees 1 more duck. How many ducks do Jeremy and Paula see?

duck

______ ducks

2. There are 2 oars in each boat. How many oars are there in 4 boats?

oar

______ oars

3. Noah counted 10 turtles on a log. 5 turtles went into the pond. How many turtles stayed on the log?

turtle

______ turtles

4. I have corners. I have fewer than 6 sides. My sides do not all have the same length. Which figure am I?

Extra Practice

1. Color the solid with only flat surfaces 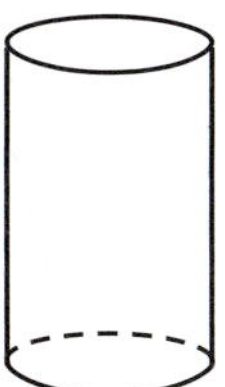 .

2. Color the solid with only a curved surface 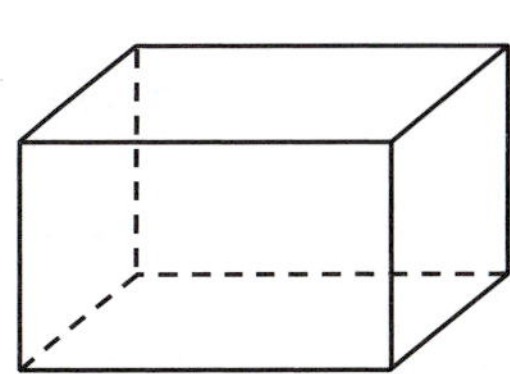 .

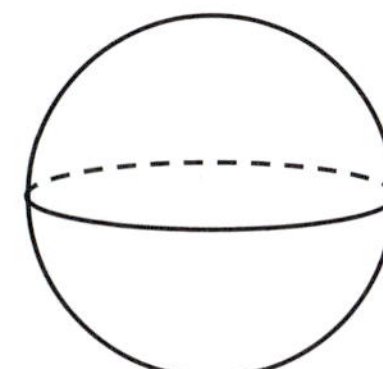

Use the solid. Write the number of flat surfaces and corners.

3. This cube has _______ flat surfaces.

4. This cube has _______ corners.

5. Color each triangle 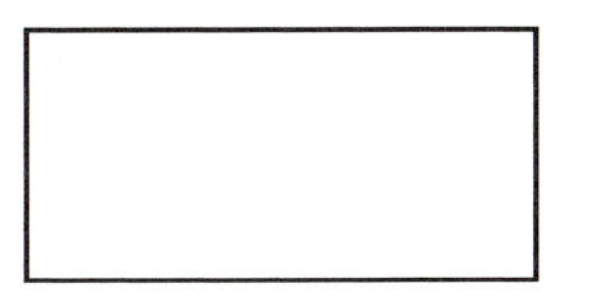 .

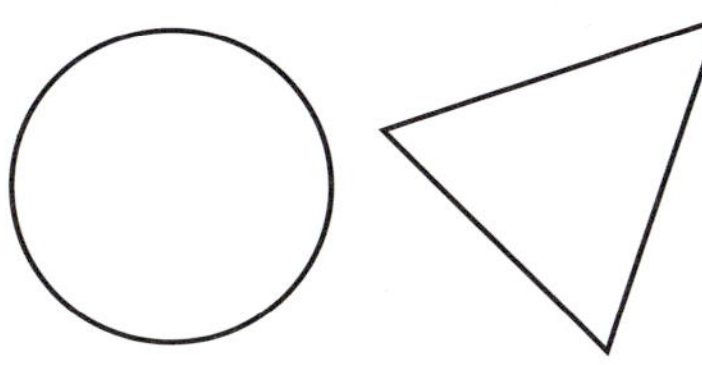 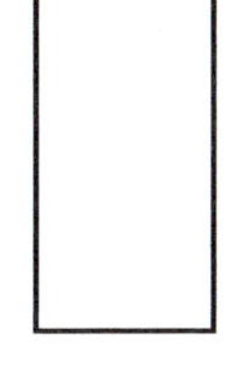 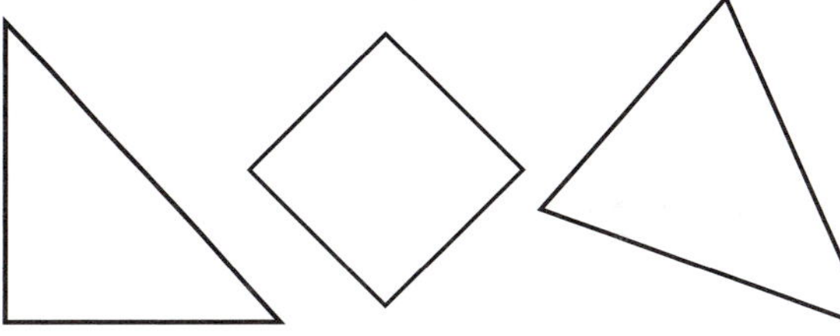

6. Use 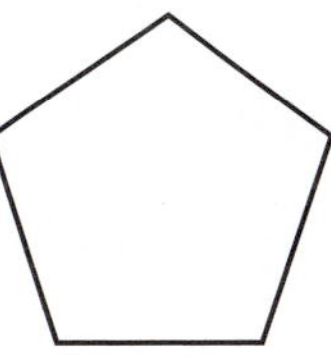 to trace each straight side.
Use ______ to circle each corner.
Write the number of sides and corners.

_______ sides

_______ corners

Problem Solving

Cross off figures that do not match the clues.
Circle the figure that is left.

7. I have straight sides.
I have only 3 corners.
Which figure am I?

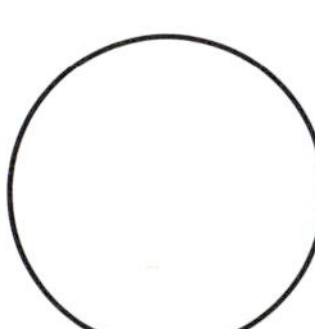  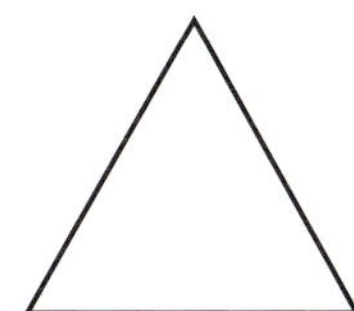

Technology
Use HMH Mega Math, Shapes Ahoy!,
Undersea 3D, Levels F, G.

Multistep Problems
Chapter 10

1. These are the types of blocks in Jason's block set. **Representation**

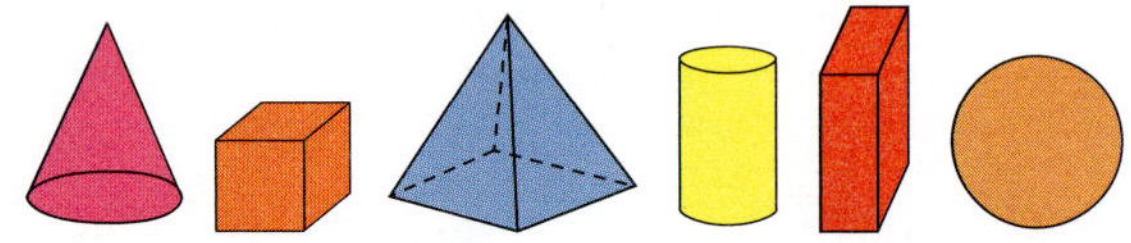

Jason wants to build a castle.

- He will use cubes and other solids that have only flat surfaces.

- The only curved solids he will use are cylinders.

- He will use fewer than 20 blocks in all.

- Draw a castle that Jason might build. Name the blocks you used and tell how many.

2. Ms. Griffith gave her class a math test on solid figures. Each student needed to circle the correct answer. **Representation**

- Circle the correct answers.

Solid Figure	How Many Sides?			How Many Corners?		
1.	0	1	4	0	1	4
2.	4	6	8	4	6	8
3.	6	7	8	6	7	8
4.	4	5	6	4	5	6

 Standards Quick Check

Look at the blue face of the figure.
Circle the name of the face.

1. 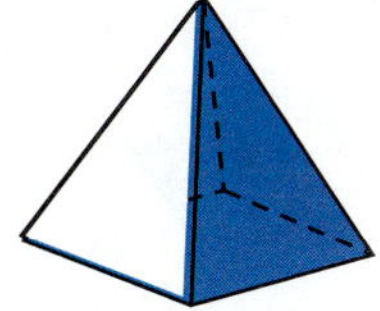

square
circle
triangle

2. 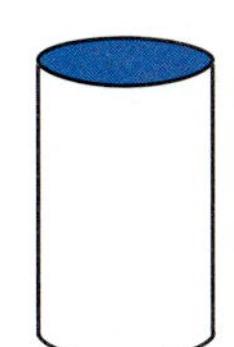

square
circle
triangle

3. 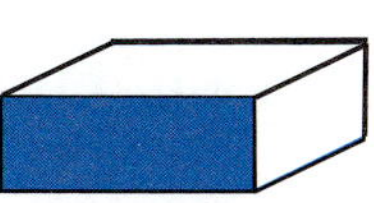

rectangle
circle
triangle

Figure Hunt!

Use the clues. Find the figure.
Write the color and name of the figure.

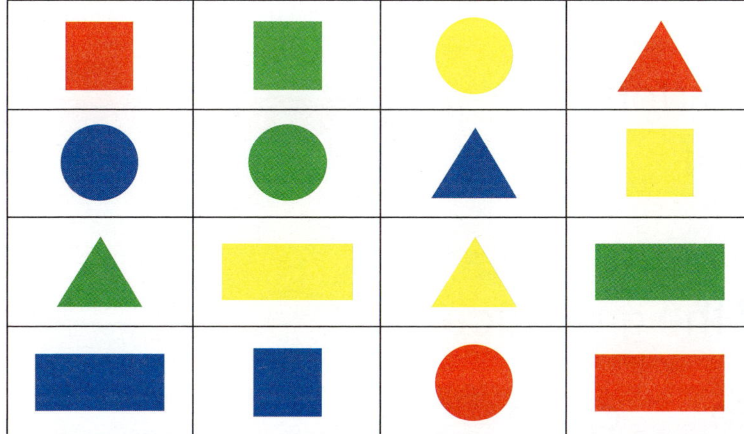

1. It has 3 sides and 3 corners. It is above a square.

It is a ____________ ____________.

2. It has 4 sides and 4 corners. It is to the right of a circle.

It is a ____________ ____________.

Supplies travel by trucks from the factory to stores. First, items are put in a can or a box. Then cartons are filled with other cans or boxes. Then large trucks are loaded, and off they go!

1. Jamal opens a carton at the store. He sees rows and rows of glue sticks.

   Circle the shape of the gray faces.

   square   triangle   circle

2. Dora opens a box of rubber bands.

   Circle the shape of the gray face.

   square   triangle   circle

3. Ramón unpacks a carton. Hundreds of boxes of pencils are inside.

   Circle the shape of the gray face.

   square   rectangle   circle

Looking Ahead to the ISTEP+
Chapter 10

Mark the best answer for questions 1–4.

1. Which figure has no corners? **1.3.1**

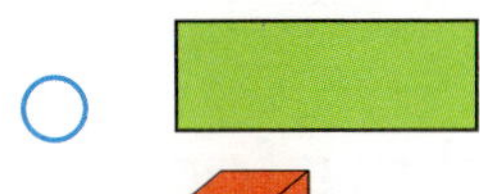
○

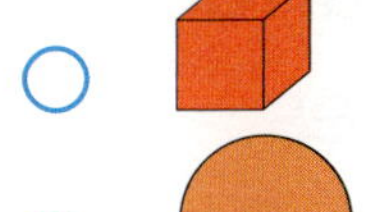
○

○

○

2. Which solid has a curved surface? **Representation**

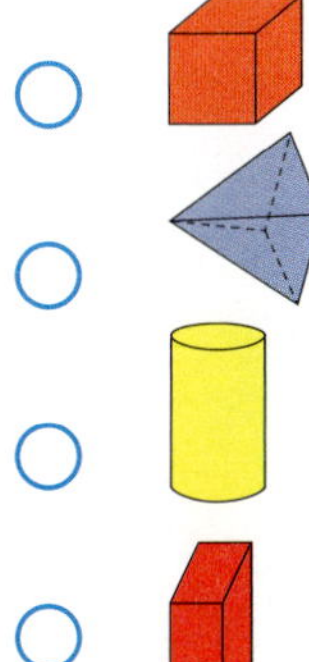
○
○
○
○

3. How many corners does this solid have? **Representation**

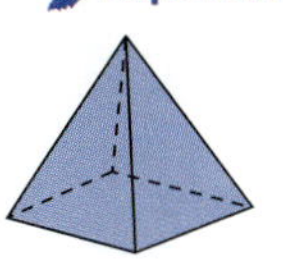

○ 3

○ 5

○ 6

○ 8

4. Which plane figure can you trace from a cylinder? **1.3.1**

○

○

○

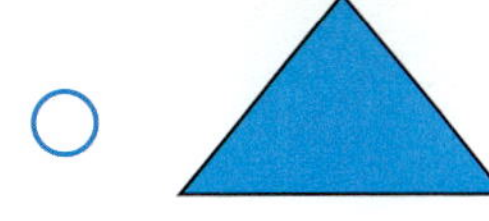
○

Mark the best answer for questions 5–7.

5. Which is **not** a triangle?

1.3.1

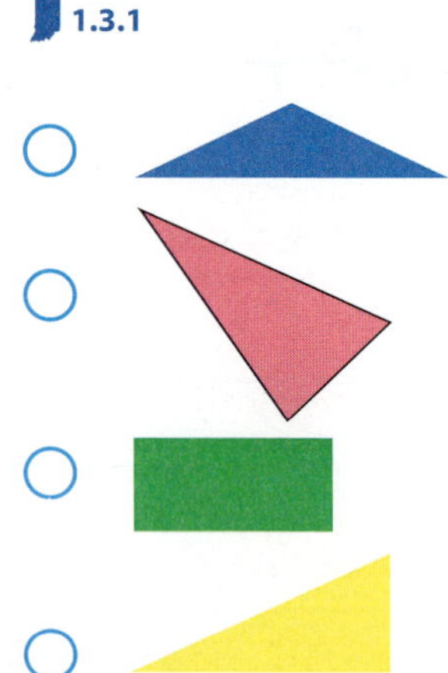

○
○
○
○

---

6. Which plane figure has 4 sides and 4 corners? 1.3.1

○ circle

○ cube

○ square

○ triangle

---

7. Which plane figure has 3 sides and 3 corners? 1.3.1

○ circle

○ cube

○ square

○ triangle

Open Ended

8. Cross off figures that do not match the clues.
Circle the figure that is left.

1.3.1

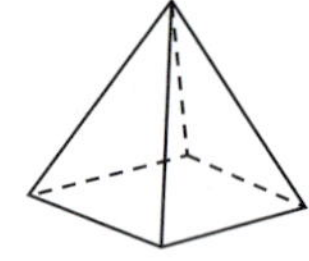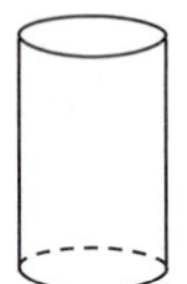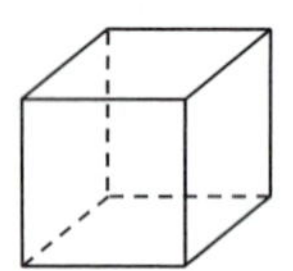

I have no curved surfaces.
I have 5 flat surfaces.
Four of my surfaces are the same shape.
Which figure am I?

Spatial Sense and Patterns

Theme: In the Sky

Fun Fact

There are many hot air balloon festivals. Hot air balloons can fly more than a half mile above the ground!

Investigate

Look at the picture. Use position words to describe one of the hot air balloons.

GO ONLINE **Technology**
Student pages are available in the Student eBook.

Show What You Know 

1. Place a red cube above the bear. Draw the cube.

2. Place a blue cube below the bear. Draw the cube.

Read the pattern. Place shapes to identify the pattern. Trace and color the pattern.

3.      

4.      

At Home This page checks your child's understanding of important concepts and skills needed for success in Chapter 11.

Chapter 11 Lesson 1

Position Words

What words help you follow directions to a place?

Vocabulary
up   down
above   below
far   near
right of   left of
next to   behind
in front of

Position words tell where objects are.

left of the bird
above the rabbit

▶ **Share and Show**   Math Board

Use the picture to solve. Circle the answer.

1. The  is to the **right of** the kite.
   What is to the **right of** the tulips?

2. The kite is to the **left of** the  .
   What is to the **left of** the butterfly?

3. The cloud is **behind** the bird.
   What is **behind** the tree?

4. **Math Talk** Find a desk and a chair in your classroom.
   Use position words to tell where the chair is.

⭐ Representation

Read the directions.
Write **A**, **B**, **C**, and **D** to place the pictures.

1. Place the 🌼 to the **left of** the 🌳.

2. Place the 🌊 **below** the 🌳.

3. Place the 🦋 **next to** the 🌳.

4. Place the 🐤 to the **right of** the 🦋.

Math Board — ## Problem Solving: Reasoning

5. Circle the true statements.

The 🟦 is to the right of the 🟥.

The 🟦 is behind the 🟩.

The 🟨 is above the 🟦.

Describe where the 🟥 is.

294

At Home Arrange four or five small toys or other objects on a table. Have your child use words such as *below, left,* and *behind* to describe the position of one of the toys. Use the clues to guess which object he or she is describing. Take turns describing positions and identifying toys.

Chapter 11 Lesson 2

Follow Directions

Position words help you find
and place objects.

Essential Question
What words help you find an object?

Vocabulary

up	down
above	below
far	near
right of	left of
next to	behind
in front of	

> **Share and Show** Math Board

Use the picture to solve. Draw to show the answer.

1. The ⛯ is **next to** the 🌳. Draw a boy **next to** the ▦.

2. The ☁ is **behind** the ✈. Draw a ball **behind** the 🌳.

3. The ☀ is **above** the 🎈. Draw a kite **above** the ⛯.

4. The ☁ is to the **right of** the ☀.

   Draw a dog to the **right of** the 🧒.

5. **Math Talk** What objects are far from the tree?
   What objects are near the tree? Explain.

Representation

Follow the directions. Use the picture.

1. Color the animal to the **left of** the . Use .

2. Color the animal **below** the . Use .

3. Color the animal **in front of** the . Use .

4. Color the animal **up** the . Use .

5. Color the animal **near** the . Use .

At Home Choose a "mystery" object in a room. Have your child ask a series of yes/no questions about the position of the object, such as "is it *above* the sofa?" or "is it to the *left of* the lamp?" until he or she can identify the object.

Give Directions

Position words help you descibe where objects are located.

Essential Question

How do you use words to locate an object?

Vocabulary

up	down
above	below
far	near
right of	left of
in front of	behind
next to	

THINK!

Use the picture. Circle the correct position word to complete each sentence.

1. The  is ______ the 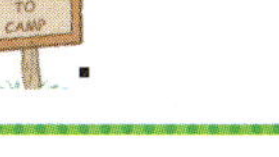 .   above   (in front of)

2. The  is to the ______ the  .   left of   right of

3. The  is ______ the  .   behind   below

4. The  is ______ the 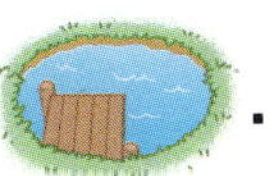 .   near   far from

5. The  is ______ the  .   next to   up

6. **Math Talk** Name two objects in the picture that are near each other. Explain.

Representation

Circle every figure that makes the statement true.

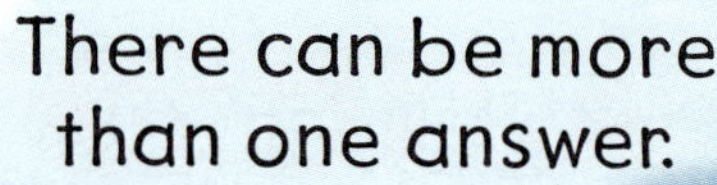

1. The _______ is **next to** the ⬤ .

2. The _______ is **above** the ▲ .

3. The _______ is to the **left of** the ⬤ .

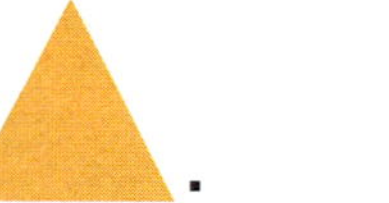

Math Board — Problem Solving: Reasoning

Use position words. Complete each sentence.

4. The ◼ is ___________ the  .

5. The ▲ is to the ___________ the  .

6. The ▲ is ___________ the  .

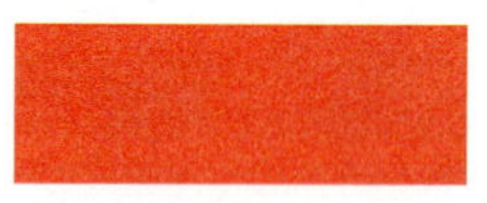

Use different words to describe the ▲ .

At Home Ask your child to draw a picture that arranges three figures with different shapes or colors. Without showing you the picture, ask your child to give directions for drawing the same picture. Then compare the results.

Chapter 11 Lesson 4

Give and Follow Directions

▶ **We Learn**

From **Start**, go up 2.
Go right 3. Where are you?

Essential Question
How can you use position words to give and follow directions on a map?

Vocabulary
left
right
up
down

▶ **Share and Show**

Follow the directions.
Draw the path. Write the place.

1. From **Start**, go up 2.
   Go right 2. Where are you?

   ____

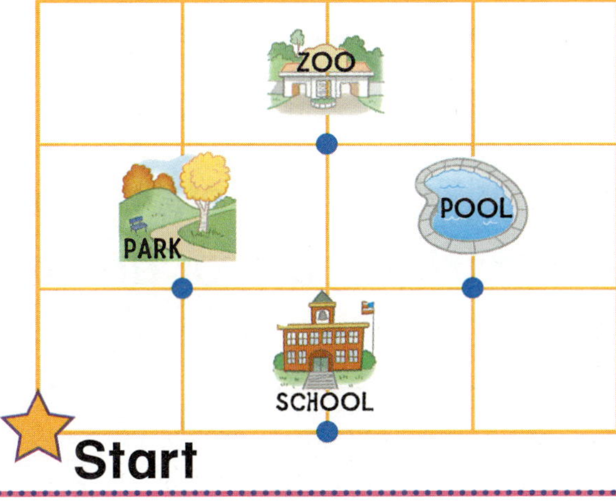

✓ 2. From the library,
   go right 3. Go up 1.
   Where are you?

   ____

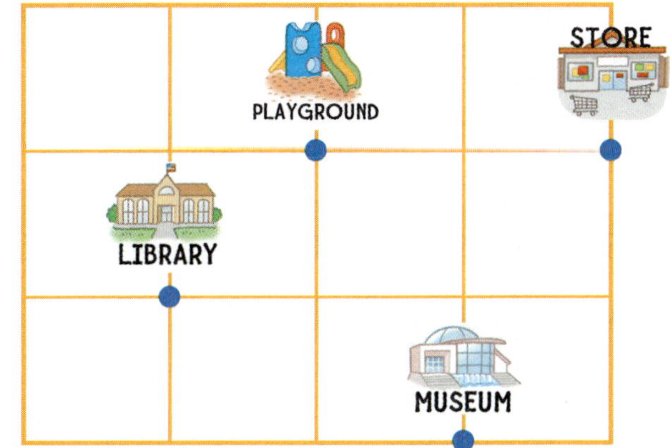

■ Representation

Follow the directions.
Draw the path. Write the place.

1. From **Start**, go right 3.
   Go down 2. Go left 1.
   Where are you?

____

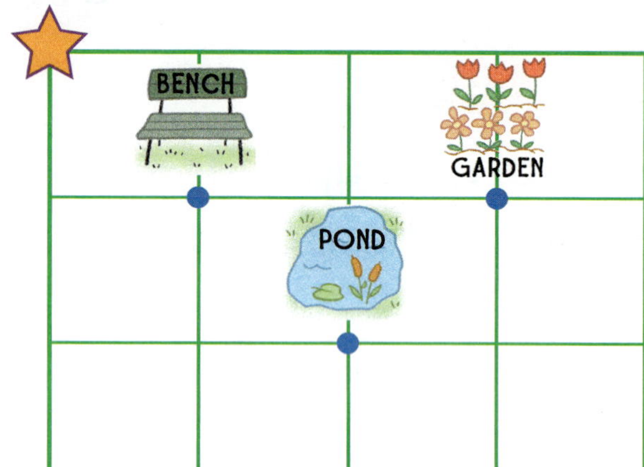

2. From the balloon, go up 1.
   Go left 1. Go up 1.
   Where are you?

____

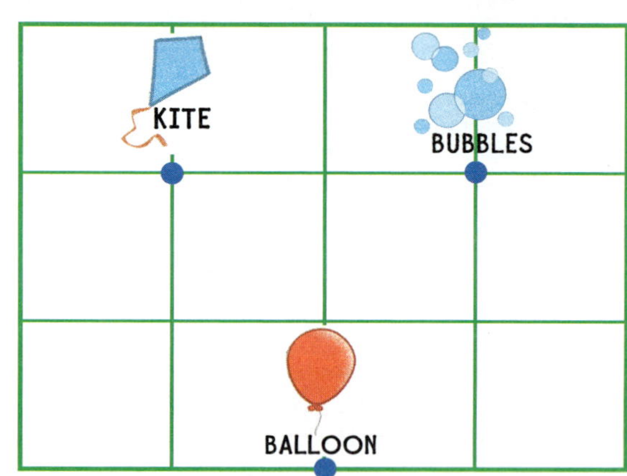

Problem Solving: Visual Thinking

3. Start at ▲. Give directions to get to the ▼.
   Write **left**, **right**, **up**, or **down**.

   Go _______________ 2.

   Go _______________ 2.

   Go _______________ 1.

   Give three different directions to
   get you from ▲ to ■.

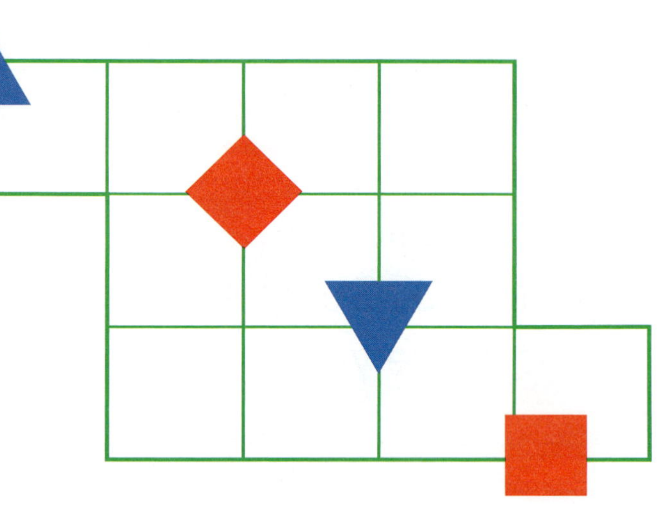

At Home Using a chair or sofa as Start, give your child two
directions to find an object in your living room. Include *left,
right, up,* or *down* and a number of steps in each direction.
Help your child draw a grid to show Start and the object.

Problem Solving Workshop

Strategy: Use Logical Reasoning

Essential Question

How can using clues help you solve a problem?

Sara paints a circle over a triangle.
She paints a square to the left of the circle.
Which painting is Sara's?

🔑 Unlock the Problem

What do I need to find?

which painting is
Sara's

What information do I need to use?

circle over a triangle

square to the left of the circle

Show how to solve the problem.
Cross out the paintings that do not match the clues.
Circle Sara's painting.

Math Talk How does your answer match the clues? Explain.

Representation

Problem Solving Strategy Practice 

Cross out the paintings that do not match the clues. Circle the answer.

1. Jim paints a square under a circle. He paints a triangle under the square. Which painting is Jim's?

2. Val paints a triangle under a circle. She paints a square to the left of the triangle. Which painting is Val's?

3. Ty paints a square next to a circle. He paints a triangle far from the square. Which painting is Ty's?

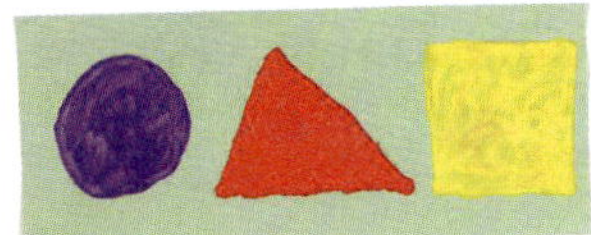 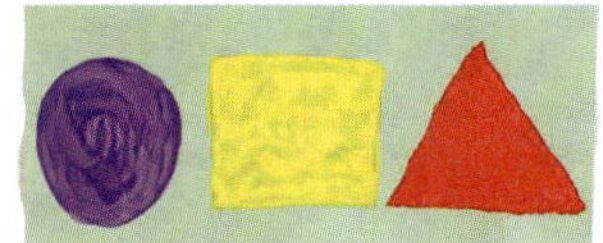 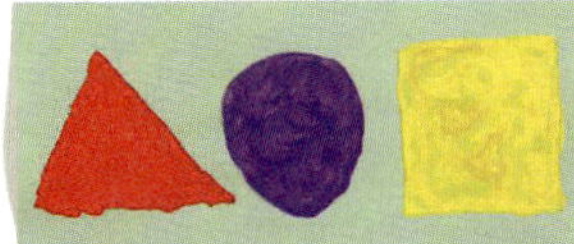

Try Your Own Problem

4. Ann paints a circle __________ the triangle. She paints a square __________ the triangle. Which painting is Ann's?

At Home Draw three different arrangements of circle, square, and triangle on separate sheets of paper. Give your child clues about the relative positions of the shapes in one of the pictures, using words such as *above* and *right of.* Have your child identify the picture being described and explain the choice.

Chapter 11 Lesson 6

Analyze Patterns

A repeating pattern has a group that repeats over and over.

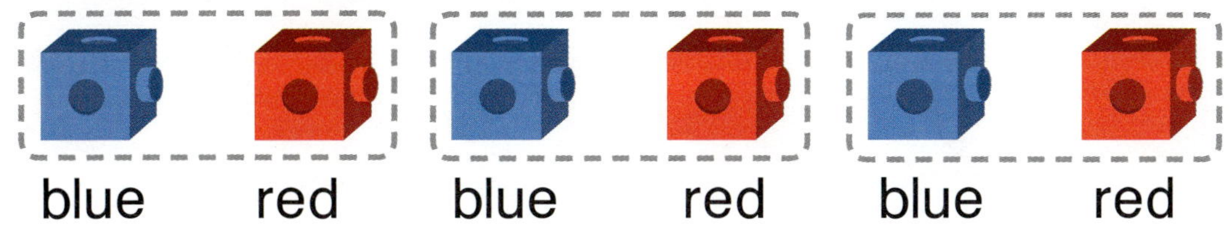

blue   red   blue   red   blue   red

Essential Question
How can you identify and describe a repeating pattern?

Vocabulary
repeating pattern
pattern unit

Connect

A group that repeats is called a pattern unit.

Use ⬤ or 🎲 🎲 🎲 to copy the repeating pattern. Circle each pattern unit.

1. 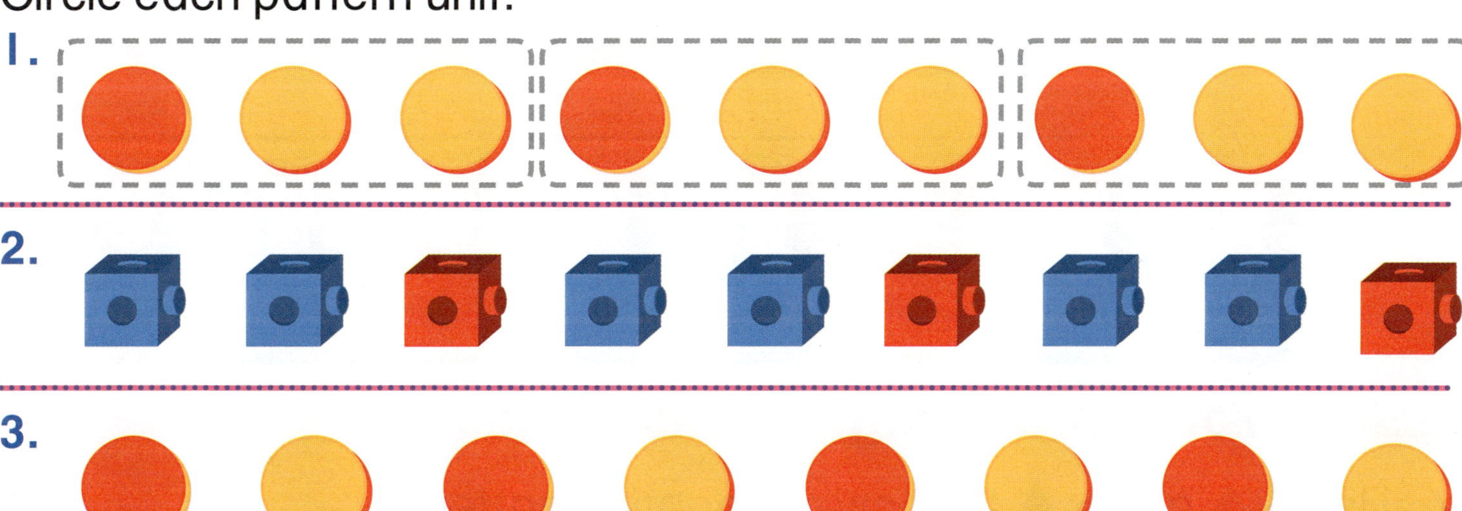

2.

3.

4.

5. 

6. **Math Talk** Explain how to find a pattern unit.

1.2.2 Create, extend, and give a rule for number patterns using addition.

Circle the first pattern unit.

1.

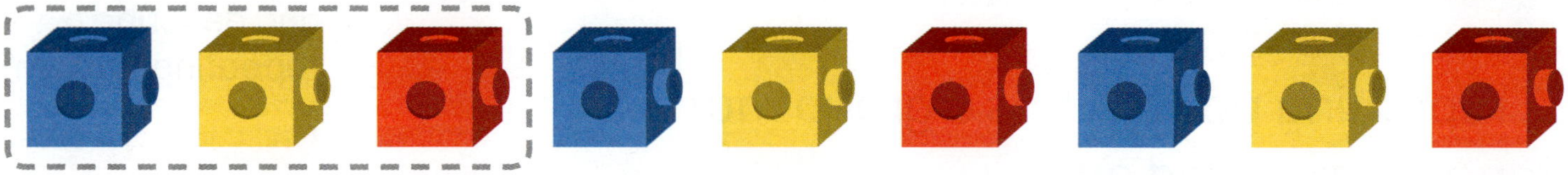

2.

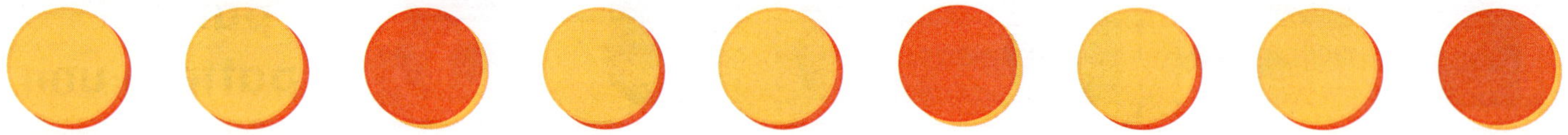

3.

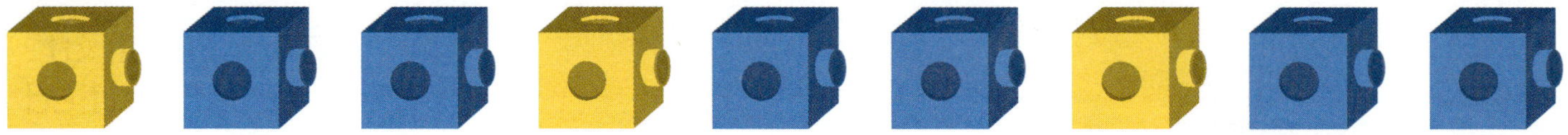

4.

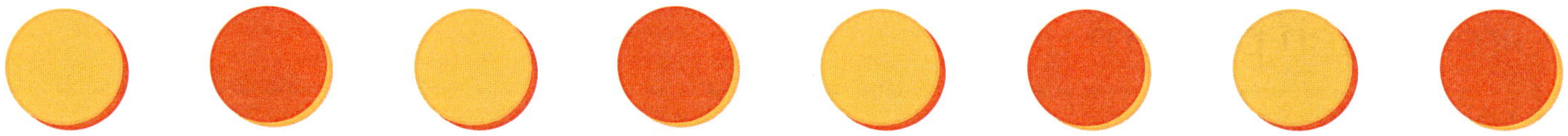

5.

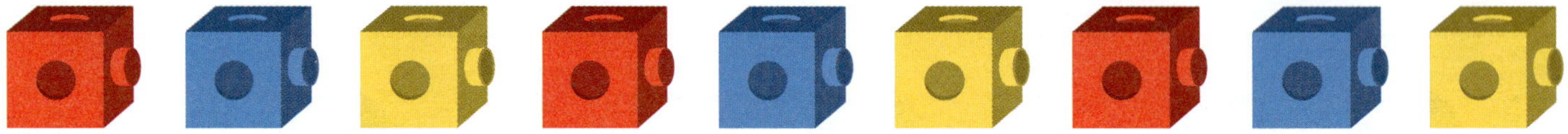

Problem Solving: Application

6. Use 3 ▲ and 6 ▲ to show a repeating pattern.
The pattern unit should repeat three times.
Draw the pattern. Circle the first pattern unit.

How do you know that your drawing shows a
repeating pattern? Explain.

Algebra: Extend Patterns

Explore

A pattern unit helps you predict what comes next.

Hands On

Essential Question
How can you identify and extend concrete repeating patterns?

Vocabulary
pattern unit

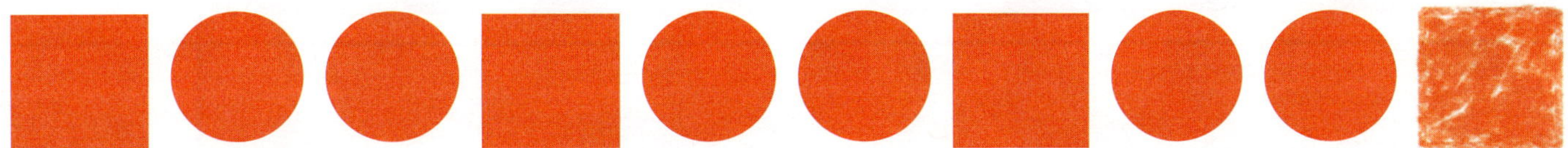

Connect

Use figures to copy the repeating pattern. Draw and color what comes next.

1.

2.

3.

4.

5.

6. **Math Talk** Predict what comes next in this pattern. Explain.

1.2.2 Create, extend, and give a rule for number patterns using addition.

Share and Show

Math Board

THINK What is the pattern unit?

Draw and color what comes next.

1\.

2\.

3\.

4\.

5\.

6\.

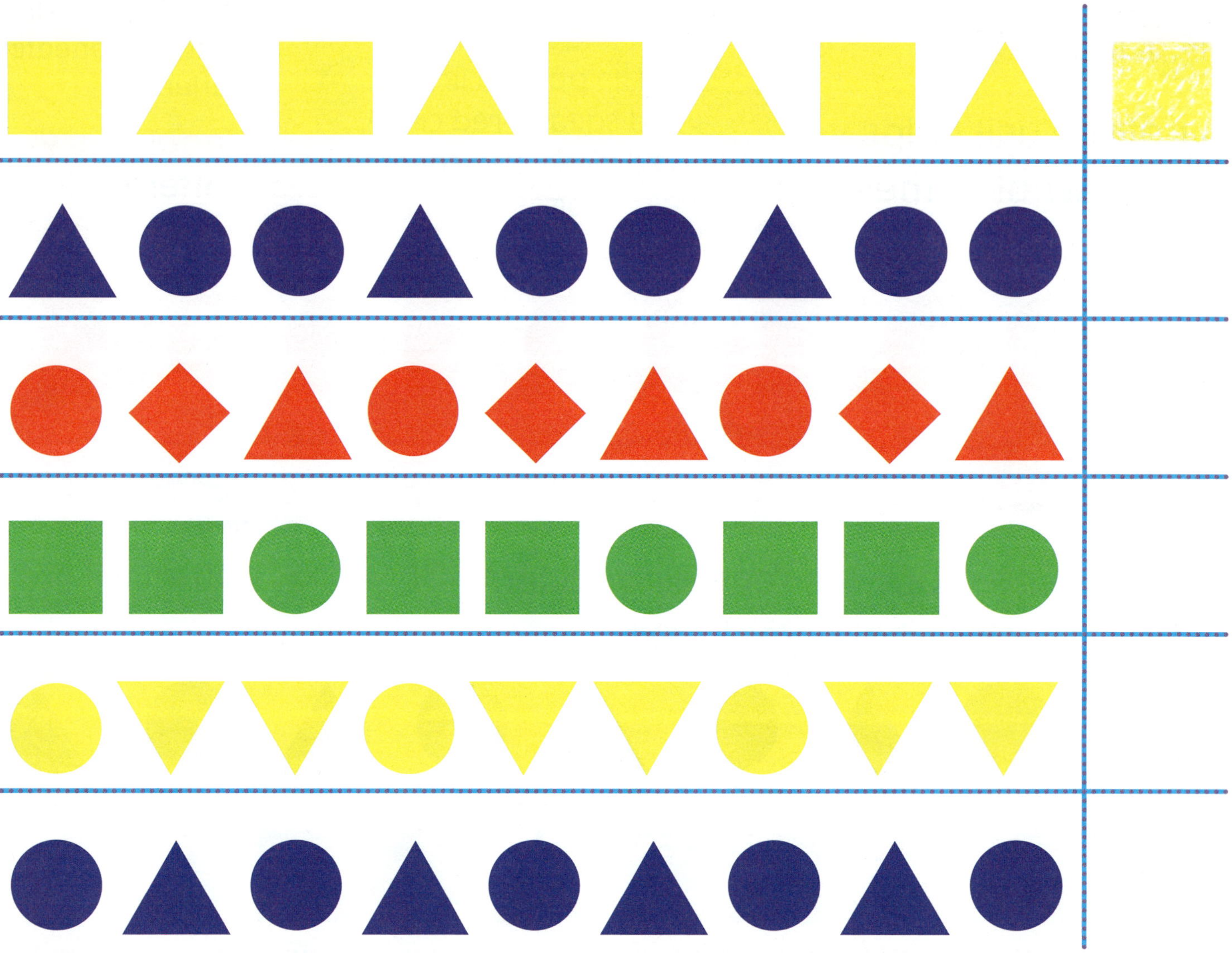

Problem Solving: Reasoning

Math Board

Draw and color what is missing.

7\.

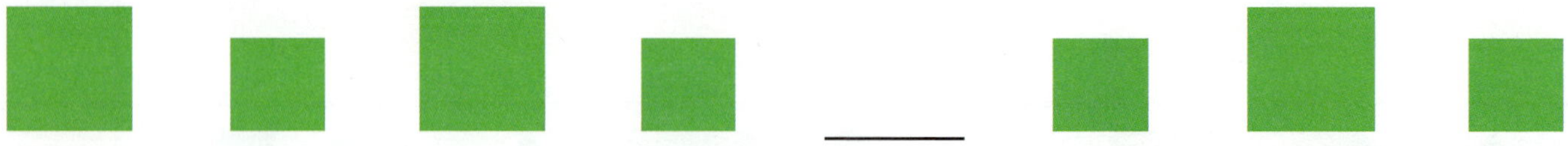

8\.

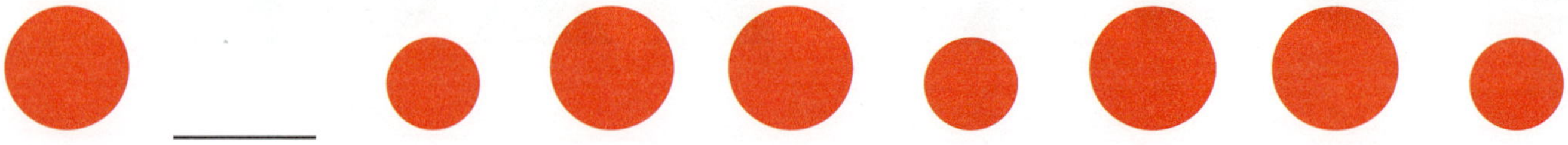

Look at Exercise 8. How did you decide what is missing? Explain.

At Home Draw figures to make repeating patterns like the ones shown on these pages. Ask your child to tell what comes next in each pattern.

Chapter 11 Lesson 8

Algebra: Create New Patterns

▶ Explore

Use the same figures to
make a new repeating pattern.
Draw your new pattern.

▶ Connect

1.

2.

✓ **3.**

4. **Math Talk** Tell how you use the same figures
to make a new pattern.

1.2.2 Create, extend, and give a rule for number patterns using
addition.

Use the same figures to make a new repeating pattern.
Draw your new pattern.

1.

2.

3.

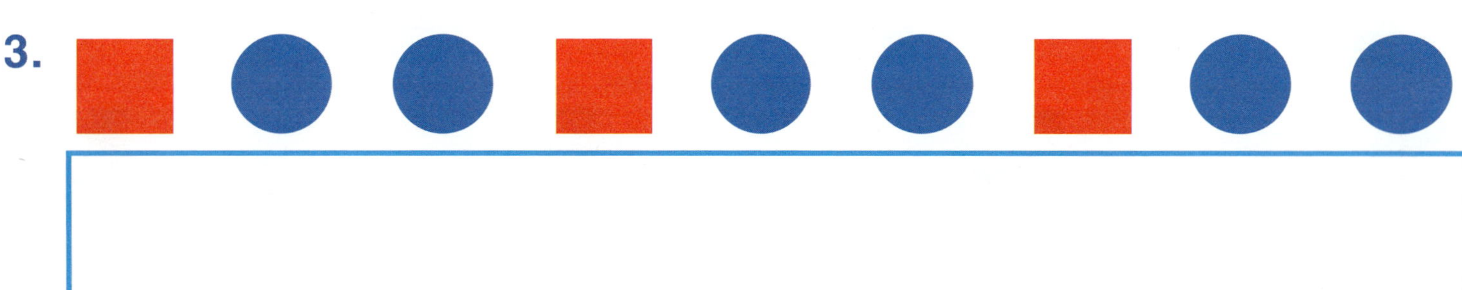

Problem Solving: Reasoning

4. Use the same colors to make a different
repeating pattern. Color your pattern.

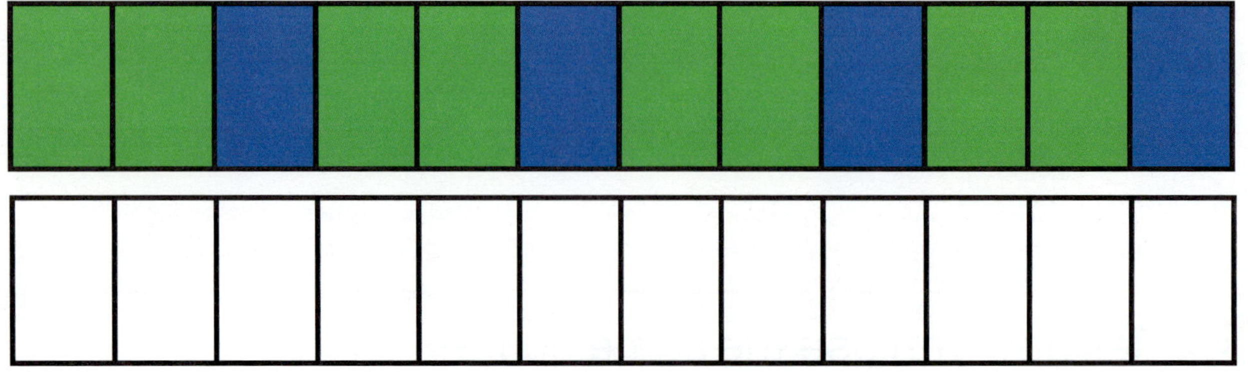

How are these patterns alike and different?

At Home Arrange two or three kinds of coins in a
repeating pattern, and ask your child to describe the
pattern unit. Have your child rearrange the coins into a
different pattern and describe the new pattern unit.

Name _______________________

Algebra: Extend Pictorial Patterns

 **We Learn**

Use a pattern unit to predict
what comes next.

car	bus	car	bus	car	bus

 **Share and Show**  Math Board

Predict what comes next. Circle your answer.
Find a pattern unit to help you decide.

7. **Math Talk** Look at Exercise 4. Predict what
the tenth object will be.

1.2.2 Create, extend, and give a rule for number patterns using
addition.

On Your Own

Predict what comes next.
Circle your answer.

Use a pattern unit.

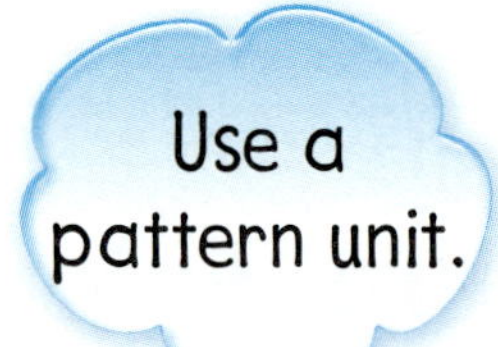

1. 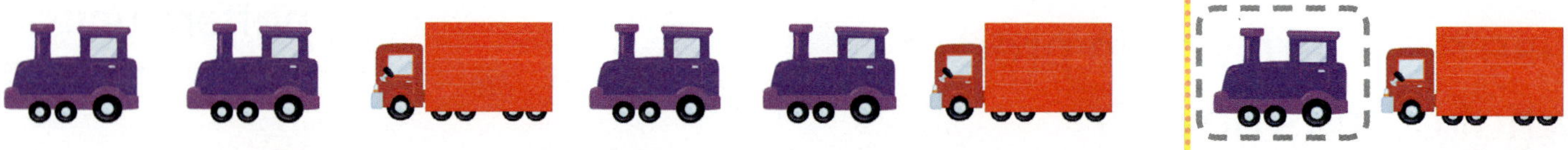

2. 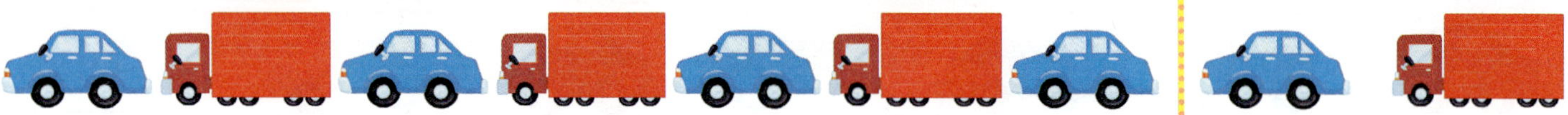

3. 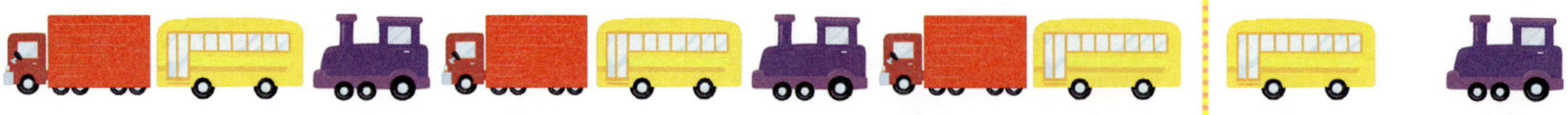

4. 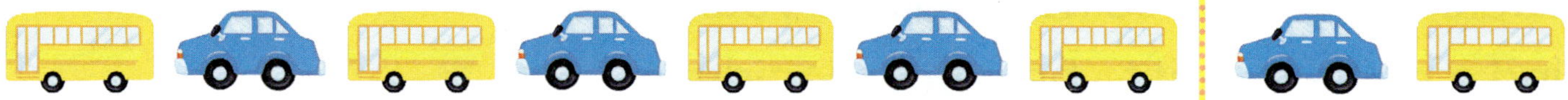

5. 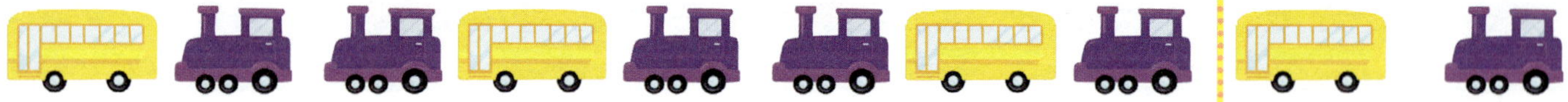

6. 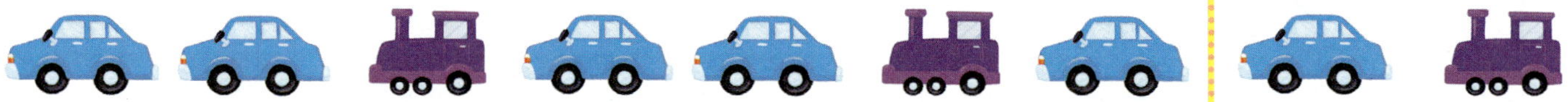

Math Board

Problem Solving: Visual Thinking

7. Color the scarf to continue the pattern.

Describe the pattern on the scarf.

At Home Have your child arrange objects in a repeating pattern and then explain what comes next.

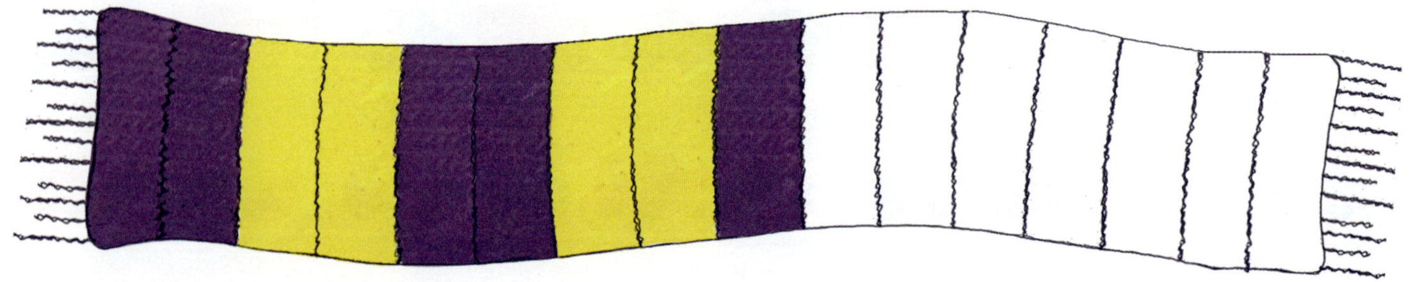

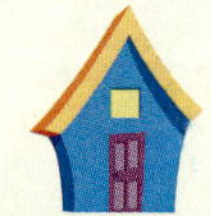

Extra Practice

1. Use 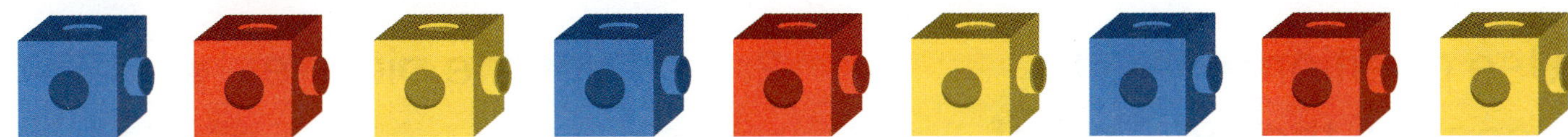 to copy the repeating pattern.
Circle each pattern unit.

2. Circle the figure
that is to the left of
the blue circle.

3. Draw and color what comes next.

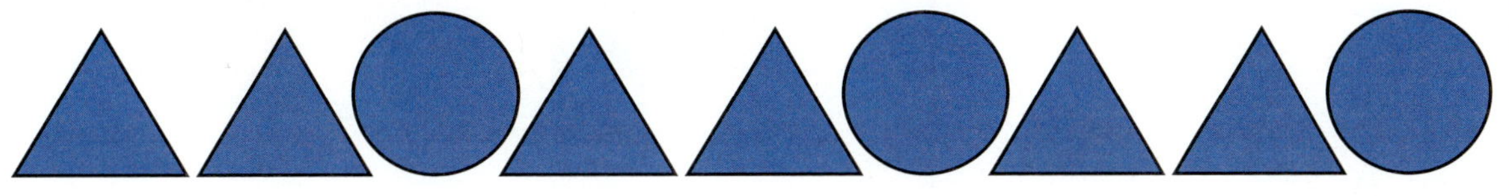

4. Predict what comes next. Circle your answer.

Problem Solving

5. Follow the directions.
Draw the path. Write the place.
From **Start**, go right 1.
Go down 3.
Where are you?

____

_ _ _ _ _ _ _ _ _ _ _ _ _ _

____

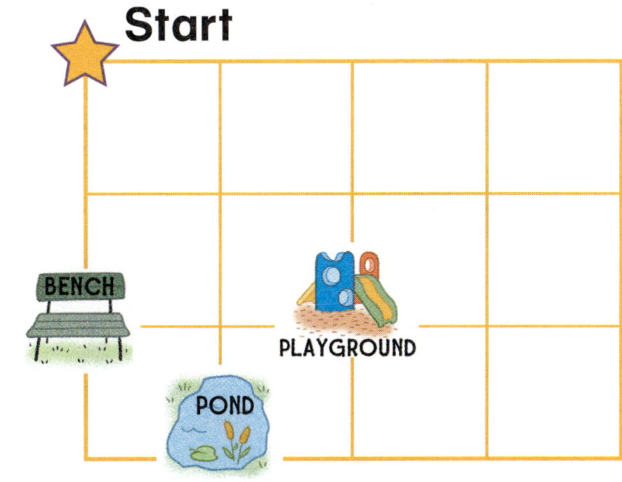

GO **ONLINE**

Technology
Use HMH Mega Math, Shapes Ahoy!,
Sea Cave Sorting, Levels B, C, F.

Multistep Problems

Chapter 11

1. Use position words to describe the location of these figures. *Representation*

- The ⬤ is to the

_______________ the ▮.

- The ⬛ is to the

_______________ the ▮.

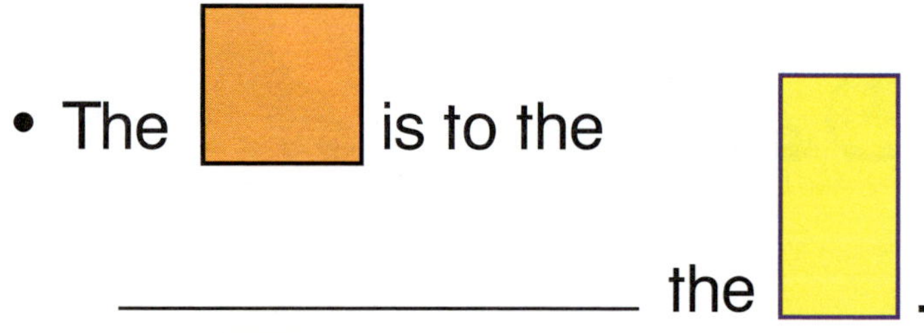

- The ▮ is _______________

the ⬤.

2. Look at the picture. *Representation*

Use position words to answer the questions.

- What is far from the house?

- What is above the house?

- What is to the right of the house?

- What could be behind the house?

Standards Quick Check

Circle the missing words.

1. The red car is to the _________ the bus.

   right of   left of

2. The bus is ______ the red car.

   in front of   behind

3. Circle the correct words.

   The  is ______ the  .

   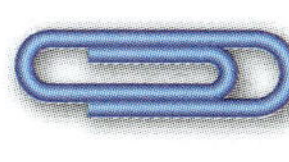

   far from   next to

Challenge H.O.T.

Use the clues to label each flower.

S is between B and N.
T is to the right of B.

_____ _____ _____ __T__

Draw or write to explain.

Thermometers measure temperature. The number in degrees tells if it is hot or cold. Wind vanes measure wind direction.

Circle the answer that completes the sentence.

1. Jessica finds the 90 degree mark on the thermometer.

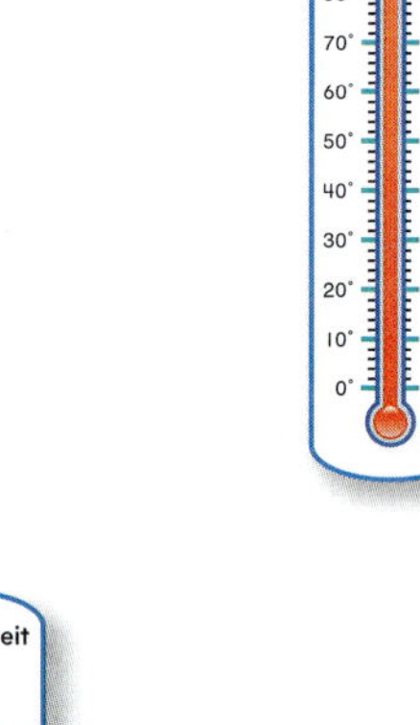

90° F is ________________ 80° F.

   above   below

2. Yoon Ki looks at the wall.

The thermometer is to the

________________ the clock.

   left of   right of

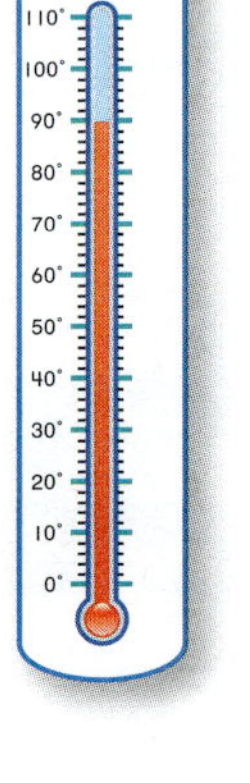

3. Emma sees a wind vane turning on the roof. The wind vane is

________________ the chimney.

far from   near

Looking Ahead to the ISTEP+
Chapter 11

Mark the best answer for questions 1–4.

Use the map for questions 1 and 2. ▌Representation

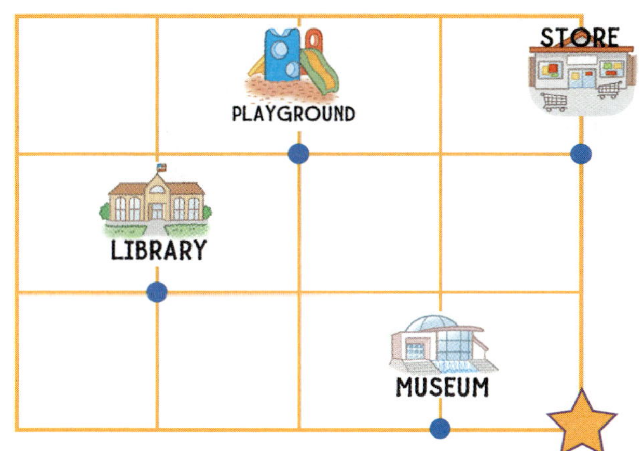

Use the picture for questions 3 and 4. ▌Representation

1. From **Start**, go left 2. Go up 2. Where are you?

- ○ library
- ○ museum
- ○ store
- ○ playground

2. From **Start**, go up 1. Go left 3. Where are you?

- ○ library
- ○ museum
- ○ store
- ○ playground

3. Which is above the ?

- ○ 
- ○ 
- ○ 
- ○

4. What is in front of the  ?

- ○ 
- ○ 
- ○ 
- ○ 

Mark the best answer for questions 5–6.

5. Which new repeating pattern can be made with the same figures? ▌1.2.2

○

○

○

○

Open Ended

Use the picture for questions 7–8. Use logical reasoning to solve. ▌Representation

7. Tim's toy is near the ●. It is in front of the ●. Which toy is Tim's? Draw Tim's toy.

6. What comes next in this repeating pattern? ▌1.2.2

○

○

○

○

8. Nan's toy is to the right of the ●. Which toy is Nan's? Draw Nan's toy.

📖 Reading and Writing Math

Write **yes** or **no** to answer each riddle.

1. I am a plane figure.
I have 3 sides.
I have 3 corners, too.
I am a triangle.

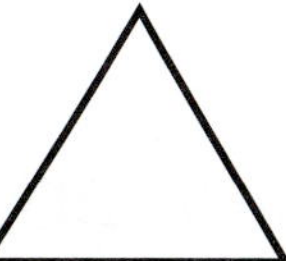

____

2. I am a plane figure.
I have 4 sides.
My sides are the same.
I am a cube.

____

3. I am a solid figure.
I look like a can.
I can slide, roll, and stack.
I am a sphere.

____

4. I am a solid figure.
I look like a box.
My faces are shaped like rectangles.
I am a rectangular prism.

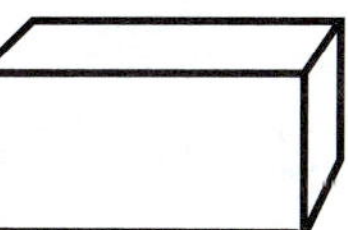

____

5. **Writing Math** Draw a plane figure.
Show two equal parts.

Name _______________________

Is It the Same?

How are the figures the same?

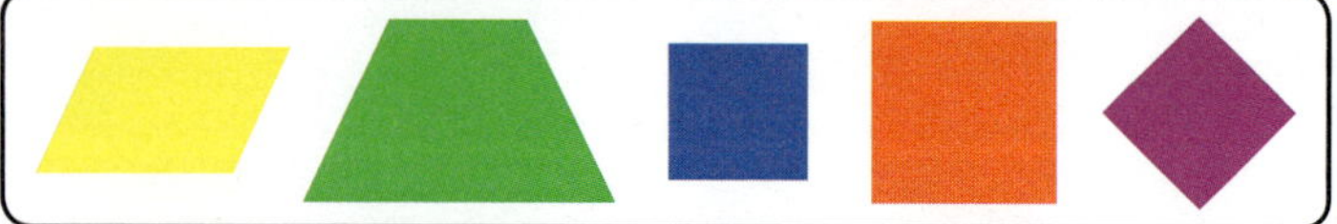

Each figure has four sides.

Reasoning

Draw a line to match each sentence with the group it describes.

1. Each figure has a curved surface.

   Each figure has 4 corners.

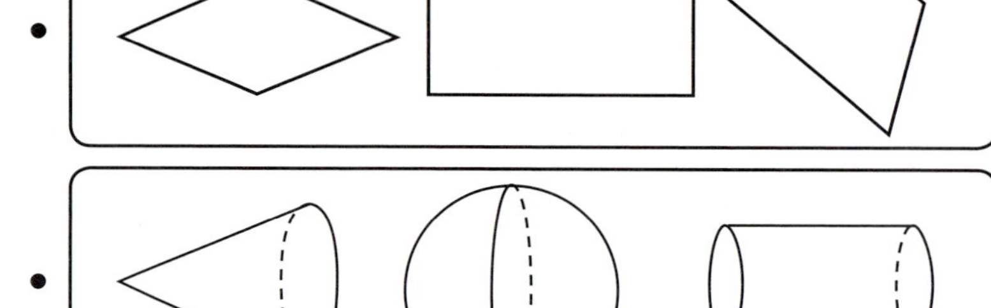

2. Each figure has 3 sides.

   You can trace each figure to make a circle.

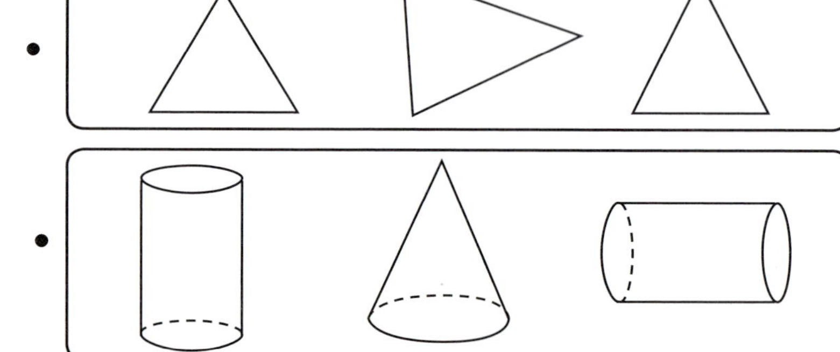

On Your Own

3. Draw 3 figures that are the same in some way. Write a rule that describes how the figures are the same.

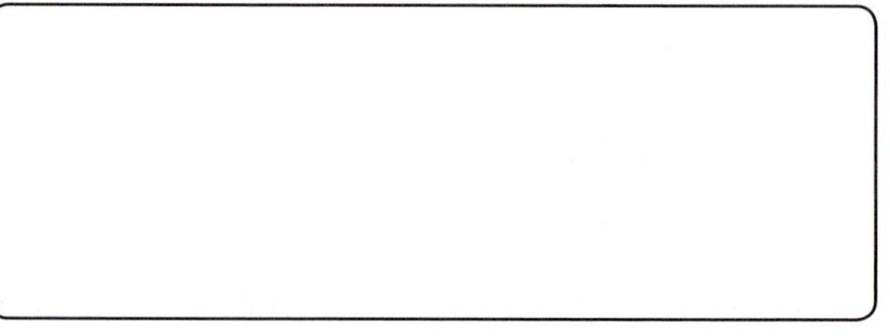

____

- - - - - - - - - - - - - - - -

____

 Look at Exercise 2. What is another rule for the top group of figures? Explain.

THE WORLD ALMANAC FOR KIDS

Cars

Not all cars have 4 wheels. Here is an example, a cable car! You can still ride one today. Have you ever been on a cable car?

The first cable cars in the United States were on Clay Street in San Francisco.

FACT·ACTIVITY

1 Color the cars to show a pattern. Use 2 colors.

2 Color the wheels to show a pattern. Use 3 colors.

3 Color the cars to show a pattern. Use 2 colors.
Color the wheels to show a pattern. Use 3 colors.

Math Talk Explain the 2 patterns you made in Exercise 3.

First Cars

The first cars did not look like cars today. What did the first car look like? Look at the picture. What figures do you see?

The first car Henry Ford built used 4 bicycle tires for wheels. It was called the Quadricycle.

Quadricycle

FACT·ACTIVITY

Use circles, triangles, squares, and rectangles to design your own car.

How many did you draw?

_____ triangles _____ circles _____ squares _____ rectangles

Math Talk Describe your car. Show and explain the different figures you chose.

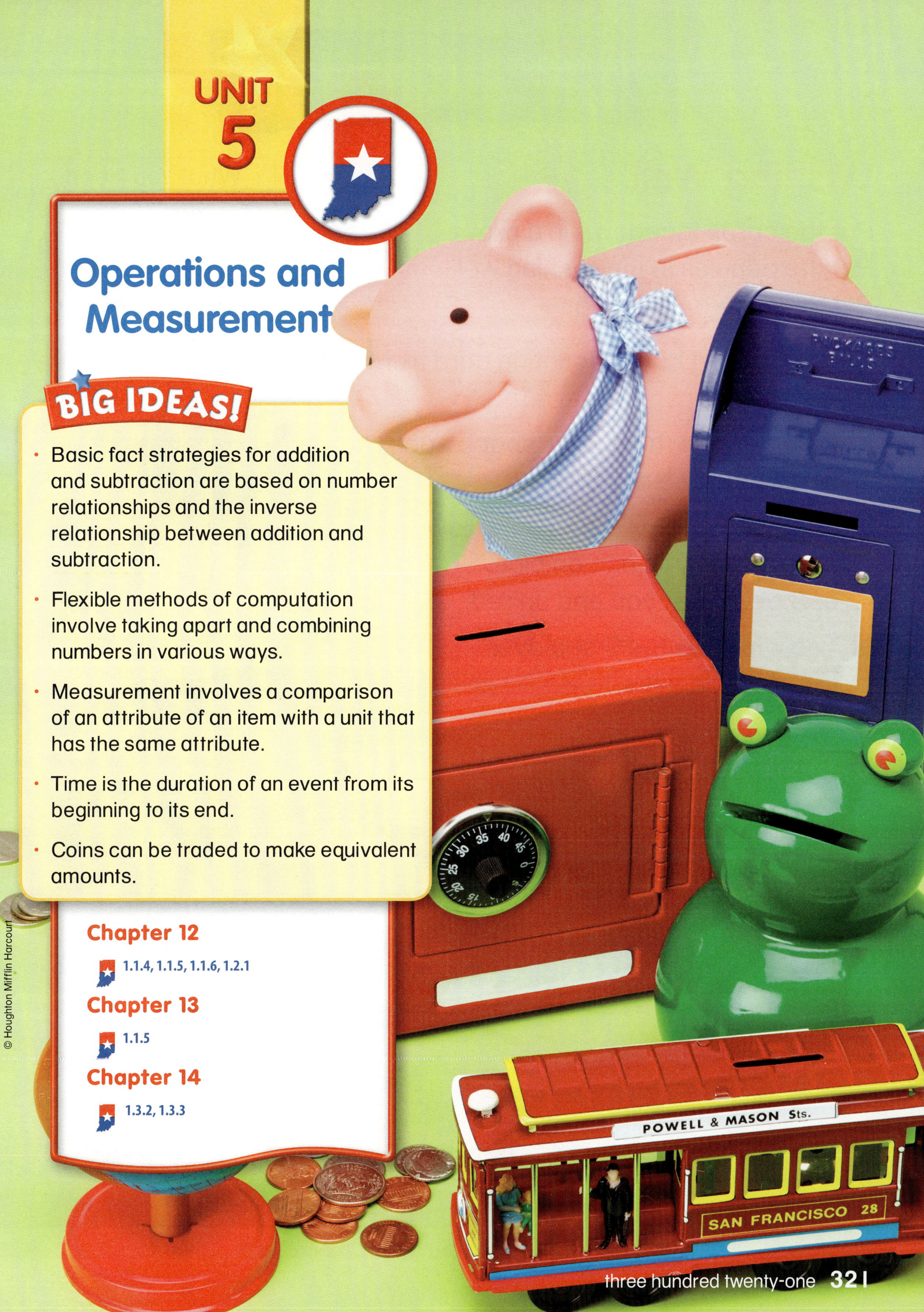

UNIT
5

Operations and Measurement

BIG IDEAS!

• Basic fact strategies for addition and subtraction are based on number relationships and the inverse relationship between addition and subtraction.

• Flexible methods of computation involve taking apart and combining numbers in various ways.

• Measurement involves a comparison of an attribute of an item with a unit that has the same attribute.

• Time is the duration of an event from its beginning to its end.

• Coins can be traded to make equivalent amounts.

Chapter 12
1.1.4, 1.1.5, 1.1.6, 1.2.1

Chapter 13
1.1.5

Chapter 14
1.3.2, 1.3.3

POWELL & MASON Sts.

SAN FRANCISCO 28

Wishing Well

Put the cards facedown in a pile.
Put the pennies in the wishing well.
Put the cube on any space.

What You Need
2 players
cards numbered 1-10
20  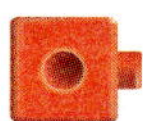

1. Take turns. Draw a counting card from the pile.

2. Count. Move the cube 1 space each time you say a number.

3. Take 1 penny if you end on yellow, 2 pennies if you end on blue, or 3 pennies if you end on red.

4. The winner is the first player to get 10 pennies.

Dear Family,

My class started Unit 5 today. In the next few chapters, I will learn further addition and subtraction, money, time, and measurement. Here are some vocabulary words and activities for us to share.

From,

____

Vocabulary

It is 4 o'clock.

minute hand
hour hand

hour minutes

 penny  nickel

 dime

You can use **inches** to **measure** length.

Family Math Activity

Help your child make a bank by covering a plastic container with paper and decorating it with crayons or markers. Make a slit in the lid for inserting the coins.

Give loose change to your child. Have your child name each coin as he or she puts the change into the bank. Use the change later to pay for a treat you can enjoy together.

Literature

These books link to the math in this unit. Look for them at the library.

- **Deena's Lucky Penny**
  by Barbara Derubertis
  Illustrated by Joan Holub
  and Cynthia Fisher
  (The Kane Press, 1999)
- **Jelly Beans for Sale**
  by Bruce McMillan
- **Game Time!**
  by Stuart J. Murphy
  Illustrated by Cynthia Jabar

Math at Home

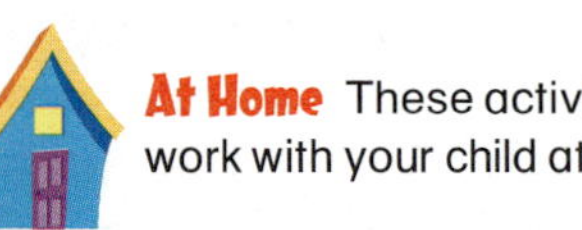

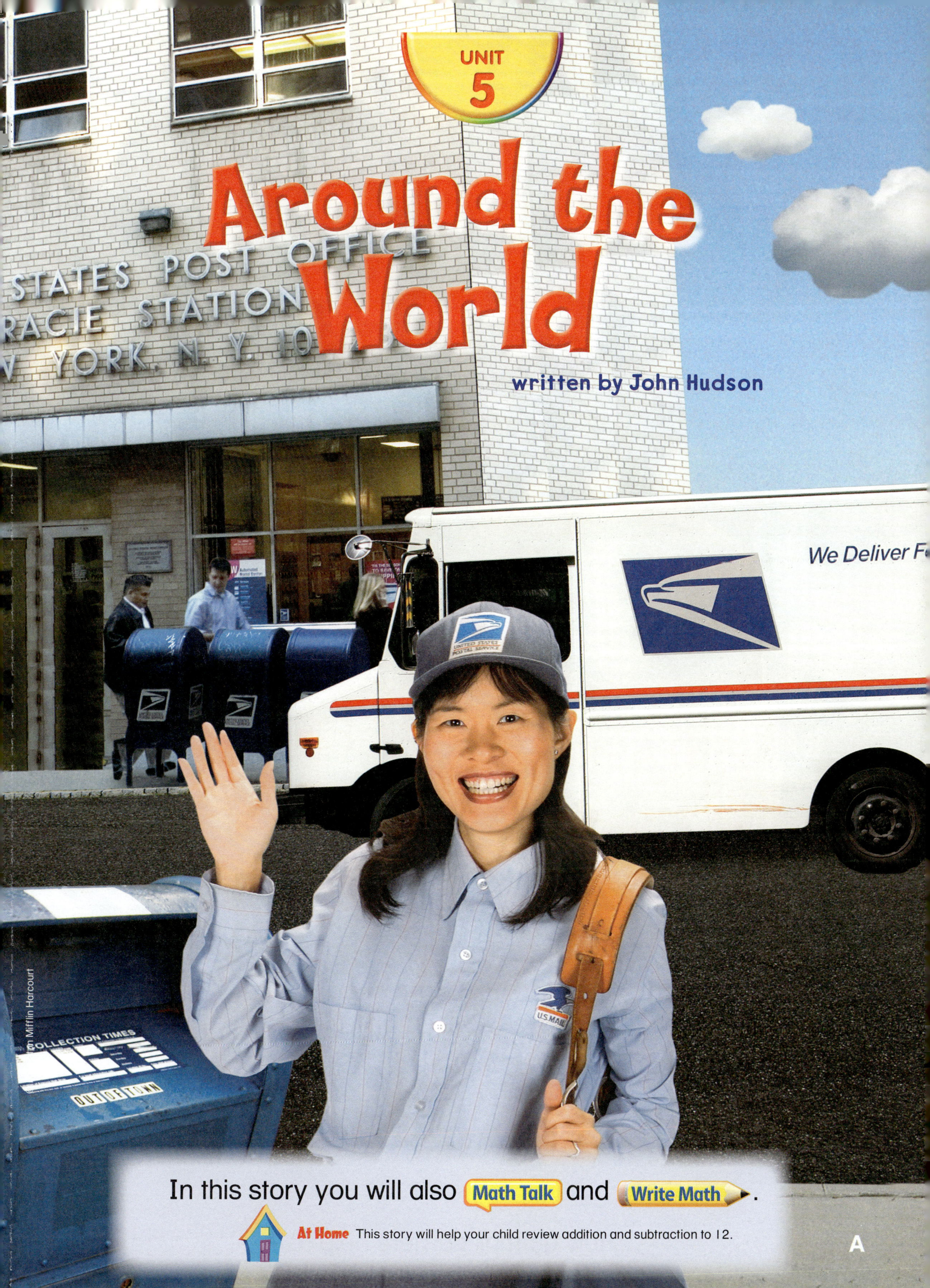

In this story you will also **Math Talk** and **Write Math**.

At Home This story will help your child review addition and subtraction to 12.

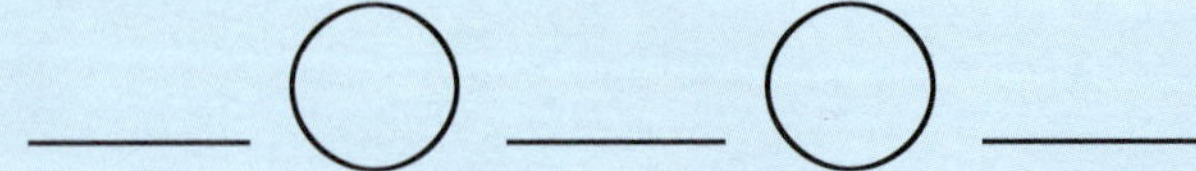

The mail carrier brings letters to
Mr. and Mrs. Jones.
How many letters does she deliver?

___ ◯ ___ ◯ ___

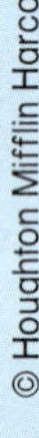

How do mail carriers help us?

The mail carrier brings packages
to the fire station. Then she brings
more packages.
How many packages does she bring?

___ ◯ ___ ◯ ___

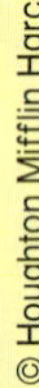

It is time for lunch.
The mail carrier eats in the park.
How many boys and girls are playing?

___ ◯ ___ ◯ ___

How do parents help us?

The mail carrier brings 12 packages to the police station. "This person has moved," says the police officer. "You need to take these back." How many packages does the officer keep?

How do police officers help us?

E

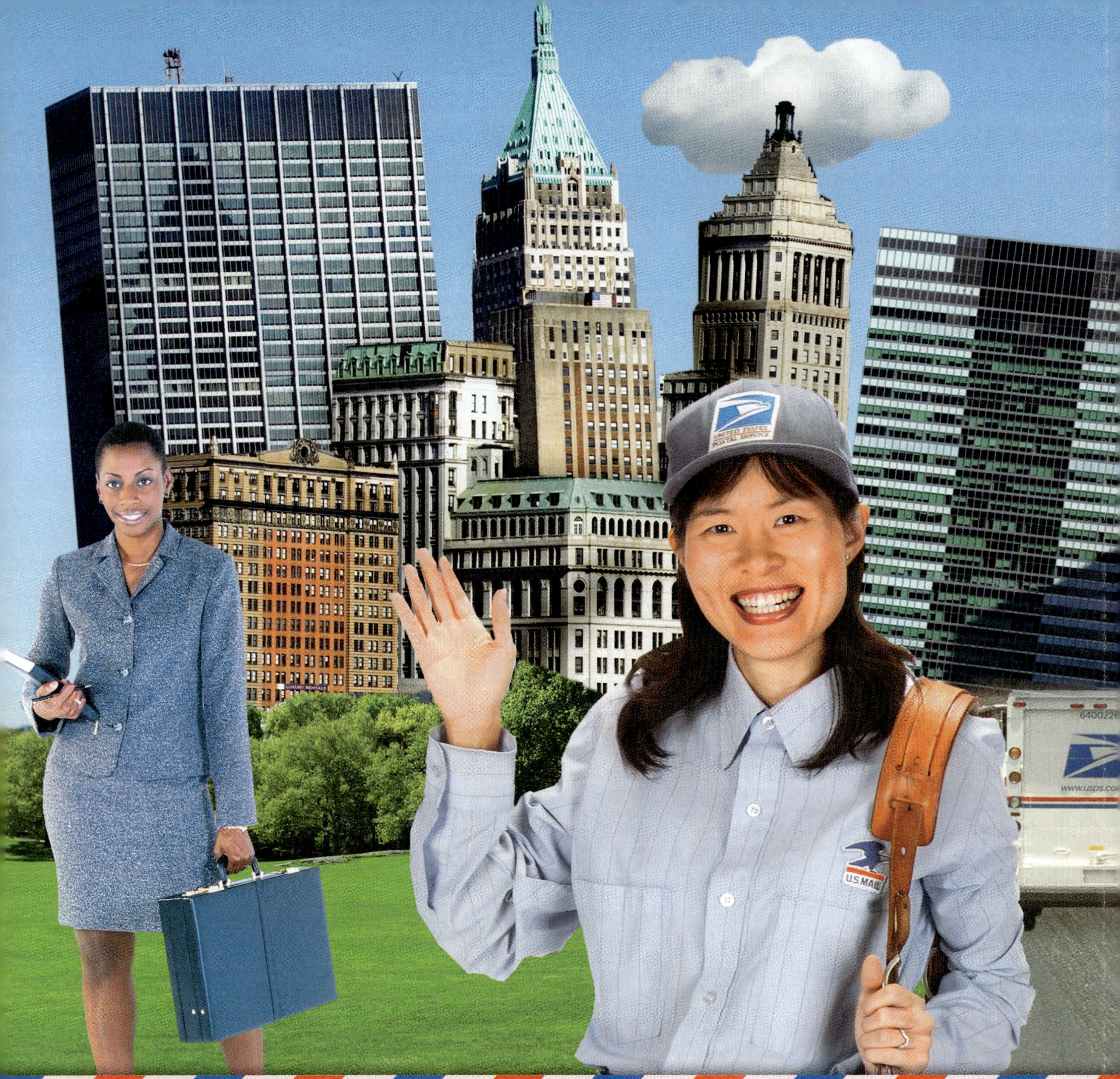

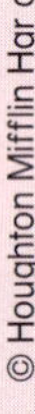

The mail carrier stops at City Hall.
She brings 8 letters for the mayor.
She brings 4 letters for the city clerk.
How many letters does she bring?

___ ◯ ___ ◯ ___

F

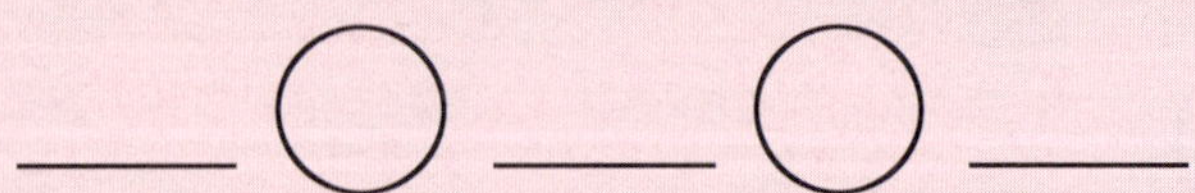

Mr. and Mrs. Jones each got the same number of letters. They got 12 letters in all. Draw the two groups of letters.

Vocabulary Review

add   difference
subtract   doubles
sum

Letters for Mr. Jones

Letters for Mrs. Jones

Write the number sentence. _____ ◯ _____ ◯ _____

Write Math ➤ Describe your number sentence. Use a vocabulary word.

____

- -

____

- -

____

G

Name ______________________

How Many Letters?

 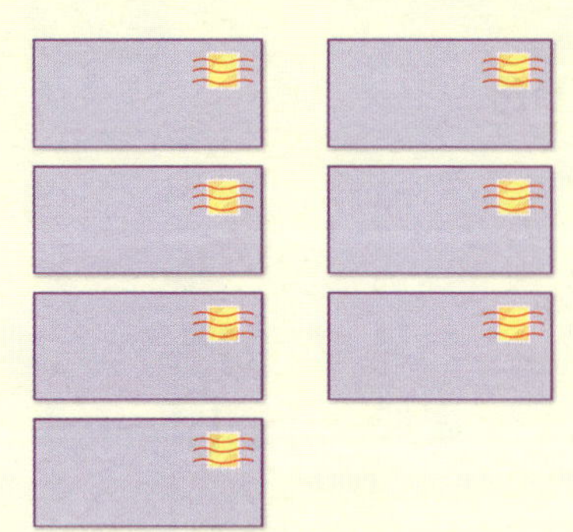

 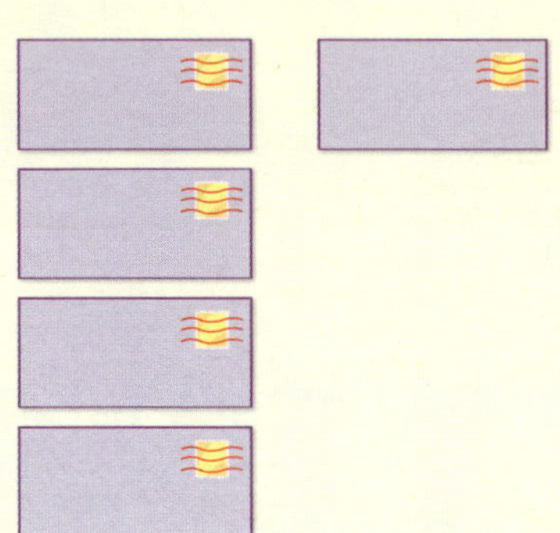

 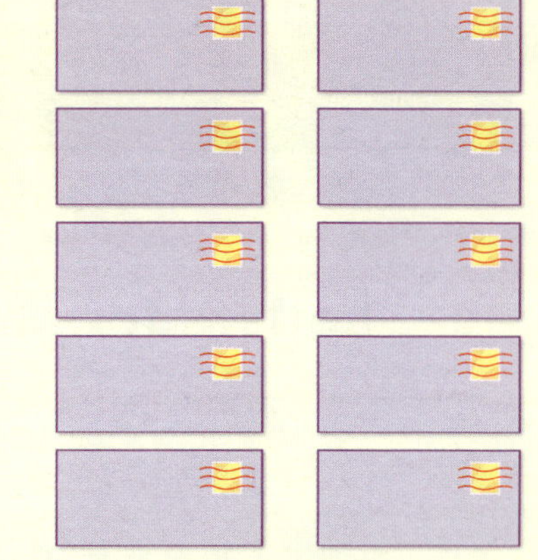

1. How many letters do  and  have in all?

___ ◯ ___ ◯ ___

2. How many more letters does  have than  ?

___ ◯ ___ ◯ ___

3. Circle the two that have 11 letters in all.

Write Math ➤ Make up an addition story about the mail carrier bringing letters to you and a classmate. Write the number sentence.

H

Addition and Subtraction Facts to 20

Theme: At the Park

Fun Fact

When a duckling hatches it stays in the nest less than one day.

Investigate

There were 18 ducks in the group. You can still see some of them. How many ducks have left?

GO ONLINE
Technology
Student pages are available in the Student eBook.

Show What You Know 

Draw lines to match. Subtract to compare.

1.

$3 - 1 =$ ___

___ more

2.

$5 - 2 =$ ___

___ fewer

3.

$6 - 5 =$ ___

___ fewer

4.

$8 - 3 =$ ___

___ more

Use the number line to count back.
Write each difference.

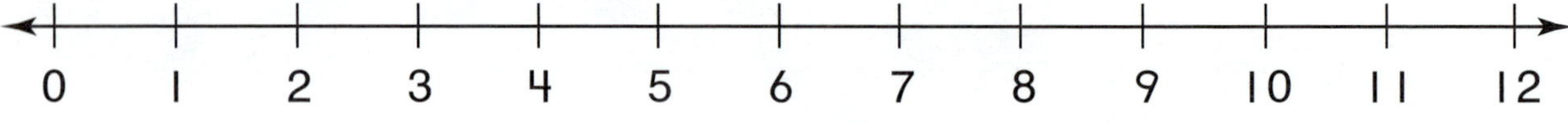

5. $7 - 1 =$ ___

6. $9 - 2 =$ ___

7. $5 - 3 =$ ___

8. $10 - 2 =$ ___

9. $10 - 1 =$ ___

10. $8 - 3 =$ ___

At Home This page checks your child's understanding of important concepts and skills needed for success in Chapter 12.

Name ______________________

Add 10 and More

Essential Question
How can you use a ten frame to add 10 and some more?

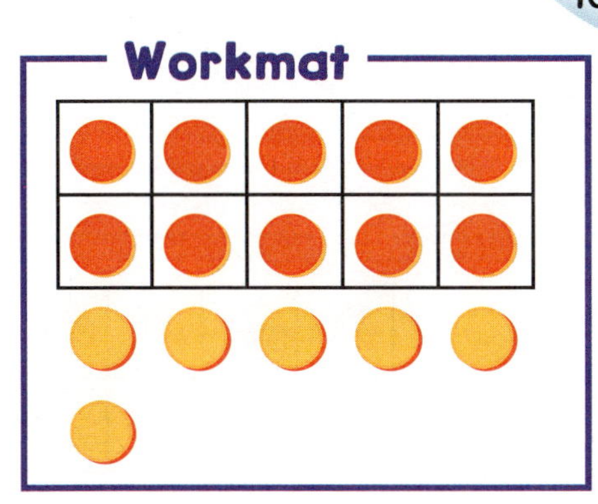

I can use a ten frame to add 10 + 6. The sum 16 means 1 ten 6 ones.

Use ⬤ and Workmat 7 to add.
Draw the 🟡. Write the sum.

1.
10
+ 3
13
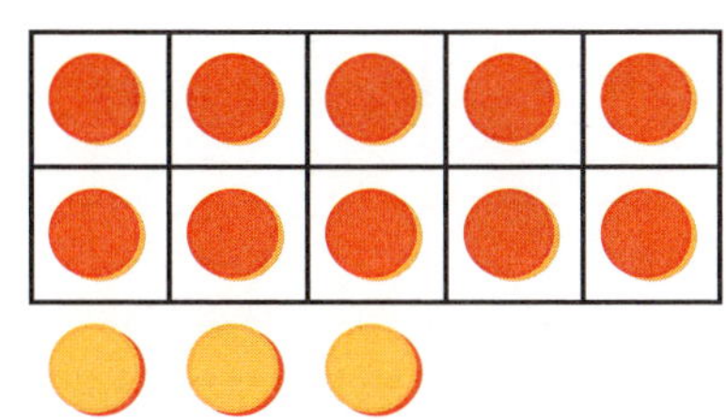

2.
10
+ 5
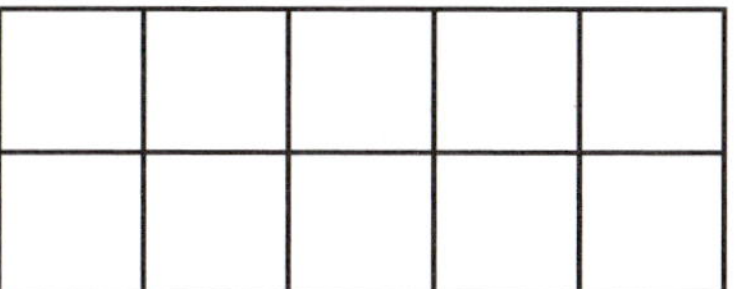

3.
10
+ 1
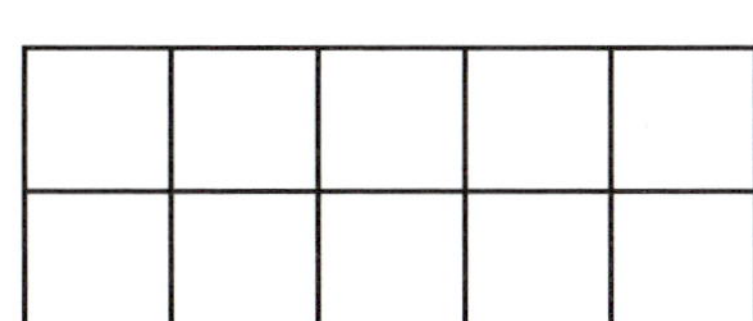

4.
10
+ 2
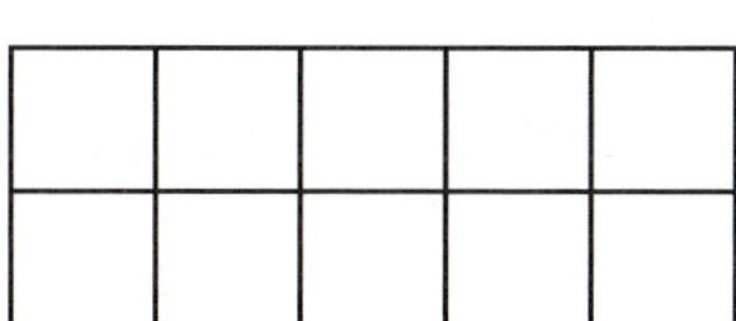

5.
10
+ 4
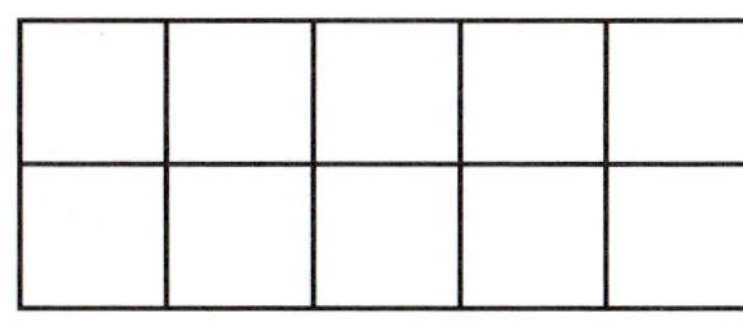

6.
10
+ 7
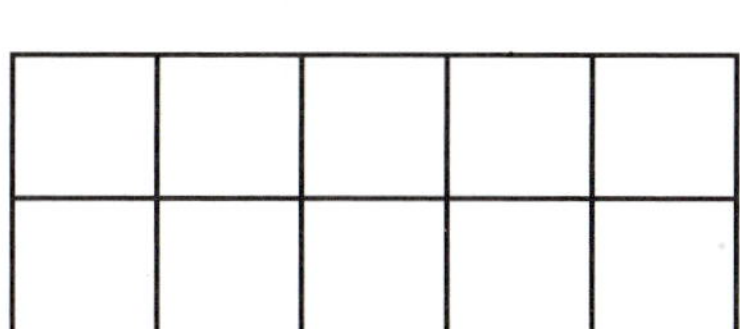

7. (Math Talk) How do you use a ten frame to add 10 + 8? Explain.

1.1.4 Show equivalent forms of whole numbers to at least 100 as groups of tens and ones. **1.1.5** Solve problems involving addition and subtraction by modeling addition of numbers to at least 100 and modeling the inverse operation of subtraction using objects.

Write the sum.

1. 10
   + 8
   ―――
    18
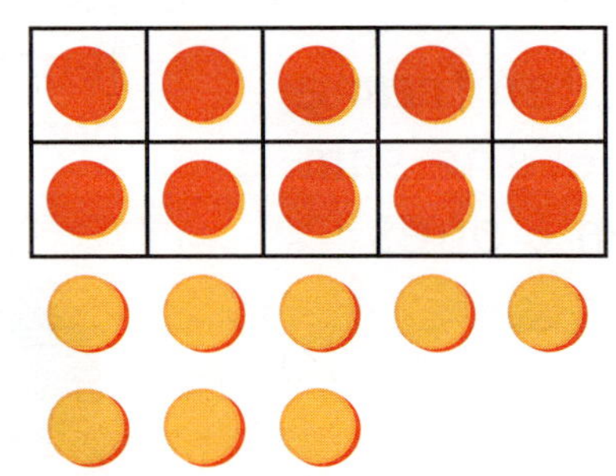

2. 10
   + 2
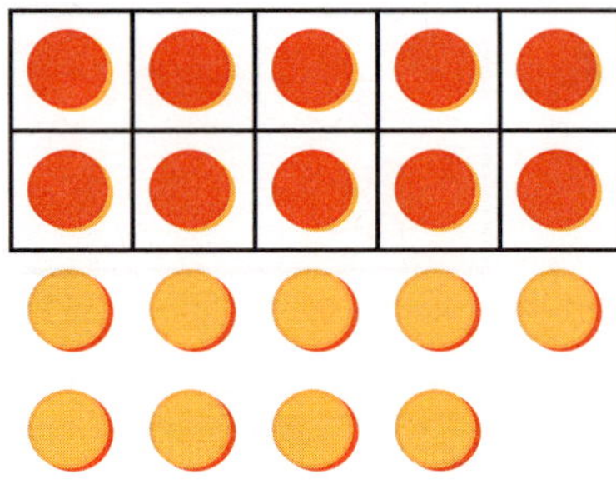

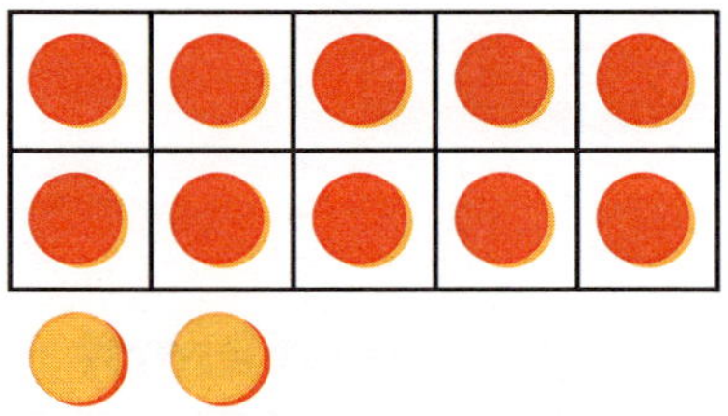

3. 10
   + 6
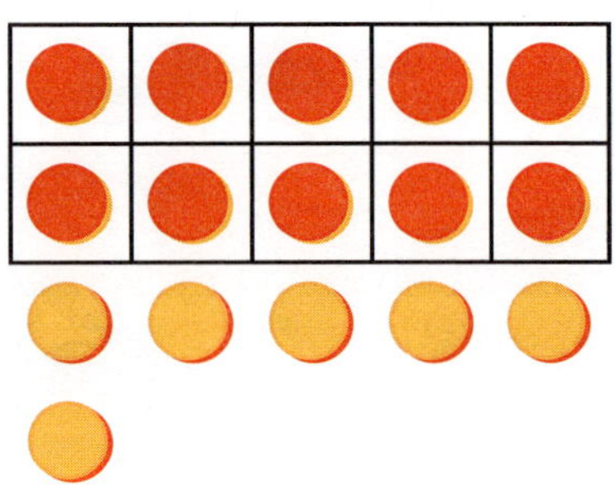

4. 10
   + 9

5. 10
   + 1

6.   4
   +10

7.   5
   +10

8. 10
   + 3

9.   0
   +10

10. 10
    + 7

Math Board

Problem Solving: Real World

11. Write the missing addend.
    Use ● to add. Draw the ●.

     10
   +[ ]
   ――――
     14

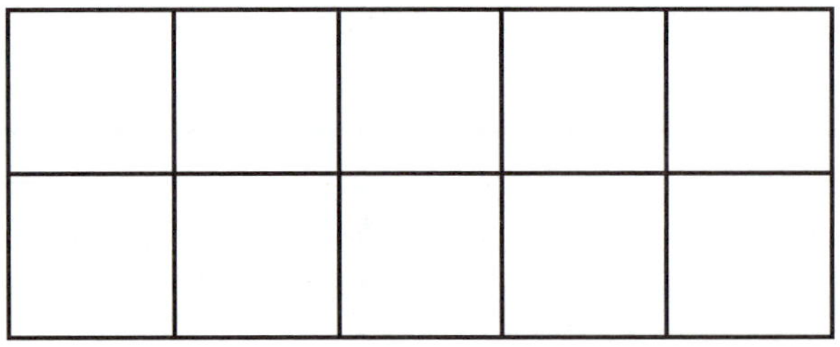

How did you find the missing addend?
Explain.

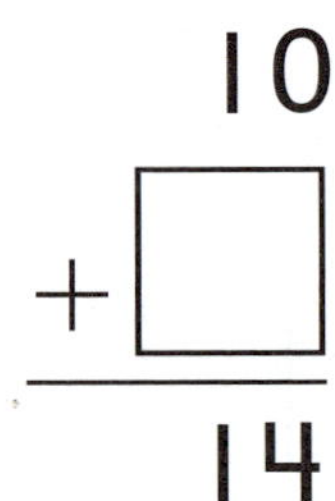

Make a 10 to Add

▶ **Explore**

Use make a ten.
Find the sum of $4 + 8$.

Put 8 🔴 in the ten frame. Then show 4 🟡.

Move 2 🟡 into the ten frame to make a ten.

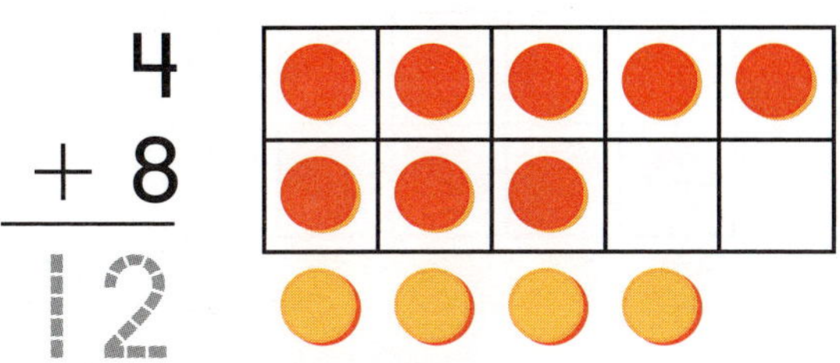

$$\begin{array}{r} 4 \\ + 8 \\ \hline 12 \end{array}$$

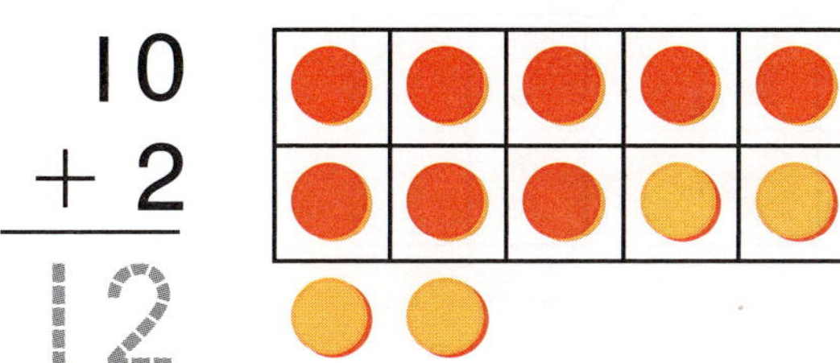

$$\begin{array}{r} 10 \\ + 2 \\ \hline 12 \end{array}$$

▶ **Connect**

Use 🟡 and Workmat 7. Show both addends.
Add. Then make a ten and add.

1.
$$\begin{array}{r} 9 \\ + 5 \\ \hline \end{array}$$
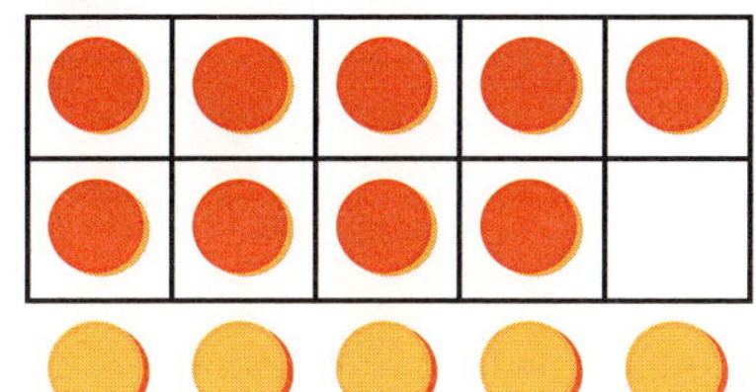

$$\begin{array}{r} 10 \\ + 4 \\ \hline \end{array}$$
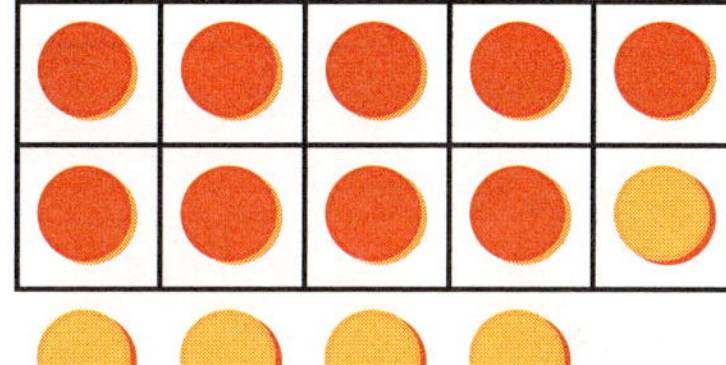

2.
$$\begin{array}{r} 4 \\ + 7 \\ \hline \end{array}$$

$$\begin{array}{r} 10 \\ + 1 \\ \hline \end{array}$$
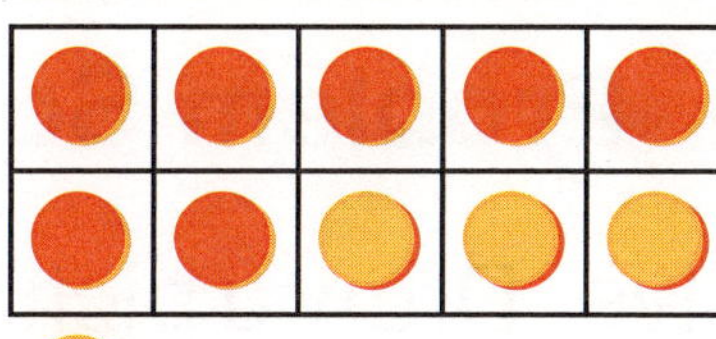

3.
$$\begin{array}{r} 8 \\ + 9 \\ \hline \end{array}$$
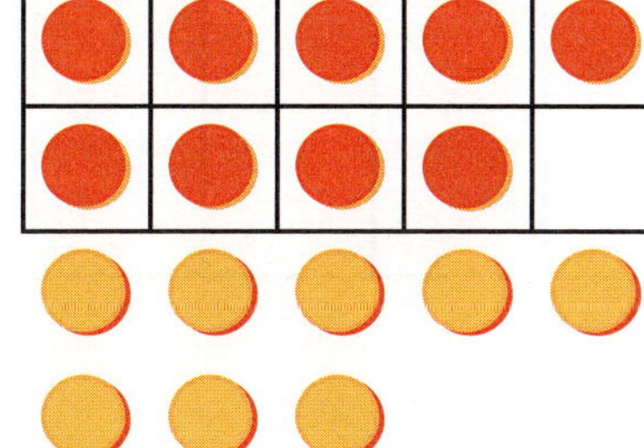

$$\begin{array}{r} 10 \\ + 7 \\ \hline \end{array}$$
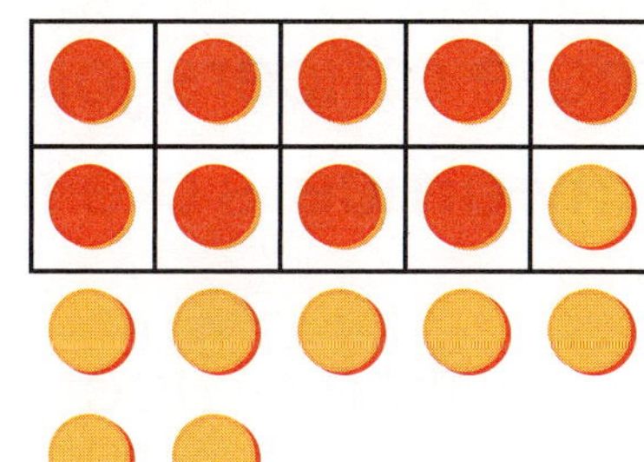

4. **Math Talk** How do you use make a ten to find the sum of $5 + 8$?

1.1.5 Solve problems involving addition and subtraction by modeling addition of numbers to at least 100 and modeling the inverse operation of subtraction using objects. also **1.1.4**

Use 🟡 and Workmat 7. Show both addends.
Add. Then make a ten and add.

1.
$$
\begin{array}{r} 5 \\ +\ 8 \\ \hline 13 \end{array}
$$
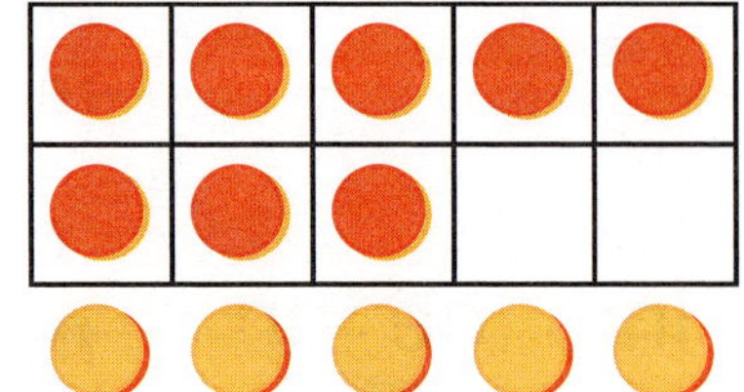

$$
\begin{array}{r} 10 \\ +\ 3 \\ \hline \end{array}
$$
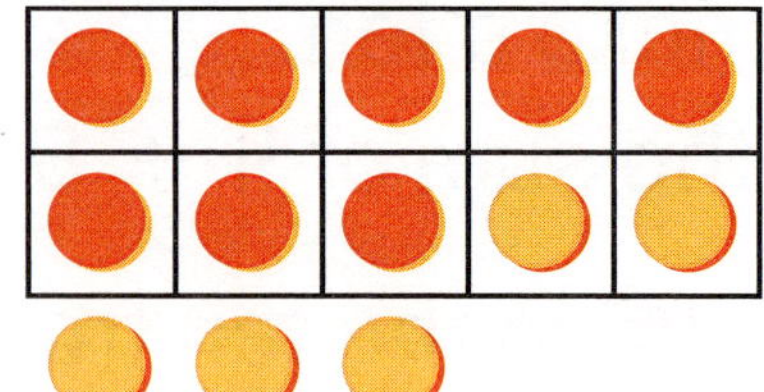

2.
$$
\begin{array}{r} 9 \\ +\ 6 \\ \hline \end{array}
$$
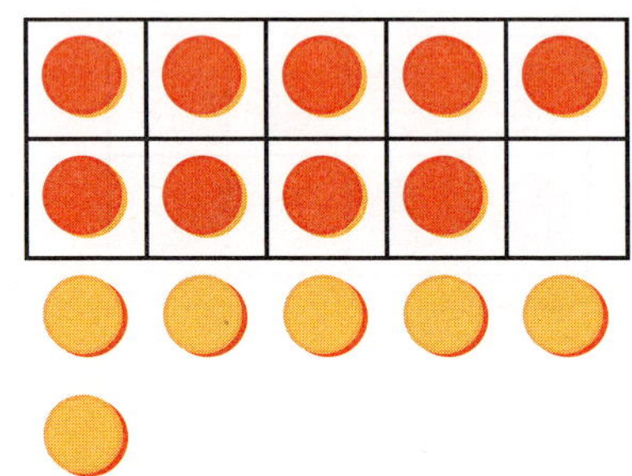

$$
\begin{array}{r} 10 \\ +\ 5 \\ \hline \end{array}
$$
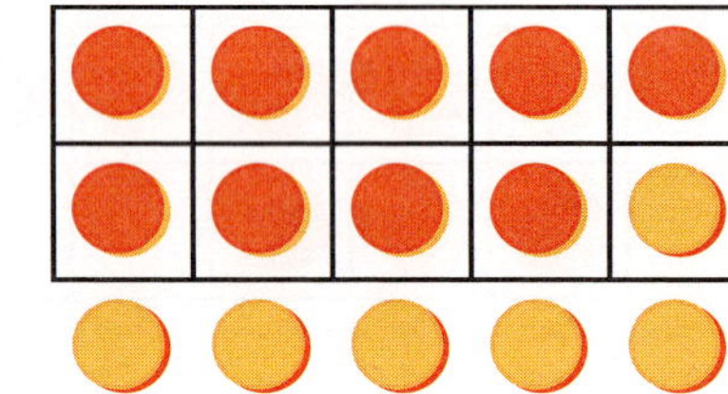

3.
$$
\begin{array}{r} 7 \\ +\ 9 \\ \hline \end{array}
$$
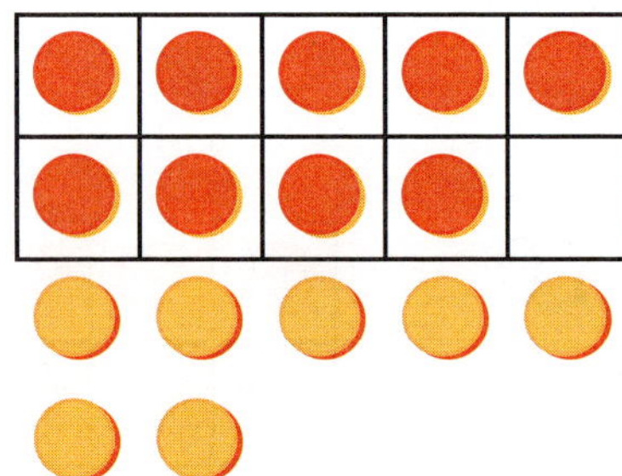

$$
\begin{array}{r} 10 \\ +\ 6 \\ \hline \end{array}
$$
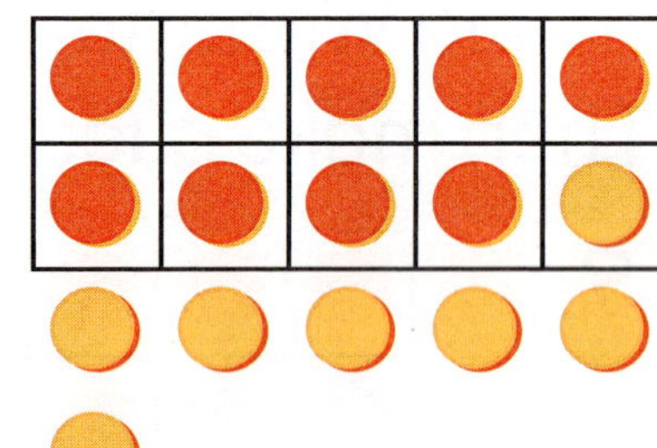

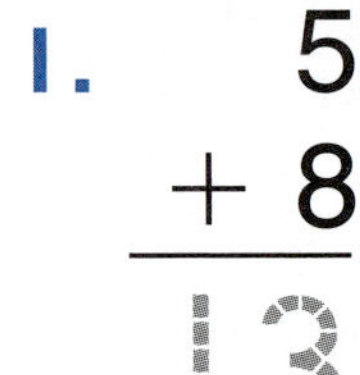

Problem Solving: Application

4. Solve. Draw a picture to check.

4 police officers lead the parade.
9 more officers join them. How
many officers are there in all?

_____ police officers

How can you make a ten
to solve? Explain.

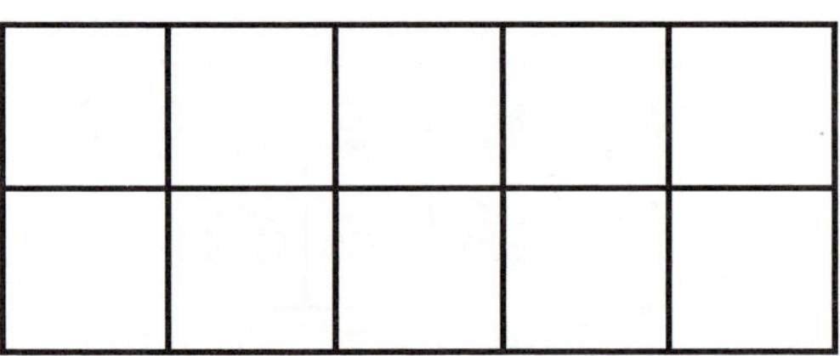

Algebra: Add 3 Numbers

▶ **We Learn**

You can choose the two addends you add first.
The sum does not change. Look for facts you know.

$$2$$
$$2$$
$$+8$$
$$\overline{12}$$

You can make a ten.

$$2 + 8 = 10$$
$$10 + 2 = 12$$

You can use doubles.

$$2 + 2 = 4$$
$$4 + 8 = 12$$

▶ **Share and Show**   

Circle the two addends that you add first. Circle
two different addends to add first. Write each sum.
Use 🎲 🎲 🎲 if you need to.

1.   7   7
         3   3
       +3   +3

2.   1   1
         1   1
       +9   +9

3.   5   5
         4   4
       +5   +5

4.   2   2
         5   5
       +5   +5

☑**5.** 2   2
         7   7
       +2   +2

☑**6.** 3   3
         6   6
       +3   +3

7. **Math Talk** Sam uses doubles to add $4 + 4 + 6$.
        Ann makes a ten. Why do they get the
        same sum?

1.1.5 Solve problems involving addition and subtraction by modeling
addition of numbers to at least 100 and modeling the inverse
operation of subtraction using objects. *also* **1.1.4**

Circle the two addends that you add first.
Write the sum.

1. 6 3 +3	**2.** 1 9 +1	**3.** 5 5 +4	**4.** 7 2 +2	**5.** 2 4 +4	**6.** 7 3 +1
7. 3 6 +3	**8.** 8 2 +2	**9.** 5 5 +1	**10.** 1 8 +2	**11.** 2 2 +6	**12.** 4 6 +4
13. 2 6 +4	**14.** 1 2 +8	**15.** 5 3 +5	**16.** 4 2 +4	**17.** 5 5 +5	**18.** 2 7 +3

Math Board

Problem Solving: Real World

19. Solve.

Jennifer gets 3 notebooks from a shelf,
3 notebooks from a box, and 7 notebooks
from a cart. How many notebooks does she
get in all?

______ notebooks

Tell two different ways you can
add to find the answer.

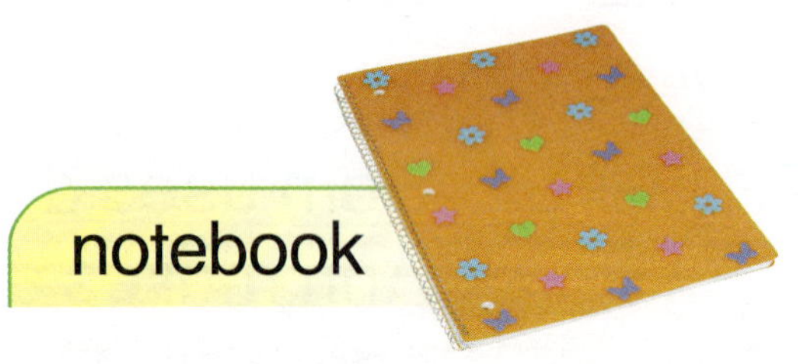

At Home Have your child show two ways to add
4 + 3 + 6. Have him or her tell which way uses make a
ten to find the sum.

Practice Sums to 20

▶ We Learn

You can use doubles, near doubles, and make a ten to find sums.

Doubles

$$8 + 8 = 16$$

Doubles Plus One

$$8 + 9 = 17$$

Make a Ten

$$7 + 4 = 11$$

▶ Share and Show

Write the sum.

1. $8 + 5 = 13$

2. $6 + 6$

3. $5 + 4$

4. $9 + 3$

5. $8 + 9$

6. $9 + 5$

7. $7 + 5$

8. $9 + 6$

9. $7 + 7$

10. $8 + 7$

✓11. $9 + 9$

✓12. $7 + 9$

13. **Math Talk** In which exercises did you use make a ten to find the sum? Explain.

1.1.6 Demonstrate fluency with addition facts and the corresponding subtraction facts for totals to at least 20.

Add.
Use the key to color.

Key
Doubles 
Near Doubles
Make a Ten

$7 + 4 =$ ______

$$\begin{array}{r} 7 \\ +8 \\ \hline \end{array}$$

$$\begin{array}{r} 5 \\ +6 \\ \hline \end{array}$$

$7 + 7 =$ ______

$$\begin{array}{r} 7 \\ +5 \\ \hline \end{array}$$

$$\begin{array}{r} 8 \\ +4 \\ \hline \end{array}$$

$$\begin{array}{r} 8 \\ +8 \\ \hline \end{array}$$

$$\begin{array}{r} 9 \\ +9 \\ \hline \end{array}$$

$6 + 5 =$ ______

$9 + 6 =$ ______

$$\begin{array}{r} 6 \\ +7 \\ \hline \end{array}$$

$$\begin{array}{r} 4 \\ +5 \\ \hline \end{array}$$

$10 + 10 =$ ______

$9 + 7 =$ ______

$$\begin{array}{r} 5 \\ +4 \\ \hline \end{array}$$

$8 + 6 =$ ______

$5 + 5 =$ ______

At Home Have your child add 8 + 5, 8 + 8, and 8 + 9. Ask your child whether he or she will use doubles, near doubles, or make a ten to solve each problem.

Chapter 12 Lesson 5

Think Addition to Subtract

You can use an addition fact to help you find the related subtraction fact.

$9 + 9 = \underline{18}$

$18 - 9 = \underline{9}$

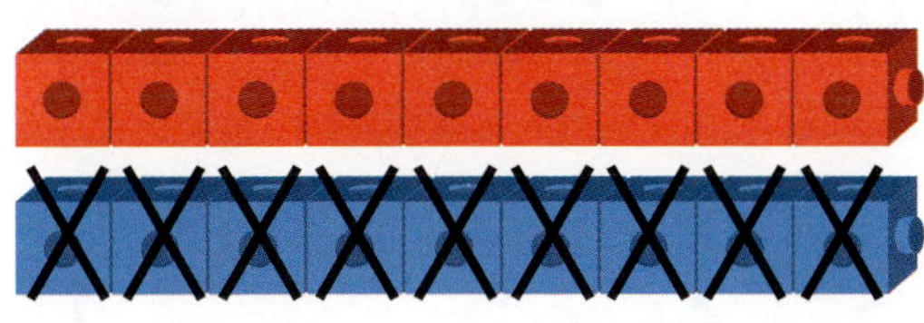

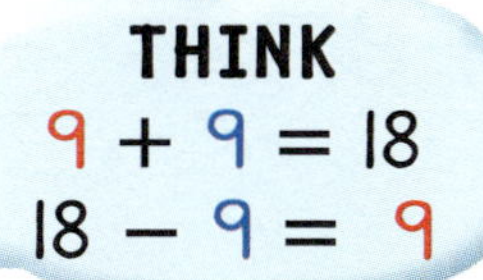

Add. Then subtract.

Use  if you need to.

1. $9 + 4 = \underline{13}$

$13 - 4 = \underline{9}$

2. $6 + 6 = \underline{}$

$12 - 6 = \underline{}$

3. $8 + 8 = \underline{}$

$16 - 8 = \underline{}$

4. $7 + 5 = \underline{}$

$12 - 5 = \underline{}$

5. $5 + 5 = \underline{}$

$10 - 5 = \underline{}$

6. $6 + 8 = \underline{}$

$14 - 8 = \underline{}$

7. $3 + 8 = \underline{}$

$11 - 8 = \underline{}$

8. $7 + 7 = \underline{}$

$14 - 7 = \underline{}$

9. $9 + 5 = \underline{}$

$14 - 5 = \underline{}$

10. **Math Talk** How does the addition fact $8 + 5 = 13$ help you solve $13 - 5$?

Essential Question
How can you use addition to help you solve a subtraction problem?

Vocabulary
subtract

1.1.6 Demonstrate fluency with addition facts and the corresponding subtraction facts for totals to at least 20.

$$9 + 6 = 15$$

$$15 - 6 = 9$$

Add. Then subtract.
Use 🔴 🔵 if you need to.

1.	7 +8	15 − 8	2.	6 +6	12 − 6	3.	7 +4	11 − 4
4.	7 +7	14 − 7	5.	6 +7	13 − 7	6.	5 +5	10 − 5
7.	9 +8	17 − 8	8.	10 + 9	19 − 9	9.	7 +9	16 − 9

Math Board

Problem Solving: Algebra

Write the missing numbers.

10.
$$8 + \square = 14$$
$$\square - 6 = 8$$

11.
$$\square + 9 = 18$$
$$18 - \square = 9$$

12.
$$4 + \square = 13$$
$$\square - 9 = 4$$

How can you find the missing numbers in
Exercise 12?

Practice Differences from 20

You can use different ways to subtract.

Use a Number Line

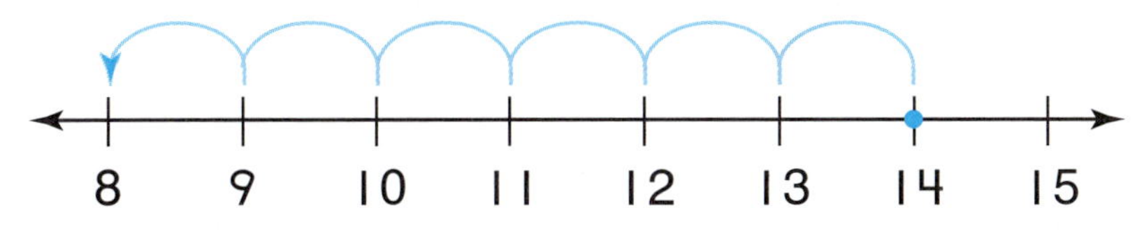

$14 - 6 = \underline{8}$

Think Addition to Subtract

Think $7 + 5 = \underline{12}$

So $12 - 5 = \underline{7}$

Write the difference.

1. $\begin{array}{r} 11 \\ -\ 2 \\ \hline 9 \end{array}$
2. $\begin{array}{r} 16 \\ -\ 8 \\ \hline \end{array}$
3. $\begin{array}{r} 12 \\ -\ 3 \\ \hline \end{array}$
4. $\begin{array}{r} 4 \\ -\ 2 \\ \hline \end{array}$
5. $\begin{array}{r} 14 \\ -\ 5 \\ \hline \end{array}$

6. $\begin{array}{r} 2 \\ -\ 1 \\ \hline \end{array}$
7. $\begin{array}{r} 13 \\ -\ 7 \\ \hline \end{array}$
8. $\begin{array}{r} 15 \\ -\ 6 \\ \hline \end{array}$
9. $\begin{array}{r} 14 \\ -\ 9 \\ \hline \end{array}$
10. $\begin{array}{r} 12 \\ -\ 8 \\ \hline \end{array}$

11. $\begin{array}{r} 12 \\ -\ 9 \\ \hline \end{array}$
12. $\begin{array}{r} 15 \\ -\ 7 \\ \hline \end{array}$
13. $\begin{array}{r} 20 \\ -10 \\ \hline \end{array}$
✓14. $\begin{array}{r} 16 \\ -\ 7 \\ \hline \end{array}$
✓15. $\begin{array}{r} 18 \\ -\ 9 \\ \hline \end{array}$

16. **Math Talk** Tell different ways to subtract $13 - 6$.

1.1.6 Demonstrate fluency with addition facts and the corresponding subtraction facts for totals to at least 20.

Subtract.
Use the key to color.

Key

Difference = 3, 4, or 5

Difference = 6 or 7

Difference = 8 or 9

$17 - 9 = \underline{\quad}$

$$16 - 9$$

$$13 - 9$$

$$18 - 9$$

$14 - 7 = \underline{\quad}$

$14 - 6 = \underline{\quad}$

$8 - 4 = \underline{\quad}$

$$15 - 9$$

$14 - 8 = \underline{\quad}$

$$13 - 6$$

$13 - 8 = \underline{\quad}$

$$15 - 8$$

$6 - 3 = \underline{\quad}$

At Home Have your child subtract 14 − 5 and 16 − 8.
Ask how he or she solved each problem.

Chapter 12 Lesson 7

Fact Families

▶ We Learn

A fact family is a group of all the related facts
that use the same numbers.

$$\underline{13} = 5 + 8 \qquad \underline{5} = 13 - 8$$

$$\underline{13} = 8 + 5 \qquad \underline{8} = 13 - 5$$

▶ Share and Show

Write the sum or difference.

Write the numbers in the fact family.

1. $9 + 5 = \underline{\qquad}$ $\qquad$ $14 - 5 = \underline{\qquad}$

 $5 + 9 = \underline{\qquad}$ $\qquad$ $14 - 9 = \underline{\qquad}$ $\qquad$ ☐ ☐ ☐

2. $\underline{\qquad} = 6 + 7$ $\qquad$ $\underline{\qquad} = 13 - 7$

 $\underline{\qquad} = 7 + 6$ $\qquad$ $\underline{\qquad} = 13 - 6$ $\qquad$ ☐ ☐ ☐

3. $7 + 9 = \underline{\qquad}$ $\qquad$ $16 - 9 = \underline{\qquad}$

 $9 + 7 = \underline{\qquad}$ $\qquad$ $16 - 7 = \underline{\qquad}$ $\qquad$ ☐ ☐ ☐

4. **Math Talk** Why is this a fact family?

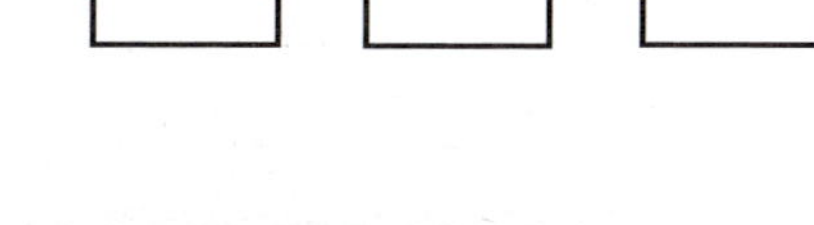

1.1.6 Demonstrate fluency with addition facts and the corresponding
subtraction facts for totals to at least 20.

1. Write each sum or difference.
Color all the facts in the same fact family to match.

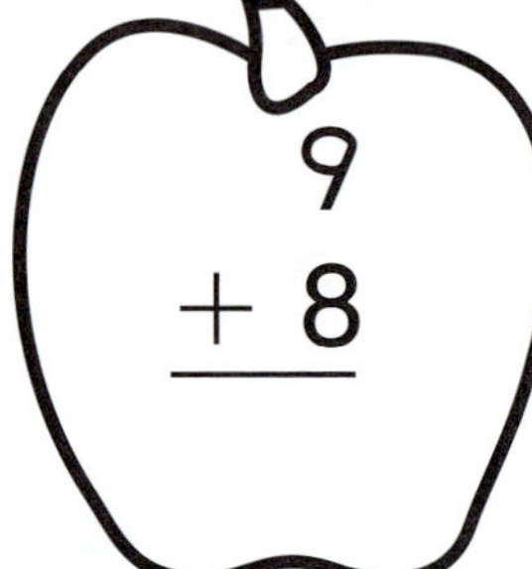

15
− 8

9
+ 8

9
+ 4

17
− 8

13
− 9

15
− 7

8
+ 6

17
− 9

13
− 4

Math Board

Problem Solving: Number Sense

2. Circle three numbers that make a fact family. Write the number sentences.

6   8   9
15   16

_____ + _____ = _____   _____ − _____ = _____

_____ + _____ = _____   _____ − _____ = _____

Use the other two numbers to write a fact family.

Chapter 12 Lesson 8

Algebra: Missing Numbers

▶ **Explore**

What is the missing number? $8 + \boxed{} = 11$

$8 + \boxed{3} = 11$

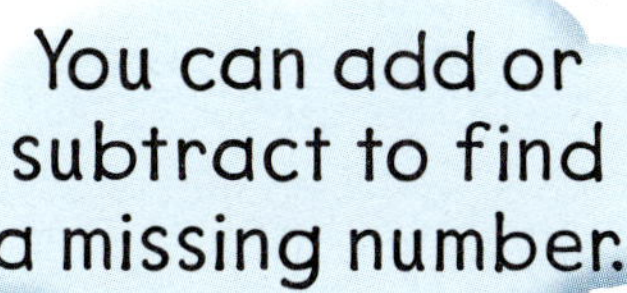

$11 - \boxed{8} = 3$

▶ **Connect**

Use ▦ and ▦ to find the missing
numbers. Write the numbers.

1.
$8 + \boxed{} = 15$
$15 - 8 = \boxed{}$

2.
$9 + \boxed{} = 13$
$13 - 9 = \boxed{}$

3.
$5 + \boxed{} = 14$
$14 - 5 = \boxed{}$

4.
$6 + \boxed{} = 14$
$14 - 6 = \boxed{}$

5.
$9 + \boxed{} = 16$
$16 - 9 = \boxed{}$

6.
$8 + \boxed{} = 17$
$17 - 8 = \boxed{}$

7. **Math Talk** How can subtraction help you
solve $\boxed{} + 6 = 13$?

1.2.1 Write and solve equations involving addition.

Write the missing numbers.
Use ▦ and ▦ if you need to.

1.
$\begin{array}{r} 7 \\ + \boxed{8} \\ \hline 15 \end{array}$
$\begin{array}{r} 15 \\ - 7 \\ \hline \boxed{8} \end{array}$

2.
$\begin{array}{r} 5 \\ + \square \\ \hline 12 \end{array}$
$\begin{array}{r} 12 \\ - 5 \\ \hline \square \end{array}$

3.
$\begin{array}{r} 7 \\ + \square \\ \hline 13 \end{array}$
$\begin{array}{r} 13 \\ - 7 \\ \hline \square \end{array}$

4.
$\begin{array}{r} 9 \\ + \square \\ \hline 18 \end{array}$
$\begin{array}{r} 18 \\ - 9 \\ \hline \square \end{array}$

5.
$\begin{array}{r} 9 \\ + \square \\ \hline 17 \end{array}$
$\begin{array}{r} 17 \\ - 9 \\ \hline \square \end{array}$

6.
$\begin{array}{r} 6 \\ + \square \\ \hline 16 \end{array}$
$\begin{array}{r} 16 \\ - 6 \\ \hline \square \end{array}$

7.
$\begin{array}{r} \square \\ + 9 \\ \hline 15 \end{array}$
$\begin{array}{r} 15 \\ - 9 \\ \hline \square \end{array}$

8.
$\begin{array}{r} \square \\ + 8 \\ \hline 13 \end{array}$
$\begin{array}{r} 13 \\ - 8 \\ \hline \square \end{array}$

9.
$\begin{array}{r} \square \\ + 7 \\ \hline 16 \end{array}$
$\begin{array}{r} 16 \\ - 7 \\ \hline \square \end{array}$

Problem Solving: Real World

10. Solve. Use ▦ and ▦ if you need to.
Rick has 7 party hats. He needs 12 hats for his party. How many more party hats does Rick need?

_____ party hats

Draw a picture to show how to solve the problem.

At Home Have your child explain how using subtraction can help him or her find the missing number in $7 + \square = 16$.

Chapter 12 Lesson 9

Create Addition and Subtraction Problems

▶ We Learn

____9____ red baskets

____6____ brown baskets

____15____ baskets in all

____6____ brown baskets

How many baskets are there?

____9____ ⊕ ____6____ ⊜ ____15____ baskets

How many baskets are red?

____15____ ⊖ ____6____ ⊜ ____9____ baskets

▶ Share and Show

Use the picture to write the numbers. Write the number sentences.

1. _____ green kites

_____ pink kites

_____ kites in all

_____ pink kites

How many kites are there?

_____ ◯ _____ ◯ _____ kites

How many kites are green?

_____ ◯ _____ ◯ _____ kites

2. _____ blue boats

_____ yellow boats

_____ boats in all

_____ blue boats

How many boats are there?

_____ ◯ _____ ◯ _____ boats

How many boats are yellow?

_____ ◯ _____ ◯ _____ boats

3. **Math Talk** Explain why the same picture can be used to show addition and subtraction.

1.1.6 Demonstrate fluency with addition facts and the corresponding subtraction facts for totals to at least 20.

Use the picture to write the numbers.
Write the number sentences.

1. _____ red flowers

_____ pink flowers

_____ flowers in all

_____ pink flowers

How many flowers are there?

_____ ◯ _____ ◯ _____ **flowers**

How many flowers are red?

_____ ◯ _____ ◯ _____ **flowers**

2. _____ blue hats

_____ orange hats

_____ hats in all

_____ blue hats

How many hats are there?

_____ ◯ _____ ◯ _____ **hats**

How many hats are orange?

_____ ◯ _____ ◯ _____ **hats**

 **Math Board**

Problem Solving: Reasoning

3. Write your own numbers for the balloons.
Write the number sentences.

_____ green balloons

_____ yellow balloons

_____ balloons in all

_____ yellow balloons

How many balloons
are there in all?

_____ ◯ _____ ◯ _____ **balloons**

How many balloons
are green?

_____ ◯ _____ ◯ _____ **balloons**

Draw a picture to show
the balloons.

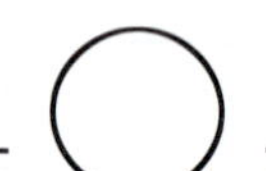

Problem Solving Workshop

Skill: Choose the Operation

Sarah buys 14 carrots.
She eats 5 of them.
How many carrots are left?

carrot

Some carrots are taken away. Subtract.

14 ⊖ 5 ⊜ 9

____9____ carrots

Chen has 6 red apples.
He buys 7 green apples.
How many apples does
he have now?

apple 

He buys more apples. Add.

6 ⊕ 7 ⊜ 13  

____13____ apples

THINK
Do I add or subtract?

Write the number sentence
to solve.

1. Mike has 6 peppers. Lisa
   brings 8 more. How many
   peppers are there in all?

   pepper

   ___ ◯ ___ ◯ ___

   ____ peppers

✓2. A store has 16 eggplants.
   Jim buys 7 of them. How
   many eggplants are still
   at the store?

   eggplant  

   ___ ◯ ___ ◯ ___

   ____ eggplants

1.1.6 Demonstrate fluency with addition facts and the corresponding subtraction facts for totals to at least 20.

Problem Solving Skill Practice

Write the number sentence to solve.

1. Lee eats 8 grapes. Then he eats 5 more. How many grapes does he eat in all?

grapes

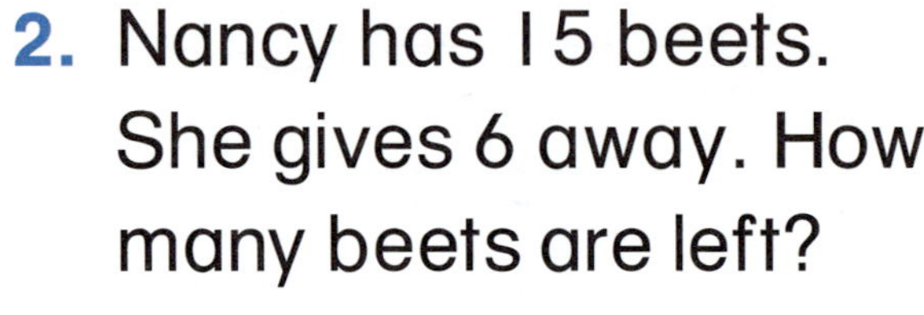

$$\underline{8} \;\oplus\; \underline{5} \;\ominus\; \underline{13}$$

$\underline{13}$ grapes

2. Nancy has 15 beets. She gives 6 away. How many beets are left?

beet

___ ◯ ___ ◯ ___

___ beets

3. Mark has 7 pears. Sara brings 7 more. How many pears are there now?

pear

___ ◯ ___ ◯ ___

___ pears

4. A store has 17 plums. Julie buys 9 of them. How many plums are still at the store?

plum

___ ◯ ___ ◯ ___

___ plums

5. Kim buys 13 oranges. She eats 4 of them. How many oranges are left?

orange

___ ◯ ___ ◯ ___

___ oranges

At Home Ask your child to explain how he or she solved Exercise 5. Discuss why he or she chose to add or subtract to solve the problem.

Extra Practice

Write the missing numbers.

1.
$$7 + \square = 14 \qquad \dfrac{14}{-7}\;\square$$

2.
$$6 + \square = 15 \qquad \dfrac{15}{-6}\;\square$$

3.
$$4 + \square = 12 \qquad \dfrac{12}{-4}\;\square$$

4. Use the picture to write the numbers.
Write the number sentences.

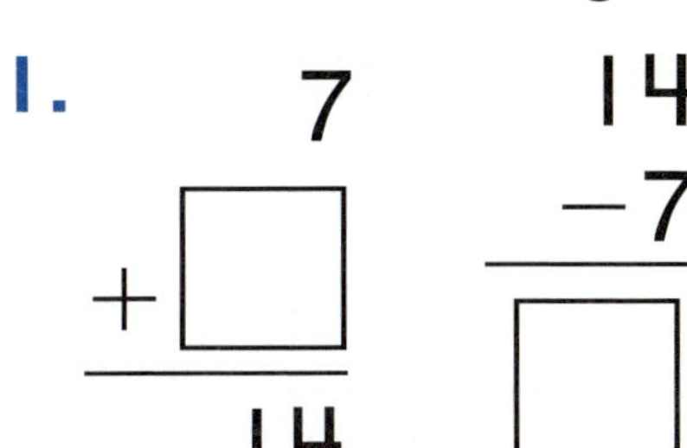

___ yellow cubes

___ blue cubes

___ cubes in all

___ yellow cubes

How many cubes are there?

___ ◯ ___ ◯ ___ cubes

How many cubes are blue?

___ ◯ ___ ◯ ___ cubes

5. Use ● and Workmat 7. Show both addends.
Add. Then make a ten and add.

$$\dfrac{5}{+\,8}$$

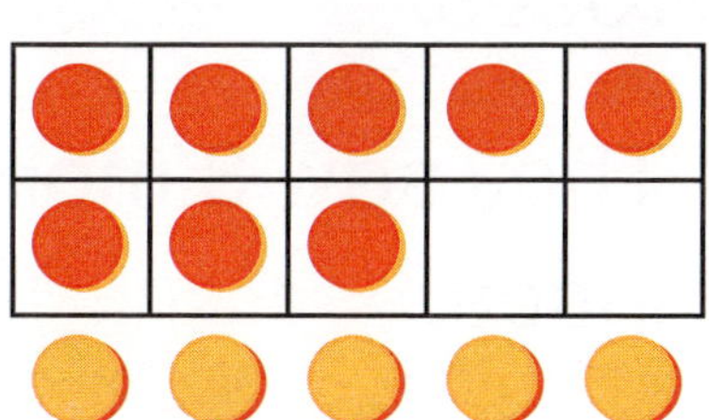

$$\dfrac{10}{+\,3}$$

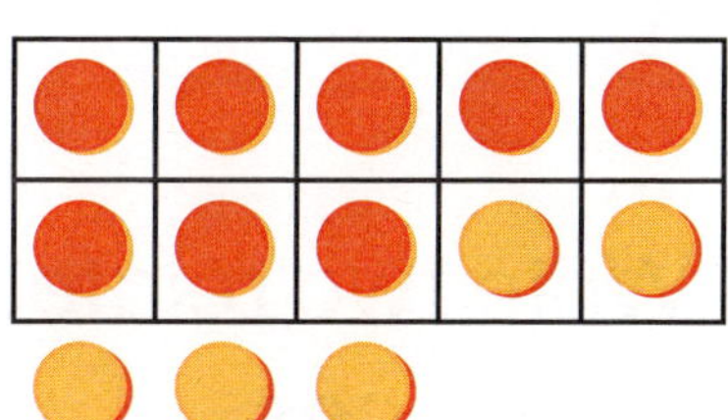

Problem Solving

Write the number sentence to solve.

6. Tim buys 13 carrots. He eats
5 of them. How many carrots
are left?

___ carrots

___ ◯ ___ ◯ ___

Multistep Problems
Chapter 12

1. Use the numbers.

1.1.5, 1.1.6

4   7   11

- Write an addition sentence using the numbers.

- Does the way the addends are ordered when you write an addition sentence make a difference? Explain.

- Write two related subtraction sentences.

2. Use the clues to fill in the table. 1.1.5

Flowers	Number
iris	
tulip	
rose	
daisy	

- The children saw 3 roses.

- They saw 1 fewer iris than roses.

- They saw 3 more tulips than irises.

- They saw 12 flowers that were not tulips.

# Standards Quick Check

Write the difference.

1. $18 - 9 =$ _____   **2.** $13 - 9 =$ _____   **3.** $17 - 7 =$ _____

4. $\begin{array}{r} 14 \\ -\ 9 \\ \hline \end{array}$ **5.** $\begin{array}{r} 15 \\ -\ 9 \\ \hline \end{array}$ **6.** $\begin{array}{r} 14 \\ -\ 6 \\ \hline \end{array}$ **7.** $\begin{array}{r} 17 \\ -\ 8 \\ \hline \end{array}$ **8.** $\begin{array}{r} 16 \\ -\ 9 \\ \hline \end{array}$

Write the difference.
If the fact is related to a doubles fact, circle it.

9. $\begin{array}{r} 16 \\ -\ 8 \\ \hline \end{array}$ **10.** $\begin{array}{r} 15 \\ -\ 7 \\ \hline \end{array}$ **11.** $\begin{array}{r} 13 \\ -\ 6 \\ \hline \end{array}$ **12.** $\begin{array}{r} 18 \\ -\ 9 \\ \hline \end{array}$ **13.** $\begin{array}{r} 15 \\ -\ 6 \\ \hline \end{array}$

Complete the puzzle.

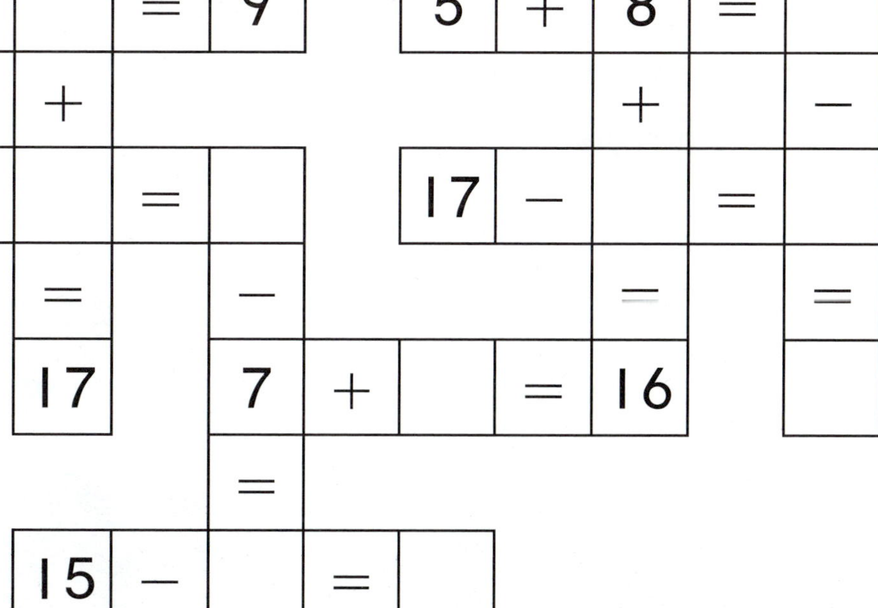

Let's Go Camping

 **Tune:** "Skip to My Lou"

Let's go camping by the sea.
Bring some friends for company.
Put your tent beside a tree.
Camping is fun for you and me!

We will count on. Start with 4.
You can do it. Add 3 more.
5, 6, 7! It's no chore!
Count on with numbers. Add some more!

We will count back. Start with 8.
Count back 2. We just can't wait.
7, 6! Subtracting is great.
Count back with numbers. Don't be late!

It's your turn to count on now.
Count back, too. Please show me how.
When you're done, please take a bow.
Count on, then count back.
Start right now!

Looking Ahead to the ISTEP+
Chapter 12

Mark the best answer for questions 1–4.

1. Which way makes 16? 1.1.6

- ○ 1 + 6
- ○ 3 + 3 + 6
- ○ 10 − 6
- ○ 7 + 9

3. What is the sum? 1.1.6

$$7 + 6 = \underline{\quad}$$

- ○ 11
- ○ 12
- ○ 13
- ○ 14

2. What is the sum? 1.1.5

$$\begin{array}{r} 2 \\ 8 \\ +\ 2 \\ \hline \end{array}$$

- ○ 8
- ○ 10
- ○ 12
- ○ 20

4. What is the missing number? 1.2.1

$$9 + \boxed{} = 18$$

- ○ 8
- ○ 9
- ○ 10
- ○ 11

Mark the best answer for questions 5–6.

5. What sum does this ten frame show? 1.1.4, 1.1.5

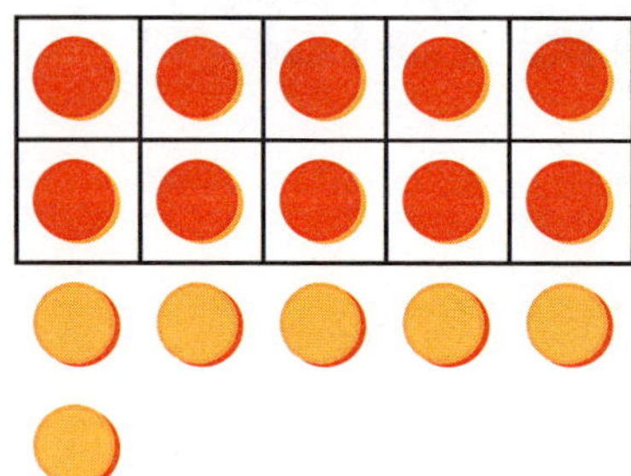

- ○ $10 - 6 = 4$
- ○ $10 + 6 = 16$
- ○ $5 + 6 = 11$
- ○ $5 + 1 = 6$

6. What is the missing number? 1.1.6

$$14 - 6 = \boxed{}$$

- ○ 7
- ○ 8
- ○ 9
- ○ 14

Write the number sentence to solve. 1.1.6

7. John has 13 oranges. He gives 5 of them away. How many oranges does John have left?

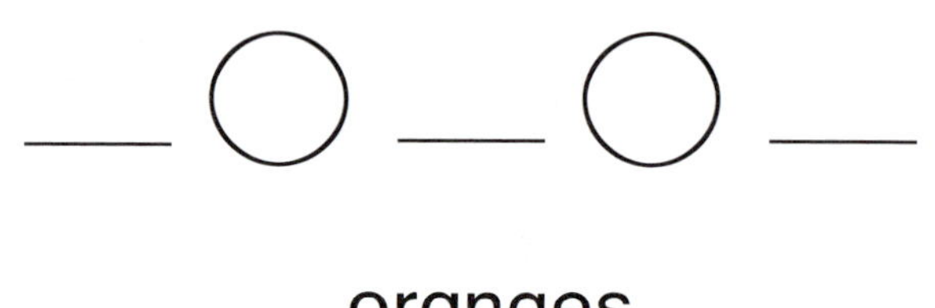

___ ◯ ___ ◯ ___

_____ oranges

Write the number sentence to solve. 1.1.6

8. Shirley has 11 crayons. She finds 5 more crayons. How many crayons does Shirley have now?

___ ◯ ___ ◯ ___

_____ crayons

2-Digit Addition and Subtraction

Theme: Birds and Trees

Fun Fact

The scarlet ibis can grow up to 2 feet tall.

Investigate

Are there more or fewer than 15 birds in the picture? Explain how you know.

GO ONLINE **Technology**
Student pages are available in the Student eBook.

Show What You Know

Write the sum or difference.

| 1. $\begin{array}{r} 8 \\ +\,5 \\ \hline \end{array}$ | 2. $\begin{array}{r} 7 \\ +\,7 \\ \hline \end{array}$ | 3. $\begin{array}{r} 6 \\ +\,9 \\ \hline \end{array}$ | 4. $\begin{array}{r} 4 \\ +\,7 \\ \hline \end{array}$ | 5. $\begin{array}{r} 9 \\ +\,8 \\ \hline \end{array}$ |

| 6. $\begin{array}{r} 17 \\ -\,9 \\ \hline \end{array}$ | 7. $\begin{array}{r} 14 \\ -\,5 \\ \hline \end{array}$ | 8. $\begin{array}{r} 13 \\ -\,7 \\ \hline \end{array}$ | 9. $\begin{array}{r} 16 \\ -\,8 \\ \hline \end{array}$ | 10. $\begin{array}{r} 15 \\ -\,8 \\ \hline \end{array}$ |

Complete the fact family.

11. $6 + 7 = \square$ $\qquad$ $\square - 7 = 6$

$\square + 6 = 13$ $\qquad$ $13 - \square = 7$

12. $\square + 8 = 14$ $\qquad$ $14 - \square = 6$

$8 + \square = \square$ $\qquad$ $\square - \square = \square$

Chapter 13 Lesson 1

Add Tens

▶ **We Learn**

30 robins are in the trees.
20 more robins join them.
How many robins are there in all?

30 + 20 = __50__

__3__ tens + __2__ tens = __5__ tens

There are __50__ robins in all.

▶ **Share and Show**   **Math Board**

Add. Write how many tens.

1. 20 + 40 = ______

______ tens + ______ tens = ______ tens

2. 30 + 30 = ______

______ tens + ______ tens = ______ tens

✓ 3. 40 + 50 = ______

______ tens + ______ tens = ______ tens

✓ 4. 50 + 30 = ______

______ tens + ______ tens = ______ tens

5. **Math Talk** In 5 tens + 2 tens = 7 tens, what does 7 tens equal? Explain.

$50 + 20 = \underline{70}$

$5 \text{ tens} + 2 \text{ tens} = \underline{7} \text{ tens}$

Add.

1. $20 + 10 = \underline{\quad}$

2. $40 + 40 = \underline{\quad}$

3. $70 + 20 = \underline{\quad}$

4. $10 + 30 = \underline{\quad}$

5. $30 + 50 = \underline{\quad}$

6. $20 + 60 = \underline{\quad}$

7. $40 + 20 = \underline{\quad}$

8. $10 + 80 = \underline{\quad}$

9. $20 + 20 = \underline{\quad}$

10. $60 + 30 = \underline{\quad}$

11. $50 + 10 = \underline{\quad}$

12. $30 + 40 = \underline{\quad}$

13. $70 + 10 = \underline{\quad}$

14. $10 + 60 = \underline{\quad}$

Math Board — Problem Solving: Real World

Use mental math. Solve.

15. Lee has 20 stickers. He gets more stickers. He has 40 stickers in all. How many more stickers did he get?

_______ more stickers

16. Sue has 10 stickers. She gets more stickers. She has 40 stickers in all. How many more stickers did she get?

_______ more stickers

Does Lee or Sue get more stickers? Explain.

At Home Ask your child to explain how he or she can use $2 + 7$ to find the sum for $20 + 70$.

Add Tens and Ones

▶ **Explore**

$$36 + 3$$

Start.

Show 36. Show 3. ➡ Add the ones. ➡ Write the tens.

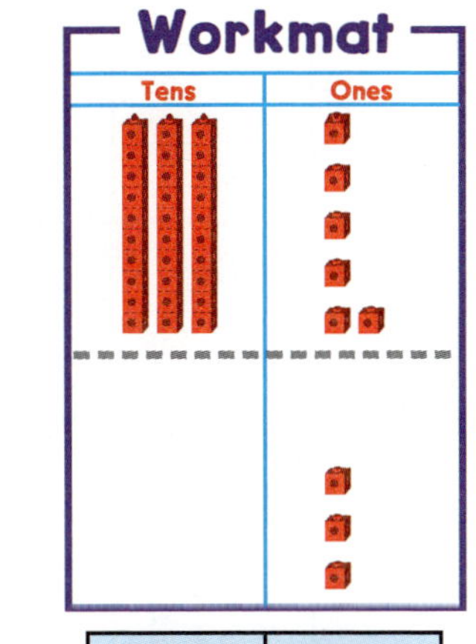

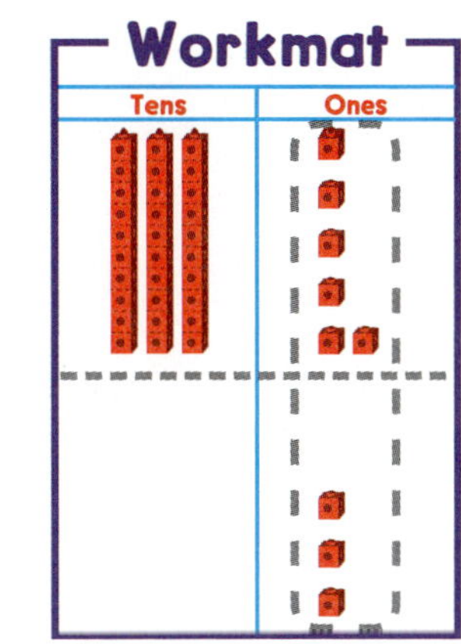

▶ **Connect**

Use Workmat 3 and  to add. Write the sum.

1.

tens	ones
3	4
+	4

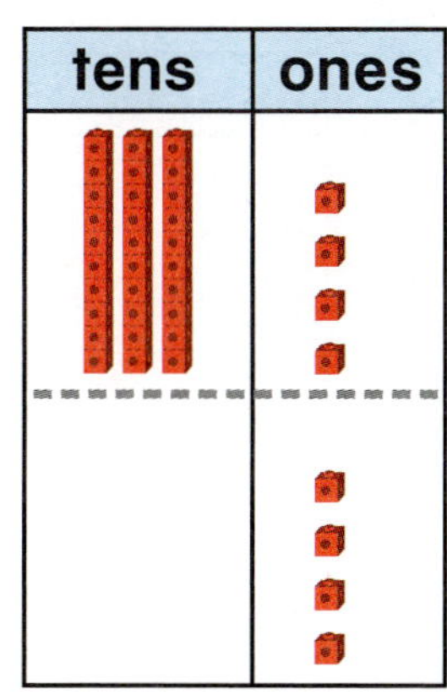

✓ **2.**

tens	ones
4	6
+	2

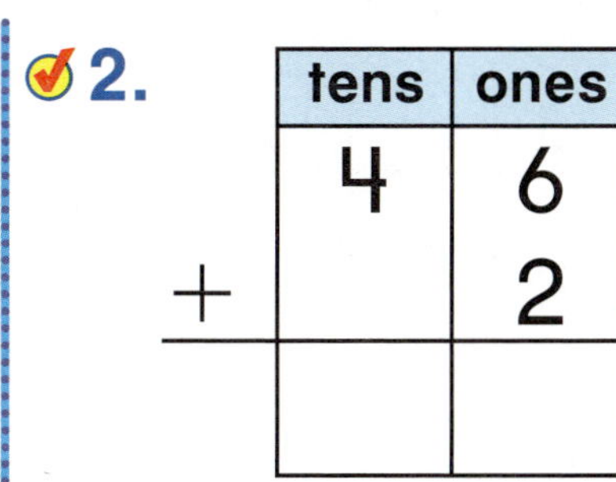

3. (Math Talk) Explain how you would find the
sum for 81 + 2 without using .

Use Workmat 3 and ▢ to add. Write the sum.

1.

tens	ones
2	1
+	8
2	9

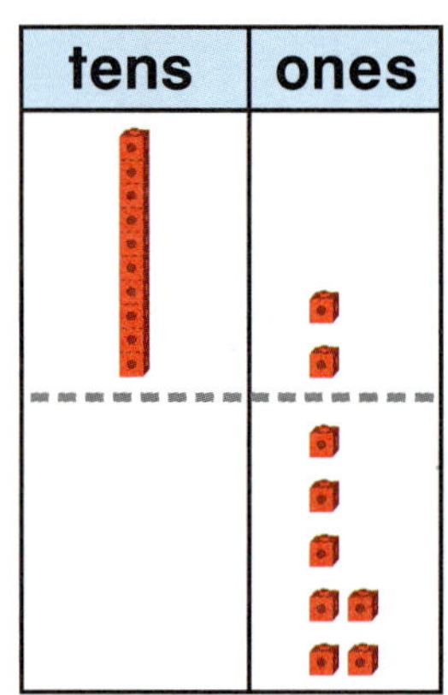

2.

tens	ones
3	2
+	6

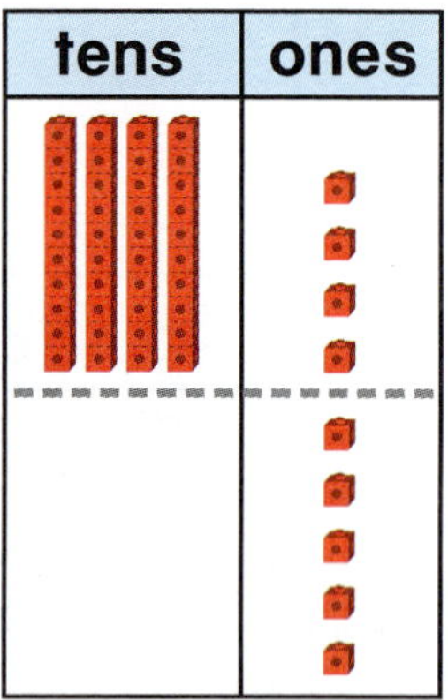

3.

tens	ones
1	2
+	7

4.

tens	ones
4	4
+	5

Problem Solving: Reasoning

Write the problem. Solve.

5.
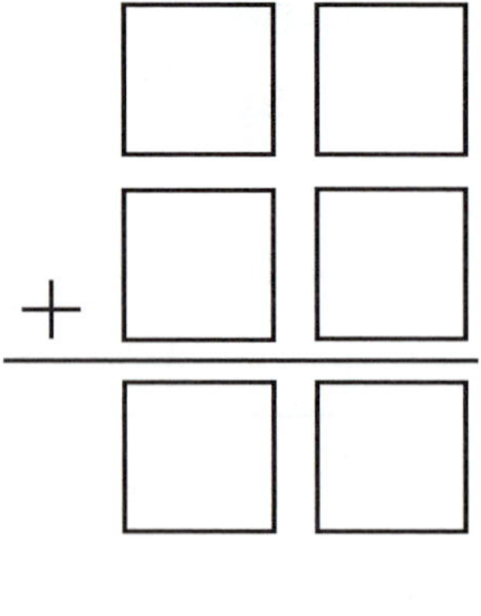

6.
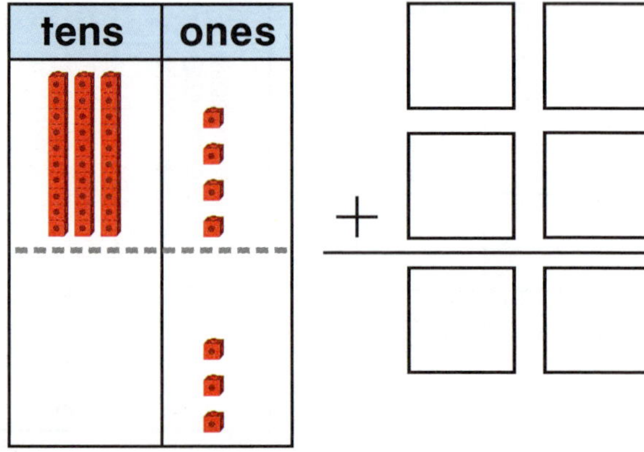

How did you figure out which number to write in each box? Explain.

At Home Give your child an addition problem similar to the ones on this page, for example, 25 + 3. Ask your child to explain how to solve the problem.

Add 2-Digit Numbers

▶ **Explore**

 Start.

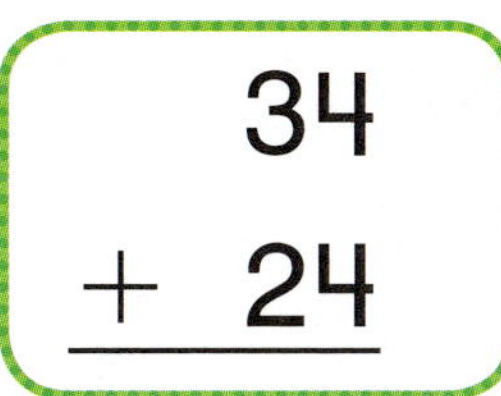
$$34 + 24$$

Show 34. Show 24. ➡ Add the ones. ➡ Add the tens.

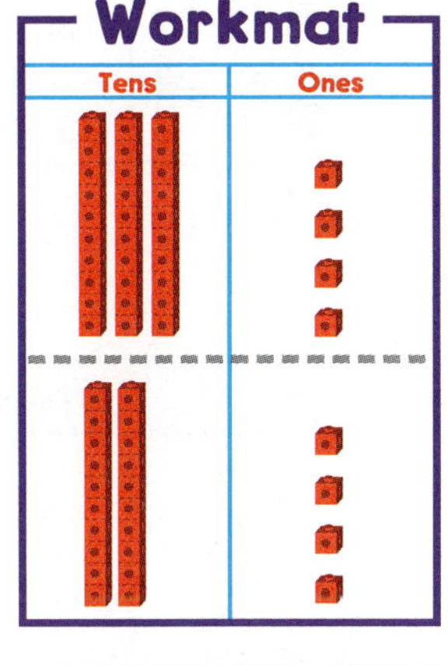

tens	ones
3	4
+ 2	4

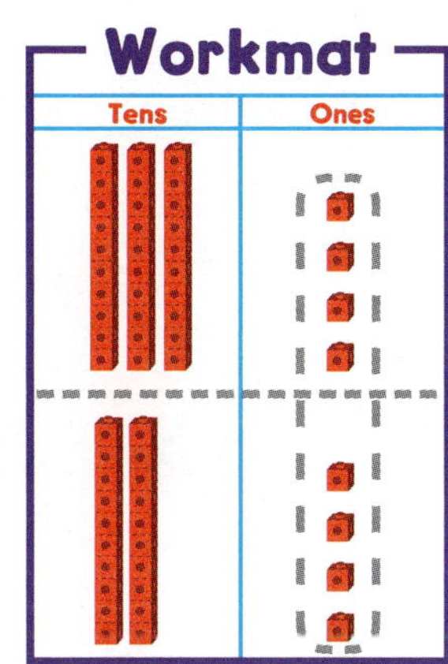

tens	ones
3	4
+ 2	4
	8

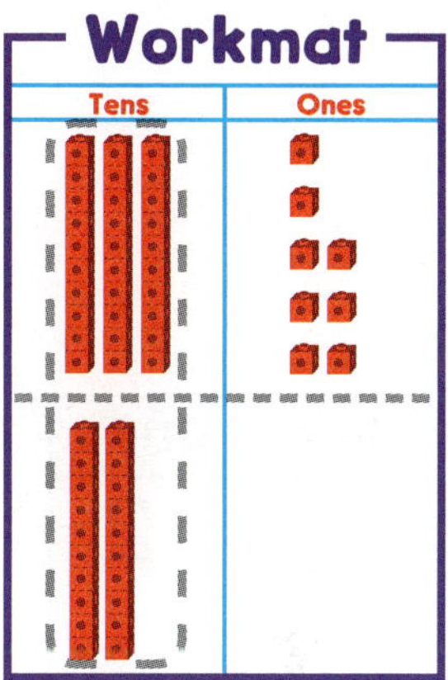

tens	ones
3	4
+ 2	4
5	8

▶ **Connect**

Use Workmat 3 and 🔳 to add. Write the sum.

1.

tens	ones
1	3
+ 3	6

✓2.

tens	ones
2	1
+ 5	7

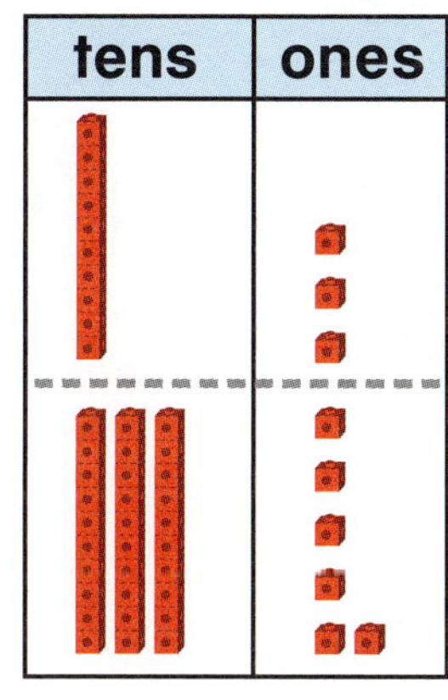

3. (Math Talk) Look at Exercise 1. What tens are added together? Explain.

Use Workmat 3 and  to add. Write the sum.

1.

tens	ones
1	2
+ 3	7

2.

tens	ones
4	1
+ 5	7

3.

tens	ones
2	2
+ 4	3

4.

tens	ones
3	4
+ 4	5

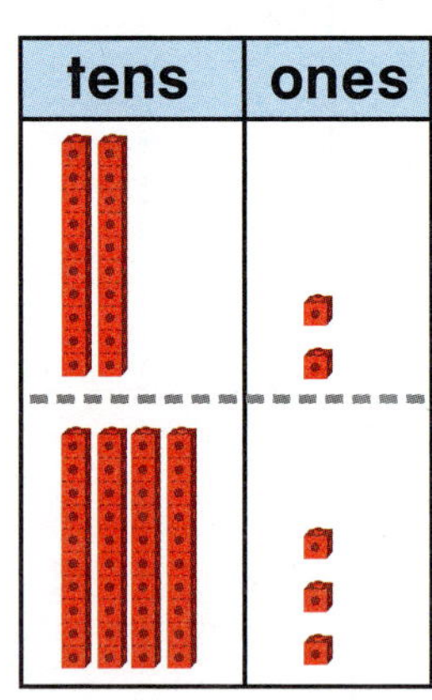

Problem Solving: Reasoning

5. Think about $34 + 24 = 58$.
Circle all of the ways to make 58.

$50 + 4 + 4$ $10 + 10 + 4 + 4$

$50 + 8$ 58

$20 + 30 + 8$

How could you make the way you did not
circle make 58? Explain.

360

Chapter 13 Lesson 4
Estimate Sums

An **estimate** is an amount that tells about how many. Without adding, circle the better estimate.

THINK
I can use tens to estimate.

Essential Question
How can you estimate the sum of a problem?

Vocabulary
estimate

Hank has 26 crayons. He finds 13 more crayons. About how many crayons does Hank have in all?

about 4 crayons

Too few.

about 40 crayons

1. Vanessa had 11 books. Then her mom gave her 8 more books. About how many books does Vanessa have now?

book
The Biggest Tree

about 2 books

about 20 books

2. Kristen picks 22 flowers on Monday. On Tuesday, she picks 26 more flowers. About how many flowers does Kristen pick in all?

flower

about 5 flowers

about 50 flowers

3. **Math Talk** Look at Exercise 1. Why does your estimate make more sense?

1.1.5 Solve problems involving addition and subtraction by modeling addition of numbers to at least 100 and modeling the inverse operation of subtraction using objects. *also* **1.2.1**

Without adding, circle the better estimate.

1. Garrett has 15 apples.
Cory has 14 apples.
About how many apples
do they have together?

about 3 apples

about 30 apples

apple

2. Amanda has 4 melons.
Brad has 3 melons.
About how many melons
do they have together?

about 7 melons

about 70 melons

melon

3. Anthony had 33 baseball
cards. Then he bought 25 more
baseball cards. About how
many baseball cards does
Anthony have in all?

about 6 baseball cards

about 60 baseball cards

baseball card

Problem Solving: Real World

Use tens to estimate your answer.

4. Mike catches 13 fish. Devin catches 9 fish.
About how many fish do they
catch altogether?

about _____ fish

Explain how you found your answer.

At Home Ask your child to tell you how he or she made an estimate for Problem 3.

Subtract Tens

▶ **We Learn**

There are 50 owls in the trees.
30 owls fly away.
How many owls are left?

50　　　−　　30　　　= __20__

__5__ tens − __3__ tens = __2__ tens

There are __20__ owls left.

▶ **Share and Show**　**Math Board**

Subtract. Write how many tens.

1.　60　　　−　　20　　　= _____

_____ tens − _____ tens = _____ tens

2.　70　　　−　　30　　　= _____

_____ tens − _____ tens = _____ tens

✓3.　80　　　−　　20　　　= _____

_____ tens − _____ tens = _____ tens

✓4.　40　　　−　　20　　　= _____

_____ tens − _____ tens = _____ tens

5. **Math Talk** In 9 tens − 4 tens = 5 tens, what
does 5 tens equal? Explain.

1.1.5 Solve problems involving addition and subtraction by modeling addition of
numbers to at least 100 and modeling the inverse operation of subtraction using
objects. *also* **1.1.4**

Essential Question: How can you use mental math to subtract tens?

$60 - 40 = \underline{20}$

$6 \text{ tens} - 4 \text{ tens} = \underline{2} \text{ tens}$

Subtract.

1. $30 - 10 = \underline{}$
2. $80 - 40 = \underline{}$

3. $90 - 70 = \underline{}$
4. $50 - 40 = \underline{}$

5. $80 - 50 = \underline{}$
6. $90 - 60 = \underline{}$

7. $70 - 50 = \underline{}$
8. $90 - 80 = \underline{}$

9. $20 - 20 = \underline{}$
10. $50 - 10 = \underline{}$

11. $60 - 10 = \underline{}$
12. $30 - 20 = \underline{}$

13. $70 - 20 = \underline{}$
14. $60 - 30 = \underline{}$

Problem Solving: Real World

Use mental math. Solve.

15. Jill has 40 stickers. She gives some stickers to Pete. Then Jill has 30 stickers left. How many stickers does she give to Pete?

    _____ stickers

16. Jeff has 40 stickers. He gives some stickers to Pam. Then Jeff has 10 stickers left. How many stickers does he give to Pam?

    _____ stickers

Did Jill or Jeff give away more stickers? Explain.

At Home Ask your child to explain how to use $9 - 7$ to find the difference for $90 - 70$.

Chapter 13 Lesson 6

Subtract Tens and Ones

 **Explore**

Essential Question
How would you find the difference for 75 − 4?

$$\begin{array}{r} 39 \\ -\ 7 \\ \hline \end{array}$$

 Start.

Show 39. ➡ Take away 7 ones. ➡ Write the tens.

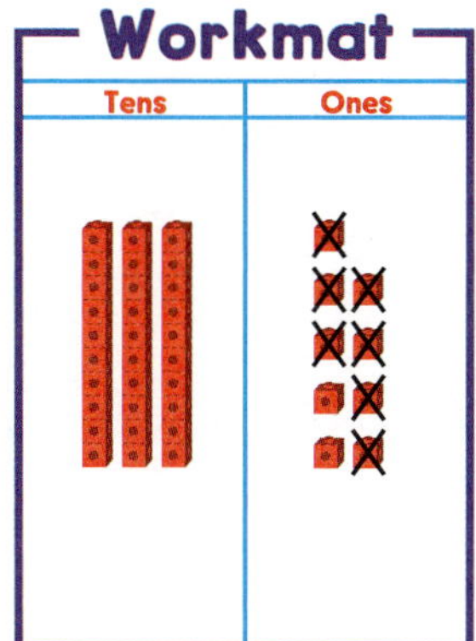

tens	ones
3	9
−	7

tens	ones
3	9
−	7
	2

tens	ones
3	9
−	7
3	2

 **Connect**

Use Workmat 3 and 🟥. Cross out to subtract.
Write the difference.

1.

tens	ones
4	5
−	2

☑ 2.

tens	ones
2	6
−	5

3. **Math Talk** Explain how you would find the difference for 98 − 1 without using 🟥.

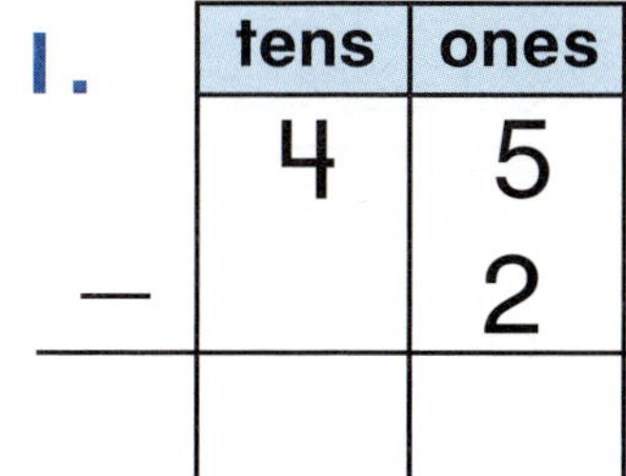 **1.1.5** Solve problems involving addition and subtraction by modeling addition of numbers to at least 100 and modeling the inverse operation of subtraction using objects. *also* **1.1.4**

Use Workmat 3 and . Cross out to subtract. Write the difference.

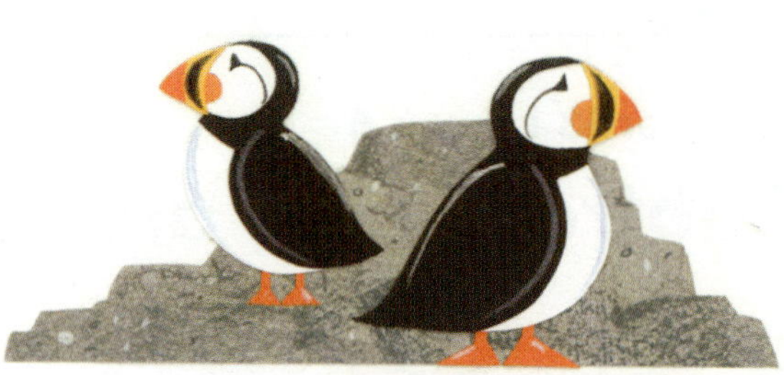

1.

tens	ones
2	5
−	3

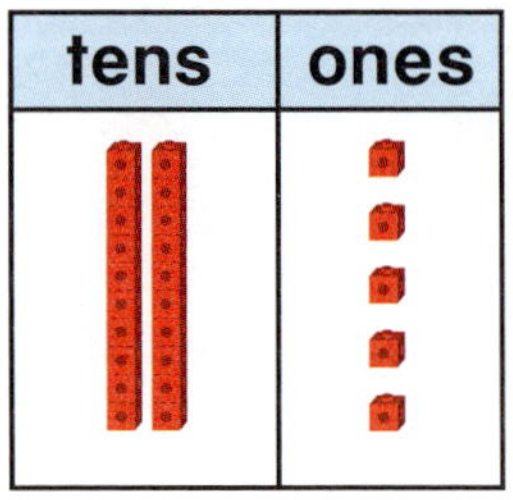

tens	ones

2.

tens	ones
4	7
−	2

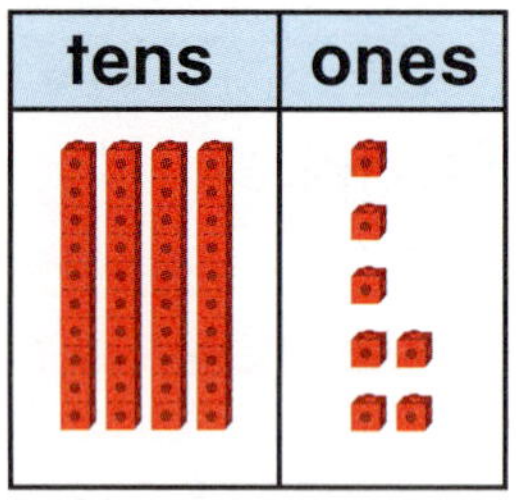

tens	ones

3.

tens	ones
3	8
−	6

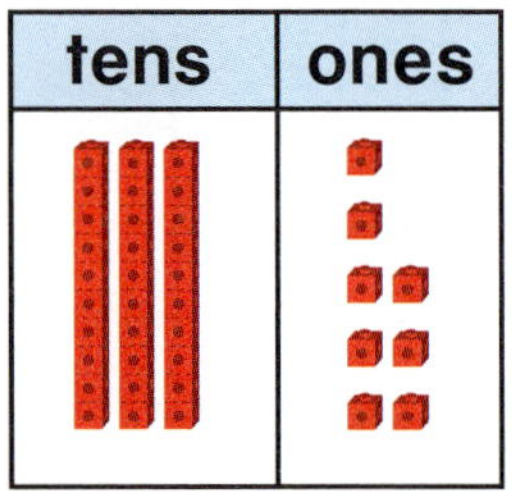

tens	ones

4.

tens	ones
1	4
−	3

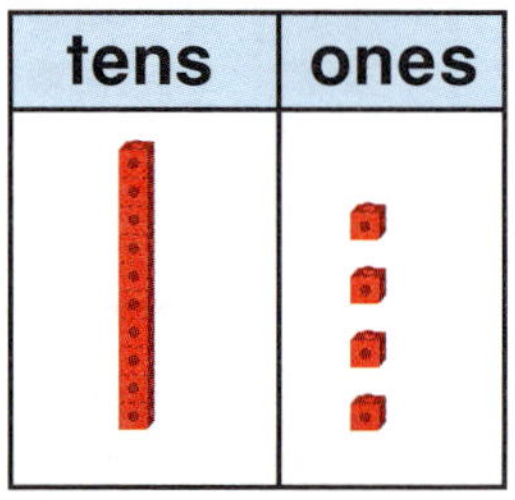

tens	ones

Problem Solving: Reasoning

Write the problem. Solve.

5.

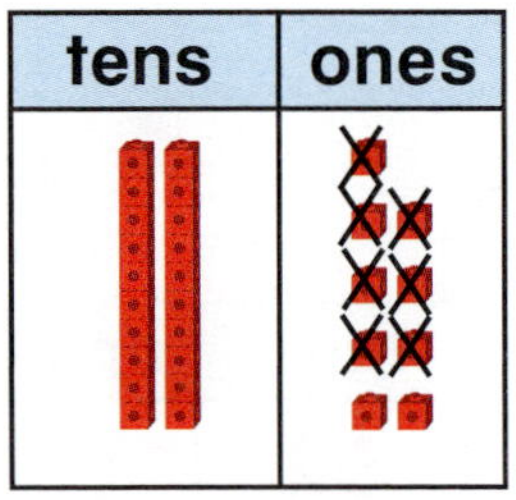

tens	ones

6.

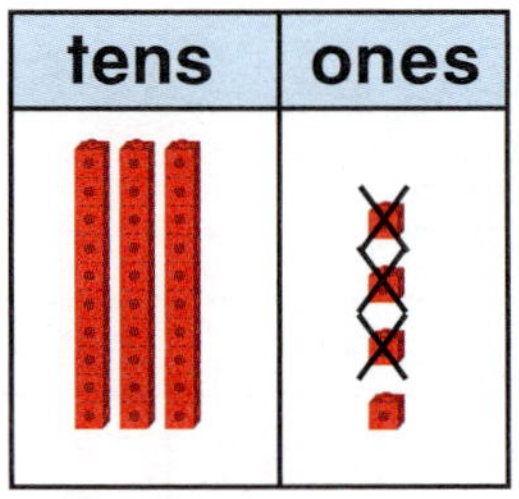

tens	ones

Look at Exercise 5. Write a math story to go with your problem.

Chapter 13 Lesson 7

Subtract 2-Digit Numbers

Explore

Essential Question
How do you subtract 2-digit numbers to show the difference?

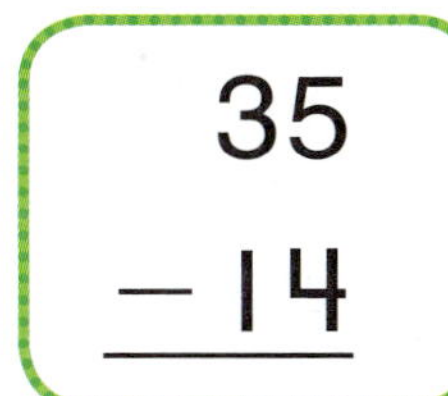

$$\begin{array}{r} 35 \\ -14 \\ \hline \end{array}$$

Start.

Show 35. ➡ Take away 4 ones. ➡ Take away 1 ten.

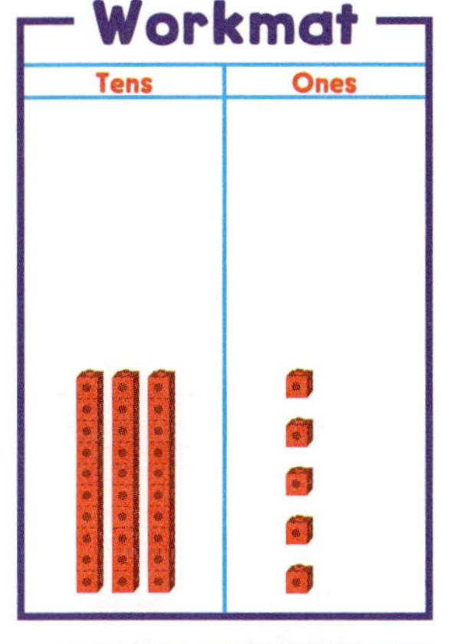
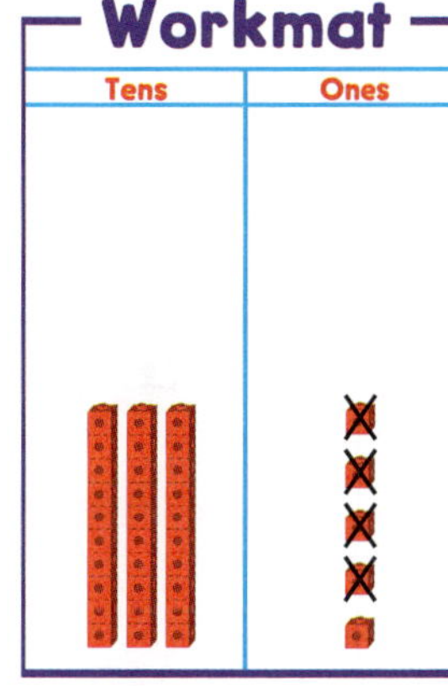
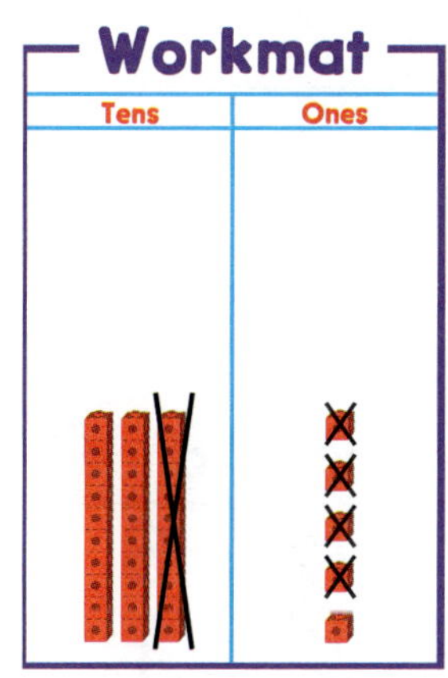

tens	ones
3	5
− 1	4

tens	ones
3	5
− 1	4
	1

tens	ones
3	5
− 1	4
2	1

Connect

Use Workmat 3 and 🔲. Cross out to subtract.
Write the difference.

1.

tens	ones
4	6
− 1	4

✓2.

tens	ones
5	9
− 2	6

3. **Math Talk** Look at Exercise 1. What tens are subtracted?
Explain.

Use Workmat 3 and . Cross out to subtract. Write the difference.

1.

tens	ones
3	9
− 1	3
2	6

tens	ones

2.

tens	ones
3	6
− 2	5

tens	ones

3.

tens	ones
4	8
− 2	1

tens	ones

4.

tens	ones
4	9
− 3	7

tens	ones

Problem Solving: Real World

5. Solve. Use if you need.

Bird Land has 58 parrots.
It gives 27 parrots to a zoo.
How many parrots does
Bird Land have left?

________ parrots

Draw a picture using to show
how you solved the problem.

At Home Ask your child to draw pictures to show how to solve 49 − 27.

Estimate Differences

An estimate is an amount
that tells about how many.

Without subtracting, circle
the better estimate.
Jake has 44 stickers. He gives 13
stickers to his brother. About how
many stickers does Jake have left?

about 3 stickers

about 30 stickers

1. Michelle had 12 markers. She gave
   her friend 6 of the markers. About
   how many markers does
   Michelle have now?

   about 5 markers

   about 50 markers

2. Sara found 37 shells at the beach.
   She gave 15 of them to her sister.
   About how many shells
   does Sara have left?

   about 2 shells

   about 20 shells

3. **Math Talk** Look at Exercise 2. Why does your estimate
   make more sense?

1.1.5 Solve problems involving addition and subtraction by modeling addition of
numbers to at least 100 and modeling the inverse operation of subtraction using
objects. *also* **1.1.4**

Circle the better estimate.

1. There are 58 children in the library. 20 go back to class. About how many children are still in the library?

about 4 children

about 40 children

children

2. There were 16 birds in the trees. 8 of them flew away. About how many birds were left?

about 8 birds

about 80 birds

bird

3. On Monday, there were 74 dolls at the doll shop. 22 dolls were sold. About how many dolls were left?

about 5 dolls

about 50 dolls

doll

Problem Solving: Real World

Use tens to estimate your answer.

4. Sam picks 48 berries. He gives 17 berries to his mother. About how many berries does Sam have left?

about _____ berries

Explain how you found your answer.

Problem Solving Workshop

Skill: Make Reasonable Estimates

Without adding or subtracting, circle the best estimate.

A parrot eats 42 seeds. Then it eats 9 more seeds. About how many seeds does the parrot eat in all?

Too few. about 5 seeds

about 50 seeds

Too many. about 500 seeds

THINK
I can use tens to estimate.

parrot

1. The library has 78 books about trees. Sam checks out 6 books. About how many are left?

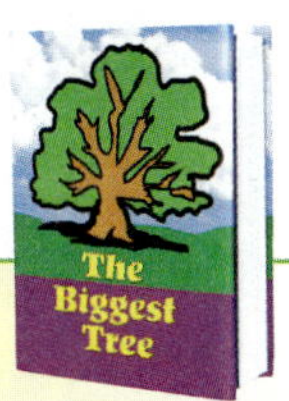
book

about 7 books

about 70 books

about 700 books

2. 32 ducks and swans are at the pond. 21 are ducks. About how many swans are there?

swan

about 1 swan

about 10 swans

about 100 swans

Math Talk Look at Exercise 2. Why does your estimate make the most sense?

Without adding or subtracting, circle the best estimate.

1. Lana counts 34 trees. Then she counts 60 more. About how many trees does she count in all?

tree

about 1 tree

about 10 trees

about 100 trees

2. There are 29 maple trees by the stream. There are 2 willow trees. About how many trees are there in all?

tree

about 3 trees

about 30 trees

about 300 trees

3. 61 birds are at the lake. 8 of them fly away. About how many birds are left?

bird

about 5 birds

about 50 birds

about 500 birds

4. Mia counts 52 birds. Will counts 45 birds. About how many birds do they count in all?

bird

about 1 bird

about 10 birds

about 100 birds

Extra Practice

Solve.

1. $70 + 10 =$ _____   **2.** $90 - 60 =$ _____

Use Workmat 3 and 🔲 to add. Write the sum.

3.

tens	ones
2	2
+	6

4.

tens	ones
3	2
+ 2	7

Use Workmat 3 and 🔲 to subtract. Cross out to subtract.
Write the difference.

5.

tens	ones
4	8
−	6

6.

tens	ones
3	9
− 2	4

Problem Solving

Without adding or subtracting,
circle the best estimate.

7. 23 ducks are at the pond.
9 of them fly away.
About how many ducks
are there now?

about 1 duck

about 10 ducks

about 100 ducks

Technology
Use HMH Mega Math, Mega Math,
Country Countdown, *Block Busters,*
Level J, K, O, P.

Multistep Problems
Chapter 13

1. Seth went to the petting zoo. He saw many animals. Use the table to answer the questions below. Show your work. 1.1.5, 1.2.1

| Animals at the Petting Zoo ||
Animals	Numbers
bunnies	14
goats	4
ducks	11
ponies	5
sheep	18

- Seth wants to pet all the bunnies and ducks at the petting zoo. How many animals will he pet?

- Seth's sister wants to pet all the sheep and ducks. How many animals will she pet?

- How many more animals did Seth's sister pet than Seth?

2. Answer the questions below. Show your work. 1.1.5, 1.2.1

- Mr. Rave needs 28 chairs for the class play. He has 23 chairs. How many more chairs does he need?

- Mrs. White brings Mr. Rave 15 chairs. How many chairs does Mr. Rave have now?

- Mrs. White takes some chairs back so that Mr. Rave only has 28 chairs. How many chairs does Mrs. White take back?

 Standards Quick Check

Use doubles or doubles plus 1. Add.

1. 8
   +8

2. 7
   +7

3. 9
   +8

4. 7
   +8

5. 9
   +9

Write the sum.

6. 20 + 2 = _____   7. 20 + 9 = _____   8. 20 + 4 = _____

Write the sum or difference.

9.   40
    +10

10.   47
     − 2

11.   35
     −14

12.   15
     +14

13.   12
     + 6

 **Challenge** H.O.T.

Juanita throws 2 darts.
Write the ways she can score 14.

_____ and _____

_____ and _____

_____ and _____

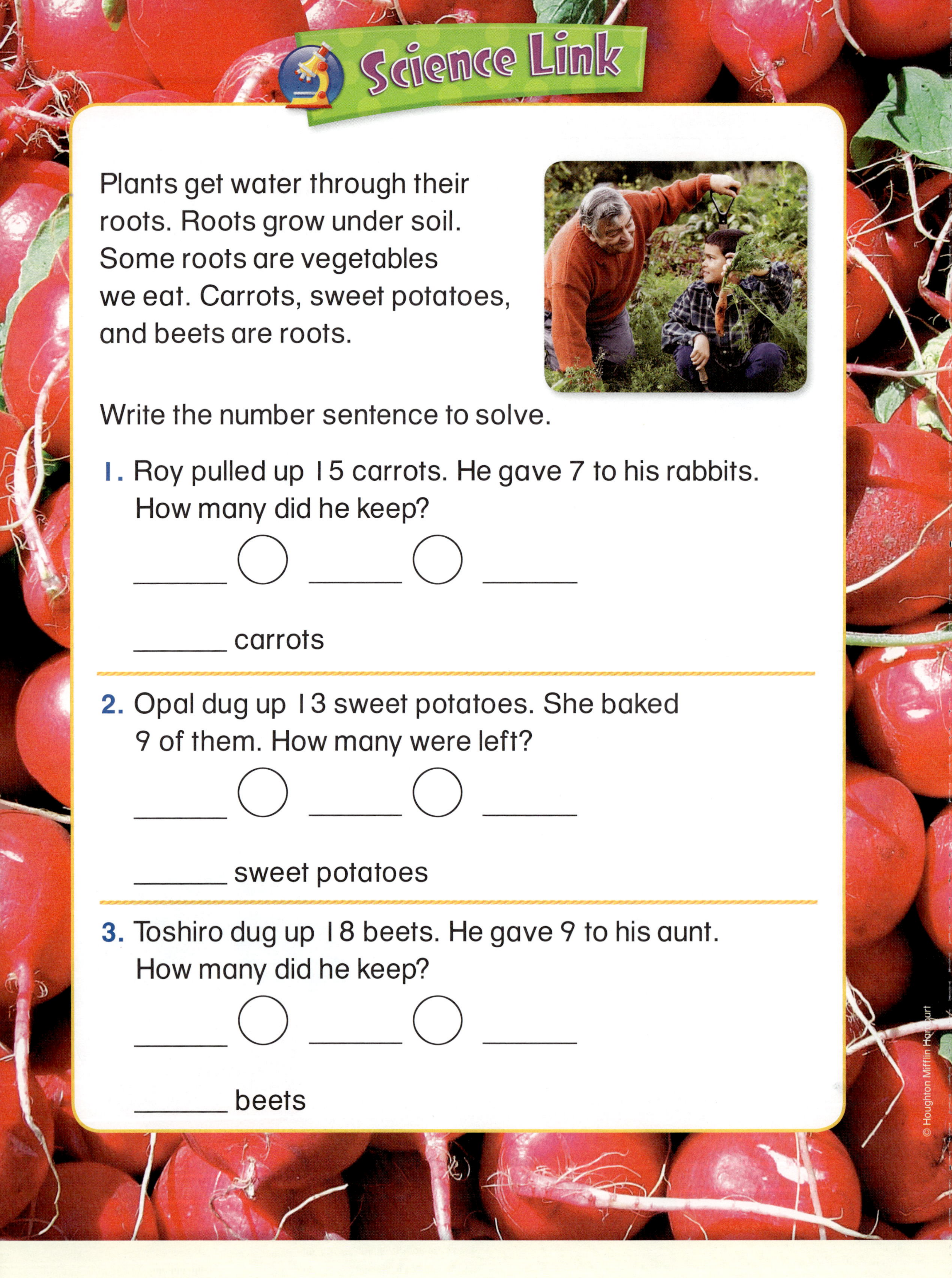

Plants get water through their roots. Roots grow under soil. Some roots are vegetables we eat. Carrots, sweet potatoes, and beets are roots.

Write the number sentence to solve.

1. Roy pulled up 15 carrots. He gave 7 to his rabbits. How many did he keep?

_____ ◯ _____ ◯ _____

_____ carrots

2. Opal dug up 13 sweet potatoes. She baked 9 of them. How many were left?

_____ ◯ _____ ◯ _____

_____ sweet potatoes

3. Toshiro dug up 18 beets. He gave 9 to his aunt. How many did he keep?

_____ ◯ _____ ◯ _____

_____ beets

Looking Ahead to the ISTEP+
Chapter 13

Mark the best answer for questions 1–4.

1. What is the sum? ▮1.1.5

$$30 + 40 = \underline{\hspace{2cm}}$$

- ○ 10
- ○ 50
- ○ 60
- ○ 70

2. What is the sum? ▮1.1.5

$$\begin{array}{r} 34 \\ + 5 \\ \hline \end{array}$$

- ○ 35
- ○ 39
- ○ 84
- ○ 89

3. What is the sum? ▮1.1.5

$$\begin{array}{r} 26 \\ + 3 \\ \hline \end{array}$$

- ○ 56
- ○ 36
- ○ 29
- ○ 23

4. What is the difference? ▮1.1.5

$$70 - 20 = \underline{\hspace{2cm}}$$

- ○ 90
- ○ 60
- ○ 50
- ○ 20

Mark the best answer for questions 5–7.

5. What is the difference? ▌1.1.5

$$48 - 16$$

- ○ 32
- ○ 44
- ○ 52
- ○ 58

6. What is the difference? ▌1.1.5

$$96 - 54$$

- ○ 31
- ○ 42
- ○ 43
- ○ 49

7. What is the difference? ▌1.1.5

$$57 - 6$$

- ○ 1
- ○ 10
- ○ 21
- ○ 51

Open Ended

Circle the best estimate. ▌1.1.5

8. The library has 87 books about birds. Tina takes out 4 of them. About how many books are left?

about 8 books

about 80 books

about 800 books

Circle the best estimate. ▌1.1.5

9. There are 39 birds. 8 of them fly away. About how many birds are left?

about 3 birds

about 30 birds

about 300 birds

Chapter 14
Measurement
Theme: At the Bank

Fun Fact
A mint is a place where coins are made. There are 6 mints in the United States.

Investigate
What coins can you use to make 25 cents?

© Houghton Mifflin Harcourt

GO ONLINE
Technology
Student pages are available in the Student eBook.

Show What You Know 

1. Skip count. Count the fingers by fives.
Write how many.

 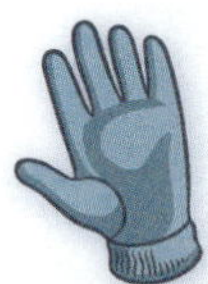 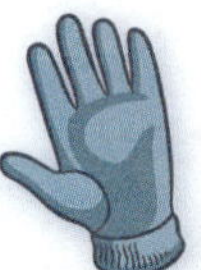 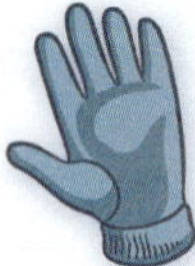 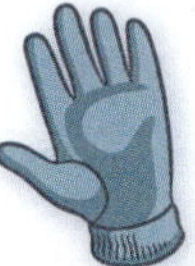

_____ _____ _____ _____ _____

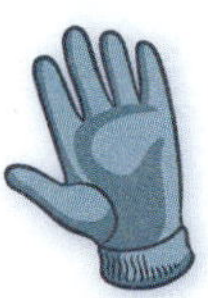 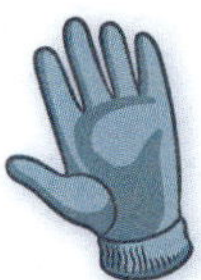 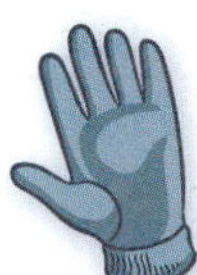 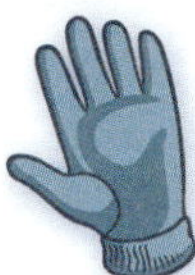 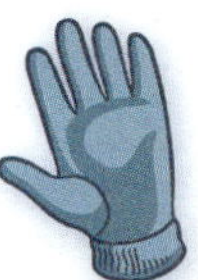

_____ _____ _____ _____ _____ fingers

2. Skip count. Count the toes by tens.
Write how many.

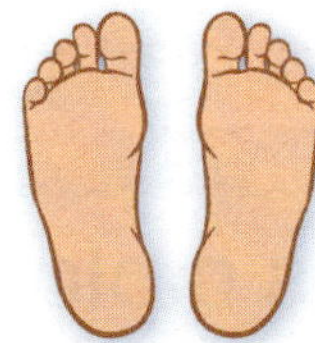 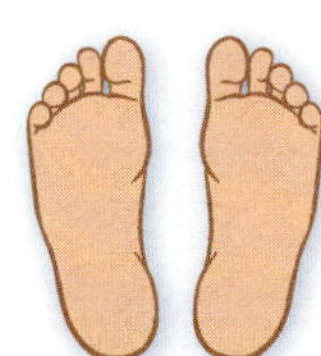 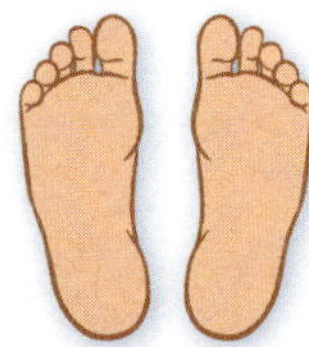 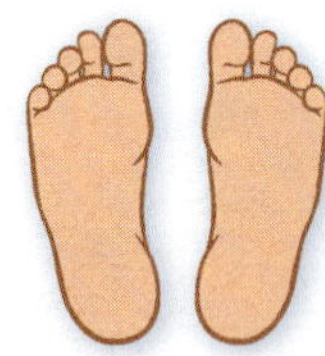 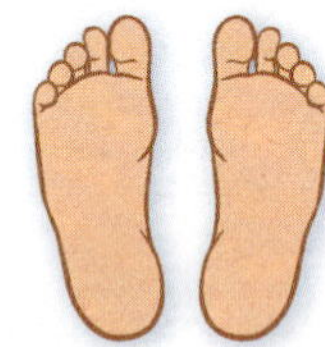

_____ _____ _____ _____ _____ toes

3. Write the number of pennies,
nickels, and dimes.

_____ pennies

_____ nickels

_____ dimes

At Home This page checks your child's understanding
of important concepts and skills needed for success in
Chapter 14.

Chapter 14 Lesson 1

Compare and Order Length and Height

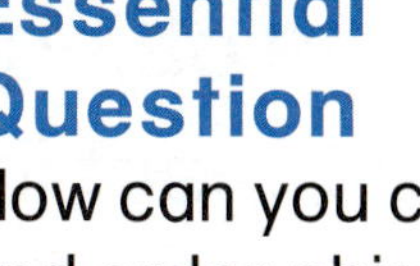

Essential Question

How can you compare and order objects by length and height?

Vocabulary

length
height
longer
taller
shorter

▶ **Explore**

Compare length and height.
Use longer, taller, shorter.

Step 1

Find the object.
Stand next to it.

Step 2

Your partner tells if
the object is shorter
or taller than you.

Use **tall, taller, tallest**
to compare three things.

tall   taller   tallest

▶ **Connect**

Is the object taller or shorter
than you? Circle.

1.

taller

shorter

2.

taller

shorter

3.

taller

shorter

4. **Math Talk** Which object above is
the tallest? Which is the shortest?

1.3.2 Estimate and measure the length of an object to
the nearest inch and centimeter.

Find the object.
Is the object longer or shorter than your hand?
Circle.

1.    (longer)

shorter

2.    longer

shorter

3.    longer

shorter

4.    longer

shorter

Order your objects from shortest to longest.
Number the pictures.

5.    

______   ______   ______   ______

Math Board **Problem Solving: Real World**

Color the longest pencil red.
Color the shortest pencil blue.
Draw a pencil that is longer than the red pencil.

6. 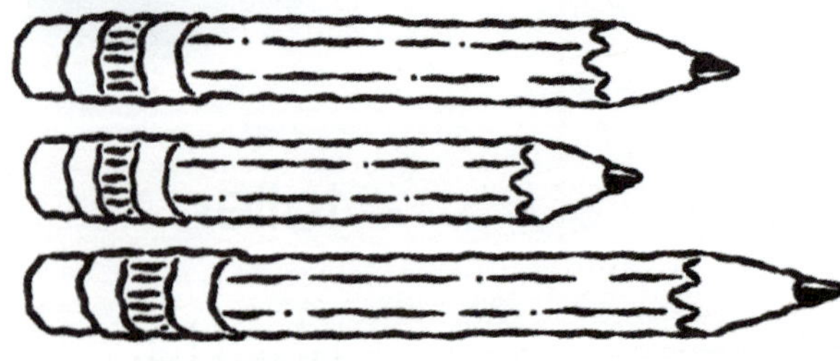

Is the red pencil still the longest? Why?

Chapter 14 Lesson 2

Use Nonstandard Units

▶ **Explore**

You can use real objects to ==measure== length.

about ___4___ ■

▶ **Connect**

Use tiles. Measure each flower.

1. 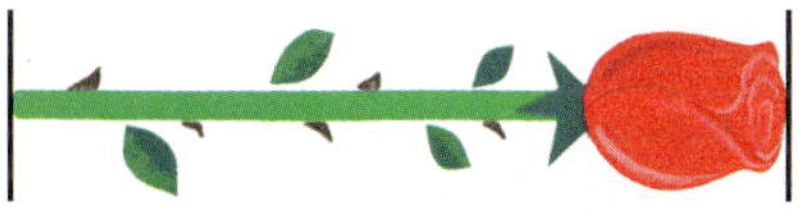 about ______ ■

2. 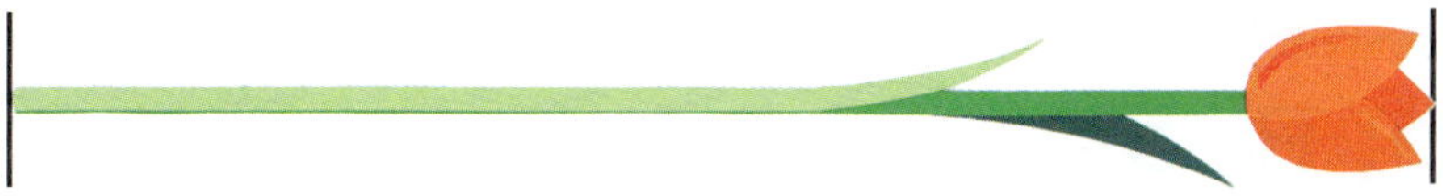 about ______ ■

✓ 3. 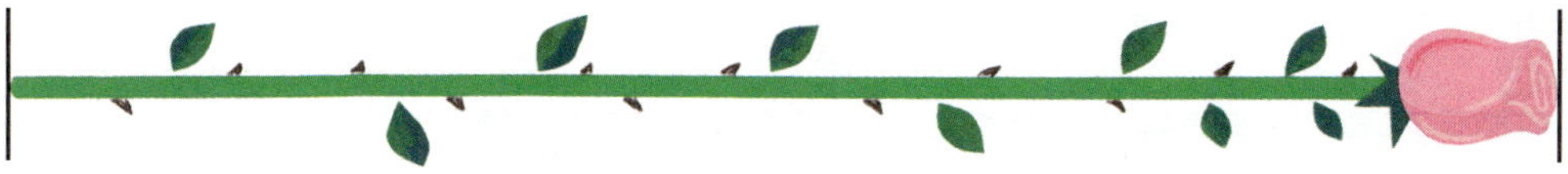 about ______ ■

✓ 4. 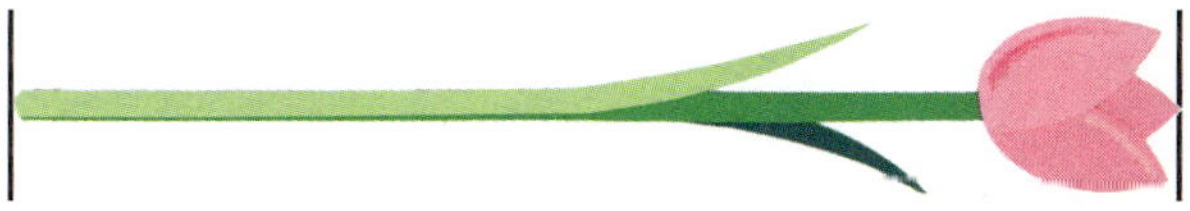 about ______ ■

5. **Math Talk** Which Exercise has the longest flower?
Which Exercise has the shortest flower? Explain.

Hands On

Essential Question
What real object can you use as a unit to measure length?

Vocabulary
==measure==

1.3.2 Estimate and measure the length of an object to the nearest inch and centimeter.

Use real objects and tiles.
Estimate. Then measure.

Object	Estimate	Measurement
1.	about _____ ■	about _____ ■
2.	about _____ ■	about _____ ■
3.	about _____ ■	about _____ ■
4.	about _____ ■	about _____ ■

Problem Solving: Reasoning

5. Circle the longer vine.

Use a string and tiles to check.
Explain how you know which object is longer.

Name _______________________

Chapter 14 Lesson 3

Inches

This paper clip is about 1 inch long.

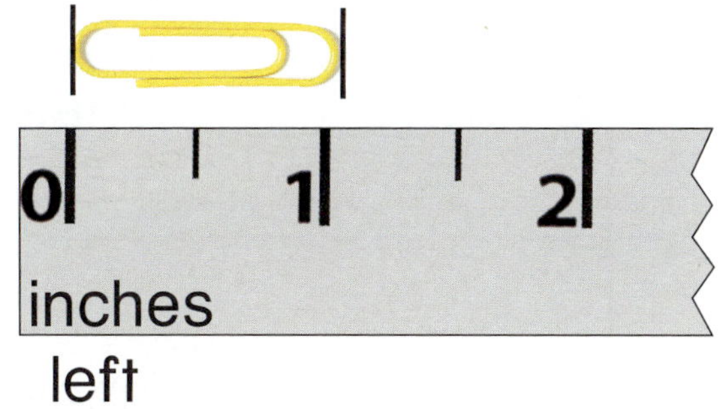

Put the 0 mark on the ruler at the left end of each object.

Use an inch ruler to measure. Circle the shortest object. Underline the longest object.

1. about _____ 2 inches

2. about _____ inches

✓3. about _____ inches

✓4. about _____ inches

5. **Math Talk** What is the error? Sara measured this eraser as 3 inches.

Use real objects and an inch ruler.
Estimate. Then measure.

	Object	Estimate	Measurement
1.		about _____ inches	about _____ inches
2.		about _____ inches	about _____ inches
3.		about _____ inches	about _____ inches
4.		about _____ inches	about _____ inches

Problem Solving: Application

5. Solve.

Mr. Hall needs a piece of rope 4 inches long.
Draw a line to show where he should cut the rope.

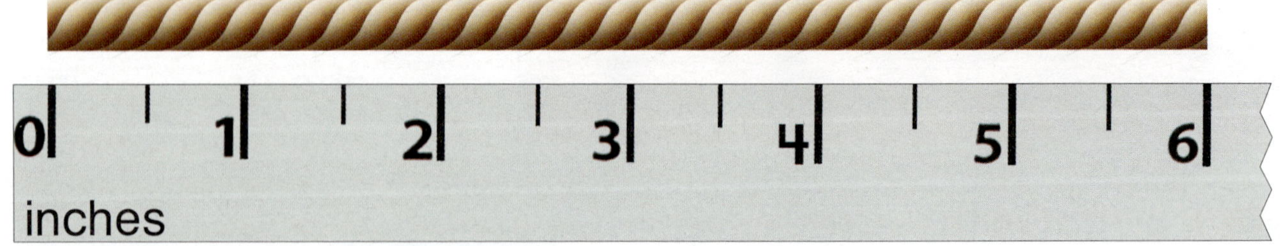

Draw a piece of rope that is 1 inch longer.
Draw a piece of rope that is 1 inch shorter.

At Home Have your child estimate the lengths of small household objects in inches and then use a ruler to measure.

Chapter 14 Lesson 4
Centimeters

▶ **Explore**

This staple is about 1 centimeter long.

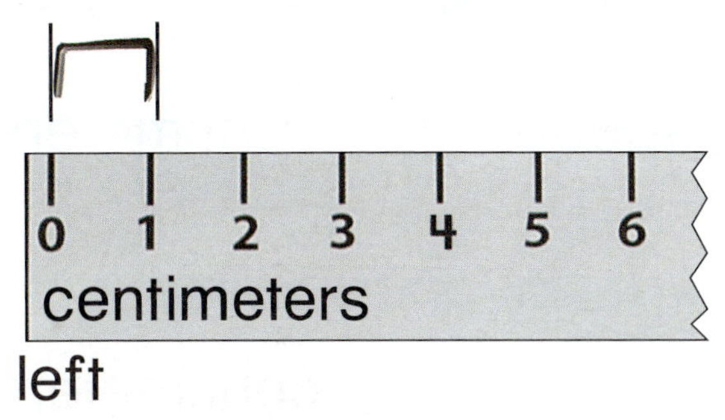

left

Essential Question
How can you measure to the nearest centimeter by using a centimeter ruler?

Vocabulary
centimeter

▶ **Connect**

Use a centimeter ruler to measure. Circle the shortest object. Underline the longest object.

1. about __6__ centimeters

2. about _____ centimeters

✓ 3. about _____ centimeters

✓ 4. about _____ centimeters

5. **Math Talk** How do you know which object is the longest? How do you know which object is the shortest? Explain.

1.3.2 Estimate and measure the length of an object to the nearest inch and centimeter.

Use real objects and a centimeter ruler.
Estimate. Then measure.

Object	Estimate	Measurement
1.	about _____ centimeters	about _____ centimeters
2.	about _____ centimeters	about _____ centimeters
3.	about _____ centimeters	about _____ centimeters
4.	about _____ centimeters	about _____ centimeters

Problem Solving: Reasoning

5. Compare the rulers. About how many
centimeters is the same length as 2 inches?
Circle your answer.

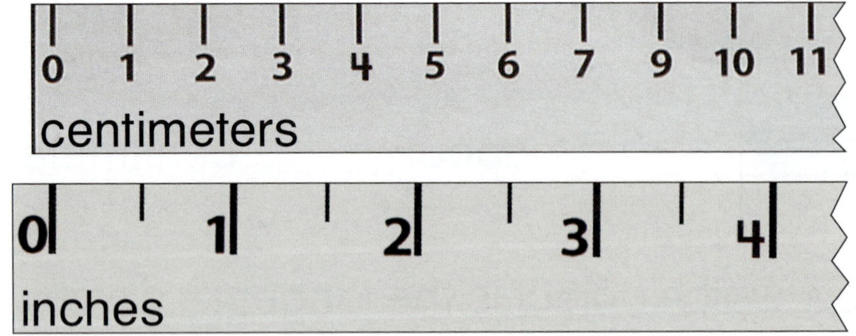

2 centimeters

5 centimeters

8 centimeters

Explain your answer.

Problem Solving Workshop

Skill: Make Reasonable Estimates 

About how many  long is the pencil?
Which estimate makes more sense?

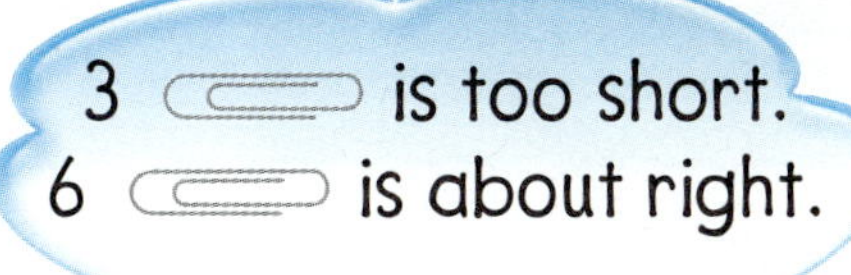

Kim estimates that
it is about 3 ☎.

Jon estimates that
it is about 6 ☎.

About how many ☎ long is each object?
Circle the estimate that makes sense.

1.

Andy estimates that
it is about 1 ☎.

Dan estimates that
it is about 3 ☎.

2.

Beth estimates that
it is about 7 ☎.

Jen estimates that
it is about 4 ☎.

3.

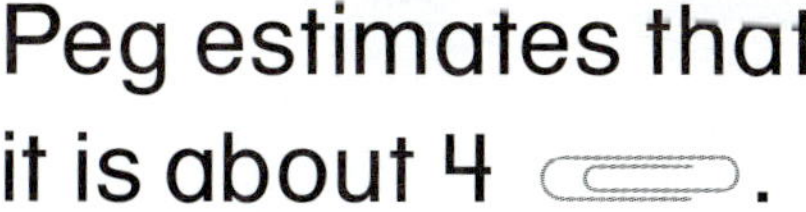

Peg estimates that
it is about 4 ☎.

Tim estimates that
it is about 6 ☎.

Math Talk Look at Exercise 3. How can you check to
see if your estimate is correct? Explain.

1.3.2 Estimate and measure the length of an object to
the nearest inch and centimeter.

Problem Solving Skill Practice 

About how many ⬭ long is each object?
Circle the estimate that makes sense.

1.

Pete estimates that it is about 2 ⬭.

Ann estimates that it is about 1 ⬭.

2.

Rob estimates that it is about 3 ⬭.

Ken estimates that it is about 4 ⬭.

3.

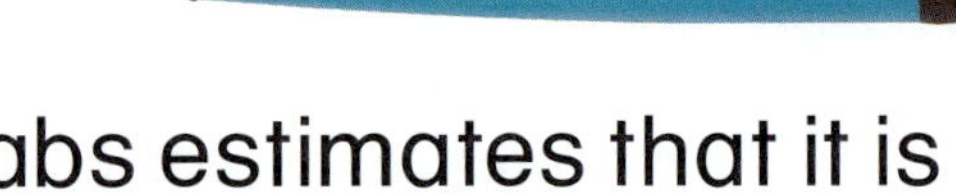

Babs estimates that it is about 5 ⬭.

Jill estimates that it is about 8 ⬭.

4.

Cam estimates that it is about 1 ⬭.

Ben estimates that it is about 2 ⬭.

5.

Mike estimates that it is about 4 ⬭.

Ella estimates that it is about 6 ⬭.

At Home Mark off a length on the floor using a piece of string. Show your child a shoe. Ask him or her to estimate how many shoes will fit on the marked length and to explain why the estimate is reasonable.

Chapter 14 Lesson 6
Time to the Hour

► **Explore**

These clocks show time to the **hour** .

It is 3 o'clock.

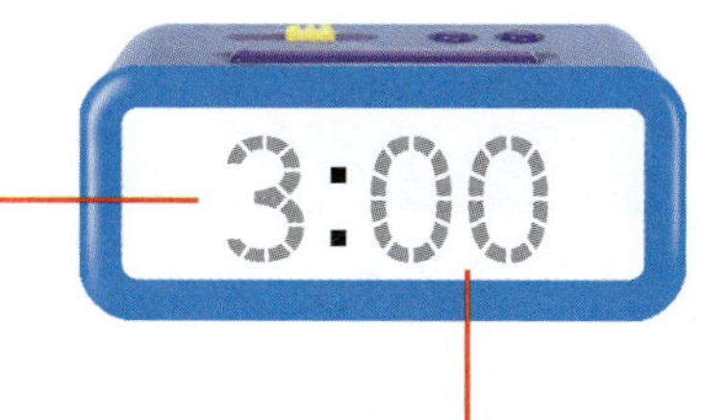

hour

minutes after the hour

The **minute hand** points to 12.
The **hour hand** points to 3.

Essential Question
How can you tell and write time to the hour on analog and digital clocks?

Vocabulary
hour
minute hand
hour hand
minutes

► **Connect**

Use a 🕐 to show each time. Write the time.

1.

5:00

2.

:

3.

:

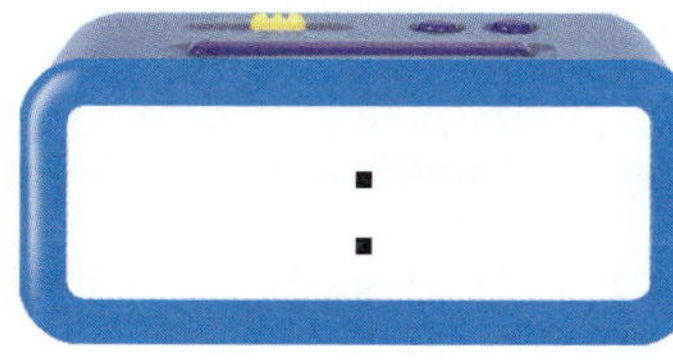

4.

:

✅**5.**

:

✅**6.**

:

7. **Math Talk** How is reading a 🕐 different from reading a ⬚ 9:00 ?

★ Representation

Use a 🕐 to show each time. Write the time.

1.

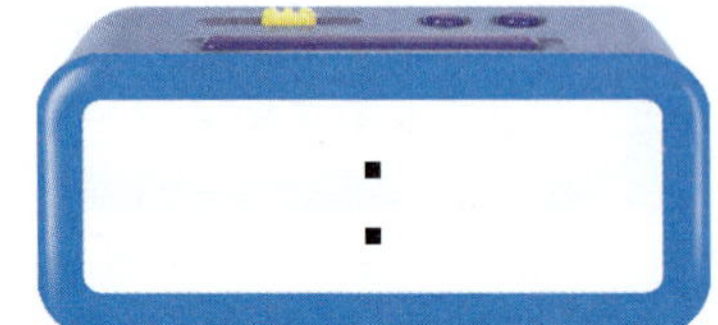
4:00

2.

:

3.

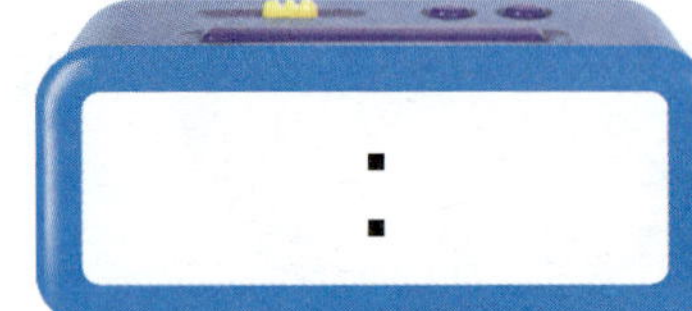

:

4.

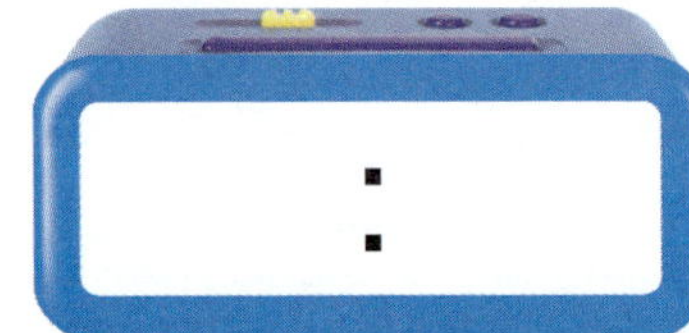

:

5.

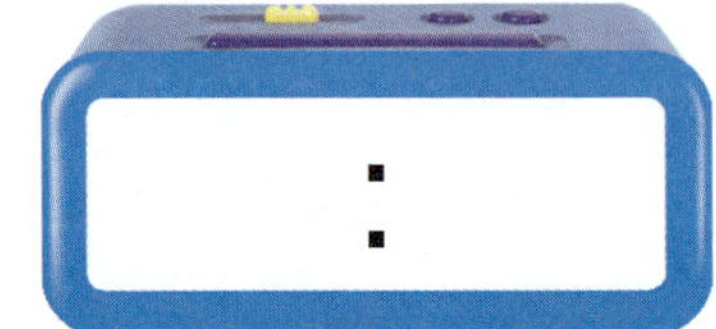

:

6.

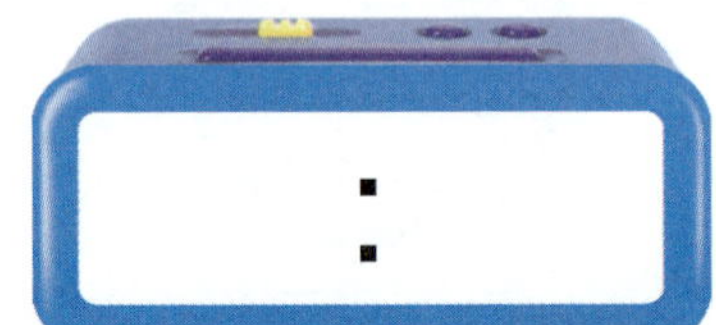

:

 Math Board

Problem Solving: Application

7. Solve.

Beth and Tim go to the park at 10 o'clock. Show this time on each clock.

Beth

Tim

Amy goes to the park 1 hour later than Beth. What time does she go to the park? Explain.

At Home Have your child practice telling time on both types of clocks and watches as you go about your daily routines.

Chapter 14 Lesson 7

Time to the Half Hour

▶ **Explore**

The hour hand is between 9 and 10.

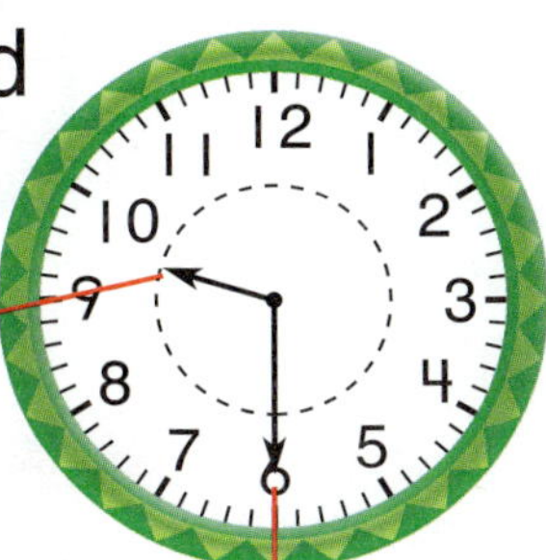

The minute hand is at 6.

minutes after the hour

hour

Both clocks read 9:30, or 30 minutes after 9 o'clock. A half hour has 30 minutes.

▶ **Connect**

Use a ⏰ to show each time. Write the time.

1.

2.

3.

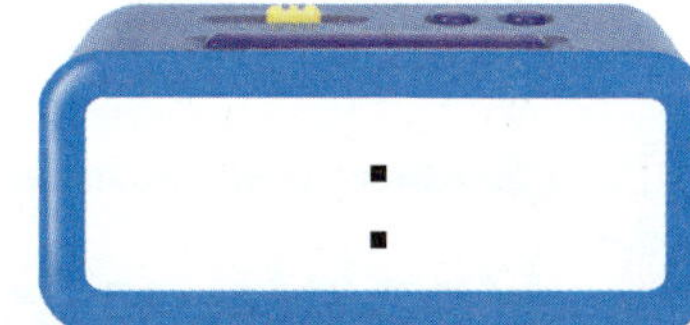

4.

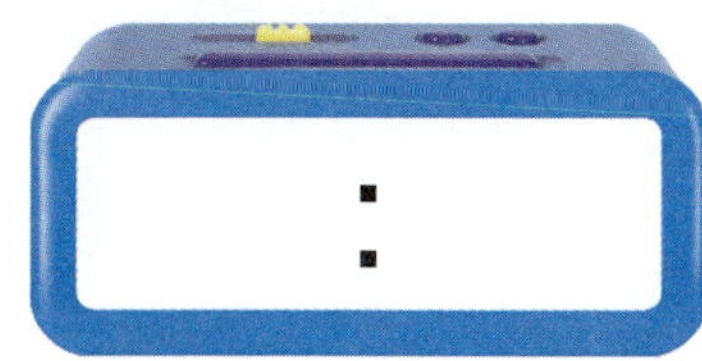

✓**5.**

✓**6.**

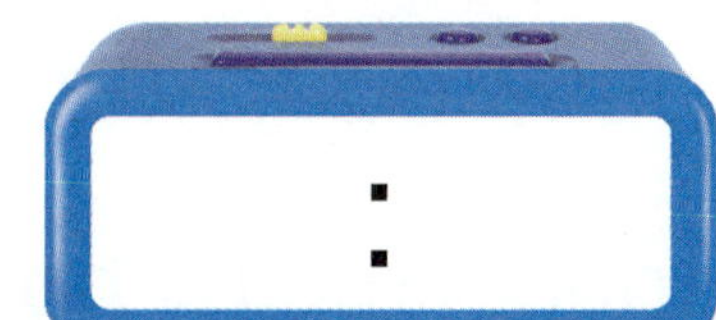

7. **Math Talk** Sam set the hands on the clock. What is the error?

Representation

Hands On ✋

Essential Question

How do you tell and write time to the half hour on analog and digital clocks?

Vocabulary

half hour
hour hand
minute hand
hour
minutes

Use a  to show each time. Write the time.

1.

5:30

2.

:

3.

:

4.

:

5.
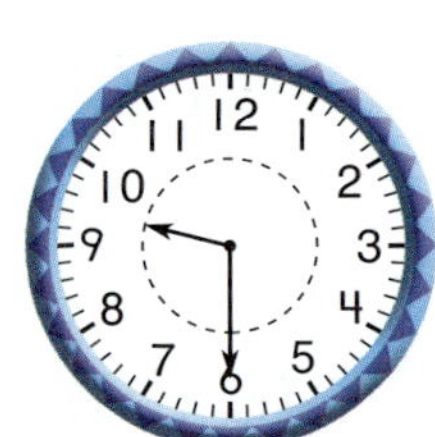
:

6.

:

Problem Solving: Algebra

Continue the pattern.
Write the times that are missing.

7. Count time by half hours.

3:30, 4:00, 4:30, ___:___, ___:___, ___:___

8. Count time by hours.

7:00, 8:00, ___:___, 10:00, ___:___, ___:___

Write a time pattern of your own.

Name ______________________________

Chapter 14 Lesson 8

Time to the Hour and Half Hour

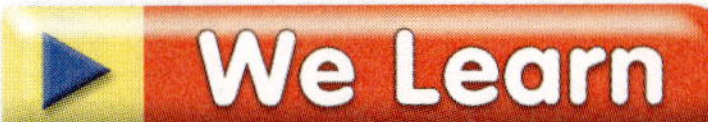

We Learn

8:00

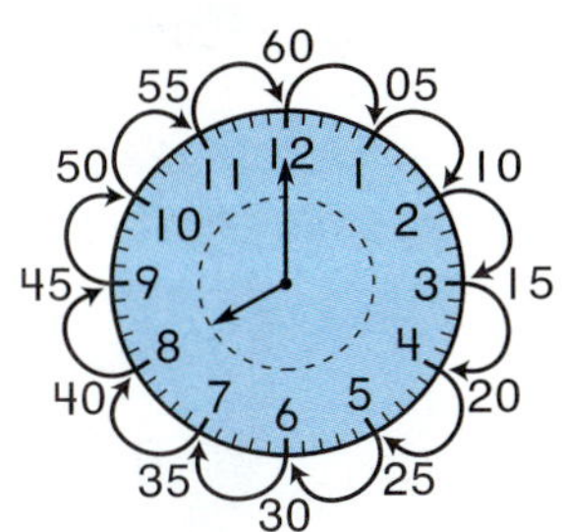

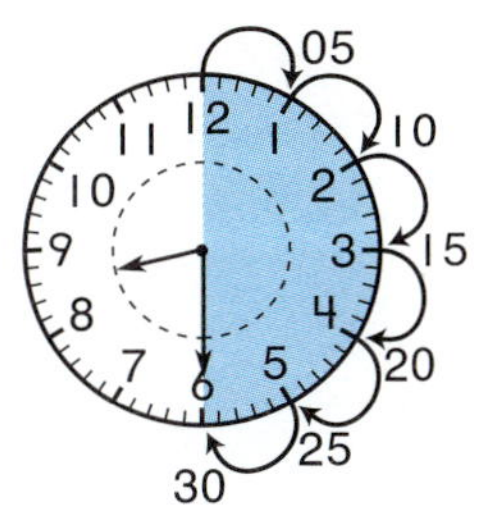

An hour has 60 minutes.

8:30

A half hour has 30 minutes.

Essential Question
How do you read and show time to the hour and half hour using analog and digital clocks?

Vocabulary
half hour
hour
minutes

Share and Show

Math Board

Read the time. Draw the hour hand and the minute hand to show the time.

1.

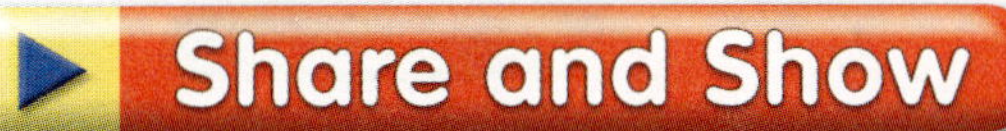

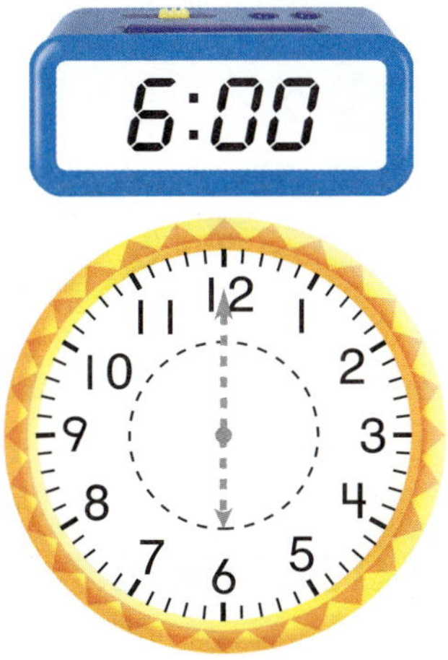

2.

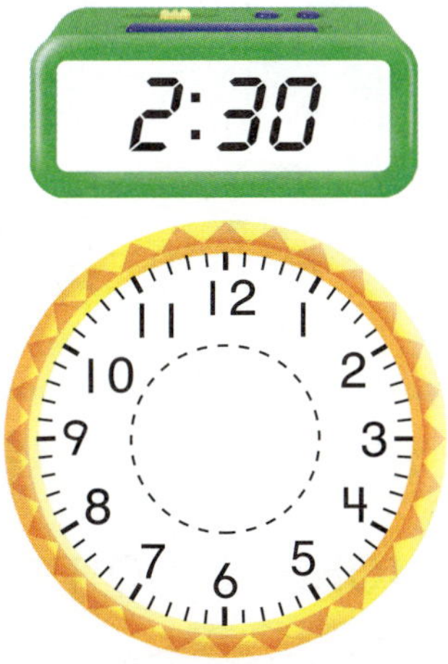

3.

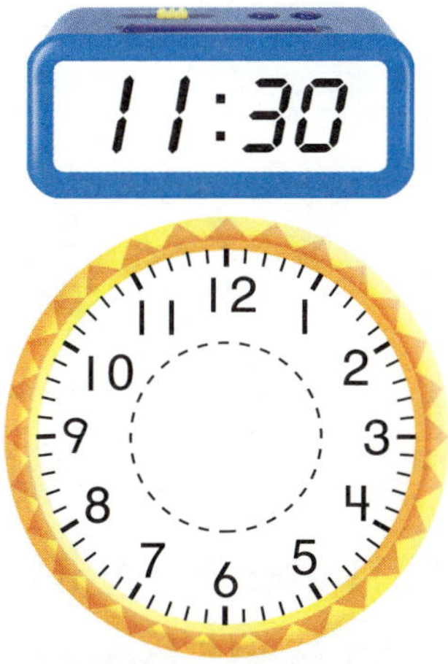

4.

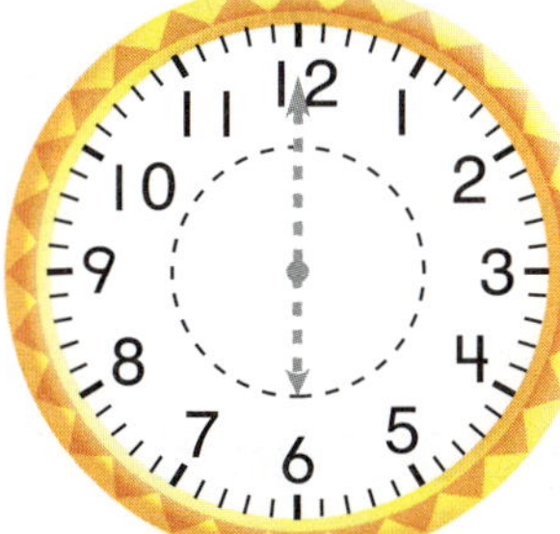

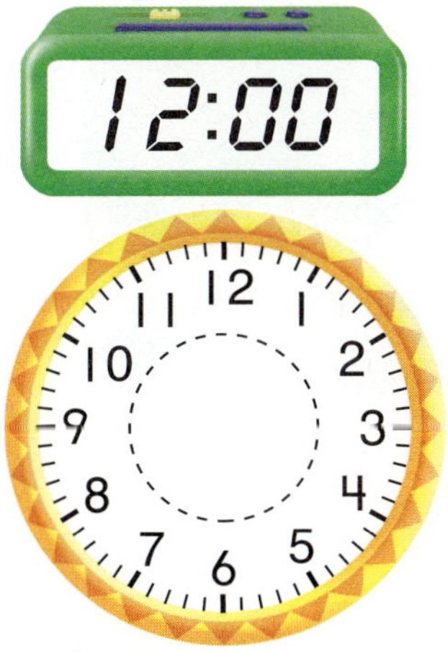

✓5.

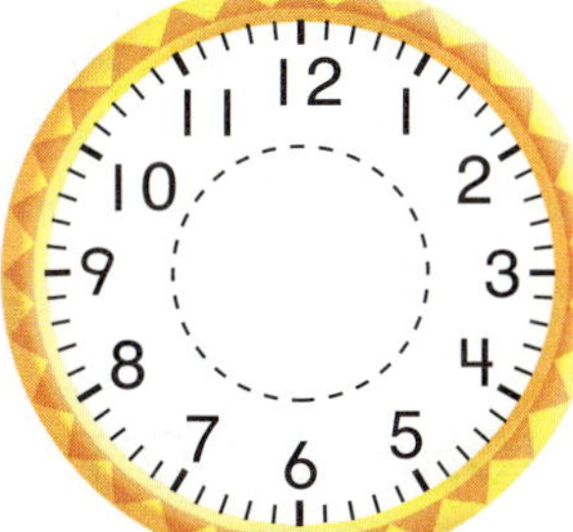

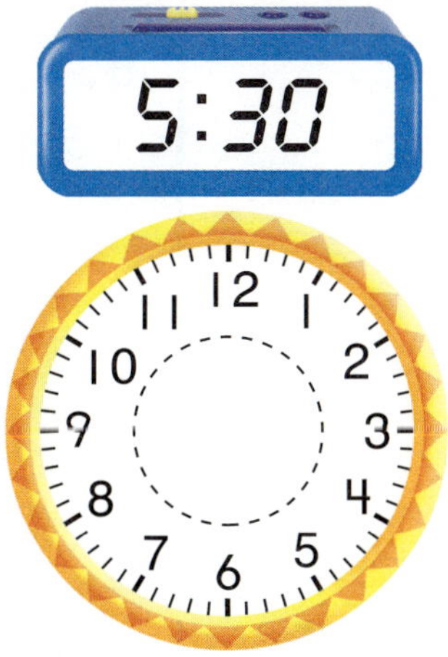

✓6.

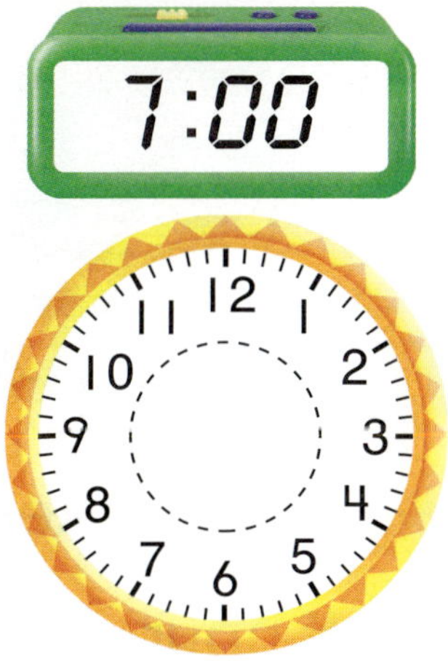

7. Math Talk How many minutes after the hour does the clock show? Explain.

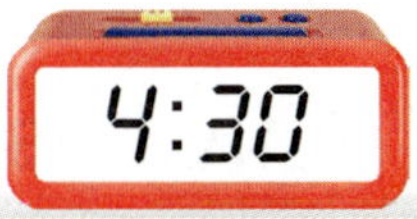

Representation

Read the time. Draw the hour hand and
the minute hand to show the time.

1. 

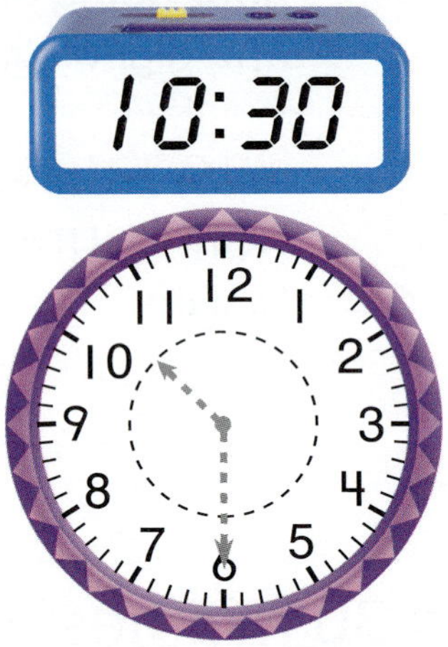

2. 

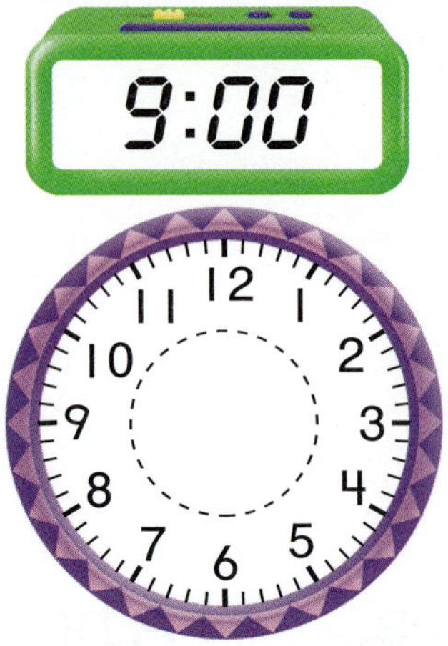

3. 

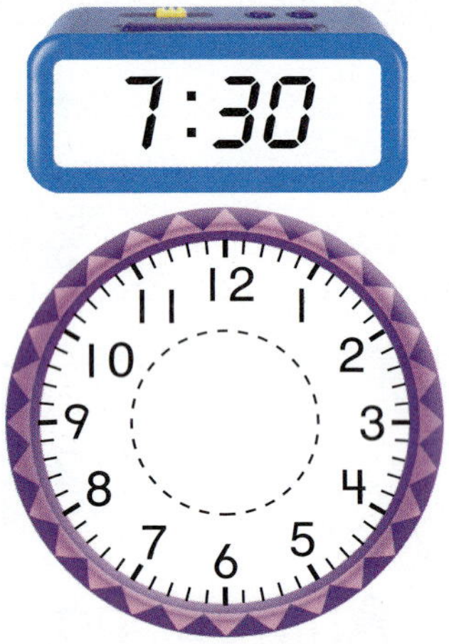

4. 

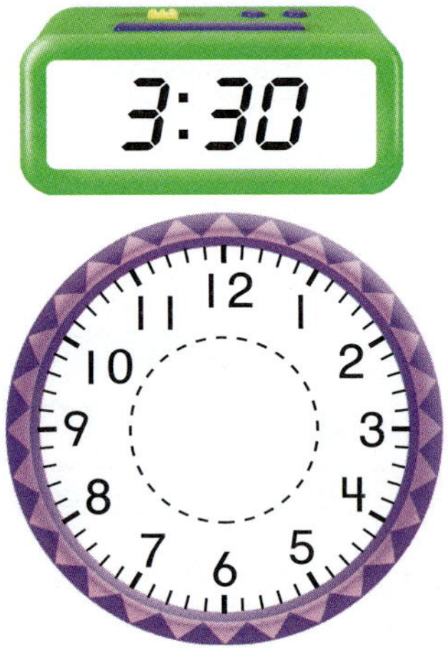

5. 

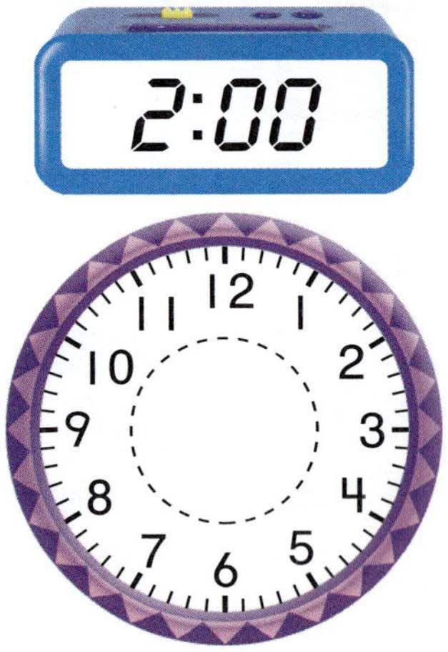

6. 

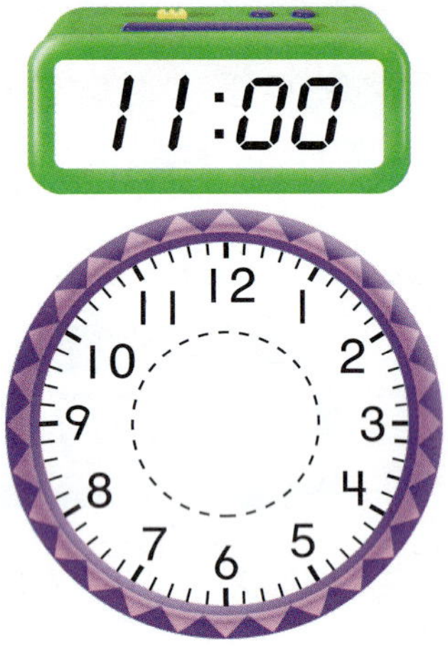

Problem Solving: Estimation

Estimate how long it would take to complete these activities.
Circle **half hour** or **hour**.

7. 

checkers game

half hour   hour

8. 

soccer game

half hour   hour

Write a list of activities you can do in about 30 minutes.

At Home Have your child perform some of the
activities on his or her list. Time each activity. Discuss
the results.

Chapter 14 Lesson 9

Pennies and Nickels

 **Explore**

 **or** 

penny

I cent

I ¢

Essential Question

How can you identify the value of pennies and nickels, and count like groups?

Vocabulary

penny

cent ¢

nickel

 **or** 

nickel

5 cents   5¢

 **Connect**

Use  and . Draw and label them.
Count by ones or fives. Write the total value.

1. 3 pennies

_____ 3¢

2. 3 nickels

_____

✓**3.** 5 nickels

_____

✓**4.** 6 nickels

_____

5. (Math Talk) How many pennies have the same value as
3 nickels? Explain.

1.3.3 Give the value of a collection of pennies, nickels and dimes up to $1.00.

Count by ones or fives. Write the total value.

1.    

1 ¢, 2 ¢, 3 ¢, 4 ¢   4¢

2.      

_____ ¢, _____ ¢, _____ ¢, _____ ¢, _____ ¢, _____ ¢ _____

3.  

_____ ¢, _____ ¢   _____

4. 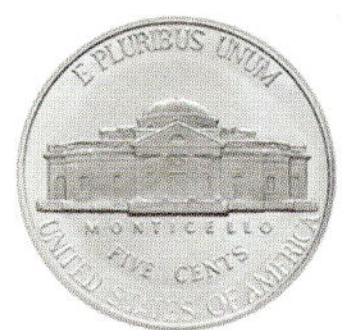   

_____ ¢, _____ ¢, _____ ¢, _____ ¢   _____

Problem Solving: Reasoning

5. Count by fives to find the value of the nickels. Write how many pennies have the same value.

_____ pennies

Explain how you know your answer is correct.

Count Collections

 **We Learn**

Count by tens. Count by fives. Count by ones.

__10__ ¢, __20__ ¢, __30__ ¢, __35__ ¢, __36__ ¢, __37__ ¢, __38__ ¢   __38__¢

Share and Show Math Board

Count. Write the total value.

1.     

______ ¢, ______ ¢, ______ ¢, ______ ¢, ______ ¢   ______

2.      

______ ¢, ______ ¢, ______ ¢, ______ ¢, ______ ¢, ______ ¢   ______

3.      

______ ¢, ______ ¢, ______ ¢, ______ ¢, ______ ¢, ______ ¢   ______

4. **Math Talk** How could you use dimes, nickels, and pennies to make 21¢? Explain.

1.3.3 Give the value of a collection of pennies, nickels and dimes up to $1.00.

▶ On Your Own

Count. Write the total value.

1.          28¢

2.         _______

3.          _______

4.        _______

5.         _______

6.          _______

Problem Solving: Reasoning

7. Solve. Draw and label the coins.

Alex has pennies, nickels, and dimes.
The total value of his coins value is 36¢.
There is 1 more nickel than there are
dimes. What six coins does Alex have?

How can you make 36¢ with 7 coins? Explain.

Extra Practice

Read the time. Write the time or draw the hands to show the time.

1. 

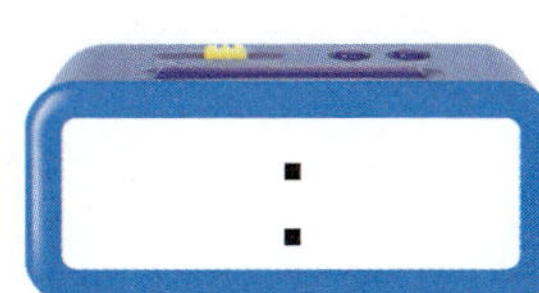

2. 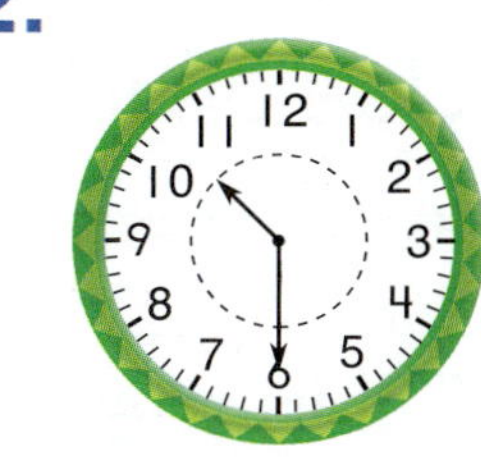

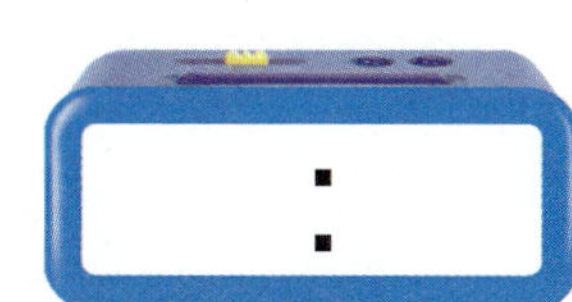

3. 

4. 

5. Use pennies, nickels, and dimes. Show one way to make 99¢. Draw and label the coins.

Problem Solving

Use 🪙, 🪙, and 🪙 to solve.
Draw and label the coins you use.

6. Emma buys a yo-yo for 52¢.
She uses 5 🪙 and 2 🪙 .
Show another way she can
buy the yo-yo.

Technology
Use HMH Mega Math, Mega Math,
Country Countdown, *Clock-a-Doodle-Doo,*
Level G, H.

Multistep Problems
Chapter 14

1. A toy car costs 47¢. Casey has dimes, nickels, and pennies in his pocket. ♦ I.3.3

He wants to use the fewest number of coins he can to buy the car.

- Show the coins Casey will use.

- Then show another way he can buy the toy car.

2. Use an inch rule to measure length. ♦ I.3.2

- Fill in the table. Use real objects in your classroom.

Object	Estimate	Measurement

- Which object is the longest?

- Which object is the shortest?

 # Standards Quick Check

Use coins. Find the total value.

1.

____ ¢ ____ ¢ ____ ¢, ____ ¢ ____ ¢ ____ ¢ ____ ¢

2.

____ ¢ ____ ¢ ____ ¢ ____ ¢ ____ ¢ ____ ¢

Draw a line to the clock that answers the question.

1. Ann starts cleaning her room at 4:30. She spends 2 hours cleaning. At what time does she finish?

2. Taro wakes up at 8:00. He gets to soccer practice 1 hour later. Soccer practice lasts for 2 hours. At what time is soccer practice over?

Oh, Yes!

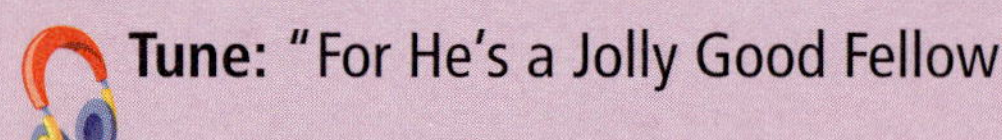
Tune: "For He's a Jolly Good Fellow"

Oh, yes! One penny is 1 cent.
Oh, yes! One penny is 1 cent.
Oh, yes! One penny is 1 cent.
1 penny is 1 cent!

Oh, yes! One nickel is 5 cents.
Oh, yes! One nickel is 5 cents.
Oh, yes! One nickel is 5 cents.
5 pennies are 5 cents!

Oh, yes! One dime is 10 cents.
Oh, yes! One dime is 10 cents.
Oh, yes! One dime is 10 cents.
10 pennies are 10 cents!

Looking Ahead to the ISTEP+
Chapter 14

Mark the best answer for questions 1–3.

1. Which coins show 21¢?

 1.3.3

2. Which is the best estimate for the length of the object in  ? 1.3.2

○ About 10
○ About 8
○ About 4
○ About 2

3. What is the total value? 1.3.3

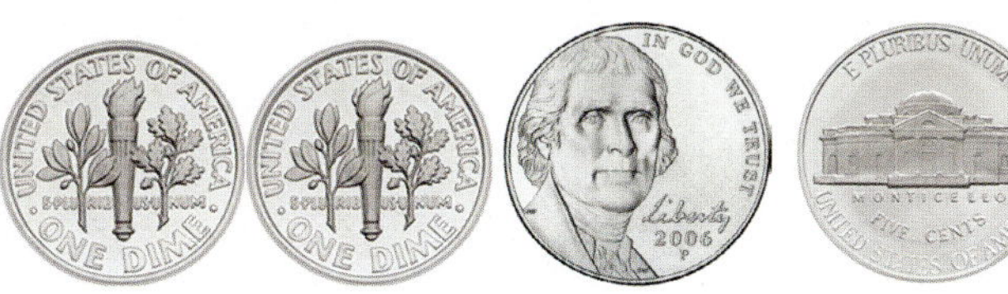

○ 20¢   ○ 30¢

○ 25¢   ○ 40¢

Mark the correct answer for questions 4–5.

4. What is the time? *Representation*

- ○ 6:00
- ○ 6:30
- ○ 11:30
- ○ 12:30

5. Which clock shows the same time? *Representation*

- ○ 
- ○ 
- ○ 
- ○ 

Open Ended

Draw and label coins to solve.

6. Dan buys a toy truck for 42¢. He uses 3 🪙 , 2 🪙 , and 2 🪙 . Show another way he can buy the toy truck. **1.3.3**

truck

7. About how many ⬭ long is the object? Circle the estimate that makes more sense. **1.3.2**

Alex estimates that it is about 3 ⬭ .

Claire estimates that it is about 6 ⬭ .

Reading and Writing Math

Tell about money and time.
Write *yes* if the sentence is true.
Write *no* if the sentence is not true.

1. A penny is worth 10¢. _________

2. A nickel is worth more than a dime. _________

3. A minute is longer than an hour. _________

4. The shorter hand on the clock
   is the hour hand. _________

5. A half hour has 30 minutes. _________

6. A digital clock uses hour and minute
   hands to show the time. _________

7. One way to read the time 3:30 is
   half past 2. _________

8. **Writing Math** Choose one of
   the sentences that is not true.
   Rewrite it so that it is true.

   ____

   ____

   ____

Joke of the Day

Question: What was the robin looking for at the library?

Answer: a _______________________

Here is how to find the answer.
- Subtract to find each difference.
- Use the code box. Find the letter that matches the difference.
- Write the letter in the box.
- What word did you spell?
- Write the word to answer the question.

Code Box							
10	16	21	25	27	36	42	51
k	w	o	i	m	e	b	r

1.
```
   47
 -  5
 ----
   42
   b
```

2.
```
   28
 -  7
 ----
```

3.
```
   24
 -  3
 ----
```

4.
```
   50
 -40
 ----
```

5.
```
   27
 -11
 ----
```

6.
```
   26
 -  5
 ----
```

7.
```
   55
 -  4
 ----
```

8.
```
   39
 -12
 ----
```

 **Math Talk** How are Exercises 2, 3, and 6 alike? Explain.

Tiny Trees

Bonsai trees are trees grown in a special way to make them very small. If left to grow normally, the same tree could grow as tall as a house. Have you ever seen a bonsai tree?

ALMANAC Fact

The smallest bonsai trees are between 2 and 6 inches tall.

bonsai tree

FACT·ACTIVITY

Use the bonsai tree to compare real objects. Make an X in the correct box.

bonsai tree

about 3 inches

Bonsai Measuring		
Object	Longer than the bonsai	Shorter than the bonsai
① new pencil		
② new crayon		
③ large paper clip		
④ eraser		

Math Talk Choose another object you think is shorter than the bonsai tree. Then compare. Explain.

Big Leaves

A pawpaw is a fruit grown in North America. A pawpaw tree has leaves that can be as long as a 12-inch ruler.

The leaf on a pawpaw tree can be 12 inches long.

FACT·ACTIVITY

About how many of each leaf do you think would be as long as one pawpaw leaf? Use a 12-inch ruler to test.

bur oak	Predict about _________ leaves Test about _________ leaves
paper birch	Predict about _________ leaves Test about _________ leaves
American elm	Predict about _________ leaves Test about _________ leaves

Math Talk Do you think a new pencil is longer or shorter than a pawpaw leaf? Predict. Then test.

Glossary

0 zero

When you add **zero** to any number, the sum is that number.

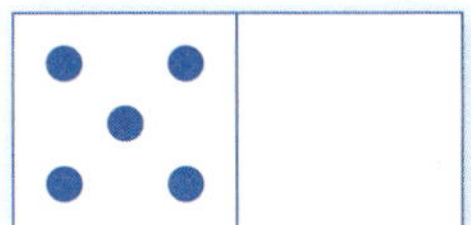

$5 + 0 = 5$

cero

above

encima

---

add

$3 + 2 = 5$

sumar

addend

$1 + 3 = 4$

addend

sumando

---

addition sentence

$2 + 1 = 3$ is an **addition sentence.**

enunciado de suma

---

after

48 is just **after** 47.

después

---

afternoon

afternoon

tarde

---

are left

2  **are left.**

quedan

B

balance

balancear

---

bar graph

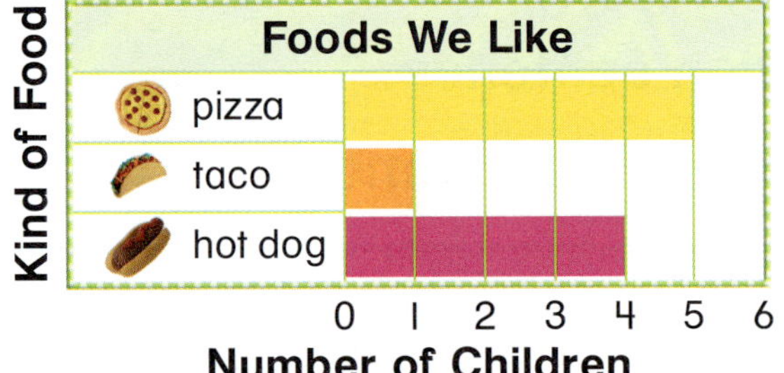

gráfica de barras

---

before

46 is just **before** 47.

antes

---

behind

detrás

below

debajo

---

beside

al lado

---

between

47 is **between** 46 and 48.

entre

C

capacity

Capacity is the amount a container holds.

capacidad

Glossary

cent ¢

A penny is **1 cent**.

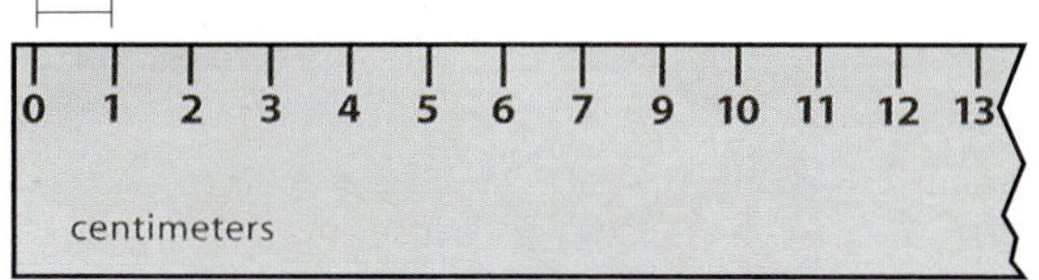

centavo

---

centimeter

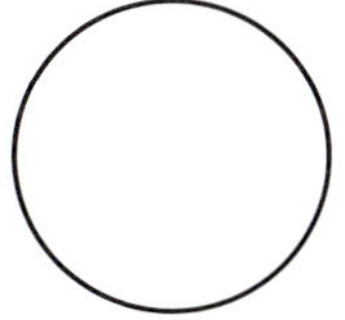

centímetro

---

circle

círculo

---

compare

Subtract to **compare** groups.

5 − 4 = 1 fewer

comparar

concrete graph

gráfica con objetos concretos

---

cone

cono

---

congruent

These figures are **congruent**.

congruente

---

corner

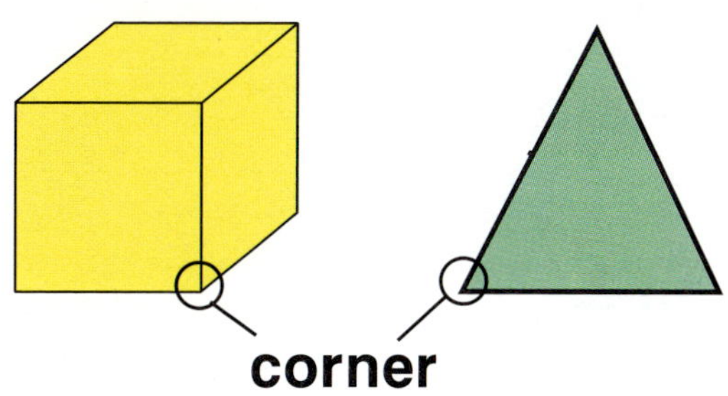

esquina

count back

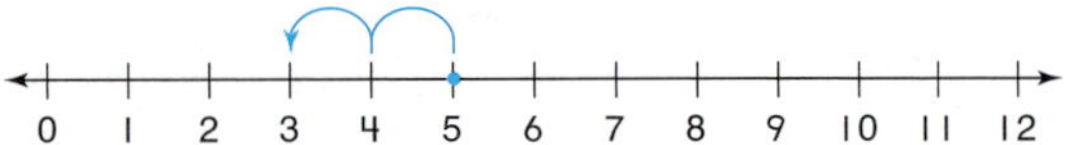

$$5 - 2 = 3$$

Count back 2.

You are on 3.

contar hacia atrás

count backward

Count backward from 63.

63, 62, 61, 60, 59

contar hacia atrás

count forward

Count forward from 63.
63, 64, 65, 66, 67

contar hacia adelante

count on

$$4 + 2 = 6$$

Say 4.

Count on 2.

5, 6

contar hacia adelante

cube

cubo

curved surface
Some solids have a curved surface.

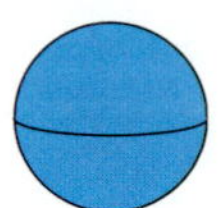  

superficie curva

cylinder

cilindro

difference
$$4 - 3 = 1$$

The **difference** is 1.

diferencia

Glossary

dime

 or  **10¢**
10 cents

moneda de 10¢

---

dollar

 **100¢**
$1.00

dólar

---

doubles

$5 + 5 = 10$

dobles

---

doubles plus one

$3 + 3 = 6$, so $3 + 4 = 7$.

dobles más uno

---

down

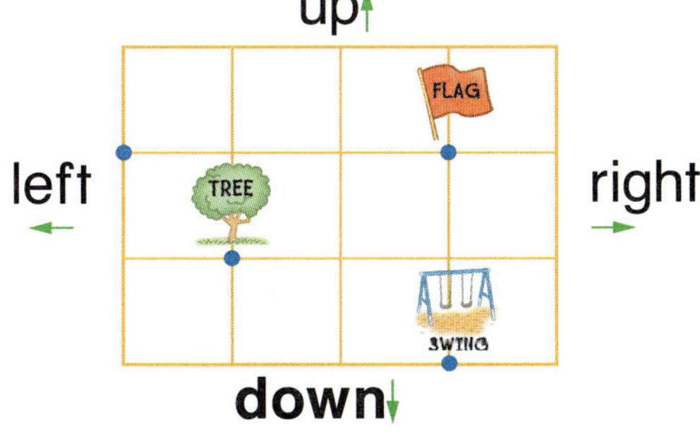

abajo

E

equal amounts

Here are two ways to make **equal amounts** for 26¢.

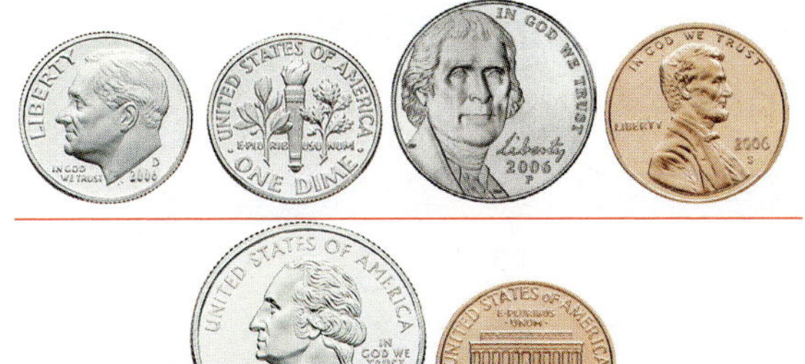

cantidades iguales

---

equal parts

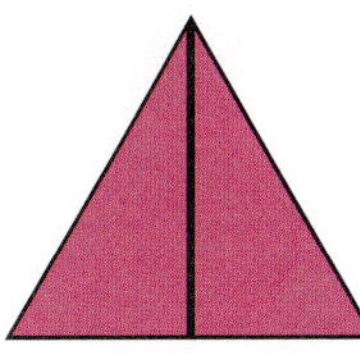

partes iguales

---

estimate

An **estimate** is an amount that tells about how many.

estimar

---

evening

evening

noche

fact family

A **fact family** uses the same numbers to make addition and subtraction sentences.

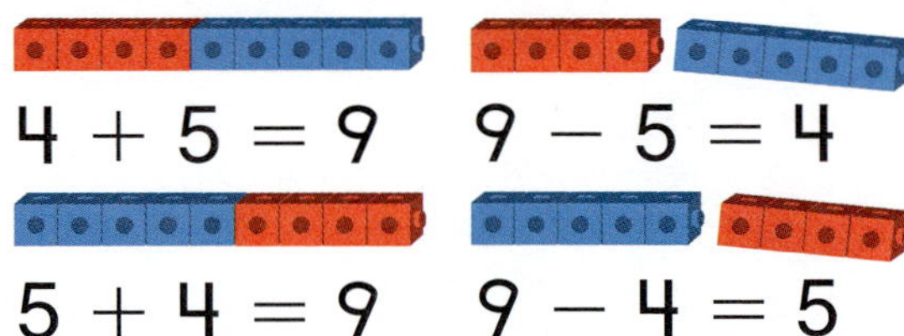

$4 + 5 = 9 \quad 9 - 5 = 4$

$5 + 4 = 9 \quad 9 - 4 = 5$

familia de operaciones

far

lejos

fewer

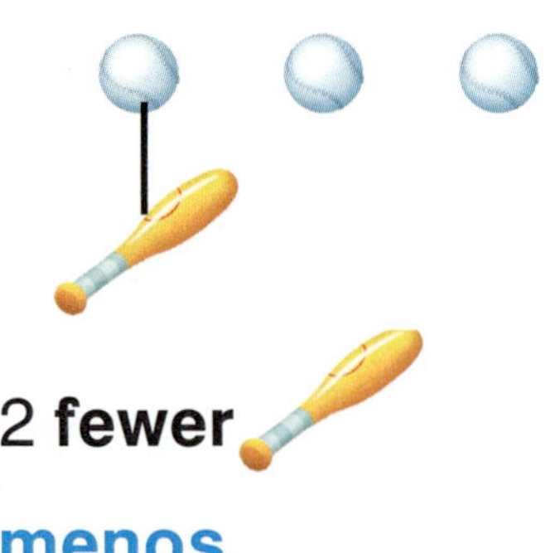

menos

first

primero

flat surface

Some solids have **flat surfaces**.

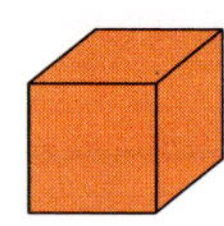 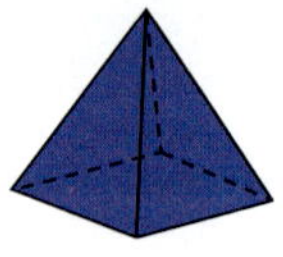 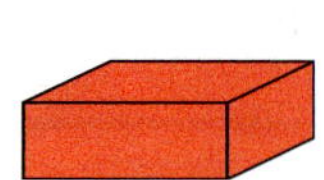

superficie plana

flip

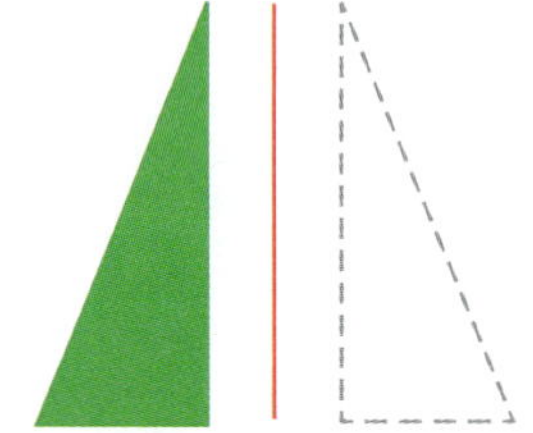

inversión

fraction

Name parts of a group with a **fraction**.
$\frac{1}{4}$ of the group is red.

fracción

greatest

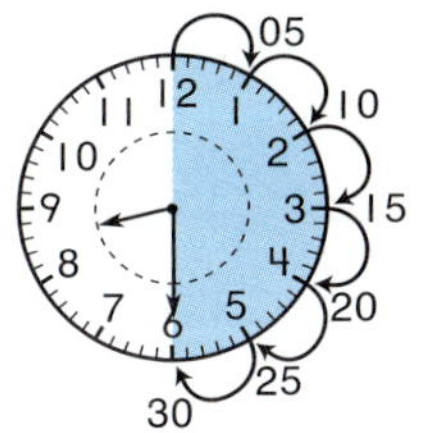

10 is the **greatest** number.

el mayor

half hour

A **half hour** has 30 minutes.

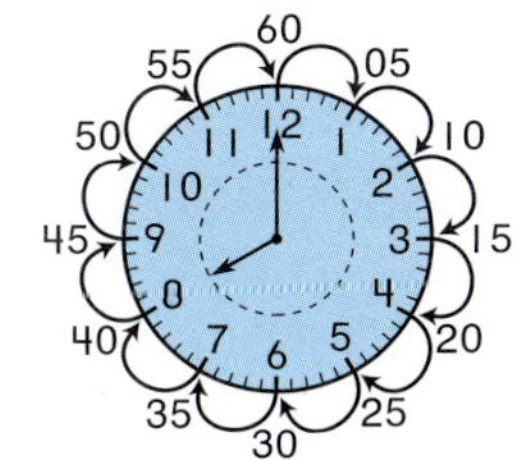

8:30

media hora

---

hour

An **hour** has 60 minutes.

8:00

hora

---

hour hand

horario

---

hundred

centena

impossible

It is **impossible** to pull a green bear.

imposible

---

in front of

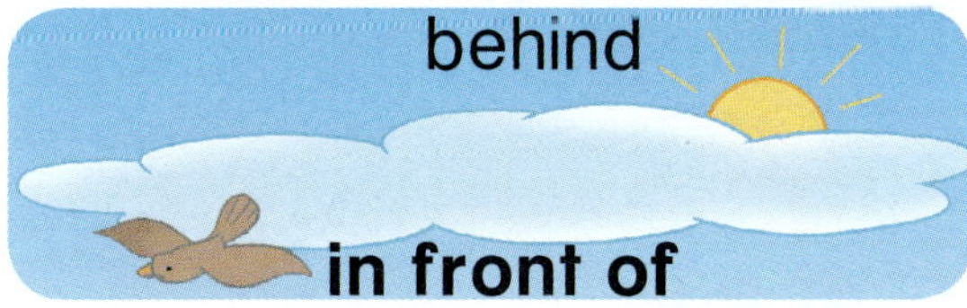

delante de

inch

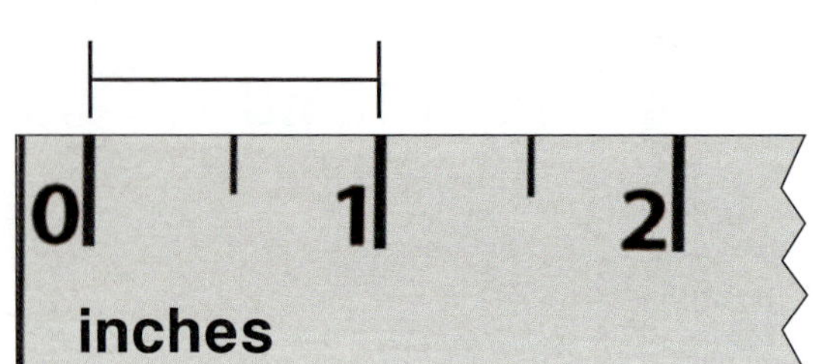

pulgada

---

inside

adentro

---

is equal to (=)

2 plus 1 **is equal to** 3.
2 + 1 = 3

es igual a

---

is greater than (>)

9 **is greater than** 6.

9 > 6

es mayor que

---

is less than (<)

9 **is less than** 11.

9 < 11

es menor que

last

último

---

least

7 is the **least** number.

el menor

left

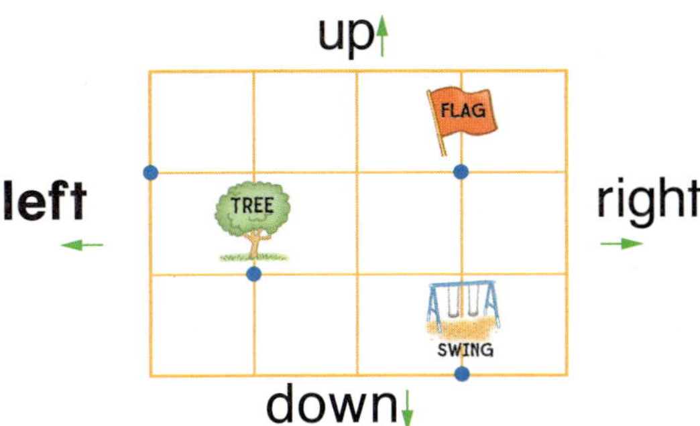

izquierda

---

less likely

Pulling yellow is **less likely** than pulling red.

menos probable

---

line plot

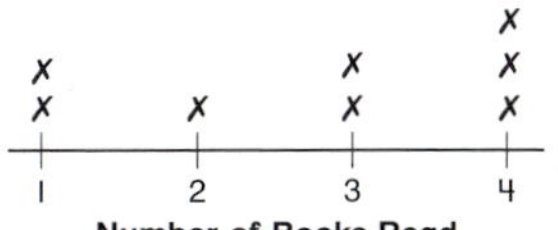

diagrama lineal

---

longest

el más largo

make a ten

Move 2 counters into the ten frame. **Make a ten**.

$$8 + 4 = 12$$

formar una decena

---

measure

Use ⬭ to **measure** short things.

medir

---

minus (−)

$$4 - 3 = 1$$

4 **minus** 3 is equal to 1.

menos

---

minutes

An hour has 60 **minutes**.

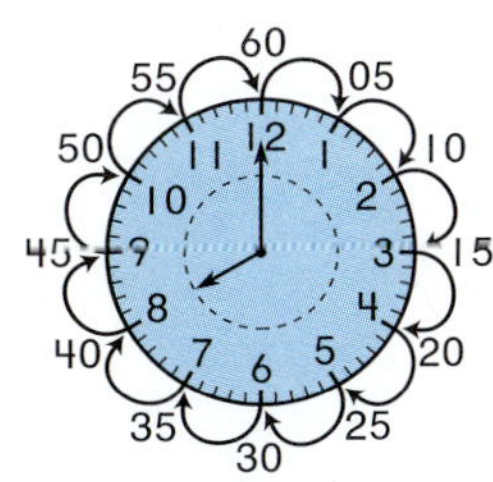

8:00

minutos

minute hand

minutero

---

month

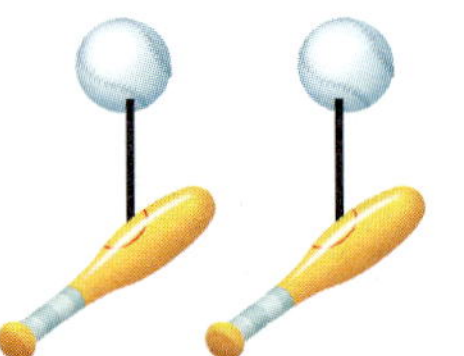

The **month** is April.

mes

---

more

I **more**

más

more likely

Pulling red is **more likely** than pulling blue.

más probable

---

morning

morning

mañana

near

cerca

nickel

 or  **5¢**
5 cents

moneda de 5¢

---

number line

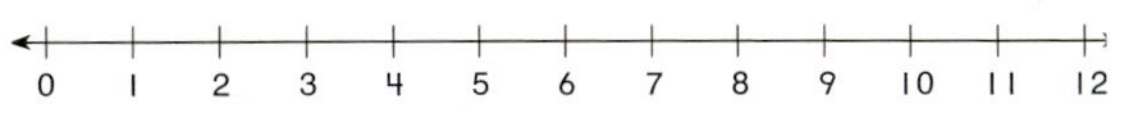

recta numérica

odd

An **odd** number of objects will have one left over when grouped into pairs.

impar

$\frac{1}{4}$ **one fourth**

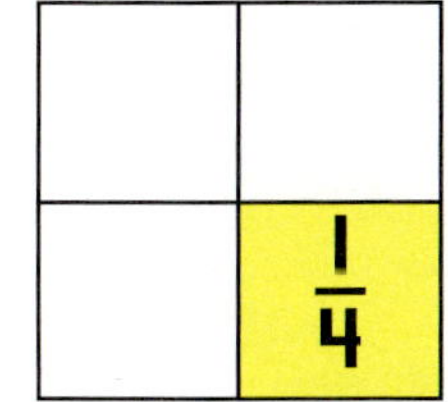

un cuarto

$\frac{1}{2}$ **one half**

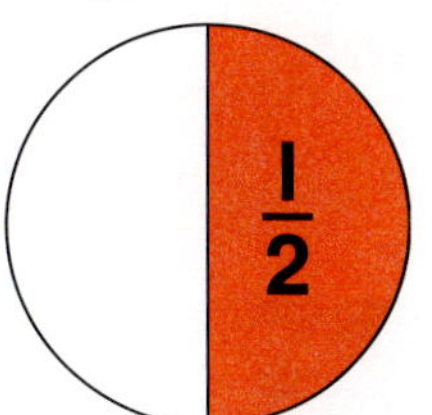

un medio

$\frac{1}{3}$ **one third**

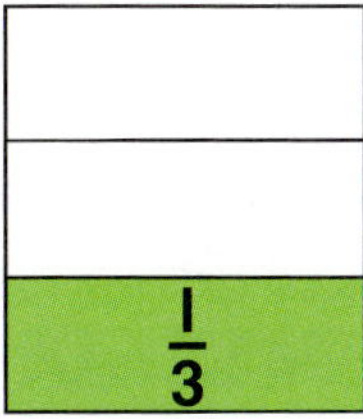

un tercio

---

one less

One less than 39 is 38.

uno menos

---

one more

One more than 39 is 40.

uno más

---

ones

10 has 1 ten and 0 **ones**.

unidades

order

You can change the **order** of the addends.

$1 + 3 = 4$ $3 + 1 = 4$

orden

---

outside

afuera

part

Add the **parts** to find the whole.

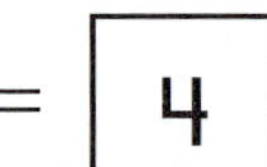

3	+	1	=	4
part		part		whole

parte

pattern

You can use a **pattern** to show all the ways to make 7.

patrón

---

pattern unit

unidad de patrón

---

penny

 or  1¢ 1 cent

moneda de 1¢

---

picture graph

Fruits We Like						
oranges						
grapes						
peaches						

gráfica con dibujos

pint

pinta

---

plus (+)

2 **plus** 1 is equal to 3.

$2 + 1 = 3$

más

---

possible

It is **possible** to pull
a blue bear.

posible

---

pound

This bag of rice weighs
1 **pound**.

libra

pyramid

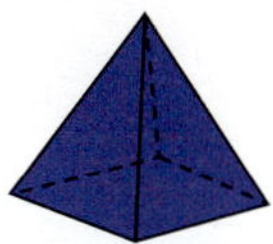

pirámide

quart

cuarto

---

quarter

 or  25¢
25 cents

moneda de 25¢

rectangle

rectángulo

rectangular prism

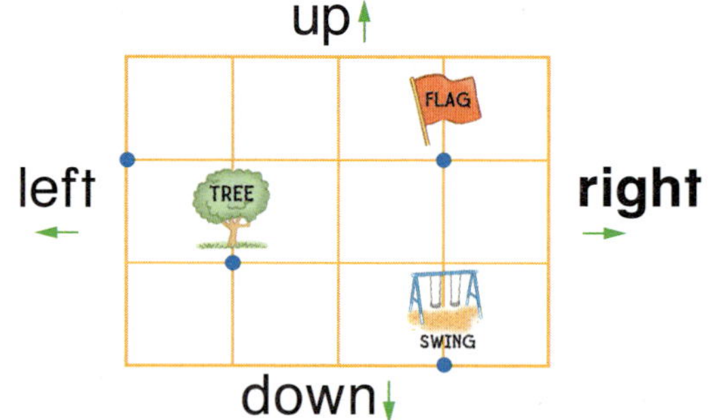

prisma rectangular

---

related addition facts

Related addition facts use the same numbers.

$5 + 6 = 11$

$6 + 5 = 11$

operaciones de suma relacionadas

---

related subtraction facts

Related subtraction facts use the same numbers.

$12 - 3 = 9$

$12 - 9 = 3$

operaciones de resta relacionadas

---

related facts

Related facts use the same numbers.

$5 + 3 = 8$

$8 - 3 = 5$

operaciones relacionadas

repeating pattern

A **repeating pattern** has a group that repeats over and over.

blue red blue red blue red

patrón que se repite

---

right

derecha

---

rule

A **rule** for this table is Subtract 1. Subtract 1 from each number.

Subtract 1	
6	5
8	7
10	9

regla

same

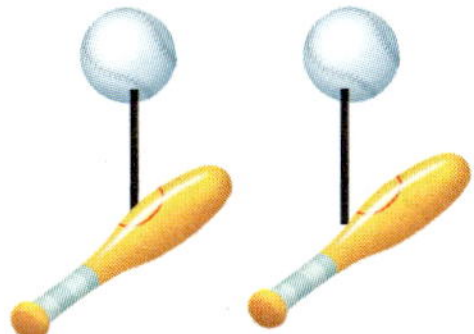

same number of  as

igual

---

same shape

same shape
la misma figura

---

same size

same size
el mismo tamaño

---

shortest

shortest

el más corto

side

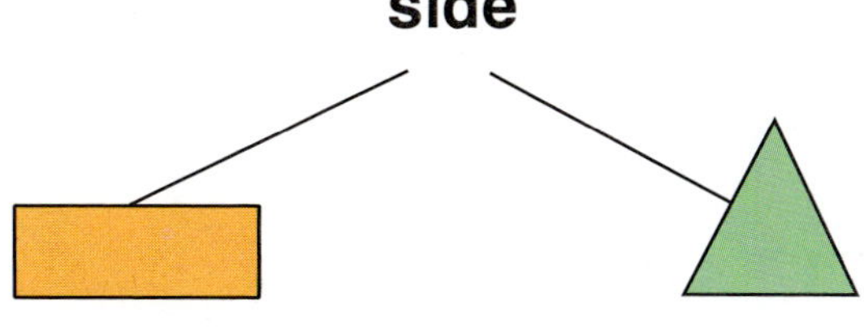

lado

---

slide

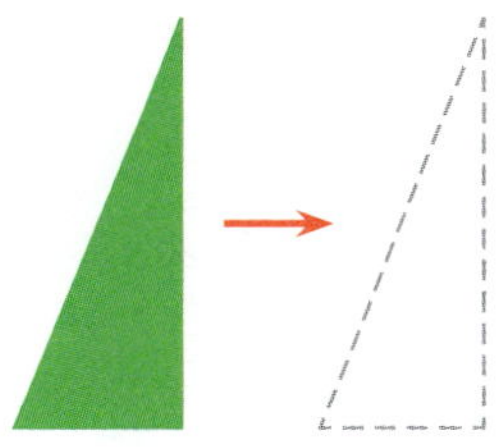

slide
trasladar

---

sort

You can **sort** these bears.
clasificar

---

sphere

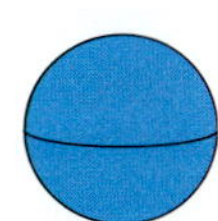

esfera

square

cuadrado

---

subtract

Subtract to find out how many are left.

restar

---

subtraction sentence

$4 - 3 = 1$ is a **subtraction sentence**.

enunciado de resta

---

sum

2 plus 1 is equal to 3.

The **sum** is 3.

suma o total

---

survey

You can take a **survey** to get information.

encuesta

T

take away

Cross out the ones you **take away**.

quitar

---

tally chart

Sports We Like		Total
soccer	ⵏⵏⵏⵏⵏ |||	8
T-ball	|||	3

tabla de conteo

---

tally mark

Each **tally mark |** stands for 1 child. **ⵏⵏⵏⵏⵏ** stands for 5 children.

marca de conteo

---

temperature

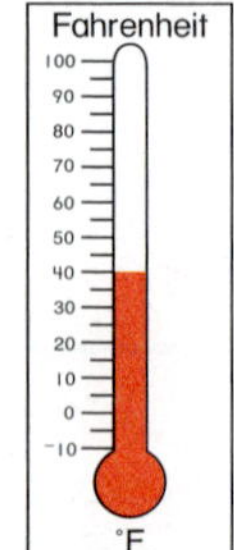

The **temperature** is 40 degrees.

temperatura

ten

decena

---

ten less
Ten less than 55 is 45.

diez menos

---

ten more
Ten more than 55 is 65.

diez más

---

triangle

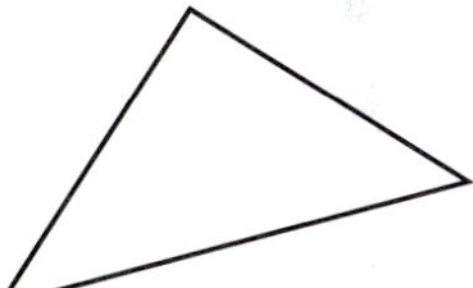

triángulo

unequal parts

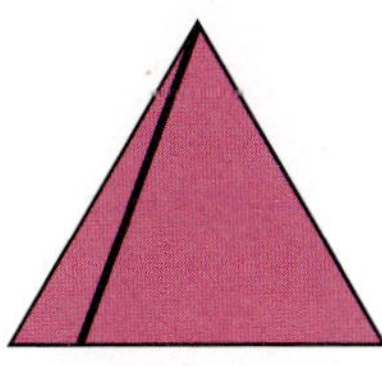

partes desiguales

up

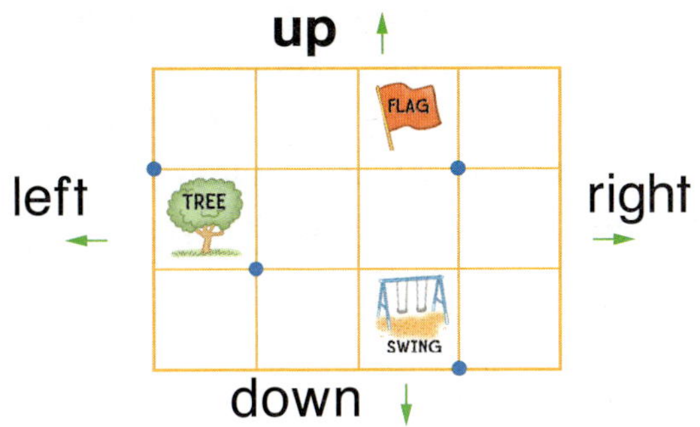

arriba

Venn Diagram
You can sort objects with a **Venn Diagram**.

Diagrama de Venn

whole
The **whole** is how many there are in all.

$$3 - 1 = 4$$
part   part   **whole**

entero

year
There are 12 months in a **year**.

año

Photo Credits

Key: (t) top. (b) bottom. (l) left. (r) right. (c) center. (bg) background. (fg) foreground.
Front Cover: (l) Wayne R. Bilenduke/Getty Images; (r) Peter Lilja/Getty Images.
Back Cover: (l) Peter Lilja/Getty Images; (r) Jerry Alexander/Getty Images.
Title Page: (l) Wayne R. Bilenduke/Getty Images; (r) Peter Lilja/Getty Images.
Copyright page: (r) Jerry Alexander/Getty Images.
Authors Page: (r) Peter Lilja/Getty Images.

Unit 1

A (c) Andre Jenny/Alamy; 19 (b) Ingram; (b) PhotoDisc/Getty Images; (b) PhotoDisc; 22 (bg) Brendan Regan; (tr) DK Images/Getty Images; 47 (cl) Corbis; 48 (tc) PhotoDisc Red/ Getty Images; (c) PhotoDisc/Getty Images; 49 (bc) D. Hurst/Alamy; 52 (bg) (tr) Dale Wilson/ Masterfile; 55 (c) Dynamic Graphics Group/IT Stock Free/Alamy; 59 (cl) Daniel Templeton/ Alamy; (bl) PhotoDisc; (cr) Artville, Imspace Systems Corp; 60 (cl) PhotoDisc; (cr) Artville, Imspace Systems Corp; 64 (br) PictureQuest; 74 (tc) Roy Ritchie/Getty Images; (c) Corbis; (c) Leah Groisberg/Shutterstock; 78 (bg) Age Fotostock/SuperStock; (tr) Bay Hippisley/Imagestate; 83 (tr) Courtesy Crayola/Newscom; 84 (tr) Giraudon/Art Resource, NY.

Unit 2

A (c) Steve Bloom Images/Alamy; B (tc) Eric Hosking/Corbis; C (tc) Gallo Images/Corbis; D (tc) Tim Davis/Corbis; E (tc) Steve Bloom/Alamy; F (tc) Gallo Images/Corbis; G (tc) John Conrad/ Corbis; H (tr) Steve Bloom Images/Alamy; 89 (c) Papilio/Alamy; 94 (br) Stockbyte/Getty Images; 102 (br) David Young-Wolff/Alamy; 105 (tc) Getty Images; (c) IT StockFree; (c) Neal Mishler/ Getty Images; (bc) Stockbyte/Getty Images; 106 (t) Gary W. Carter/Corbis; (c) Gary Black/ Masterfile; (b) William Gottlieb/Corbis; 107 (bc) Corbis; 112 (bl) Ingram; (tr) Ingram; 113 (c) Steve Bloom/Alamy; 116 (br) Corbis; 124 (tr) Corel Stock Photo Library; 125 (tc) Ingram; (bc) Shutterstock; (tcl) Ingram; 126 (tc) Corbis; (cl) PhotoDisc/Getty Images; (b) Paul B. Moore/ Shutterstock; (bc) Dennis Sabo/Shutterstock; 130 (bg) Lang Yiu/Corbis; (tr) Rolf Bruderer/ Corbis; 132 (br) Ingram; (cr) Kevin Schafer/Alamy; 133 (c) Shin Yoshino/Minden Pictures; 152 (t) PhotoDisc; (tc) PhotoDisc; (bc) PhotoDisc; (b) PhotoDisc; 158 (br) Mike Hill/Alamy; 161 (tr) Renee Lynn/Corbis; (inset) Mark Newman/Photo Researchers, Inc.; 162 (tr) AP Images; (c) Mike Hill/Getty Images; (bl) Corbis; (cl) Li wei sc/Imaginechina; (br) Li wei sc/Imaginechina.

Unit 3

167 (c) Darren Robb/Getty Images; 177 (tl) Artville, Imspace Systems Corp; (tl) Ingram; 178 (br) Corel Stock Photo Library; (br) Ingram; 190 (cl) PhotoDisc; (cl) Corel Stock Photo Library; 191 (c) Bobo/Alamy; (b) Artville, Imspace Systems Corp; 194 (bg) Shaun Cunningham/Alamy; (tr) Keith Brofsky/Brand X Pictures/Age Fotostock; 196 (r) PhotoDisc; (r) Ingram; 197 (c) Bill Frymire/Masterfile; 204 (br) Ingram; 216 (bg) Simon Jauncey/Stone/Getty Images; (tr) Michelle Garrett/Corbis; 219 (c) Steve Satushek/Getty Images; 245 (tr) Avner Richard/Shutterstock; (br) PhotoDisc/Getty Images; 246 (bl) Danny Smythe/Shutterstock; 247 (br) PhotoDisc/Getty Images; 250 (bg) Steve Allen/Alamy; (tr) Ariel Skelley/Blend Images/Alamy; 255 (c) PhotoDisc; 256 (tr) David Madison/Getty Images; (cl) PhotoDisc; (c) PhotoDisc; (r) Image Club Graphics; Image Club Graphics.

Unit 4

A (bc) Lester Lefkowitz/Getty Images; B (tr) Lester Lefkowitz/Getty Images; C (br) Justin Kase/ Alamy; D (tl) Tomasz Gulla/Shutterstock; E (tr) Justin Kase/Alamy; F (tl) Imageshop/Alamy; G (tl) Justin Kase/Alamy; H (tl) Imageshop/Alamy; (cr) Lester Lefkowitz/Getty Images; 261 (c) Nick Dolding/Getty Images; 268 (tc) Linda Z/Shutterstock; 270 (t) Linda Z/Shutterstock; (t) PhotoDisc; (t) Shutterstock; (t) PhotoDisc; 284 (tc) PhotoDisc/Getty Images; (c) Image Source/ SuperStock; (bl) Ingram; 288 (bg) Robert Llewellyn/Corbis; (tr) Lester Lefkowitz/Corbis; 291 (c)

Thomas Hallstein/Alamy; 314 (tr) Paul Collis/Alamy; (br) Tony Freeman/PhotoEdit, Inc.; (bg)
Stock Connection Distribution/Alamy; 319 (inset) Richard Cummins/SuperStock; 320 (cr) MPI/
Getty Images.

Unit 5

A (t) Rudi Von Briel/PhotoEdit, Inc.; (cr) Sarah Hadley/Alamy; C (tr) Getty Images; (tr) Image
Source/Getty Images; D (cr) Photodisc Blue/Getty Images; (cl) Ingram; E (tr) David Hiller/Getty
Images; (t) Jochen Tack/Alamy; (tc) Robert Brenner/PhotoEdit, Inc.; F (tc) Williams Manning/
Corbis; (tr) Bob Daemmrich Photography, Inc.; H David Hiller/Getty Images; H Image Source/
Getty Images; H Photodisc Blue/Getty Images; 325 (c) Konrad Wothe/Minden Pictures; 347
(tc) Artville, Imspace Systems Corp; (bc) PhotoDisc/Getty Images; (bl) PhotoDisc/Getty Images;
348 (tl) Artville, Imspace systems Corp; (c) Brian Leatart/Jupiterimages; (c) Lukasz Janicki/
Shutterstock; (bc) Artville, Imspace Systems Corp; 355 (c) Roland Seitre/Peter Arnold, Inc.; 364
(tc) Artville, Imspace Systems Corp; (c) Artville, Imspace Systems Corp; 370 (br) Digital Stock/
Corbis; 373 (tr) Steve Bloom Images/Alamy; (bc) ImageState/Alamy; 374 (tc) Corbis; (c) Lynn
M. Stone/Alamy; (c) Ottfried Schreiter/imagebroker/Alamy; (bc) PhotoDisc; 375 (bc) PhotoDisc/
Getty Images; 378 (bg) Visual Communication/Alamy; (tr) Dan Kenyon/Taxi/Getty Images; 380
(cr) PhotoDisc; 381 (c) Mel Yates/Getty Images; 392 (tc) Ingram; 398 (br) Stockbyte Platinum/
Alamy; 406 (tr) D. Hurst/Alamy; 409 (tl) Richard Hutchings/Corbis; 410 (tr) D. Hurst/Alamy; 413
(tr) Trinette Reed/Zefa/Corbis; (bl) Corbis; 414 (cl) Dorling Kindersley; (c) Matthew Ward/Getty
Images; (bl) Fujio Nakahashi/Getty Images;.

Glossary:

426 (b) Artville, Imspace Systems Corp; 426 (br) Ingram.

All other photos Houghton Mifflin Harcourt libraries and photographers; Guy Jarvis,
Weronica Ankarorn, Eric Camden, Don Couch, Doug Dukane, Ken Kinzie, April Riehm, and
Steve Williams.